T.B.

W9-ARH-364

"Give me one good reason why I shouldn't kill you."

The man dressed in black had told Renee to lie down and put her feet against Brent's feet. "I told you to get down on the ground, bitch." He scowled. Renee quickly dropped to the ground, then inched forward until the bottom of her sandals rested against the soles of her husband's tennis shoes. She lay as stiff as a cadaver, her arms and hands fixed rigidly by her side. The gunman held the pistol at Brent's head. Brent's face was the color of ash.

Brent cried, "Please don't shoot me."

"Give me one good reason why I shouldn't kill you."

Brent's heart jumped into his throat. It was probably the greatest test of Brent Poole's fleeting twenty-four years. Without flinching, he swallowed hard and answered with the thought dearest to his heart.

"Because I have a daughter that I love very much," Brent said bravely.

The gunman's eyes narrowed. He shoved the cold steel underneath Brent's chin and lifted him off the ground. Brent was off the ground and nearly on his knees when the man squeezed the trigger.

FE 01 '06

DANCE OF DEATH

DALE HUDSON

PINNACLE BOOKS
Kensington Publishing Corp.
http://www.kensingtonbooks.com

Some names have been changed to protect the privacy of individuals connected to this story.

PINNACLE BOOKS are published by

Kensington Publishing Corp.
850 Third Avenue
New York, NY 10022

Copyright © 2006 by Dale Hudson

All rights reserved. No part of this book may be reproduced in any form or by any means without the prior written consent of the Publisher, excepting brief quotes used in reviews.

If you purchased this book without a cover you should be aware that this book is stolen property. It was reported as "unsold and destroyed" to the Publisher and neither the Author nor the Publisher has received any payment for this "stripped book."

All Kensington Titles, Imprints, and Distributed Lines are available at special quantity discounts for bulk purchases for sales promotions, premiums, fund-raising, and educational or institutional use. Special book excerpts or customized printings can also be created to fit specific needs. For details, write or phone the office of the Kensington special sales manager: Kensington Publishing Corp., 850 Third Avenue, New York, NY 10022, attn: Special Sales Department, Phone: 1-800-221-2647.

Pinnacle and the P logo Reg. U.S. Pat. & TM Off.

First Printing: February 2006

10 9 8 7 6 5 4 3 2 1

Printed in the United States of America

For Deborah, DJ and Deegan

Acknowledgments

It's an old cliché, but this book would have never been possible without the help and cooperation of my family, friends and associates.

First and foremost, I would like to express my appreciation to Jack and Marie Summey and Jane Lovett. Thank you for your continued kindness and your willingness to share information, even at the risk of casting dark shadows on yourself and your family.

A debt of gratitude is owed to Detective Terry Altman, Captain Sam Hendrick, and many other members of the law enforcement and medical emergency team who provided valuable information and shared their special insights into the Brent Poole case.

I am also grateful to Attorney Bill Diggs for his contributions and giving me access to his files. Some of the same courtesies have been extended to me from attorneys Ralph Wilson, Greg Hembree, Fran Humphries, Tommy Brittain, and Morgan Martin. These officers of the court have never said no to my request for an interview and are always willing to assist in any way.

Thanks also to my agent, Peter Miller, who so gracefully presented this project, and to Michaela Hamilton and B. Tweed at Kensington Publishing Corporation.

Many thanks goes to my writing partner and close friend, Dale Dobson. Your continued faith, friendship, and encouragement has helped me through this project and many more like it. Included in that same list is longtime supporter and friend Jo Clayton.

To my friends and business associates who protect and keep me financially afloat while I am writing and ignoring my day job: my attorney, Ralph Stroman, my accountant, Morgan Lewis, my banker, Richard Causey, and my associates in the Eldercare business, attorneys Bruce Robinson Jr., Dennis Worley, and Paul Ekster—you have my deepest gratitude.

A special thank-you goes to Edward and Kathleen Burroughs for your long and devoted friendship. You've always been there to keep us laughing and lift our spirits when we've needed it the most.

I would like to thank Kimberly Renee Poole, who has revealed the most intimate and deepest secrets of her life. That really took a lot of guts!

Finally, my deepest and heartfelt appreciation is reserved for my faithful and loving wife, Deborah, and my creative and high-spirited children, DJ and Deegan. You not only give me the time to write, but still continue to support me when my obsession fuels me at three o'clock in the morning and on holidays.

And to my mom, I'm eternally grateful for your encouragement and your continued love and support. I just wish Dad was still around to enjoy it. He'll always be the greatest story-teller in my life.

For the wages of sin is death.
    —Romans 6:23

CHAPTER 1

Every man likes to think he is a great lover.

Brent Poole grabbed his wife's hand and followed the panorama of crystal sand juxtaposed and running north between the Atlantic Ocean and the dunes. As they walked from their hotel parking lot, past a strip of private beachfront houses and onto the darkness of one of the last miles of undeveloped maritime forest along the beach, it dawned on Brent just how romantic Myrtle Beach was.

What a wonderful place to fall in love all over again, he thought.

Like so many lovers before him, Brent was mesmerized by the rhythmic waves breaking into rivulets of bubbling foam and spilling out onto the white sand. With his wife walking next to him, he felt so warm and alive. So sexually aroused.

Brent giggled like a schoolboy. "Let's do it over there." He locked onto Renee's arm and pulled her from the surf into one of the many hollows hidden in the dunes. Unfurling a beach towel, as if it were a white sail that had been lifted from a flagship, he spread it across the sand for them to lay on.

"I don't think anyone will see us here," he whispered.

Renee smiled and began unfastening her jeans.

Frigidity had never been at the top of Renee's shortcomings list. She and Brent had always been experimental when it came to intimacy. The way she saw it, most people joined the "mile-high club," but this adventure was a little more daring than that. The thrill of making love in the open and being seen really turned them on.

A sharp breeze whipped across the ocean and onto the beach, cooling their naked bodies. When they finished making love, Brent rubbernecked the sand hills, curious to see if there was an overly inquisitive person idly standing by. He'd thought he had chosen an isolated spot on the beach, but he wasn't certain. The last thing he needed at this point and time in his life was to discover some wide-eyed pervert had been hiding in the dunes, spying on him and his wife. He had grown weary of people like that. Consumed by lust. Always goggling and gawking. Envying their relationship.

Brent dressed, then helped his wife up and back into her jeans. He reached down and grabbed the beach towel and with a quick light motion shook it to remove the sand. He handed Renee her pack of cigarettes, which had spilled out of her jeans, then slid his watch over his wrist.

He looked at the time. It was almost midnight. In the distance, they could see the headlights of a truck driving past them on the beach. Renee poked him on the shoulder, then asked, "What are those headlights doing on the beach?"

"Oh, it's probably a police officer making sure no one was doing what we just finished doing." He laughed out loud. "Just think if we would have been any longer, we might have gotten caught in the act."

Although the thrill of "being seen" truly excited the Pooles, they had no real desire to get caught by the police. The possibility of going to jail for engaging in a lewd act or indecent exposure on the beach didn't necessarily appeal to either of them.

"We better start walking toward the hotel." He nodded at the lights shining ahead from where they were staying. He grabbed her hand and led her out of the dunes. The Carolina Winds Resort Hotel at Seventy-sixth Avenue was only five blocks away. "We promised not to keep the baby-sitter waiting."

Brent and Renee headed southward along the shore and toward the resort. They talked about their 2½-year-old daughter and marveled over her day at the beach. It was Katie's first trip and she had been captivated by the unfathomable seashore and the mysterious deep blue ocean that stretched before her. She had reveled especially in the time spent with her daddy, making mud pies and digging holes in the sand, where the waves crashed and ran gently to the shore.

As the Pooles strolled toward their hotel, they noticed a man dressed in long black pants and a long-sleeved black sweatshirt. He was in the dunes about twenty yards to their right, near a small hurricane fence, and was walking in the opposite direction. With temperatures that had soared past the nineties earlier that day, leaving the night air hot and muggy, they wondered why someone would be wearing winter clothes in June.

Brent looked back and was startled to see the man had turned around and was now following them. Alarmed by the stranger's appearance, he quickened his pace. Keeping his back turned toward the stalker, he cautioned Renee not to look behind her.

"Just keep moving forward," he told her. "Don't give him any opportunity to stop us." Sensing imminent danger, he hurried them down the beach. He believed the guy would back off once they reached the lit perimeter at the hotel.

Somehow, though, the man ran ahead of Brent and Renee, jumped out in front of them, and blocked their pathway. He was a large man, over six feet tall, with a big body and a big head. He was wearing a black ski mask. When they stopped and took a step backward, the stranger raised a semiautomatic 9mm pistol and pointed it at them. The gun was black and looked almost like a plastic toy gun.

Brent froze. Letting the beach towel fall from underneath his arm, he slowly lifted his hands with palms facing outward toward the jittery man. He wondered what he wanted with them.

"Get down on the ground." The man's deep voice was muffled inside the thick ski mask. He was jumpy. Clearly on edge. *Probably on some kind of dope*, they both imagined.

Brent hesitated. He first turned his head toward Renee, then back at the robber, as if he had recognized something familiar about his grumpy voice. He was certain she had recognized it, too. But before he could speak, the gunman lunged forward and tackled him to the ground. Brent fell backward, momentarily losing his breath when the burly man slammed down on him. The man's legs were the size of tree trunks. They pinned Brent's arms and buried them in the sand like small artifacts.

"I told you to get down on the ground!" the man shouted in the wind. He pointed the black muzzle and held it at Brent's head.

Brent felt as if his head had been riveted to the ground. He had a Swiss Army knife in his pocket, which he had bought at a flea market two Christmases past. But even if he could have gotten to it, it would have been useless against this rotund man wielding a 9mm and an itch to kill. He figured it was best to do exactly as he said and give him what he wanted.

But just what did he want with them? Brent's face searched for an answer. *Was he a robber? A rapist? A killer?*

The man in black wasted no time in telling them that what he wanted was for Renee to lie down and put her feet against her husband's feet. "I told you to get down on the ground, bitch." He scowled.

Renee quickly dropped to the ground, then inched forward until the bottom of her sandals rested against the soles of her husband's tennis shoes. She lay as stiff as a cadaver, her arms and hands fixed rigidly by her side.

The gunman eased upward, keeping Brent's arms pinned underneath his legs. Still straddling his body, he held the pistol nervously at his head. "Give me everything you got," the man said, holding out his open left hand toward Brent.

Brent nodded his head. Keeping a close eye on the pistol, he lifted his backside, retrieved his wallet and surrendered it to the gunman. Then he took off his watch and gave it to the man.

Renee was shaking so badly she couldn't get her rings off her fingers.

The robber swung the gun away from Brent and pointed it toward her.

"Hurry it up, bitch!" he shouted at the same time he slid the muzzle underneath Brent's chin.

"I'm trying . . . I'm trying," Renee mumbled through

clinched teeth. She removed her wedding rings from her left hand and a diamond ring from her right hand, then handed them to him.

"Is there anything else?" the robber demanded. He jerked the gun away from underneath Brent's chin and started waving it in his face again.

"Yes, my wedding ring," Brent answered somberly. As always when he got excited, his eyes had turned clear blue.

The masked man kept the gun aimed at Brent's head while he freed Brent's arms. "Then give me that, too," he snarled.

Brent anxiously pulled on the small band of gold and pried it from his finger. Beads of perspiration trickled down across his face and fell on his shirt. He stared into the eyes of this crazed man hiding behind a ski mask and begged for his life.

"Please, I'll give you whatever you want, just don't shoot me," he pleaded.

The gunman turned around and looked at Renee. He lowered the gun's muzzle, pressing it once again to Brent's forehead.

Brent held his breath. His arms were numb. He shut his eyes.

Renee didn't want to witness what she knew was going to happen. She saw the gun resting against Brent's forehead and closed her eyes when the man's index finger flexed, then slowly curled around the trigger.

There was a maniacal laugh. The gunman squeezed the trigger.

Click.

Nothing more. Only silence.

Renee opened her eyes. The gun had misfired. Brent was still alive.

The gunman was enraged. He squeezed the trigger again.
Click. Click.

The gun misfired again. The man anxiously rolled the gun over in his hand and ejected the brass cartridges.

Brent's eyes widened. His teeth shone white from the moon's glow as he clinched them in fear. He could see the robber was having difficulty getting his gun to fire. He released the breath he had been holding and tried to sit up.

Renee lifted her head and watched the man slapping the gun with his hand, as if that was what was needed to fix it.

He's not going to kill him, she thought. *This has to be a joke. He's going to get up and run away now.*

Brent's face was the color of ash. His skin tightened against his face.

When the man raised up to fix his gun, Brent leaned forward just far enough to lift his arms in a submissive gesture. Begging for his life a second time, he cried, "Please don't shoot me."

The man sneered back at him, then exchanged glances with Renee. He pointed the gun at Brent and pushed it back against his head, forcing him down to the ground.

"Give me one good reason why I shouldn't kill you."

Brent's heart jumped into his throat.

It was probably the greatest test of Brent Poole's fleeting twenty-four years. He had always been a happy-go-lucky person—just a whimsical kid who believed his whole life was still waiting ahead of him. He never, in his wildest dreams, imagined being in a position where he would be forced to bargain for his life. But without flinching, he swallowed hard and answered with the thought dearest to his heart. "Because I have a daughter that I love very much," he said bravely.

The gunman's eyes narrowed. He shoved the cold steel underneath Brent's chin and lifted him off the ground. Brent was off the ground and nearly on his knees when the man squeezed the trigger a fourth time.

Only this time the gun didn't misfire.

Pow!

The blast of the 9mm handgun rang out in the dark night like a firecracker.

Brent never heard the shot. And, doubtfully, he never felt it.

His head snapped backward as the spiraling bullet rocketed from the gun's black muzzle and burst through his skin. It pierced his tongue, blasted through the roof of his upper mouth, speeding behind and ripping through his brain. The chunk of lead finally slammed against his skull and embedded itself into the boney surface. His body stood upright momentarily as if suspended by the force of the blow. Then, as if someone had let go of the rope, he fell to the side and crashed to the ground.

Thud.

The limp body sounded like a fallen sack of potatoes.

Brent's brain was already torn and hemorrhaging when the gunman knelt down beside him. With no regard for human life, the shooter placed the gun above Brent's left ear and fired a second round into his brain.

Pow!

In killer's terms, he "finished him off."

The noise from the second shot echoed inside Brent's head. Even though the triggerman wanted to make certain he was dead, it wasn't necessary. In a split second, with his first shot, he had already robbed Brent of all consciousness.

Renee Poole had witnessed it all.

The shooter turned around, stepped toward her and lifted her T-shirt.

She was startled. She had given him all of her jewelry and Brent had given him all of his jewelry and his wallet. There was nothing else left to give him. She lay there frightened, but waited until the man finished, then watched as he ran off toward the dunes.

Brent lay motionless in the white sand. Spurts of crimson blood oozed from his open wounds and drained across his head and shoulders. His garbled moans grew weaker. His breathing shallower. He was dying.

Renee got up on her knees and called out to her husband. "Brent . . . Brent . . . ," she said softly through her tears. She saw the wet, sticky blood trickling from his head, sliding lazily across his face. It sounded like water moving over rocks in a creek. She prayed, "Oh, God, please let him be okay." Brent was dying, but she didn't know what she could do to save him.

William Brent Poole Jr., just ten minutes earlier, had been celebrating his third anniversary. Loving and caring for his wife. Making plans for their child and their marriage. And sharing hope that marked their future. It didn't seem right.

The masked man did not yet understand the magnitude of

the tragedy he had inflicted on the night of June 9, 1998, when he shot Brent Poole at close range, putting two bullets in his brain and leaving him for dead. A young life had suddenly been snuffed out at the threshold of his adulthood.

For the next twenty months, the inexplicable logic of why someone would have wanted Brent Poole dead would become the greatest challenge for both Brent and Renee's family. An enormous amount of time, money, energy, resources and manpower from seven divisions of police authorities in South Carolina, North Carolina and Virginia would dedicate themselves to solving that riddle. Ultimately, the answer to that question would be determined by a court of law and the American justice system.

CHAPTER 2

Renee was alone and frightened.

She sat still and looked at her husband as he struggled to live. He was still hanging on, but not by much. She stared at his body as he spasmed involuntarily. His blood continued to pulsate from the open wounds underneath his chin and above his left ear. Dripping from his head and onto the sand, it formed a bright red narrow stream, crawling over the sand and flowing toward the sea.

Renee felt as if somebody had poured hot molten lead into her stomach. The unavoidable trauma of having witnessed the shooting had been much too intense. She found it difficult to breathe and unconsciously kept pulling at her T-shirt. Her ears roared as if her head were being held down in a five-gallon bucket of water.

He needs help, she silently repeated over and over. *He needs a doctor.*

Renee tried to stand and felt the blood drain from her head. Her knees buckled. She tried again, but couldn't get her body to cooperate. Her brain seemed paralyzed.

"Get help, get help," she kept mumbling.

Renee finally swayed to her feet. She wanted to help Brent, but didn't know what to do. Everything was in a fog—like she was in some two-bit movie. Not really in it, but just standing on the outside watching the images of the shooting. In her mind's eye, the reel was stuck and the same scene played over and over again.

You've got to get help, a voice inside kept repeating.

Renee was determined to override her physical body. She looked around, but there was no one else on the beach. She stood still and screamed, but nothing came out. She tried to scream a second time. Still nothing. Remembering the lights from the police car earlier on the beach, she looked to see if it was still there. It was.

Yes, I see it. There. On the beach. A truck was coming toward her at about one hundred feet away. She'd stop the truck and get somebody to help her. Walking away from Brent's body, she staggered down the beach like a sunburned wino who had just finished off his last pint.

Even though it was near midnight, Myrtle Beach was still pulsating with people, mainly tourists and families beginning their summer vacation. Out on the boulevard, cars were backed up for miles, bumper to bumper. While the neon and fluorescent lights flooded the heart of town, a crowd of people in shorts and T-shirts strolled back and forth from the Pavilion Amusement Park and ocean to the hundreds of high-rise hotels and cottages that bordered the beaches. She could hear their laughter floating with the wind, but they were oblivious to Renee's pleas for help, the robbery and the shooting on the beach that had just occurred within a few blocks from them at Eighty-first Avenue North.

Twenty-three-year-old patrol officer Scott Brown had been assigned to the special unit of the Myrtle Beach Police Department (MBPD) officers that patrolled the beaches. Trained in both first aid and lifesaving procedures, this young and athletic officer seemed well-suited for the job. Brown was well-liked and respected by those who frequented in and around the beach.

At approximately 11:30 P.M., that Tuesday, Officer Brown had been policing the north end of Myrtle Beach, just past Eighty-first Avenue North. As he continued cruising northward, he saw a Caucasian female dressed in a white T-shirt and blue jeans who was coming out of his headlights and over to the driver's side of his truck. She was not running and did not seem to be in a hurry, just advancing toward him at somewhat of a meandering pace. Even though she was the only person he saw in this area, he didn't pay any particular attention to her. To him, she was just another beach walker.

As Brown drove closer, he wasn't sure if she was walking toward or away from him. He looked around to see if there was someone else behind him, but didn't see anyone. It was very common for beach walkers to lose their sense of direction, then stop him and ask for guidance or instructions.

It had been a little breezy on the beach that night, and because of that, both of the windows in Brown's truck were up. Just as his vehicle approached the girl, she crossed the headlights onto the driver's side, and showed just enough of a wave to get his attention.

She is going to ask me a question, Brown thought as he rolled his window down. He stopped in front of the attractive, dark-haired girl and stared at her. Early twenties. He leaned out the window and made eye contact.

"Can I help you, ma'am?"

The girl's hands were cupped and placed over her mouth, as if she were trying to catch her breath. She dropped her hands and calmly said, "Someone just shot my husband."

"What?" he blurted out, not expecting to hear that. Even though there had been a few strong-arm robberies on the beach, where someone had assaulted a tourist and demanded money, he had never heard of anyone being shot.

"Someone shot my husband," she repeated again.

He didn't know what to think. The girl kept her hands over her mouth and nose and was crying into her hands. She wasn't screaming or wailing, but had told him she had just witnessed her husband getting shot. He expected her to be upset, maybe even suffering from some type of emotional shock.

"Where is your husband?" he asked.

She pointed across the hood of the car and to the right-hand side, where the headlights pierced the breaking ocean waves.

Brown followed her penciled finger. He was not accustomed to seeing dead bodies lying on the beach at night. This was something of an anomaly—dead birds or dead fish, maybe—but never dead bodies.

The girl kept pointing toward the ocean. "He's down there."

Brown turned his vehicle in the pointed direction and switched on the takedown lights. The white lights from his truck illuminated the area. He hoped she was making this story up. In his many lone nights on the beach, he'd encountered a number of persons suffering from mind-altered states, usually brought on by the consumption of alcohol or drugs, but none of them had ever claimed to have witnessed a murder. As he edged the truck closer toward the surf, he spotted what appeared to be a body lying in the sand at a distance of some sixty to eighty feet away.

Brown's heart skipped a beat. It was pumping adrenaline to his brain like a two-horsepower sump pump. "I am going to be out of my truck," he radioed the dispatcher, who logged the call in at 11:45 P.M.

Brown wasn't sure at first glance if it was indeed a body on the beach or not. He needed to keep the girl close to him and asked her to walk with him while he took a look. As he moved forward, his suspicions were confirmed, however, when he saw the form of a white male, unconscious, lying faceup in the sand. The victim was wearing blue jeans, a button-up striped shirt and white tennis shoes. His feet were facing the dunes and his head was pointing toward the water. It was a grotesque sight. His face was covered with blood. Some of the blood had pooled behind his head and spilled out and onto the sand, then formed a trail that reminded him of a sleek kite's tail.

Brown stood over the body and looked for wounds. He felt as if his feet had been nailed to the ground. He wanted to pull his eyes away, but he couldn't. The individual had been shot in the head and he stared at the fresh blood dribbling down both sides of his face and dripping off his head. To the right of the body, he saw what looked like a white beach towel with a blue fish blazoned across the front. For a brief moment, he thought he was going to get sick. It quickly passed and his attention was redirected toward the body.

As he leaned over to inspect the body, the girl beside him fell to her knees, then grabbed the man's hand. She began to cry and tremble. He felt a lump in his throat. In her lap, he noticed a pack of Marlboro Light cigarettes and what appeared to be a wedding ring in her hand. She was twisting the band of gold around and around in her hand as if she were screwing the cap on a bottle of pop.

It didn't take Brown long, just a matter of seconds, before he realized the potentially dangerous scenario. The truck's takedown lights and headlights were beaming down on them and the body, lighting up the area like a football field. There he was, standing over the body, and she was kneeling beside it. They were both wearing white shirts. Sitting ducks for a shooter who might have decided to come back and finish the job, intent on eliminating the sole witness. He knew the dying man needed attention, but if he stayed to help him, he could be jeopardizing his and the girl's safety. His main objective suddenly shifted from aiding the victim to getting them safely back to the truck.

"We need to get out of here," he blurted out, his eyes focusing hard on the sand dunes. He reached down and tapped the girl lightly on her shoulder.

She didn't move.

He placed his hand in the middle of her back and lifted her up. "Come on, we've gotta get out of these lights."

She nodded.

The slender girl let go of the injured man's hand and rose to her feet, then stepped away from the body and started running alongside Brown. When they reached the truck, he fumbled inside for his portable radio.

In technical police jargon, he announced, "This is Officer Brown. We've got a shooting here on the beach at Eighty-first Avenue. I need help. I repeat, I need another officer."

CHAPTER 3

Officer Scott Brown's call for police assistance was executed at 11:51 P.M., some six minutes after his first transmission. After making the call, he opened the door of his truck and slid the girl in the driver's seat, then fixed himself in the apex of the door. Taking the oath of his duty "to serve and protect" to its highest level, he shielded her with his own body. With the threat of a killer still in the perimeter, there wasn't much he could do for the injured person. His first responsibility was to take cover and protect his witness. And that meant he had no choice other than to sit still, watch over the body and wait for the ambulance to arrive.

Brown tried to calm himself. "Ma'am, can you tell me what the shooter looked like?" His palms were sweaty.

"All I can remember is that he was dressed in black clothes and had a ski mask covering his face. He robbed us and ran toward that way." She pointed in the direction toward the sand dunes, slightly south of the Eighty-second Avenue beach access.

"You say he robbed you?"

She nodded.

"What did he take from you?"

She gestured with her hands and touched her chest lightly, telling him she had been robbed of some necklace or other piece of jewelry. She was still trembling and crying and kept her hands cupped over her mouth and nose.

Brown shook his head, keeping his eyes peeled toward the sand dunes.

Private first class L. D. "Lewis" Aiossa, with the MBPD, was also on duty and had heard Brown's distress call. It took him only a few minutes to drive from Seventieth Avenue on King's Highway to Eighty-second Avenue North and cross over to the beach access. When he whipped his patrol car in at the access, he parked behind several vehicles, boxing them in. He knew they were potential witnesses and made damn sure they weren't going anywhere. Guaranteed. They'd have no choice but to sit and wait until he moved his car.

Aiossa hurried onto the wooden walk deck that led to the beach, where he spotted Officer Brown about 125 yards south. Brown was standing at the truck with his patrol lights on and talking with a female. As Aiossa moved cautiously toward them, he spotted in the shadows of the truck lights a body lying in the sand. The person had obviously been shot in the head, as indicated by the blood trail that flowed from his head and colored the sand.

"What happened here?" he asked, standing a few feet from the body.

"We had a robbery and a shooting." Brown stepped away from the truck and gestured at the body. "The man's wife was able to describe the assailant as a man of unknown race, medium build, dressed in all black with a black mask. Heading westbound from this position on the beach, he ran toward the dunes."

Aiossa radioed the information to 911 and asked for assistance from the emergency medical services (EMS). He needed medical attention for the victim and additional officers to help locate the shooter. The Myrtle Beach Fire Department (MBFD) was the emergency services closest to the scene at Eighty-second Avenue. Operating from the same building, Fire Unit #121 and Medic #22 shared responsibilities, servicing the northern area of the beach as both the fire department and the ambulance service. In the event of a critical situation, they would both respond.

Don Askey was a fire engineer for Myrtle Beach's Fire Unit #121. Because the officer normally in charge was on medical leave with a knee injury, Askey, a thirteen-year veteran, became the acting senior man responsible for directing three firemen and two paramedics. Years of alternating his workdays between fire fighting and construction work on the beach had deepened his tan and chizzled his six-foot body into a muscular 235 pounds. Perfect for the physical demands this job required.

It was almost midnight when the 911 operator dispatched Askey's unit. He and his coworkers had just finished cleaning up the station and equipment and were preparing for bed when they got the call about a gunshot wound. They loaded up their equipment and drove the engine out of the station house, following closely behind the ambulance.

On the way to Eighty-first Avenue, Askey discussed the call with his partners and they agreed there was something unusual about it. To their knowledge, a shooting had never occurred in this secluded area of the beach. Tourists normally stayed away from there. Askey commented further that he had responded to a lot of calls in his tenure with the fire department, some of them being gunshot wounds, but he couldn't recall if any of them—be it suicide or homicide—were ever committed on the beach itself. And in the thirteen years he'd been here, he had never responded a single time to this stretch of isolated beach.

Askey had heard only one complaint about this area near Eighty-first Avenue, and that was in relation to a homosexual group that would meet and gather at the beach access. He recalled someone in his unit relating an incident whereby this person let a friend borrow his four-by-four jeep one summer to go on the beach. He left it parked at the Eighty-second beach access and returned later to find several pamphlets advertising the Offshore Drilling club and other gay bars. They had been shoved in the console area of the open jeep.

The men got a good laugh out of Askey's story. It helped to ease the mounting tension.

Askey's vehicle arrived at the beach access a second ahead

of the medic unit. Both rescue teams quickly parked and grabbed their equipment. As they hurried down the board-walk, they could see the two officers on the beach standing near the truck talking to a young girl. One of the officers, Aiossa, saw them and came running to the end of the boardwalk to help carry their equipment. He led them through the sand and onto the beach, about 150 feet to where the lights from the truck in-tersected and illuminated the body lying in the sand.

Even though the receding tide had washed away the soft sand from the beach, the rescue squad still found it extremely difficult to maneuver while carrying all their life-support equipment. Every second counts when someone is dying, but carrying all that life-support equipment across the beach was easier said than done.

The five men quickly set down their equipment, fell to their knees, and went to work on the critically injured patient. Their patient was a Caucasian male who appeared to be in his early twenties, five feet six and was estimated to weigh about 150 pounds. They couldn't tell much of what he looked like, as his head was covered in blood. As they huddled around the wounded man, they could see the silhouette of a gunshot wound. He'd taken a hit at least once. Underneath the chin. After assessing the wound, they were convinced this young man was close to crossing death's door.

The fire-fighting paramedics Eric Tier and Sammy Vest strapped a heart monitor on their patient to see if he was still alive. They were able to pick up a faint heart rhythm.

"This guy is really fighting to live," Tier remarked. He had learned from many years as a paramedic working on old people how to recognize quickly those who retained the will to live. In this young man's face, he saw a very strong desire to live.

Believing their victim was viable, the paramedics began ad-vanced lifesaving procedures. While Tier suctioned the blood from the wounded man's mouth and throat and inserted the breathing tube, Vest was busy positioning the IV needle into his arm.

The thirty-seven-year-old Tier had responded to many gunshot victims in his career as a paramedic and knew how sensitive the head was to any blunt trauma. He had also seen CAT scans and X rays of a speeding projectile as it entered the soft tissue of the brain and ripped through the delicate vascular system. He once witnessed a ballistic test where a bullet was fired into a vat of Jell-O to demonstrate the shock waves that occur as a result and learned the same principle applied when someone was shot in the head. As the bullet enters the soft tissue of the brain, the shock waves emit tremendous pressure in all directions, known as "cavitation," and will result in death, if not quickly relieved.

"It's severe head trauma," Tier said, gritting his teeth. "This guy doesn't need a paramedic, he needs a surgeon."

Tier had recognized his patient's biggest problem was his breathing. He needed CPR, so he called out for a flat board. But before they could do the chest compressions, he knew they had to get him out of the sand and onto a hard surface.

As paramedics Ginny Gregory and Charlie Miller joined in and worked feverishly on the patient, Don Askey could not help but overhear the young girl's story. Ten feet behind him on the sandy bank, she sat with the patrol officers, crying, and telling them what had happened. How they had been robbed and how her husband had been shot. Askey looked over his shoulder and stared expressionless at the girl for a few seconds. He heard bits and pieces of the conversation, then turned back around and focused on his patient. What he heard did not jive with what he saw. But, of course, he was less interested in the conversation behind him than he was with her wounded husband in front of him and what was going on there.

Askey's eyes locked on the crowd of onlookers and curiosity seekers who had begun gathering at the top of the beach. He watched to see if any of them fit the robber's description as given to the officers by the victim's wife. While the paramedics lifted the body and placed it atop the flat board, he glared toward the crowd like a bodyguard, looking for any sudden movements. If the shooter was still out there, he could just as easily take him out and the others who were trying to keep his intended victim alive. It was a trying moment. For his safety and the safety of his crew, he needed to get the victim out of there as soon as possible.

One of the patrol officers, who had just arrived on the scene, backed his four-by-four truck out on the beach so the firefighters and paramedics could load the victim into the back. The rescue team climbed in beside their patient and rode the short distance down the beach to the awaiting ambulance at the Seventy-seventh Avenue access. They were mindful every second of the way that a sniper, who could easily pick them off from his perched position, could be lurking nearby. For all they knew, this might have been a robbery, a drug deal gone bad or even a random killing. But whatever it was, it was as plain as the noses on their faces that whoever had shot this guy had wanted him dead in the worst way.

The injured patient was still alive when they loaded him from the truck, and he was still breathing when they slid him into the ambulance. Up until this time, the paramedics believed he had sustained only one gunshot wound—the one underneath his chin. But, once inside the cab, they could see in the light that he had taken a second hit. There, an inch above his left ear, was another bloody, gaping hole.

When the paramedics found out that the young man had two gunshot wounds, they were skeptical. The chances of him surviving were slim with one bullet to the brain. Now, with two bullets to the brain, it looked hopeless. In all likelihood, they knew he would be hard-pressed to make it. And, even if by some miracle he did survive—didn't have to be a brain surgeon to figure that one—the outcome would not be in his favor.

At approximately 12:20 A.M., the ambulance headed toward the Grand Strand Regional Medical Center (GSRMC). With the blasting siren dividing the traffic like the parting of the Red Sea, they made the five-mile trip in a quick few minutes. When the ambulance came to a screeching halt underneath the covered breezeway leading to the emergency entrance, the rescue team jumped out of their vehicle like a pit crew at the Southern 500. Hurriedly they transferred their patient inside and headed for the trauma room, where the medical staff anxiously awaited.

On the way down the hall, Don Askey stared at the young man lying on the gurney still fighting for his life and wondered how this could have happened.

He's so young, he thought, *with so much to live for and so many good times ahead. What kind of sicko would want to kill him and steal all of that away from him?*

CHAPTER 4

Myrtle Beach, South Carolina, holds a special place in many vacationers' hearts. Situated between Charleston, South Carolina, and Wilmington, North Carolina, it is in the center of a sixty-mile hemispherical beach known as the Grand Strand. As expected, the Atlantic Ocean is the greatest attraction to the Grand Strand, but there are other year-round features. As their brochures boast, there are "100 plus golf courses, world class fishing, five entertainment theaters, numerous hotels, fabulous campgrounds, and 1,650 dining choices that also entice visitors to return year after year."

Long considered one of America's favorite family-vacation destinations, Myrtle Beach is nestled along the Carolina coastline between the Atlantic Ocean and the Atlantic Intracoastal Waterway. It is the hub of the Grand Strand Area—sixty miles of beach that extends from the Winyah Bay, near Georgetown, all the way to the sleepy town of Little River, at the North Carolina border. Few vacationers had ever seen this area until sometime in the early 1900s. Simply known as "New Town," this beautiful landscape of rolling dunes and giant oaks standing guard over wide sandy beaches, bound by the Waccamaw River on one side and the Atlantic Ocean on the other, was nearly inaccessible. These natural geographical boundaries forced early travelers in pursuit of summer recreation to ferry across the river, then ride in wagons all the way from the river to the beach. In the 1700s, two Native American tribes inhabited the area's coastline, and in the 1800s, treasure-hunting pirates, like Captain Kidd and the infamous Blackbeard, frolicked along the shores. These notorious, rabble-rousing pirates found the fickle waters along the Atlantic coast a perfect looter's hideaway. But, by and large, the pristine coastline remained primarily undiscovered and remote. Most of America's population never even heard about this treasure until the first decade of the twentieth century.

The real visionary for the Grand Strand as a resort area has to be credited to Franklin G. Burroughs. This prolific businessman not only owned and operated a timber and turpentine firm in the nearby town of Conway, but held the titles to nearly two-thirds of the surrounding lands in Horry County. Burroughs was so confident in the coastline's potential as a tourist attraction that he purchased nearly eighty thousand acres along the shoreline and then constructed a railroad and bridge, leading from Conway, across the Waccamaw River, to make the beach accessible. He built the beach's first hotel, the Seaside Inn, in 1901, and initiated the first of many novel ideas to attract visitors.

The first vacationers to New Town were enchanted with its natural beauty, and, like Franklin Burroughs, they found the gentle climate and inherent charm of the beach irresistible. The development of seaside cottages and small boardinghouses sprang up rather quickly. Eleven years later, the Grand Strand got a huge boost from another entrepreneur, Chicago businessman Simeon Chapin. It was Chapin himself who convinced Burroughs that they shared the same passion and that he would make him a good business partner. As a result, Burroughs sold Chapin nearly half of his stock in his real estate company and the two men formed a new joint venture for the purpose of developing residential and commercial properties. Recognizing their vision was finally going to become a reality, the two men started pumping a lot of money into the Grand Strand, ultimately becoming the largest single developer in the area. Their company, Myrtle Beach Farms, still exists today and continues as one of the most powerful and dominating forces on the Grand Strand.

In 1936, when the Intracoastal Waterway cut through the heart of the Grand Strand, it supplied New Town with customers using shipping and commercial crafts. It, too, was a huge boost to New Town's economy. Two years later, after the citizens had been granted a town charter, they decided to hold a contest to rename this quaint resort area and the name "Myrtle Beach," ironically submitted by Franklin Burrough's wife, was chosen in honor of the abundant supply of wax myrtle trees and shrubs found along the coastline.

As odd as it may seem, Myrtle Beach's growth and push for a bigger and better resort expansion was spawned not by an individual, or a group of individuals like Burroughs and Chapin, but by a natural disaster. In 1954, Hurricane Hazel—as welcome as a yard of pump water—crashed into Carolina shores in the dark of night with wicked winds exceeding 130 miles per hour. As if they had been constructed from matchsticks, cottages and hotels along the coastline were leveled as easily as the wind rustling through fallen leaves, then washed out into the ocean. The storm's 18½-feet-deep water surge rolled into the city of Myrtle Beach with waves that broke at rooftop heights and climbed over traffic lights and telephone lines. Property damages in South Carolina alone were estimated at $27 million.

But, in spite of nearly everything in Myrtle Beach being destroyed by the hurricane, the city's key leaders and real estate developers dug in and started rebuilding. Stronger winds require stronger trees, and this time their blueprints called for larger and more lavish projects that could withstand the forces of the ocean. Not surprisingly, developers noticed as the building permits increased in Myrtle Beach and along the Grand Strand, so did the number of tourists.

In less than three decades, the city found itself at the heart of the fastest growing metropolitan area in the United States. Guests from all over the world were coming to enjoy the Grand Strand's beaches and an incredible range of activities, entertainment, shopping and dining. It seemed as if there was no end to the economic boom in the 1960s and '70s.

It was in the late 1980s when Myrtle Beach's continued

growth launched the establishment of an alternative industry dedicated to the country music and entertainment venues. Businessman/musician Calvin Gilmore was the first to grasp the ripe opportunity. He billed his country music theater, The Carolina Opry, as a live-music and comedy-variety show that rivaled any theater in Branson, Missouri.

A year later, the popular Southern country band Alabama followed with its own amphitheater. The group had actually gotten their start in Myrtle Beach in the 1970s, performing for tips in shot glasses at a little dive known as The Bowery. For almost a decade, Alabama had worked on their music at the little nightclub near the Pavilion on Ocean Boulevard before moving to Nashville and becoming a big hit. They returned full circle in the 1990s, and built yet another attractive country phenomenon, The Alabama Theater.

A short time later, dinner theaters, such as Dolly Parton's Dixie Stampede and Medieval Times, moved to Myrtle Beach, adding to the growing circle of big-name entertainment. Soon, other stars, like the Gatlin Brothers, Ronnie Milsap, Crook and Chase, EuroCircus, and Snoopy on Ice, built comparable theaters with their names on lit marquees out front.

In 1998, the same year the Pooles chose to vacation at the beach, Myrtle Beach and its resident population of about thirty thousand year-round citizens played host to more than 10 million visitors. Tourists from all over the country found Myrtle Beach with its warm year-round climate and comfortable, relaxed lifestyle to be the perfect vacation haven. The Grand Strand's wide variety of affordable attractions, including countless oceanfront resorts, hotels, condos and campgrounds, as well as some of the best retirement communities and beautiful beach houses on the east coast, were getting noticed by both national and world travel magazines.

"Myrtle Beach has something for everyone," one magazine touted. "There's no better place in the world to be than Myrtle Beach for safe, family fun!"

CHAPTER 5

The 1998 tourist season had been a particularly busy one for the MBPD. First, the Canadian vacationers had arrived in March for the Canadian-American Days Festival. As in previous years, the thousands of northern neighbors had chosen to escape the cold of winter during Ontario's school vacation week and travel to Myrtle Beach to celebrate the festival and enjoy the commencement of spring. Next, the Grand Strand had been bombarded in May by nearly two hundred thousand motorcycle enthusiasts, who came to observe Biker's Week and fraternize with other devotees. And then in June, the area had been inundated with hoards of graduating high-school and college students eager to kick off the summer season with the high-energy experience traditionally known as Sun Fun Week. All three of these festivals had included parades down the boulevard, beach games, athletic competition, live music, beauty pageants and other creative activities. And because these events were spread out all over Myrtle Beach and the Grand Strand, the men and women who labored to guarantee both residents and visitors a reasonable assurance of peace, security and safety often found themselves overworked and shorthanded. They longed for a few weeks of normalcy before the Fourth of July's onslaught of holiday tourists.

On Tuesday, June 9, 1998, MBPD officers and employees were counting down the last minutes to the end of their midnight shift. The tens of thousands of young adults celebrating Sun Fun Week had all gone home and given way to a much more subdued and older family crowd. Giving the police a reprieve, the Grand Strand reverted back to the more relaxed tone of a family resort, where hotels and motels provided activity programs and paid almost as much attention to the children's needs as to the adults.

MBPD Homicide detectives Terry Altman and Jim Joyce were two of ten investigators who had been scheduled for duty on June 9. Their shift began earlier that day at 4:00 P.M., and they were taking a breather before it ended at midnight.

It had been a slow night—skate duty, they call it—for Altman and Joyce. Actually, the recess had been quite enjoyable as the detectives finally had the time to tie up some loose ends. In the middle of their shift, they'd gone out, had a nice dinner, walked and drove around a little bit. All in all, it had been an easy, laid-back evening.

When Len Sloan, the third-shift detective, arrived, he saw that Altman and Joyce were already packed and waiting to go home.

"Hey, Sloan, it's a shame you gotta stay here all night with nothing to do," Altman teased. Sloan was one of the first persons he had met when he joined the police department. Charles Dickens could not have imagined a simpler, more humble and likable character than Sloan. The two friends laughed and joked with each other.

Suddenly their horseplay was abruptly interrupted by Brown's urgent message on the radio. In layman's terms, his message was: *We've got a shooting here on the beach at Eighty-first Avenue. I need help, I repeat, I need another officer.*

The detectives were accustomed to tuning into police radio messages and had developed a certain sense in distinguishing from the inflection of the voice as to whether it was something other than a normal call. When they heard Brown's message, they recognized the incident was very serious and violent. They assumed he had gotten in a fight with someone, that he was in trouble and needed help.

Shots must have been fired by the officer and maybe some-one had fired at him, they concluded.

Radio calls transmitted from the beach patrol and other pa-trolmen didn't routinely bring the detectives out to investigate the scene. A supervisor on duty, being of the rank of corpo-ral and above, would respond, assess the situation and deter-mine if a detective was needed.

"Well, we'll see you later," Altman and Joyce teased Sloan. "We're going home."

Technically, they could have. But, as all detectives know, in-cidents often occur at the end of the shift that require them to work until the job is done, and sometimes for the duration of the night and into the next day. Brown's plea for help sounded to them like there had been a shooting. If they were going to get called later at home anyway, they figured they might as well go up there and get it over with.

"Come on, Detective Sloan"—Altman chuckled, slapping the bespectacled, chunky man on the back as they walked out the door—"we'll go up there with you, help you out as much as we can, and then we'll call it a night. Then you can take over."

Since Eighty-first Avenue was a little less than five miles from the police station, it didn't take the detectives long to drive to the crime scene. Each detective had driven his own assigned Ford Crown Victoria, just in case they might have to disperse and go to different areas. One after another, they pulled into the beach access at the crime scene and started walking across the boardwalk, which cut through the dunes and led toward the beach.

For tourists who happened to be at the access or out on the beach, it was a curious sight to witness the police cars rush in and to watch these men dressed in coats and ties march out on the beach. For those who didn't know better, it appeared as if the FBI had landed and were storming the beach.

By now, a small crowd of witnesses and rubberneckers had heard the commotion and curiously gathered around the Eighty-first beach access to see what was happening. As the detectives walked down toward the beach, they met a couple of young men walking up toward the boardwalk. The guys were

all young, tanned and looked like surfers. Detective Altman
stopped and started talking with them. The other two detectives went on ahead to the crime scene area.

"You guys know what's going on here?" Altman asked the
teenagers.

"Yeah, we heard there was a shooting." A slim, blond-
headed guy with a silver earring dangling from his right ear
spoke up first. "But we don't know anything about it. We were
farther down south on the beach and saw the action around the
boardwalk, so we started walking up. But we didn't see or hear
anything. All we know is that somebody got shot on the
beach."

Altman pulled out his pad and jotted down their names, ad-
dresses and phone numbers, then stepped off the boardwalk
and onto the soft sand. In the headlights of the patrol truck,
he saw his partners talking with Scott Brown. He was relieved
to know the officer had not been injured.

The soft, yellow sand clung like gold to the detective's
shoes. He took a few steps, then hopped onto the smooth sand,
where the tide had washed and hardened the beach. He noticed
an area indented with a number of footprints and marred by a
long trail of blood. Knowing someone had been shot, he
guessed it must have been the girl he saw perched in the
driver's side of the truck with the door open. But as he got closer,
he could see she wasn't injured. Sitting behind the steering
wheel, she was positioned with her feet resting on the wide running boards of the truck, where she could just step out of the
truck had she wanted to.

From a distance, Altman studied the attractive, dark-haired
girl dressed in blue jeans and a white T-shirt. She was just casually there, half out the door with her hand clasped. She
looked a little pale to him, but she didn't look upset or hurt
in any way.

"Hey, Sloan, come here for a second." He waved his partner toward him. When Sloan walked over and stood next to him,
Altman turned his back to the truck so the girl couldn't hear
him. "She wasn't the one that was shot, was she?" he said,
thumbing back toward the truck.

Sloan shook his head from side to side. "Oh, no, she wasn't shot. It was her husband."

"Then where's the body?"

"EMS has already responded and taken him to the hospital."

Altman turned around and stared at the girl sitting in the truck. She appeared to be very calm for someone whose husband had just been shot. He turned back to Sloan, then asked, "You want to fill me in on what happened?"

"Yeah, the girl's name is Renee Poole. She and her husband, Brent, had been taking a stroll on the beach when they were robbed by this guy dressed in black clothes. He robbed them, then shot Brent in the head. Although the medics said they expected the worst, he was alive when they left in the ambulance."

The Myrtle Beach Patrol Unit (MBPU) had begun securing the perimeter. They were closely guarding the crime scene and logging every person coming and going into the area. Corporal Gary Kalkwarf, the second-shift supervisor of the beach patrol, placed a call to the Horry County Police Department (HCPD), requesting the use of their tracking dogs. If the shooter was still in the area and hiding somewhere in the dunes or around the beach on Eighty-second Avenue, the police might have a chance with the help of the dogs at finding him. Kalkwarf was afraid the ocean breeze blowing the salt water across the beach would make it very difficult for the tracking hounds to pick up the perpetrator's scent. In fact, the chances were zero to none the dogs would be able to follow the trail, yet Kalkwarf told them he was still willing to give it a try. The Myrtle Beach crime scene investigation team had also arrived and were waiting on the dogs to finish tracking the trail before they began their work.

When Altman looked around and saw all the officers on scene, he quickly deduced it wasn't necessary for all of them to be there. He suggested Jim Joyce take Renee back to the police department and obtain her statement. It would be to her benefit to get her away from the crime scene, and the quiet and still atmosphere at headquarters would help calm her and give her an opportunity to think. Perhaps then, she could provide additional information about the suspect.

Len Sloan agreed to remain at the crime scene, help manage the operation, and call the on-duty detective supervisor if needed. Altman thought it was best if he went to the hospital to check on the victim. From what he had been told, it was doubtful if he'd be able to get a statement from Brent Poole at the hospital. Nevertheless, he could get some information from the emergency responders and ask the doctors to shed some light on the situation.

As additional police officers arrived, they were immediately placed one hundred yards both north and south of the position in an attempt to expand the protection of the crime scene. Officers were also positioned around the surrounding area of the residences along the beach leading up to access and beyond, in case the killer was still lurking in the area.

As anyone who's connected to police work knows, the first forty-eight to seventy-two hours are the most critical in solving a homicide. It has been proven in two-thirds of the homicide cases that are solved, the police have been able to apprehend the suspect within twenty-four hours. Needless to say, there is a window of opportunity to solve a case within forty-eight hours and the chances of it ever being solved fall dramatically after that time period.

Because those first forty-eight hours were so critical in solving Brent Poole's murder, a staggering amount of work had to be completed. Murders in Myrtle Beach are very uncommon; as a result, everyone in the police department had been called out to work his/her magic. While crime scene technicians conducted the initial examination of the crime scene and collected physical evidence, additional officers and detectives were busy securing the crime scene and locating witnesses to interview.

A good crime technician is worth his/her weight in gold. Just by closely examining a crime scene, an adept technician can readily obtain a tremendous amount of information, often pinpointing exactly what took place and in what order, as well as why the crime took place and who is responsible. That is, if the murder scene has not been heavily contaminated.

The problem with this particular crime scene was that it had been.

All criminologists will agree a crime scene begins to deteriorate the moment a person enters it—just the very act of examining a crime scene damages the scene. And the more people who enter it, the more damage is done and the greater the potential for an irrevocable error.

The MBPD crime scene technicians didn't have the luxury of working an undisturbed crime scene. The biggest obstacle they had to overcome was there had already been half-a-dozen people or so who had entered the murder scene. It wasn't that the damage done to the crime scene had been committed out of ignorance or lack of training, but all with good intentions. Brent Poole was still alive when EMS responders arrived and granted it was more important to try and save his life than worry about preserving the crime scene. Crime scene technicians would have to determine what was trace evidence and what had been brought in or taken out by the emergency responders. Any of their trace evidence could have been deposited or taken away by any of the responders at any time. The technicians knew from the very beginning how easy it could be for them to make a mistake and have it come back to haunt them at a later date.

One advantage to the crime scene, however, was that the murder had been committed in a public place. Since the beach was a public place and there was a fair amount of traffic in and around that location, the odds were in the police's favor they'd find witnesses who had observed what had occurred. Witnesses are always easier to find and talk to during the embryonic stages of investigation, and their memories are generally more accurate and susceptible to recall soon after the crime has occurred. Collecting verbal evidence from witnesses was as vital to solving this crime as collecting the physical evidence.

The MBPD would be diligently searching for any clues that would lead to a suspect and help solve this case. Using high-intensity lights, they would be required to spend the majority of their time on their hands and knees sifting through the sand and closely examining the ground around them. In general, they'd hoped the evidence collected that early morning would tell them not only what the killer left behind, but what he left that shouldn't have been and what wasn't there that ought to be.

Supervising officer Aiossa began collecting a few of the fifty-five-gallon drums that were being used as garbage cans and taped off a fifteen-by-fifteen perimeter around the crime scene. While the others were taking care of the crime scene, he walked back to where the six people whose cars had been blocked, and now were sitting at the Eighty-second beach access, waited to be interviewed. The frustrated bystanders told him in colorful language they didn't recall seeing anyone coming out or going on the beach or any vehicles leaving suddenly, but thought they had heard something that sounded like fireworks on the beach.

While the crime scene technicians waited to work the murder scene, the Horry County tracker and his dogs continued to work the area around the beach access and in the dunes in hopes the dogs would be able to pick up the scent of the killer. There was also a very narrow window of opportunity for the tracker's hounds to locate and capture the perpetrator, but they would utilize any and all attempts.

Perhaps, the tracker shrugged to the officers standing nearby, *this just might be our lucky night.* If this mysterious killer—this man dressed in black—was somewhere in the area, he wanted to make sure the dogs found him and put him away before he killed again.

"You guys continue to keep a close watch out for the killer," Corporal Kalkwarf admonished his men. "We've already got one innocent victim dead, we don't want to make it two."

CHAPTER 6

Renee Poole never remembered getting in the police car. She was still dazed and unbelieving at what had taken place on the beach.

"Ma'am, are you okay?" The voice was sympathetic. "We're here at the police station." A tall, thin and dark-haired man opened her door.

Renee nodded and stepped out of the car. His voice sounded like it was coming from a fog. She couldn't escape the image of her husband being shot. She remembered the shooter as his finger tightened over the trigger, the jerk of his hand when the bullet exploded, the roar of the gun as it left the muzzle and blasted into Brent's head, and the thud of Brent's body falling onto the sand. She gagged as she thought about the raw scent of blood that spilled from his head wounds and pooled onto the sand. She remembered these things, but knew she couldn't do anything to change them.

Renee desperately needed someone to hold her close. To tell her she was safe. To say that everything was going to be okay.

Detective Jim Joyce escorted his key witness out of the car and into the Myrtle Beach headquarters on Oak Street. Over the years, there were several incidents along the Grand Strand where a couple had been robbed and/or assaulted. The MBPD particularly frowned on incidents that involved tourists visiting. It wasn't beneficial to the city and to the businesses in the area. Any news reports of such incidents were certain to frighten other tourists. Detective Joyce was aware that although this crime was committed in a remote area of the beach, the implications would be the same. No one wanted rumors circulating that the beach was no longer a safe place to visit.

More important though, Detective Joyce focused on the fact that Renee and her husband had been victims of a serious crime. Although he had not received the official word from the hospital, he sensed from the talk at the crime scene that Brent Poole was probably not going to survive his injuries.

Joyce contacted Mary Stogner, the MBPD's victim's advocate on call. The police department had just implemented the advocacy program and Stogner was one of three staff members. Their primary function was to console the victim, assist them with any paperwork and provide them with general information on counseling and other services available to them as a victim. Renee Poole was just the type of person who needed their help.

"I'm sure she's frightened," Joyce told Stogner as he walked her to the room where Renee was sitting. "This is not a good situation for her family. She and her husband are both in their early twenties and they've got a little girl."

Stogner sympathized with Renee Poole, virtually a stranger in town, now the victim of a violent crime. Thinking she needed someone to talk to, she pulled up a chair and sat across from Renee. She introduced herself and calmly asked, "Is there anything I can get you?"

Renee nodded. "Yes, I need a cigarette. I think I left mine on the beach."

"I'll see if I can bum a few from the officers. What kind do you smoke?"

"Marlboro Lights. But I'm so desperate, I'll smoke about anything you can find."

Stogner talked with Renee for about thirty minutes. When she was certain she was strong enough to provide a statement, she notified Detective Joyce.

"He's just going to ask for some general information about you and your husband and the crime," she assured her.

"Thank you. You've been very pleasant," Renee said flatly.

"That's what we're here for." Stogner reached under her desk, pulled out a small stuffed animal and handed it to Renee. "Please let me know if we can be of further assistance."

Renee managed to smile. She wasn't sure if the stuffed animal was for Katie or for her to keep for comfort. But she did need something real to hold on to since everything else at that moment seemed make-believe.

Renee's interview with Detective Joyce began at 12:45 A.M. When the detective asked where she was staying, she stated again that she needed to call the hotel and speak to her baby-sitter. Joyce then stopped the interview and requested that someone call the hotel and check on the situation.

Renee had stopped crying and was relatively calm when the interview resumed. Speaking very softly, she explained slowly what had happened earlier on the beach.

Joyce eased forward in his chair and took notes on a yellow legal pad, not wanting to interrupt her as she talked. She told him all about the man dressed in black and how they had been robbed. The silence stretched out afterward. The slight tremor in Renee's voice returned.

"And he went back over to my husband, and my husband said, 'Please, don't shoot me.' And he said, 'Why shouldn't I?' My husband said, 'Because I have a daughter that I love very much.' Then I heard the gun go off."

Joyce groaned. He uncrossed his legs underneath the table and sat up straight in his seat. "Do you know how many times it went off?" he interjected.

"I heard it click a couple of times. I think there were two shots."

"Did it click *more* than two times?"

"Yes, I think I heard it click a few times before I heard the actual shots."

Renee described what exactly had been stolen and provided a description of the man dressed in black. He then asked her, "And when he was talking to you, could you tell if he had any type of accent? Or maybe a deep voice?"

"I don't remember. I don't think it was very deep, though."

"Was he taller or shorter than you?"

"Taller. I think I'm five three. He was a lot taller than me, but not taller than you."

Joyce stood up and turned to the side, then sat back down. He was taller than the man she had remembered seeing. "And that's all he said to you, 'Get down on the ground and give me everything'?"

"Yes, everything. Money, jewelry, wallet, everything."

Joyce laid his pen down on the yellow pad.

"Okay. Uh . . . do you have someone else here that you're staying with?"

"No, but I need to speak with the baby-sitter at the hotel."

Joyce stood up slowly. "What time were you expected back?"

"We were supposed to be there at twelve A.M., so she needs to be relieved," Renee pleaded.

Joyce planted his hands on the table. He looked at his watch. It was a few minutes before 1:00 A.M.

CHAPTER 7

Thirty-one-year-old Terry Altman had been working with the Myrtle Beach Police Department for seven years. Altman was a local boy, having graduated from Socastee High School in 1985. Like most teenagers who live in and around Myrtle Beach, he had worked part-time after school in the food-and-beverage industry. It had helped pay for his education at Coastal Carolina University, where he was awarded a Bachelor of Arts degree in political science, in 1991. A few months later, he applied and was accepted as an auxiliary officer with the Myrtle Beach police force. In November 1992, he was hired as a full-time police officer, assigned to the traffic division, working five-day ten-hour shifts.

Altman had found his niche and went on to graduate from the eight-week officer's training at the South Carolina Criminal Justice Academy. In February 1993, he was reassigned to a patrol shift. For three years, he alternated from a uniformed patrol officer, back to the traffic division, until finally being promoted to the investigative division with the Myrtle Beach Police Department.

Detective Altman had been assigned to the homicide-investigative division for only two years the night he drove to the hospital to investigate the robbery and shooting of Brent Poole. If he had to guess, he'd say he had already investigated anywhere from twenty-five to thirty dead-body calls. That was the one part of the job he disliked the most, and probably the reason why he had not chosen a career in medicine. He made no bones about it. He wasn't fond of dead bodies.

Altman walked through the electric doors at the Grand Strand Regional Medical Center (GSRMC) emergency room and turned into the emergency room's lobby. A few people were sitting in chairs and couches, idly reading magazines or watching the wall-mounted television. He smiled at an elderly couple standing at the nurse's desk and waiting to be processed, then eased around them to the trauma unit, where he believed Brent Poole would have been taken. To the right of the nurse's station in the trauma unit, he recognized several personnel from the fire department, who were retrieving their equipment and completing the last of their paperwork. From the grim look on their faces, it was apparent the situation for their patient looked hopeless.

Don Askey, the emergency responder from Unit #121, had already completed his paperwork and was leaning against the nurse's station. His body was washed in sweat and the gritty sand from the beach still clung to his clothes and skin liked yellow mud. He looked as if he'd just lost his best friend.

"How's it going?" Altman anxiously asked.

"Not so good." Askey shook his head, then rolled his eyes toward the trauma unit. "They're still working on him."

The rooms in the trauma unit were petitioned on the side and front by cloth curtains. In an opening between the curtains, Altman could see Brent's lifeless body lying on the table in the middle of the room with the team of five nurses and doctors surrounding him. They were working on him, frantically trying to bring him back to life. Plastic tubes protruded from the young man's mouth. Blood covered his face and dripped down onto the table and fell to the floor.

Altman stepped toward the nurse's station and stood by Askey. He could always count on Don for an honest opinion. He whispered, "So, what's your assessment of this situation?"

Askey gazed at the detective with a bewildered look on his face. He hadn't realized until now the significance of what he had overheard the young girl say on the beach. He wiped his mouth with the back of his hand, then leaned in toward the detective. "I'm not sure what she told you about how this happened, but it didn't happen the way she said it did."

Altman shifted his feet and turned his head slightly toward the fireman to make certain he didn't miss a word. Through the opening in the curtain, he could see the trauma team was still busy working on the victim. He guessed they had been successful in keeping him alive.

Askey continued: "I'm telling you, man, there's just something not right about this situation." He lifted his hands, palms upward, in front of his chest, and shrugged. "A young couple is robbed on the beach. He gets shot twice. In the head and at close range. But nothing happens to the girl? Maybe it's just me, man, but this whole thing doesn't make sense."

Over the years, Altman had learned to listen to the opinions of other professionals when he investigated a case. Every discipline had its own way of looking at things. Their own perspective. Even still, each individual approached things differently and had his own opinions. But he'd learned first impressions were almost always correct. He always made it a point to tell Askey and the others how much he appreciated their insight.

Altman talked to the other paramedics before they left the hospital. He thought about what Askey and the others had told him. They had confirmed some of what he had recognized earlier back at the crime scene. Their feelings about this case were nearly the same as his and their suspicions as contagious as the common cold.

After the emergency responders exited, Altman stood alone at the nurse's desk and stared at the heart monitor through the opening in the curtains. In just the few minutes while he was there, there had been the trace of a slight bounce flowing across the gray screen. That had changed. Now he watched as all the life seemed to flow out of the victim—eventually changing the fluttering beep to one single, flat line. Brent Poole was dead.

Altman sat down in a chair and took a deep breath. Although the trauma team had refused to give up and continued working on their patient, he realized Brent probably wasn't going to be revived.

At 12:21 A.M., the emergency surgeon, Dr. James Duffy, decided there was nothing more the trauma team could do. Duffy took a deep breath, waved his hands out in front of his chest and signaled them to stop. After halting his team's efforts, Duffy made one more last assessment, then pronounced their patient dead.

Altman stood at the nurse's desk and watched the members of the despondent emergency trauma team, RN Barb Plaxco and RN Ronnie McDonald, as they filed out of the petitioned room. The other trauma nurse, Rose McKay, had already started completing the charts at the nurse's desk, and she leaned over to Altman and whispered, "This is a terrible shame. It hurts me so much to see something like this. He was so young and such a good-looking man. Makes you wonder, who would want someone like him dead?"

Altman nodded. She was as right as rain.

As the trauma unit dispersed from the room, Altman reached for the phone at the nurse's desk and called Detective Len Sloan at the crime scene. It was important when there was a murder case for Altman to follow protocol and contact everyone who was needed to respond. His call to Detective Sloan would be the first of many he would have to make that night to get all the responsible persons in the right places to investigate this case. He asked Sloan to contact Sergeant John King, who was the supervising detective on duty.

"You can pass the word that Brent Poole just died," Altman said over the phone. "You might want to notify the county coroner as well."

Officially, the Poole case had just been updated from a shooting to a homicide. From Altman's previous experiences of working murder cases, he knew the implications of losing Brent Poole. Brent had been his only other witness. Not only was it going to make his job more difficult, now that half of his sources were gone, but it would be the beginning of another all-night ordeal of tracking down leads, interviewing, and seeking information that would escalate into a marathon of full proportions. Altman had already worked his eight-hour shift, and he called his wife to warn her he might not be home to see her again until the next day.

Altman's stomach tightened in knots.

As Altman watched and waited from the nurse's desk, Corporal David Grazioso, the crime scene specialist with the Myrtle Beach Special Operations Section (MBSOS) for the night shift, stepped into the room. He spoke with Altman, then followed him to the petitioned room where Brent's body still lay on the gurney.

"Graz," as he was known to his fellow officers, had been called out at midnight and arrived at the crime scene at 12:15 A.M. Asked to stand by and wait until the dog team had finished tracking the area, he had begun processing the crime scene some fifteen minutes later. At approximately 12:30 A.M., he had started snapping pictures, drawing charts, and examining the crime scene for potential evidence. He then drove the short distance to the GSRMC for the purpose of photographing the body and collecting further evidence.

When Altman was certain the room had been vacated, he and Grazioso entered through the partitioned curtains. As was the standard procedure with all gunshot incidents, any person present at the crime scene would be tested for the presence of gunpowder residue. Grazioso had already swabbed the hands of the victim's wife back at the crime scene, and was there to perform an Atomic Absorption Analysis kit on Brent. The results would determine if he had fired a handgun in defense or taken his own life.

Both samples from Brent and Renee Poole would be sent the next day to the forensics lab at the State's Law Enforcement Department (SLED) and tested for the presence of gunpowder residue. If either of the fatal wounds had been the result of a weapon fired from the victim or his wife, or the tests proved they had fired a weapon, then the case would abruptly take on new proportions.

Grazioso was also there to collect and bag the victim's clothing for evidence, but until he found a couple of nurses to help him, that would have to wait. A fourteen-year veteran of the MBPD, he knew all too well how difficult it was for one person to remove the clothing from a dead person. When he found out from Altman that the nurses were busy with another emergency in the trauma room, and it would be about an hour before they could send someone to help him, Grazioso became concerned.

"I really need to get back to the beach," he told Altman.

As a crime scene specialist, Grazioso had covered the waterfront and Ocean Boulevard section of the beach and responded to calls for service where the crime scene had simply vanished. Washed away by the rising ocean tides. And there was that same risk with this case. He knew it was his responsibility to remove and bag the clothing, but under the circumstances, he needed to return back to Eighty-second Avenue as quickly as possible. Fortunately for Grazioso, Detective Altman was there to assist.

"Go ahead, Graz," Altman told him. "As soon as I finish talking with the doctor, I'll get a few of the nurses to help me and we'll get it for you."

Altman sat at the nurse's station and waited until Dr. Duffy had cleaned up, then asked for a few minutes of his time.

Duffy discussed the severity of the victim's wounds as Altman followed him in the curtained room. "There are two gunshot wounds." A frown stretched across Duffy's tired face. He looked beat. "One just inferior to the left ear, which was a close-range or loose-contact-type wound."

Altman slid a pair of latex gloves over his hands. He sidestepped a pool of blood that had dripped on the floor and moved in to take a closer look at the wounds.

Duffy pointed to a hole on the side of the head, to where there was soot, carbon fragments and pieces of skin tissue clinging to the entrance site. "There is a projectile found in this area, the parietal occipital or posterior aspect of the head," he said in anatomical terms. "The other one is a wound under the chin. This, of course, is a contact wound, as you can see the muzzle of the gun was in direct contact with the skin."

Altman could see the muzzle imprint in the skin. He winced at the thought.

"There is no powder residue around this wound site,"

Duffy continued. "Probably an indication that all of the residue had gone into the wound when the bullet passed through his chin and into the top of the head."

Duffy placed Altman's gloved fingers on Poole's scalp. Altman could feel the fragment of a bullet underneath.

This was the first time Altman had ever touched a dead body. A few years ago, he would have never imagined himself being asked to touch a bullet lodged beneath someone's scalp and above his brain. As he massaged Brent's scalp and felt the lead underneath, he was queasy at the thought of what damage the bullet might have done on the underside of Poole's skull.

Duffy held up the X ray of Brent's skull and pointed to where the two bullets were lodged in the brain. As he explained the significance of the small white spots against the black of the negative, Altman grimaced at the estimated number of fragments of bone that had been shattered upon impact and the delicate tissues ripped by the path of the speeding bullet.

The doctor shifted his weight. "As you can see, there are no exit wounds." He continued tracing with his finger the projectory angles of the bullets through the brain, which ended in two star-shaped patterns where they both were lodged.

Altman felt faint, but quickly shook it off. "Which one of the bullets do you think killed him?"

"Well, either one of them would have been enough to have killed him. In fact, after seeing this X ray, you wouldn't think that anyone would have ever lived after suffering a gunshot wound through the head like this. Even if it was just for a moment, there was just no way he could have survived those bullets."

Altman took a few steps backward away from the body and started peeling the gloves off his hands. He'd hoped Dr. Duffy was about to confirm his suspicions.

"So, what do you make of all this, Doc?"

Duffy looked at the X rays for a second time and, without hesitation, answered, "I think this kid got executed."

Atlman affirmed that was what he needed to know.

The detective thanked the doctor, walked out of the room and turned down the hall. He felt light-headed. He needed a stiff drink of water. On the way back from the water fountain, he noticed Robert Edge, the county coroner, standing in the hall talking with Dr. Duffy. The doctor had also briefed the coroner on Brent's injuries and showed them to him.

"Is it okay to remove the victim's clothing for evidence?" Altman asked Edge after he had finished talking with the doctor.

Edge nodded his approval.

Altman had never before taken the clothes off a dead body. And he wasn't too thrilled about having to do it this time. "I'll have to borrow a couple of hospital nurses and ask them to do it," Altman mumbled as he walked away from the coroner. He wished now he hadn't been so quick to volunteer his services.

Altman found RN Mary Ellen Darragh in the hall and asked her if she would assist him in removing Brent's clothes. Darragh wasn't aware of the detective's revulsion for dead bodies. She did not know it was his first time to undress a body.

"I will get his clothes off for you, but you will have to help me," she told him.

Altman was eager to get back to the crime scene and share the information he had learned from the emergency responders and the confirmation he'd received from the doctor. But he couldn't until Brent's clothing had been collected and his body settled in. He could have waited until another nurse was free, but if it had to be done and he had to help do it, then he wanted to get it over with as soon as possible.

"Okay. If we're going to do it, let's do it now before I change my mind," Altman reluctantly agreed.

Darragh grinned at the detective, whose face had quickly turned the color of a red plum.

Altman pulled a white handkerchief from his back pocket and nervously swiped it across his brow. "I'll be in the trauma room waiting for you."

Darragh shook her head and smiled.

Altman walked into the trauma room and stood over the body a second time. Recalling the doctor's information about the wounds, he stared at Brent's head, cringing at his bloodied and bruised face. The blood had coagulated on both sides of his face in splotches and was a sharp contrast with the young man's thick brown, curly hair and against his fair complexion. His mouth was open; his white teeth separated by the plastic endotracheal tube. An IV of saline solution was still stuck in his arm. His lifeless eyes were an astonishing crystal-clear blue.

If only Brent's lips could have moved, Altman knew he could have told him a lot of things. He just wished Brent would have lived long enough to tell him what had happened. It would have made his job a lot easier and explained a lot of unanswered questions.

But there were answers that no one, including Brent, would ever be able to give him. That was his job. He would have to find out those answers on his own. That was what he got paid for.

"Okay, Detective, we're ready," Nurse Darragh announced as she entered the room. She had several other nurses, Patty Rathner and Maureen McGinty with her. As they began removing the clothes from the body, a striped shirt, trousers, socks, underwear, and tennis shoes, Altman collected them and dropped them in bags. Those that had any blood on them were placed into a biohazard bag, which was a red plastic bag designed to prevent the blood from seeping out.

Altman handled Brent's clothing very carefully. He realized the potential of obtaining these items for the forensic team and not wanting to destroy any evidence that could later match the killer. There was a lot of blood on Brent. His shirt was soaked in blood and the blood from his head had seeped onto the gurney.

Altman didn't know how much, if any, debris from the killer had stuck to the victim's bloody clothing. If he had struggled at all, it was possible that a hair, a fiber or a piece of flesh that belonged to the shooter may have bedded itself in the blood. If that was the case, then it would be one of the clues they would be looking for to pinpoint the murderer.

When they finished undressing Poole and packing his clothing away, Altman noticed the hair on Poole's legs and pubic area had been shaved. *Must have been a racing cyclist,* he thought. Looking at his taut body, he guessed Brent would be the type that rode at least one hundred miles per day.

Altman had been a cyclist at one time and knew why a rider

would want to shave his body hair. It made it easier to apply ointments and medicine to the body after a hard race and also eliminated the possibility of "road rash." When a biker takes a fall, the hair on the body will get caught between the skin and the asphalt, and will literally be pulled out by the roots, resulting in an even deeper and more abrasive skin tear.

He made a mental note to ask Brent's wife about this. Perhaps her husband rode cycles as well, and he'd learn that the two of them had something in common after all.

Darragh and the other nurses draped a white sheet over Brent, then notified the county coroner that the victim was ready to be pronounced dead. Altman called Lieutenant Bill Frontz, who had since responded to the scene and advised that he was still at the hospital with the coroner.

"Do you want the autopsy to be performed at the Medical University in Charleston or here at Grand Strand Regional Medical Center?" Altman asked.

"Here at the Grand Strand Hospital," Frontz responded. "You'll have to ask him to call Dr. Edward Proctor, the forensic pathologist, and schedule an autopsy."

Altman waited with the others for the coroner to examine Brent's body, then pronounce him dead. After he finished his business, Altman gave him the instructions for the autopsy. The coroner called Dr. Proctor and learned the autopsy would be scheduled for 1:30 P.M. that same day.

Altman helped the nurses wheel the body out of the trauma room. They rolled Brent's body down the hall, behind the cafeteria and into the refrigerated morgue, where the autopsy would be performed. As Brent Poole's body was being transported down the hall, Altman looked back behind them. A trail of blood followed behind them every five to ten feet. One of the nurses alerted a maintenance man and he shadowed them, the entire 150 feet to the morgue, with a mop and bucket and cleaned up the blood along the way. Once inside the morgue, the gurney carrying Brent's body was placed alongside several other bodies covered in white sheets.

Altman's stomach churned. No one said a word.

Altman felt a chill running up and down his spine, like the

brain freeze he got as a little boy when he ate his ice cream cone too quickly. He casually passed it off to the nurses as the temperature in the morgue, but privately knew better.

Having completed his job at the hospital, Altman thanked the nurses for their help in disrobing and securing Brent's body. He said his good-byes, then went outside and stood in the parking lot in the night air. The sky looked like an ocean of black and deep purple. The moon looked as if it was hiding its face behind a cloud, perhaps ashamed of what had been witnessed earlier on the beach.

CHAPTER 8

Captain Sam Hendrick was accustomed to his phone ringing late at night. A light sleeper by design, he rolled over in his bed to answer the phone.

"Sorry to wake you, sir," Sergeant John King drawled, "but there's been a shooting at the beach we think needs your attention."

King was the on-duty supervisor at the MBPD Investigation Division. It was his responsibility to notify the higher-ranking detectives about a serious case or a shooting. He had been a policeman for fourteen years, inching his way up from a detention officer to sergeant in the investigative unit. Ten of those years, he had worked under Hendrick's command. In fact, the two had been working together so closely that King had developed a sense of when he thought Hendrick needed to be called in on a case. He was convinced this shooting was definitely one of those times.

"What have you got, John?" Hendrick cut the lamp on beside his bed, then patted his wife back to sleep.

"Hate to get you out of bed for this," King apologized, "but it looks like we have a homicide on the beach. I've already called the lieutenant. I thought you both would want to be in on this one."

Hendrick had been in law enforcement for twenty-six years—as long as he and his wife, Jennie, had been married.

They both accepted the fact his job was always going to be a forty-hour-plus week. Like most police officers, when Sam wasn't working, he was thinking about work. This would not be the first or the last time he would have to crawl out of bed after midnight, put on a coat and tie and drive to the beach to investigate a murder.

Hendrick straightened his tie in the mirror, kissed his wife good-bye, then headed out the door. Without saying so, they both knew it would be some time before he would see his family again. On his way out the door, he remembered being told over the phone that the young man who had just been shot on the beach was twenty-three years old. His own son, Sandy, had just turned twenty-one.

It was a little after 12:30 A.M. when Captain Hendrick arrived at the Eighty-first Avenue beach access. As he stepped off the boardwalk and onto the beach, there was an assembled crowd of law enforcement officers to greet him. Hendrick recognized there were two elements in working a crime on the beach that he could always count on. Regardless of the time of year, he always found the beach windy at night, and he always had a heck of a time walking on the beach without the gritty sand clinging to his shoes and clothes like a layer of glue.

As chief of the Investigation Division, Hendrick not only had the control of the day-to-day operations with the detectives, narcotics and crime scene investigations, but at any time a major crime occurred every department fell under his jurisdiction for chain of command. Although he didn't directly supervise the beach patrol, he had jurisdiction over them and anything that related to this crime scene. Hendrick expected a full report from every department who was working this case.

"What have you got so far?" Hendrick asked, singling out his sergeant.

Sergeant King looked up. "Good morning, Chief. We've got a robbery here, where this one guy was shot. Wife was with him, but she wasn't shot. She's our only witness. Detective Joyce has her at the station now interviewing her."

"What is it she said she saw?" Hendrick wanted to know.

King held up his notepad in the light shining from the

trucks still parked on the beach. "She told us someone wearing a mask and dressed in black came up from behind them on the beach, robbed them and then shot her husband."

King lowered his pad and stepped toward Hendrick. He led him a few feet away, cupped a hand around his mouth as a shield, then said in a low voice, "We got the call about ten minutes ago that he died. Detective Altman is still at the hospital talking with the doctors and emergency responders, hoping they'll be able to shed some light on the situation."

Captain Hendrick and Sergeant King walked over to the cordoned area of the beach, which was being spotlighted by the beach patrol trucks. Careful to stay outside of the immediate crime scene area so as not to contaminate the evidence, they observed from a distance the pool of crimson blood that stained the beach's white sand.

"The wife said the robber made her and her husband lie on their back with their feet together before asking for their money and jewelry," King continued. "And then, for no apparent reason, he shot her husband." He paused. "Said he shot him in the head. Shot him twice."

Hendrick thought about what he had just heard. A few of the details King had given him were a little odd, but he had learned over the years to reserve his comments until all the facts of the story were in. Victims of serious crimes often experience confusion or momentary memory lapse due to the shock and trauma of the moment. Until they got the complete story from the victim's wife, he would take a wait-and-see posture.

"The robber shot him here." King pointed as they walked around the back side of the yellow-taped area, which was about the same square footage as the standard boxing ring. They moved in for a closer look. The evidence collection team was busy sifting through the sand, searching for any morsel of a clue to the crime. An additional officer, Dean Mayer, who was particularly gifted with a metal detector, had been called in to help examine the area.

King motioned toward the officers, then reported what had already been found.

"They've located several spent shells, so we know the

robber shot the guy here. We believe he then took off at a northward angle toward the beach access. The dogs were able to pick up his scent to the beach access, but then they lost the trail there. We figured that is where the gunman probably got into his parked car and drove off."

"What have you got by way of footprints?" Hendrick asked.

"Well, there were so many people in and out of this area to begin with, especially when the paramedics came down here to treat the body," King said, "I am afraid we don't have anything solid in that department."

King knelt down and grabbed a handful of sand. He shook his head as if the fault lay with the grainy material he now had squeezed between his palm and fingers. "Besides, you know how this soft sand is. It never gives a good print." He opened his hand and let if fall in one clump to the ground, then brushed his hand off against his pants pocket.

"How about the patrol officer, what does he know?"

King nodded toward the officer standing by his truck. "Officer Brown, who found the couple, is over there with his supervisor, reviewing his report."

Hendrick looked over at the young, clean-shaven and white-walled officer.

"Brown did say he noticed one thing in particular about the victim's wife that was unusual," King continued. "She had told him the robber made her and her husband lie on their backs, with their feet together before he robbed them. He said when she first approached him on the beach, to say that her husband had been shot, he asked her to sit in his truck. Yet, when she got out of his truck some time later, he looked closely at the back of her shirt and noticed there was no sand on it. Nor was there any sand on the back of the cloth-covered seats where she had been sitting."

"On the back of her pants, either?" Hendrick asked with a quizzical look.

"No, sir. There was nothing on her pants or the back of her shirt."

"How about blood?" Hendrick pressed. "Any blood on either her shirt or pants?"

"There was a tiny drop of blood on her pants and some on her hand. But, other than that, there was nothing."

"And you said she is our only witness of what went down?" Hendrick reiterated.

King answered in the affirmative.

Hendrick walked King away from the crime scene and toward Officer Brown and his supervisor, who were standing at the truck. He wanted to hear it again from the patrol officer and get his perspective.

Hendrick being to summarize the facts. More so for himself than Sergeant King. "So, in essence, we got the robbery of a young couple. The husband is shot and the wife is not. The wife is the only person we have at this point who knows what happened, and the only person we can get any information from."

"It's the only one we know about so far," King confirmed. "We believe there might have been other witnesses, but we don't have any at this time."

"Well, we can't count on finding another witness, so it is possible this girl is all we've got. And, given that her husband is dead, she just might turn out to be the only witness to the shooting." Hendrick scratched his head. He didn't like the direction this case had taken. "We've got no choice at this point but to stay with the girl and get all we can out of her, if we're ever going to find out what happened here."

"Yes, sir," King snapped.

"I agree with that."

Hendrick stepped up to Officer Brown and his supervisor, huddled around the lit truck. The additional information from Officer Brown could be the piece of the puzzle they needed to help solve this case. Brown repeated what he'd told his supervisor. Hendricks recognized immediately the officer was no raw recruit. Fortunately, this three-year veteran was a well-trained, astute and observant officer, everything Hendrick had aspired for all his men.

"And you're sure, Officer Brown, there was no sand anywhere on her front or backside?" Hendrick asked.

"No, sir." Brown gestured with his hands. "The only sand

I saw on her was on the knees of her jeans. Now, I did see a large amount of sand in my front seat when she exited my vehicle. She had to have gotten that on her when she and I checked on her husband. She had knelt down beside him and held his hand. I'm certain that's where the sand on the seat of her pants came from."

Hendrick pulled King aside again. "John, we've got to get to this girl. We need to get her story from her and get it fast!"

"Yes, sir, I understand. She is important."

"She is more than important," Hendrick emphasized with great emotion, his hands flapping. "This whole case may depend on her and her testimony. In fact, if we don't get it, we may never be able to solve this murder."

While serving in the army, Hendrick had played a little poker. Although he was never very good at it, he had learned a thing or two about human nature. The men in his outfit who consistently won were those who knew how to read and play other players. If they were ever going to solve this case, he needed a man like that: someone who was a natural at pinpointing changes in facial expressions and reading body language, someone who could hone in on the smallest sigh or bead of sweat on the upper lip, someone who could use that emotion and get the person to betray his or her true feelings.

That someone, Hendrick knew from the very beginning, was Detective Terry Altman.

CHAPTER 9

Detective Altman left the hospital, then drove back to the crime scene to meet with Lieutenant Frontz and Captain Hendrick. This was the first murder on the beach they had ever worked.

"Good to see you back, Altman." Frontz chuckled when he saw Terry walking toward him. "The chief's got some news for you."

Thinking there had been some new development in the case, Altman felt his hope rise. He quickened his pace and headed toward Hendrick, who was still talking with Sergeant King. Maybe he would say they had found the killer and they could all go home and get some sleep. But that was not to be.

"At this point and time," Hendrick stated, "it's crucial that we put our best foot forward and assign who we think is the best person for the job of lead detective. Unfortunately, we've got to play the hand we've been dealt. We have one living witness—the widow—and she's the only person we have to tell us what happened. Now, that's scary."

"Yes, sir, I agree," King added.

"It looks like her story might be all we've got, so we've got to get her to show us the hand she's playing. I'm telling you, solving this case is going to depend solely on the person we choose to get information from that lady sitting in our office.

And it's going to take someone like Altman to get the truth out of her."

King nodded.

When Hendrick informed Altman he had been appointed the lead detective on this case, he responded jokingly, "Oh, crap, that's all I need."

For the next thirty minutes, Altman briefed Hendrick and Frontz and shared what he had learned at the hospital, especially that of Dr. Duffy's candid opinion. They, in turn, provided him additional information they had garnered from the crime scene. By now, the crime scene evidence team had completed their search, and the three detectives were able to walk through and examine the bloodied area. They studied the scene and discussed the found evidence and the "how's and why's" this murder could have occurred.

"We found two spent nine-millimeter cartridges," Hendrick told Altman. "There was one on top of the sand to begin with. Then we found another one when we brought in Officer Mayer, who skimmed the sand with a metal detector. He is the expert at finding things buried beneath the ground. I don't think anything else was there or he would have found it."

Altman pictured in his mind's eye the shapes and casts of a 9mm cartridge—silver casing and copper jacketed with hollow expansion points. A chill suddenly passed over his body. These were synonymous with the two bullets the killer had fired directly into Brent's head that shattered his brain.

"Another four live cartridges were found," Hendrick continued. "All of these I believe came from the same nine-millimeter gun. Three were found on top of the sand by Grazioso when he processed the crime scene. The fourth one had been hidden under the sand and was found by Mayer and his metal detector."

Corporal Grazioso walked over to the group, holding an evidence bag.

"Good so far, Graz," Altman chimed in. "What else you got for us?"

"We found a beach towel, a button, some loose change and a pack of Marlboro Light cigarettes near the bloodstain on the beach," Grazioso reported.

"All these probably belonged to the victim," Altman speculated.

Grazioso dug down deeper in his bag and pulled out a Swiss Army knife. "One silver knife," he said as he held it out in front of Altman for examination. "It was closed when we found it, so I doubt it was used at the crime scene."

Altman watched the knife as Grazioso turned it over in his gloved hands. He wondered if there had been a struggle. If the knife belonged to Brent, then why hadn't he used it. Remembering the gunshot wounds to Brent's head, Altman wondered if he had had time to defend himself at all.

Grazioso reached down in his bag again.

"Oh, and most important, when we were digging in the sand, we found this buried along beside a penny." Grazioso dropped a small gold wedding band into Altman's open hand. "We believe it belonged to the victim's wife."

Altman stared at the wedding band resting in his palm. He thought about the value of his and his wife's own wedding bands. They were certainly worth more than a penny each, and he would at the drop of a hat fight anyone who attempted to wrestle it from his or her hand. But, he wasn't too sure he would be willing to give up his life in exchange for their rings.

After talking with Grazioso, Altman did his own bit of canvassing through some of the blue garbage cans that were down in the area. He hoped he might find anything that would provide a clue to this murder. Of course, that had already been done by the other officers, but he went through them again anyway. He wanted to make certain nothing had been overlooked.

It was important for Altman to get into the right frame of mind and begin formulating his own thoughts and perspective about this case. He had, for all intents and purposes, just been named the lead detective.

CHAPTER 10

While Renee Poole continued talking with victim's advocate Mary Stogner, Detective Joyce called Don Myers. Myers was working the security division of Nations Bank and gave him the name of George Ross. He was in charge of the central office and supervised the persons that handled debit and credit cards. Ross made several calls and finally connected Joyce with their Charlotte, North Carolina, office, which was tracking any activity of the Pooles' stolen plastic cards. There was a flag on any card activity, but so far the cards had not been used.

Detective Joyce thought it odd that the robber hadn't used the debit card or a single credit card. In nearly all of these type cases, the robber tries to access the card as quickly as possible to avoid eventual detection.

"Are you sure there's been no report on any of these cards?" he asked.

"Yes, sir. I've checked it twice," the cordial lady in the Charlotte office confirmed.

Joyce hung up the phone and had just started walking back toward the interview room when he was called back. It was Detective Altman calling to tell him Brent Poole had died at the hospital. The long and thin man hung up the phone and slowly walked to Stogner's office. He looked as burdened as an old plow horse.

Renee must have recognized the glum in Joyce's sullen

cheeks when he walked in and closed the door behind him. "How's Brent doing?" she asked apprehensively. Joyce shook his head, then answered softly, "He didn't make it."

Renee's stomach tightened. She felt her body begin to shake and heard a voice trying to comfort her. Her head dropped. She hadn't been told anything about Brent. She knew nothing about what hospital he had been transferred to or that he had been in surgery. Fighting to contain her tears, she didn't want to believe what she was hearing. It was all still like a bad dream. From the outside, she saw someone that resembled herself sitting in that chair and listening to these people trying to tell her something, but she couldn't comprehend what it was.

Renee got sick again and had to go to the bathroom. When she came back to the office, she took a seat in the same chair and found herself staring across the desk at a large, red-faced man with a permanent scowl. She swallowed hard.

"Mrs. Poole, I am the Myrtle Beach captain of investigation, Sam Hendrick," the burly man said quietly, looking at her through rose-tinted glasses. "Is there anyone you need to call?"

Renee cleared her throat. "I need to call Brent's parents." Mary Stogner handed her a pencil and a piece of paper and Renee wrote down the number, then slid it across the desk. "They live in Clemmons, North Carolina."

Hendrick dialed the numbers, then patiently waited until he heard a female answer on the other end. He identified himself and asked if this was the home of Bill and Agnes Poole. It was. "Ma'am, I'm sorry to have to tell you this, but I have some bad news about your son. He's been in a terrible accident here at the beach."

Dead silence. Hendrick thought he did hear her eyelids blink.

Law enforcement officials normally try to be very sensitive when notifying the victim's family members of an impending death. It's common knowledge that bad news always seems to come unexpectedly by phone in the middle of the night. And when that happens, the police believe it is easier to receive disturbing news from a known person rather than a complete stranger. Captain Hendrick believed Brent's parents would prefer hearing the account of their son's death from their daughter-in-law rather than the police.

Hendrick handed the phone to Renee and whispered, "Why don't you tell your mother-in-law what happened."

Renee took a deep breath, grabbed the phone, and proceeded to tell Agnes how they had been robbed and Brent had been shot.

Agnes listened for a few minutes, then started screaming, "What do you mean? How can my son be dead?"

Renee's contorted face turned blood red. She gritted her teeth, then pursed her lips and handed the phone back to Hendrick without looking at him.

Hendrick closely observed the naive-looking girl sitting before him in blue jeans and a T-shirt; she could pass for sixteen. He and Brent's mother continued talking a few minutes about her son's murder.

"If my son is dead," Renee overheard her mother-in-law shout, "then you need to look at his wife."

Renee cocked her head like one of the gray squirrels that scampered along the power lines from the tall oak trees to the police station. When Agnes mentioned John Frazier's name, Renee looked down and stared at the floor with the face of someone who had just grabbed the shit end of the stick.

Hendrick offered his sympathy to Mrs. Poole, then hung up the phone. The room was so quiet one could have heard a mouse pissing on cotton.

"I need to call my parents," Renee quickly blurted out. She recited the phone numbers and the chief slowly punched them in. Her parents also lived in Clemmons, a small town nine miles southwest of Winston-Salem, North Carolina.

When the phone rang at the home of Jack and Marie Summey, it was two o'clock in the morning. Marie answered the phone, then woke her husband from a deep sleep. There was an emergency and it was their daughter Renee calling.

"Now, calm down," Marie told her hysterical daughter. "I want to make sure I heard you correctly."

"Mama, something terrible has happened!" Rene exclaimed. "Brent has been shot!"

"What do you mean shot?" Marie mouthed the words to her husband, who had sat up in bed. He was still half-asleep.

"We were robbed by somebody on the beach and he shot Brent," Renee cried.

"Oh, no!" Marie exclaimed. "Is he okay?"

Renee hung her head. She couldn't answer.

At the very time Marie was waiting for an answer, the call waiting signal beeped. Knowing it had to be in reference to this same incident, Marie told Renee she was putting her on hold and took the call. It was Agnes Poole. And she was as furious as a howling northern wind.

"Have you talked to Renee?" Agnes shouted.

"Yes, I have heard some of it," Marie answered, trying to keep her sanity. "I have Renee on the other line."

"Well, don't you think something is going on?" Agnes's voice blasted through the receiver.

Jack got out of bed and started getting dressed. When he saw the color and expression in his wife's face change, he took a deep breath. It was going to be a long night.

"I don't know what you mean," Marie answered. "In fact, that is what I am trying to find out right now."

"You know very well what I am talking about," Agnes fired back.

"I am telling you I don't know what in the hell is going on, Agnes."

"Well, you don't seem too upset about it," Agnes said sarcastically.

The accusation rubbed Marie the wrong way. "Let me find out what's going on and then I'll call you back." She clicked the phone once and was beeped back to Renee. "That was Brent's mother on the other line." She paused and tried to catch her breath. "Please tell me what in the hell is going on!"

"Mama, Brent is dead!"

"I don't believe it. That sounds like a sick joke to me."

"He is, Mama! He's dead!"

Marie nearly dropped the phone. It couldn't be true, she

thought. She did not want to believe what she was hearing. Her mind must be playing tricks on her. Anxiety crawled across her body and started stinging her like a swarm of backyard fire ants. She thought about it, then decided she wasn't going to believe it until she heard it from another party.

"I still don't believe it, Renee. It's not true," she insisted. "Put someone else on the phone."

Renee handed the phone back to Captain Hendrick, who calmly relayed the news of Brent's death to Marie. After talking a few minutes with the detective, Marie asked him to put Renee back on the phone.

"Where is Katie and who has her?"

"She's at the hotel with a baby-sitter."

"Well, your father and I are going to drive to Myrtle Beach. We'll go to the hotel, relieve the sitter, and wait for you there. You and Katie can ride with us back to North Carolina. And until everything is settled, you two can stay at home with us."

Renee agreed to meet them. "Katie's at the Carolina Winds Hotel, Mama. Room six-oh-four. The baby-sitter's name is Mrs. Murphy."

After Marie finished talking with Renee, Jack picked up the phone and called the Pooles' residence. Bill answered the phone. In the background, Jack could hear Bill's distraught wife crying and screaming, "Oh, my God, no! Oh, my God, no!"

"Bill, we are so sorry to hear about Brent," Jack said. "He was like the son we never had. We all loved him and are just as hurt as anyone by this."

Bill was so grief-stricken that he could hardly respond. He thanked Jack for his call.

"I want to apologize to the both of you," Jack told him. "When your wife called us a little while ago, we had no earthly idea what had happened. If there is anything we can do, please let us know."

He promised he would.

After speaking with the Summeys, Bill Poole called his son, Craig, who lived in nearby Lewisville, and his daughter, "Dee." He could barely get the words out of his mouth before his two children gasped in horror.

The bond between thirty-five-year-old Craig Poole and his younger brother was very strong. It had grown even stronger when their daughters were born within fifteen hours of each other 2½ years ago. When his father told him what had happened, Craig dropped the phone in great anguish and collapsed against the back of the bed. His brother's death hit him like a ton of bricks—it didn't make sense. "Why would someone want to shoot Brent?" he cried out to his wife, Amy.

Craig couldn't control his emotions. All he could think about was Brent's daughter. Little Katie was his heartbeat, his little princess.

For Brent's older sister, Deanne Mishler, the tragic news was worse than anything she could have ever imagined. There was a ten-year difference between Dee and Brent; and even today, she still doted on him like he was her baby. As she fell into her husband's arms and sobbed, she suddenly realized how unprepared she was to grieve. She started thinking of all the neat little letters Brent had sent her after she had married and moved away from home.

"This little boy would write me letters"—Dee sobbed—"He would say, 'And Ginger (their dog) says 'ruff-ruff.' He would send me three dollars in the envelope with a note: 'This is for you to play Ms. Pac-Man,' he'd write."

Dee was absolutely convinced that this would be the ultimate test of her family's love and faith in God. She called her parents back on the phone and learned they were going to drive to Myrtle Beach and find out for themselves exactly what had happened to Brent. When she arrived, the pain that ripped through her parents' home was more than she could stand. Her mom and dad sat across their bed, weeping, trying to understand how this could have happened. They were clutched in an iron fist of trauma.

The three of them agreed that Bill should call the Myrtle Beach police and make certain they knew all the facts. Detective Joyce took their phone call. "Has Renee told you everything that's been going on with their marriage?" he asked curtly.

"I'm not sure, what do you mean?" Joyce asked.

"Well, there had been some trouble with their marriage for a long time. Brent and Renee had just gotten back together. She was seeing a guy by the name of John Boyd Frazier. We think he or his friends might have something to do with our son's death."

"That certainly is very useful information. We appreciate you calling us."

"And I think if you push her hard enough, she could possibly tell you who killed Brent," Poole added before hanging up the phone.

"If there's any truth to that," Joyce assured him, "then we'll get to the bottom of it." Too early to tell, but the detective believed the information could be very useful in solving this case.

When Detective Joyce walked back into the interview room and asked Renee to explain what her father-in-law was referring to, she said without great concern, "Oh, I moved out of the house for a week and stayed with a friend named John. That's all that's been going on." It was nothing significant.

Joyce asked Renee for John's full name and address, then excused himself from the room. Just in case, he phoned the police in Winston-Salem, North Carolina, while Renee talked with Mary Stogner and Captain Hendrick and completed the last of the paperwork.

"Can you have someone do a check on a Caucasian male, six feet one, two hundred twenty-five pounds, by the name of John Boyd Frazier? We want to make certain he has been home all night."

Shortly after 2:15 A.M., Jack and Marie Summey threw a few things in a overnight bag and left for Myrtle Beach immediately. In their haste, they had forgotten to brush their teeth or comb their hair. During the drive, they talked about the possibility of Renee being involved with John Boyd Frazier, but didn't see how she was involved in all of this.

"My throat and stomach are so raw," Marie said. "They couldn't hurt any worse than if I'd swallowed a handful of double-edged razor blades."

Jack told her he felt some of the same pain. "We'll just have to straighten it out when we get there," he said, attempting to calm his wife. "We've always taught our daughter to tell the truth and we have to trust she will do just that."

CHAPTER 11

Earlier in the night, Captain Hendrick had established a temporary command post at Eighty-first Avenue. It was there, near the crime scene, where he had huddled with his men to remind them of the urgency for gathering all the information they could on this homicide. In 1993, when Hendrick attended the FBI Academy, he had been trained for similar situations, which required the teamwork and cooperation of multiple officers to finalize an outcome. He had already experienced many complex investigations whereby his management and coordination skills had been tested to the max. Once again, he knew it would require his best efforts in managing his personnel to solve this case.

"We have a difficult situation here," Hendrick had cautioned his right-hand man, Sergeant King. "I am afraid the crime scene isn't going to give us much; so when you finish up here, I want you to go back to the police station and interview the Poole girl. I am certain she has already given her account of what happened by now, but I want to make certain we don't miss anything."

In the few short hours Renee Poole had been at the Myrtle Beach police headquarters, she had alternated her time between the interview room, the bathroom, and outside the building when she insisted she needed a cigarette. So far, the police had gotten little information from her. If this was a cat-

and-mouse game she was playing, she was coming off curiously reticent and seemingly gentle as a week-old kitten.

Detective Jim Joyce had been the first to interview her, then carefully listened to her story a second time after he had confronted her with the information passed on to him from her in-laws about her liaison with another man. One thing he noticed early in their conversations was that when he asked about her marriage and the trip to Myrtle Beach, Renee's speech was even and spontaneous. But when it came to specifics about the shooting and the shooter, she'd hesitate and stammer before she replied. It was almost as if he had asked questions she wasn't prepared to answer and was searching to find the answers. And the way she shifted her body uneasily in the chair when asked about John Boyd Frazier convinced him he was getting the runaround. He had a hunch her relationship with her husband wasn't all peaches and cream.

"I think she's holding back, Chief," Joyce said to Hendrick while Renee was taking a smoke break. The two men readily agreed. For some reason, she was unwilling to give up detailed information about her affair with Frazier and they wanted to know why.

"I've asked Sergeant King to interview her as well," Hendrick said in a low voice. "We really need to know what happened last night on the beach. I hope she understands how crucial it is that we get that information back to the other units who are still out in the field and working on the case. How does she expect us to find her husband's killer if she doesn't tell us the truth about what happened?"

It was 3:00 A.M. when King first arrived at the police station. Renee Poole was still talking with Detective Joyce and victim's advocate Mary Stogner. King tapped on the door and called Joyce out of the room.

"How is she doing?" King asked.

Joyce looked through the glass window at Renee, then answered, "She's calm and seems to be holding up okay."

"Is there anything I need to know before I talk with her?"

"Yes," Joyce said, quickly reviewing his notes. "There was

some information given by Brent Poole's family about her having an affair. You might want to mention that."

Always the meticulous dresser, Sergeant King looked at his reflection in the glass door and straightened his tie before going in to interview Renee. For as long as he could remember, there had always been a strict dress code with the Myrtle Beach detectives. It didn't matter whether it was twelve noon or three o'-clock in the morning, every detective was to be dressed in a coat and tie whenever he went out to investigate a crime. King accepted the fact that it might appear to some that he was out of place—and to others, it looked awkward or unusual, especially on the beach in the summer months. But the dress code distinguished them as professionals and projected an appearance that they knew what they were doing. King believed all those officers in suits reflected the professional image they were trying to project.

King chuckled at some cases where people even made the comment afterward that they knew they were in trouble when they saw all these men in suits. They mistakenly imagined the FBI was after them.

At three in the morning, such as was in this case, King believed this dress code gave him the edge he needed. To him, it conveyed the right impression to be sitting in front of this witness polished down and dressed in a starched shirt, a tie and a sports jacket rather than sitting there in blue jeans and a T-shirt.

The detective's *GQ* image was of little significance to Renee Poole when he stepped in the room at 3:37 A.M. and introduced himself to her. She had been at the police station for almost three hours now and wanted to go home. She wanted to check on her daughter and take her home with her. She needed to see her parents.

"Mrs. Poole, I know you have talked with several other officers tonight," King began, dismissing both Joyce and Stogner from the room. "But I would like to talk with you about last night." He pulled out a chair and sat down directly in front of her. "I want to talk to you so that I can get a feel for what has happened to you and your husband."

Renee sat rigidly in the chair, staring straight ahead, unsmiling, with big brown eyes and the slender, tanned body of a teenager. In her lap sat a small stuffed animal.

King never apologized for her having to stay at the police station all this time. He had been told that other than her daughter, she was alone and was waiting for her parents to pick her up. The drive from Clemmons, North Carolina, he calculated, was a good four hours away. He guessed she had no choice either way but to sit and wait.

King listened as Renee began to tell her story. He told her he'd do his best to understand all the facts and would only interrupt her for clarification when it was necessary. Throughout the interview, she remained very calm. She was never hysterical, but at certain points within her story, she would pause, then cry for a few seconds before continuing on. Even though King saw Renee as "nonemotional," her demeanor didn't seem to be anything out of the ordinary. In his years as a police officer, he had seen it both ways. Some victims he had interviewed were very quiet and seemed to be in shock, while others were hysterical and emotionally beyond themselves.

King had tried long ago to stop assessing people by their emotions. He wanted to be fair to Renee. To give her the benefit of the doubt. She was a total stranger. He had never seen her nor had he been exposed to any previous behavior prior to this interview, and he had no comparison between her past and present behavior. He had no idea of what was "out of character" for Renee and did not want to judge her prematurely.

King asked Renee to go through her story a second time before he started pressuring her for more information. When she finished, his eyes moved reflexively toward her and he shook his head uncomprehendingly. Wanting her to know he didn't buy her story, he asked insistently, "When you and your husband went to this bar, did you have anything to drink?"

Renee was caught off-guard. "He had a Lynchburg lemonade and I drank two margaritas," she said weakly.

"Then, you went to the beachwear store and bought a beach towel?"

"Yes, a beach towel. It was a good-size towel, with an aqua-color design on it."

"And on to the ATM machine at Nations Bank to draw out some money? How much did you get?"

"Fifty dollars. It was so we could pay the baby-sitter."

"But you didn't go directly to your room, but instead went for a walk on the beach heading north?" King asked with a hint of sarcasm.

"We walked for about a half-mile, walked up a little ways, just kind of looking around, having conversation. Walked past, I guess, it was the last house on the left before you come to the wooded area. We found a spot, then laid the beach towel down."

"How long did y'all stay there doing that?" King asked.

"Maybe ten or fifteen minutes."

"Just talking?"

"Well, we made love," Renee blurted out. "It was something he wanted to do. And with it being our anniversary."

Renee slumped in her chair. The words flowed as easily as syrup from King's mouth, making her feel all the more comfortable. She let her guard down.

While the witness relaxed, King continued to probe, asking for specific details about the robber and the shooting of her husband. She told him again about the man dressed in black and how he had attacked them. Said she couldn't tell if the man was white or black.

Renee said she had heard two shots and thought the shooter had sort of a deep voice, but King sensed her statements lacked the normal general convictions that conveyed truth. He had a feeling she was making it up as they went along.

Near the end of the interview, King looked at Renee accusingly, then asked, "Is there something you're not telling me that you think I would find out later and would want me to know about it now?"

Renee's face tensed. She shifted uneasily in her chair. She hesitated, then decided to give him the whole song and dance about her affair with John Boyd Frazier.

"Uh, I know that when the other detective . . . ," Renee sputtered, "when he called my mother-in-law, I don't know what she said to him, but he asked me if there was something, you know that—that I was leaving out . . . and, uh, my husband and I did have problems a little while ago. I moved out and moved in with a friend for about a week. And, uh, it was a male friend."

King grew silent and listened intently as Renee continued to explain about her affair. She was clearly nervous and it showed.

"And my husband accepted the fact that I moved in with him, you know. He knew he was a friend . . . but I had slept with the guy and I told my husband that I had."

King faked a surprised look. "This is the friend you're talking about?"

Renee nodded vigorously.

"And, shortly after that, I moved out and moved back in with my husband. And he accepted it. We agreed to work everything out. We were gonna go to counseling. I talked to this guy a few times since then, and my husband told me, well, you know, I don't have a problem with you being friends, just—you know—just don't see each other."

King's mannerisms and voice remained stern. "What type of problems did you and your husband have?"

"My husband and I?"

"Yeah."

"I left him because he didn't pay me enough attention," she said emphatically. She looked down at the floor, then glanced nervously back at King. He kept staring at her like she was lying. "I didn't feel like he paid our daughter enough attention. And he realized that and wanted me to move back home."

"How long did y'all have this problem before you actually left?"

"My husband works second shift and he was hardly ever at home and we had just gotten a computer. And he was on it, you know the time he was at home." She shrugged indifferently. "A few months . . . for a while . . . we just never really talked about it."

"How long were y'all married?"

"We've been married three years."

"Three years . . . and when did the problem start?"

"I guess when I got the computer or shortly after."

"How long ago was that?"

"I think we got it a little over a year ago."

"A year ago?"

"Maybe," she said doubtfully, staring at the floor again. Then with renewed interest as if she had just gotten a sudden burst of energy, she looked up and rushed ahead with words shooting out like rapid fire from an automatic pistol. "He just started playing on it a lot in the past few months. But once I brought it to his attention and I left and we talked out our differences and everything, I went back home and he didn't mess with it anymore."

When King asked her pointedly if Brent had ever gotten physical with her, she said, "No. Not once. Yes, Brent had only gotten upset a few times, overreacted and started throwing things, but other than that, [we] were always able to work things out."

King was surprised that she was babbling and running off at the mouth like she couldn't stop. But he wasn't going to correct her.

"I talked to John about mine and Brent's problems. I told him I was gonna leave my husband. I was gonna move out. And I told him I didn't have anywhere to go and he told me I could come home with him. He said he worked third shift and that he would never really be there anyway. So, if I took a job during the day, we would never really see each other. We both agreed to do that and I moved out and he helped me move in with him. I called my lawyer and told him what I had done. He said, 'Well, you know maybe that wasn't such a good idea.' I said, 'Yes, well, I really didn't have anywhere to go.'"

"How about a girlfriend?" King asked, encouraging her to continue. "Couldn't you have called her?"

"Uh, yeah, I called her and told her the day I left."

"No, I mean, any reason why you didn't move in with her?"

Renee wrinkled up her nose and lightly shook her head from

side to side, as if a foul odor had just permeated the room. King continued to watch her closely. It seemed to him as if she were feeding off her own excitement and fear. The more she talked, the more she got wrapped up in telling her story. She acted like she couldn't stop herself from talking.

"She and her fiancé . . . She works at a dance club . . . an adult entertainment club. . . . He works in Virginia and has a small son that stays with him. They lived in a two-bedroom apartment. There really wasn't a lot of room there. My friend has a decent-size house and lived by himself, so I just moved everything in there."

"So, you met this friend when?" King asked.

"I met him March of last year," Renee said. "We were friends and so I moved in with him for five days."

"Okay, there was no doubt that this guy, John, had some interest in you?"

"Yes."

"And the feelings were mutual?"

"Right."

King was quiet. He wanted Renee to tell him what she thought this relationship meant to her. If she got off-course, he would steer her back.

"Well, we were friends to begin with," Renee rambled on. "And I guess once I moved in with him, I kind of changed."

"What do you mean by 'I kind of changed'? Was it a change in you, your husband or your friend?"

"No, what I mean was that there was a change in our relationship," Renee clarified. She didn't appear too shocked by her own revelation, and quickly blurted out, "It became a sexual relationship."

King thought about what Renee had told him. If he understood her correctly, she meant the relationship had become something very serious. He always understood a relationship with a friend as someone you could sit down and talk with about your problems. But when she confessed they had had a sexual relationship, for him that meant something more in depth than sharing a Happy Meal at McDonald's.

"Now, you said the relationship had gotten physical and that the feelings were mutual between you and John?" King asked, wanting Renee to confirm that fact a second time.

"Yes."

"And you two had a brief affair, where you left your husband, moved out of your home and lived with John for five days before returning to your husband?"

"That's right."

"And your husband knew about this affair and was okay with it?" he asked doubtfully.

Renee thought about if for a moment, then laid out the whole scenario. She and John had been communicating just about every day while she was still living with her husband. She admitted even though they lived forty miles away from each other, that never stopped them from being together.

"Even before I moved out, I would go over to John's house and take my daughter with me. We'd just kinda hang out, watch movies and do other things."

King suddenly felt a cold knot growing in the pit of his stomach. He asked her, "Did you ever tell your husband you were leaving?"

"No, I didn't tell him I was leaving," Renee said, void of any emotion.

"What did you do? Just pack up and leave?"

"Yep. And he had no idea what I was doing."

"Did he have any idea what was going on between you and John? I mean, did he have any idea that there was . . . maybe someone else?"

"Nah," Renee said, her voice a kind of verbal shrug. "Well, I think maybe he thought it, but he never said anything to me. And when I told him, you know, he was a friend, ah, he kinda . . . He talked to John and then we all three got together on the phone and talked about it."

"This was afterward or was this before you moved in with John?"

"After I moved in."

"And you'd call back and talk with your husband, and then John would get on the phone, too?"

"Yeah. All three of us would be on the phone. And, ah, we

would—would solve a lot of . . . ah . . . solve a lot of our problems that way. You know, just kinda getting everything out in
the open."

The whole idea was becoming a little too bizarre for King.
He liked and had dated hordes of women—by the skin of his
teeth, he had managed to remain single. Although he was certainly not an expert on the female psyche, he did recognize
men and women didn't always see eye-to-eye on different
issues, especially when it came to sex, love and romance. He
guessed it was the "men are from Mars, women are from
Venus" type of thing. But Renee's version of her marital relationship was starting to sound a little too kinky, even for
King's taste. Of course, in his line of work, he had heard and
had seen worse.

"So, how did he feel about you sleeping with John?"

"He didn't like it very much, but, ah, he . . . he said that he
loved me and he wanted our marriage to work. And I told him,
'Yeah, that I did, too.' That our daughter needed us."

"How did John feel about that?"

"Ah, he wasn't delighted with it, but he knew that—that
Brent was my husband and we had had seven years together."
Renee paused, then almost offhandedly in her sexy country-
girl accent, she stretched out the words: "Almost seven years
together. Katie did need her father. She, you know, needed us
to be together." She then assured King she and Brent had been
able to work through it all and came to the beach for romance
and to revive their once-broken relationship.

King kept his eyes glued on her. Her striking eyes appeared
more rounded than before. He sat staring silently at them. But
it was really her voice he had noticed the most. Her voice was
as cold as a Thanksgiving turkey frozen in a Frigidaire freezer.

"I did the wrong thing by leaving," she said. "What we really
needed was just some time apart. To really think about what
was going on."

Renee also admitted after she and John Boyd Frazier severed
their relationship, they had stayed in touch and remained
friends. She said John was there to help counsel her through
her separation. She had planned to get a job and save up

enough money to rent an apartment, hoping to earn enough income to live on her own, and that most of the times when John called her, he would just be asking her how everything was going.

"And he wasn't trying to get you to come back?"

"No. No. He—he knew that once I decided to go back home to my husband, he'd leave well enough alone."

King was astonished. "He wasn't trying to get you to sleep with him again?"

"No."

"Did he just cut that out completely or did that come after a period of time?"

"Uh, he never really wanted me to come back. He—he, more or less, respected my decision, and I told him, you know, that we could remain friends because that's what we had started out as."

"And he was happy with that?"

"Yeah, I just told him I'd talk to him when I needed friendly advice, and if I needed someone to talk to."

King pursued the matter a few minutes longer, then abruptly changed directions. "Any other problems you and your husband ever had, other than that?"

"No," she replied without any emotion, confident she had nothing to hide. "No. I think that was really about it."

"How about his parents? Did y'all get along?"

"Oh, yes."

"Did they know about you and John?"

"Yeah."

"What were their feelings about that?"

"Disappointment, disappointment," Renee said in her little girl's voice. "Uh, it's just that his parents are Christian people, and, uh, they forgave me for it and, uh, I forgave them for judging me. You know, about what I did. And, uh, we—my husband and I—started going to church. Uh, pretty much as soon as I moved back home. And, uh, his mom bought me a Bible. She treats me like her daughter. Uh, they forgave me for it, and, uh, it doesn't come up in conversation. We just kinda really don't talk about it."

"Do you think John would do something like this to your husband?" he asked darkly.

Renee froze like Bambi caught in high beams. "Oh, no. He, uh, he knew how well we were getting along. Uh, my husband and I actually—we're trying, uh, we were trying to have another baby. And, uh, you know, I told John, you know, that we were gonna get remarried and, uh, that my husband was wanting to have another baby. And, uh, he was happy that I was happy, you know that—that we were actually making things right. Because when we got married, it was, uh, I was three months pregnant and it was kinda rushed. And we just wanted to do things right. To start over."

It was obvious Renee had some hidden secrets and King was digging them up as fast as he would have dug clams at a clambake. He looked at his watch. It was 4:40 A.M. He debated the pros and cons of continuing, but could feel his own legs and back begging for a rest, so he ended the interview.

Renee stood up slowly, as if the motion weren't easy, then stretched her tired body. She closed her eyes and tried to think of Katie. Walking over to the window to get a better look, she could see the moon had completely disappeared behind a layer of clouds. The shadowy fears of night held her eyes open as her brain attempted to corroborate parts of the blurry night. She stuck her face against the window and sank into a low and lonely depression. She wanted to throw up, but there was nothing left inside her.

As Renee thought about her situation, the facts were becoming more and more alarming. She blinked her eyes. This was worse than a dream. This was a nightmare.

CHAPTER 12

Detective Jim Joyce telephoned the Winston-Salem Police Department (WSPD) sometime around 3:00 a.m. and requested an officer to be dispatched to the home of John Boyd Frazier. Joyce told the desk sergeant that Frazier was a white male, stood approximately six feet one and weighed 225 pounds, and lived at Kingswell Drive in "Old Town." He was a suspect in the Brent Poole murder.

The desk sergeant dispatched the information through the department's mobile data terminal. Officer Darrell Mills, a seven-year veteran, received the request from the communications center at approximately 5:00 A.M. Unfortunately, when the call appeared on the computer terminal in Mills's car, there was just a written report with instructions to attempt to verify Frazier was at home. There was no indication of urgency. Thinking he had received a routine call, he didn't hesitate to stop the driver of a vehicle who nearly collided with his police vehicle after running a red light. While Mills was writing the citation, the desk sergeant contacted him again.

"What's your estimated time of arrival?" the dispatcher asked him.

Mills completed the transaction, then took the extra time to admonish the reckless driver prior to returning the call on his cell phone to headquarters.

"I've been delayed with a vehicle committing a seven

twenty-six," he answered. "I just finished the citation and on my way to the location now."

"You need to get over there ASAP," the dispatcher urged. "We've got a possible murder suspect and we need to verify his whereabouts."

Mills shoved his foot down on the gas pedal and proceeded immediately. He arrived at Frazier's neighborhood somewhere between 5:20 A.M. and 5:25 A.M. Driving slowly through the community of homes, he spotted the number of Frazier's house on the mailbox and stopped his car.

A concrete driveway led from the street and continued inside a Cyclone fence area behind Frazier's house. Mills cautiously got out of his car and eased toward the fence to get a better look. A gray Acura Integra was parked inside the fence, some forty feet away. The gate was locked.

The officer had no way of knowing if the Acura had recently driven inside the fenced area. It hadn't occurred to him at the time to check it for dew or to see if the engine was still warm. Knowing that Frazier could have been somehow involved in a murder, Mills had decided it was best to downplay his visit. To make as little hoopla as possible. It not only reduced his personal risks, but it decreased the chances of frightening or alarming Frazier. The last thing he wanted was to become engaged in an early-morning shoot-out with some frightened suspect scared out of his wits.

Frazier's neighborhood was very quiet in the early hours of that Wednesday morning. It would still be a while before his neighbors awoke and started their day. Mills stood on the front porch, seemingly unnoticed, and peered in through a small side window next to the front door. Uneasiness still hung heavily in the air. The air caught like a pair of fists in Mills's lungs, then slowly slipped out between his teeth. He knocked firmly on the door and waited a few minutes. No one stirred. He looked through the window again. Still pitch-black inside. Either John Frazier was sound asleep or he was nowhere to be found. Mills knocked a second time, only harder this time. Still no response.

Just as Officer Mills had decided no one was home and was

heading toward his car, a light came on in one of the back bedrooms and he heard footsteps pounding down the hall. The officer stopped a few feet from his car and waited for the door to open. When it did, Mills found himself staring at a large Caucasian male with tousled, thin black hair and eyes too large and too black.

Dressed in a bathrobe and a T-shirt, John Frazier stared back at the uniformed police officer standing in his yard, unflinching, as if there were nothing left inside to shine outward. He seemed startled and even a little nervous. Maybe even a little flustered.

Mills eased back toward the front porch, then apologized for his intrusion at such an odd hour.

"Are you John Boyd Frazier?"

John nodded. He looked like a bear who had just been awoken from his hibernation.

Frazier's appearance, however, didn't mean anything to Mills, since there's never been a laundry list of rules on how someone should react when a police officer shows up at one's house, unannounced, at 5:30 A.M. He had seen the same look many times before when he had awaken others at such odd hours. Some expressions were valid, as Mills was often called upon to deliver alarming or heart-stopping news. But not always. It wasn't unusual for him to field a request that later proved to be initiated by a prankster or an angry lover with nothing better to do than waste police time and disturb someone's early-morning REM sleep.

"There's been a missing person's report filed on you in South Carolina," Mills announced, offering John a little more information. "I'm just trying to find out if you're at home."

The two men exchanged glances.

Mills kept his face blank of expression and tried to relax. He couldn't tell if John was alone, and he didn't appear to be drunk or under the influence of drugs. The only sign of emotion he could see in John was a slight nervousness. He hadn't expected him to open the door and invite him in for a cup of coffee, but most people in this situation would want to explore if further.

"I have a cousin that lives in Myrtle Beach," John offered, straightening his robe. "His name is Mike Frazier. Maybe it's him they're talking about. But as you can see, he's not here."

"Is that your car parked in the back?" Mills asked, hoping to secure additional information.

John shrugged rather smugly. "No, that belongs to a friend of mine, Kayle Schettler. I loaned my car to him and he let me borrow the Acura."

"Can you give me an address on your friend?" Mills inquired, reaching for a notepad in his front pocket.

"Um, well, uh, that would be difficult to say." John looked away from the officer as if his memory banks had closed and were not scheduled to reopen until later that day. "I can tell you how to get there," he said, shaking his head as if trying to kick start his brain. "He lives a few miles down the road from here, but I can't for the life of me tell you the address."

"Okay, if you could give me his name again and I'll see if I can't locate an address."

"Kayle Schettler," John said softly, spelling out each letter in his friend's name. "It's spelled: K-A-Y-L-E. S-C-H-E-T-T-L-E-R."

After jotting down Schettler's name, Mills didn't ask John for any further details concerning the whereabouts of his car or why he was driving someone else's car. Had he asked, Frazier would have told him that he and Kayle had been friends since high school and it wasn't out of the ordinary for the two of them to switch cars. Kayle was a crackerjack mechanic and worked at Cloverdale Shell on Cloverdale Shell Avenue in Winston-Salem. He had worked on John's car before, and on several previous occasions had offered to loan him his Acura to drive until he returned John's Blazer.

On Monday, June 8, John had driven up to the service station around noon and asked if Kayle could work on his car. The front end of his Blazer had been making a noise and he wanted Kayle to see if he could fix it. Since they had switched cars in the past, John then asked if he could borrow Kayle's car. Even when he told Kayle he would need to borrow his car through Thursday, Kayle never hesitated. After all, what are friends for if not to help out when one was in a bind?

But Mills never asked for an explanation about John's car and he never offered. He apologized again to John for disturbing him then excused himself. He wasn't there to harass or accost him, and accepted the fact that he had accomplished his mission. John was at home so he left it at that. Unfortunately, he still hadn't thought about walking to the car and placing his hand on the hood to feel if the engine was still warm—a sure sign that the car had been driven recently.

Inside his patrol car, Mills telephoned communications at headquarters and told them he had found John Frazier, at home. Several minutes later, he received another request from the MBPD. They wanted him to locate Frazier's car, described as a black Chevrolet Blazer with a personalized tag. The tag was a North Carolina plate with a "first in flight" airplane insignia and had the word "NERVUS" blazoned across it.

Mills telephoned the name of John's friend he had written down and asked the dispatcher to verify an address. He was given Schettler's address at Brandemere Lane Apartments and drove straight to the adjacent parking lot and located John Frazier's vehicle. Since he had been told there had been a shooting last night in Myrtle Beach and that John was a suspect, there was a good possibility this black Blazer had been there also. But when he checked it out, he found the vehicle to be cold and John's friend at home and asleep in bed.

CHAPTER 13

Anything worth doing is always worth doing twice. Maybe even three times.

When Detective Altman finished searching the crime scene area a second, then a third time, he drove back to the MBPD station. Captain Hendrick was already there, meeting with the detectives between their interviews with Renee. They had become suspicious of Renee due to her inconsistencies in what they knew and what she had told them. Although the detectives believed at this time she was not involved in the shooting, they were convinced, however, that she could identify the shooter. They just didn't understand why she insisted on not doing so.

"We contacted Brent's family and they told us some pretty hairy stuff about Brent and Renee's marital problems," Hendrick immediately advised Altman.

Altman gulped a swallow of lukewarm water before entering the interview room to refresh himself. He winced. The water wasn't very palatable. It was now 5:10 A.M. He had been going at it since yesterday afternoon.

As Altman and Hendrick talked about it, they clearly understood he and Sergeant King had the advantage at this point. They were in control of the situation. Not only was Renee Poole on their turf, so to speak, but she hadn't been lawyered up as of yet. Still, they teetered a fine line in inducing their subject to talk. At any minute, she could refuse to answer their questions, ask to see a lawyer, and bring their interviews to a screeching halt.

"Up to this point, we've attempted to keep her talking," Hendrick related. "We've tried to impress upon her that she's not under suspicion. That no one is planning to arrest her, as we have no cause to, and that we're merely just wanting to take her statement. Trying to get all the facts straight in our minds."

Their plan had worked. Renee had not asked for a lawyer, and until then, they would continue to interview her. Hendrick assured Altman that he, too, didn't like the smell of things and his previous suspicions had been greatly intensified after talking with Brent's parents. He was confident the two detectives, with just the right amount of pressure, could wrestle the truth away from her.

"Take your time," the chief cautioned Altman as a trainer would instruct his star athlete from his corner of the ring. "This might be our only chance to get what we need from her. If for some reason a lawyer shows up and wants to stop the interview, then you can count on us to stand at the door and prevent that from happening. She's not going to get a lawyer until she asks for one."

Altman walked into the sparsely furnished room. Sergeant King sat at the table across and directly facing Renee. Altman pulled his chair up beside her and next to King. In classic textbook style, the two well-trained detectives physically boxed her in. Forming what is known as the interrogation-style triangle, they created a powerful physical rendering of how they wanted Renee to perceive her present circumstances. As they stared at her fiercely, the air suddenly grew cold.

Renee shifted nervously in her seat, then leaned back slightly as if to draw a breath from the unencumbered air. She should have known sooner or later the posse would come gunning for her, and she guessed this was it. Had she not been so mentally and physically drained, she would have easily figured out these were no ordinary cops. What she didn't know was that King and Altman had worked as a team many times before. Investigative work had long ago infiltrated their blood and they'd been given many opportunities to perfect their dog-and-pony show. They had played this game many times before and did it well, knowing exactly how and when to feed off each other.

"Ms. Poole, I'm Detective Altman. I know you have already told your story several times tonight, but unfortunately, I was working on something else involving your husband at the hospital and haven't gotten all the details. I've just been getting bits and pieces of it, here and there, so if you could . . ."

Renee looked typically tired and worn. Dark circles like half-moons hung underneath her eyes. She repeated what she had already told King. She obviously felt comfortable enough with the two men to share confidences about her marital problems, but assured them she and her husband had worked all that out before they came to the beach. As she talked about her troubles, her voice sounded weak and vulnerable.

Renee began by explaining how she and Brent were high-school sweethearts and how they had been a couple for about seven years. She said she had dated just three other people besides Brent, and only because he had broken off their relationship while they were dating.

"He broke up with me just to go out with someone else," she said in a voice as flat as her eyes were blank. "I was upset about it, but we still remained friends. He would call me and talk to me about his problems with his girlfriend and I would give him advice."

Altman sat back in his chair and rolled his eyes toward Sergeant King, as if to say, *Just great, we got ourselves another fucking Dr. Laura.*

Renee shook her head, then said adamantly, "It was all good advice." It was like she was just another simple, sincere, and forthright girl, trying to help her boyfriend work things out with his girlfriend. "But when he got ready to go to college, he broke up with her. . . ." She paused and bit her lower lip, then suddenly changed directions. In a gleeful voice that sounded much like a teenager, she blurted out, "And I just recently found out that he didn't cry when he left her. That he came straight to my house and cried."

Altman stared at her with a curious look.

Renee then answered her own question. "Because he wanted me to go back with him and we started dating again from there."

"And how long ago was this?" Altman interjected.

"'93 maybe?"

"And when you guys would break up, would you go out with other people also?"

"Yeah."

"And how did Brent feel about that?"

"He really didn't say."

"He never told you he didn't like you going out with other people," Altman snapped.

Renee shook her head again. "He was usually involved with someone." She shifted her hands restlessly in her lap and reminded the detective it was Brent who had broken up with her to go out with someone else and not the other way around.

"Well, how did you feel about him going out with other people?"

"Uh, I wasn't happy with it, because I loved him. But I knew within a couple of weeks, he'd come back," she said lightly.

With that taken care of, Altman decided it was time to move on down the trail. He was confident Renee would soon learn this was not his first ride at the rodeo. "And how has your relationship been since 1993?" he asked, inching steadily toward her adulterous behavior.

"Uh, it's been really good," she said quietly, otherwise her manner entirely uncontrived. "We got married. I was three months pregnant when we got married. We had a pretty good marriage up until a year ago, uh, until we bought a computer."

Sergeant King glanced toward his partner, signaling that she was giving Altman the same old soft-shoe routine she'd tapped out earlier for him. She claimed Brent had started staying on the computer six months after they got it. That he worked second shift and was never at home. And he wasn't giving the family the kind of attention they needed.

Altman had been around the romantic block more than a couple of times, too. He wasn't buying it, either.

When Altman asked Renee what was it that Brent was doing on the computer that she didn't like, she said he was spending too much time on the Internet. She at first told the detectives he was looking for things for their four-wheeler, that they both had four-wheelers. She said he had bought her a four-wheeler for her birthday so she could be with him. But then she changed her story that he was really searching into adult pornographic sites.

After some probing, Renee admitted she would sit down with her husband and they would look through these pornographic sites together. But she said their troubles really started when they bought games. "Some of these games," she added, "could be played over the Internet, and Brent would go in and find someone to play games with him." She didn't specify what kind of games, but the detective had a sneaky idea what she was implying. Renee said she didn't like it because Brent was on the computer all the time when he could have been helping her with Katie, cooking meals, cleaning or doing anything besides that.

Altman curiously asked Renee if she stayed on the computer as much as her husband.

"Not near as much as him," she answered quickly. "When he went to work, I'd do things with my daughter instead, like taking her to the park or visiting either with my or his parents." With a look of disgust, she added that Brent's addiction with the computer had been going on for about a year and she just got tired of him not paying her and Katie any attention. When asked if she thought Brent was seeing someone else, she shook her head doubtfully. She was sure their problem was the computer. She was almost certain nobody else had come into Brent's life.

"What about your life?" Altman asked, leaning into her. Their faces nearly touched. "Has anybody popped up?"

"Yes, a guy named John," Renee answered. She took a few minutes to explain how she and John had met, had become friends and how their relationship had blossomed from that point on. She said Brent didn't have a problem with that at the time. That he was not the jealous type. So, if she wanted to have male friends, he didn't care, as long as they were just friends.

Altman glared at her unbelievingly, then asked, "Just how often did you see John?"

"John and I talked on a daily basis," she admitted. "I would take my daughter to his house to watch Disney movies and run errands. Since my husband worked the second shift, I would always go to John's house about three or four in the afternoon and stay until nine or ten that night."

"How does your daughter feel about him?" Altman asked.

"Oh, she liked him. She liked him a lot. And he liked her, too."

"And that didn't bother Brent at all?"

That sounded strange to Altman. Brent was her husband and any red-blooded male that he knew would launch a solid protest against that relationship. The husky homicide detective was intrigued when Renee said her husband didn't have a jealous streak in him. And, even more so, when she detailed but yet casually dismissed her mysterious behavior.

"Every day I would check in with Brent while he was at work. But when he would ask what I was doing or where I was at, I would never mention John or that I was at his house. I always told him I was doing something different or what I was planning to do later." She claimed this charade had been going on for about a year before Brent ever caught on. Then, of course, last month she had decided to leave her husband and move in with John.

"So there's a little bit more going on besides you just going over and watching movies and stuff?" Altman asked. "I mean, is this a sexual relationship that has evolved between you and John?"

Renee grew silent. She stared at the detective for a few seconds. She nodded nervously. Her eyes darting first from Altman to King, then back to Altman. Her hands shifted again in her lap.

"I—I did have sex with h-him," she stammered, "but the last time was probably about a month ago. I do remember I was having sex with John when I left my husband and moved in with him. I think maybe that was the last time, right before

I had left to come back home." She clarified she had only moved in with John for a week.

Altman moved in closer, attempting to crowd her and close the space that opened between them. "So, how did Brent take it when you moved in with John?"

Renee shifted in her seat and leaned away from the detective, giving herself some breathing room. "Ah, he knew we were friends and he didn't really have a problem with it," she said, starting a sentence, then stopping abruptly, leaving them hanging in midair. "Uh, he met John, and, uh, we would all three get on the phone and have conversations to help us resolve some problems. Uh, get everything out in the open. You know, maybe there was something I told Brent that I didn't tell John or I told John and didn't tell Brent. And, uh, we'd get everything out in the open and discuss it and we'd solve all our problems."

Despite the fact that Renee seemed to be surprisingly relaxed and untroubled while Altman talked with her, he could not help but believe she was spinning a web of lies. He was astonished that two men in love and having sex with the same woman could calmly sit down together and iron out their difficulties. That didn't sound like anybody he knew.

"Now, let me get this right," the befuddled detective insisted, "you're saying things about getting stuff out in the open. How would you discuss things? Was it just a mutual agreement? Like, 'Brent, I'm doing this now' and he would say, 'Oh, that's fine.' Or would it be you guys arguing about it?"

"Oh, no, we wouldn't argue about it. He would ask me a question and I would tell him. John would be on the phone and he would confirm it or disagree with It. Just depending on what was said."

"Well, in speaking with his parents, they wouldn't say that. They said you guys were fussing and fighting all the time."

"No, no, we had our arguments," Renee admitted haltingly. "Yeah. We had our arguments, but they weren't really severe." She said their last argument was about two weeks ago and it was about John.

"About two weeks ago?" Altman snapped angrily. "And this is when Brent found out that you'd slept with John?"

"No, he knew prior to that." For the first time, Renee's voice cracked. "I think he just started thinking about things. It was bothering him. He would call me at home. If I weren't at home, he would page me or call his mom to see if I was there. He became just really antsy about where I was at. And, uh, you know, I'd call in and check in with him and tell him, you know, where I was at."

Altman's head shot forward as he started applying pressure. "And what would you say, it seems just a little strange that you're calling your husband when you're living with somebody else just to let him know what you're doing?"

Renee didn't say anything. She didn't have to. The detective's chagrin told her what he was thinking.

"And when you decided to move back in with Brent, how did John feel about that?"

"He wasn't really happy about it." Renee's lips started trembling. "But he just told me, 'Well, you know, that's your decision. I hope everything works out, you know.' And we agreed to remain friends, 'cause that's how we originally started out."

He stared at her expressionless. Unsmiling, in a far seeing place.

"We're *friends*," Renee quickly corrected. She could feel her legs starting to tremble. "And, uh, I talked to my husband about him and he talked to John about it. Everybody agreed, you know, that was fine. As long as everybody knew what was being said, that was fine."

Altman didn't believe her. "And at no time did Brent ever get jealous over John?" he asked.

"He was upset that I slept with him, yes. But he didn't get jealous over him."

"I don't understand it," the detective shouted suddenly, his arms flailing about. "Brent was twenty-four, and you're twenty-one. You've only been out of high school a few years, still pretty young age to handle an open marriage like that. I remember how jealous kids are in high school. If your boyfriend even sees somebody else even looking at you, usually they're going to flip off the handle or want to fight this other guy."

Renee assured the detective that John and Brent were never like that.

"No. Brent's not a violent person. He had a really bad temper at one time, but he's gotten over that. We've talked about [it] and we had been going to church and everything. He's really not a jealous person. He knows I don't have a lot of friends."

Renee whined to the detectives that she only had one friend, Cynthia Hanson, the girl who had introduced her to John. Altman asked for her phone number and Renee gave it to him, even though she said Cynthia wasn't up to date on her relationship with John. Renee drew in a quick breath, then let it out slowly. "I've been pretty much a loner all my life," she wanted the detectives to know. "I've never really had any friends. Even in high school, I didn't have any friends."

Given Renee's looks, the detectives didn't believe that was true. Altman tried not to show his frustration and asked, "Doesn't it seem a little strange that you're carrying on a relationship with another guy and you're living with your husband and child?"

"Right." Renee felt helpless.

"I mean, don't you think that's strange?"

"To an extent, yeah, but we were friends to begin with and my husband knew that," she tried to say convincingly. "I think the only reason it bothered him is that I slept with him. Brent would listen to our conversations and he knew what was being said, so he really didn't get too upset about it. He knew what all we talked about."

When pressed, Renee said that Brent was ecstatic when she came back home for good. John wasn't very happy about it, though. He even told her to get somebody to move herself, that he wasn't going to do it. But she said John did respect their decision and that he had only been over twice. The invitations for him to come over and see her had been at Renee's request. Brent didn't know John had been over, because she didn't tell him. She said she was afraid he'd think something was going on.

Renee claimed she'd only been at John's house once since

she had moved back home, and only to pick up her things. She claimed John was not mad that she had gone back to Brent. She swore nothing was going on, that they would just talk about her and Brent's relationship. She did admit that John had been calling her daily since she moved out of his house, but insisted that Brent didn't have a problem with that.

The seasoned detective found her story hard to believe, so he took aim and attempted to shoot it full of holes. "What would you talk about with John in relation to your relationship with Brent?"

"Well, John knew that we were going to church," Renee said, her red eyes now glistening. "That we were going to church and that we were gonna start going to counseling." She quickly corrected herself. "Uh, my husband was gonna set up an appointment for us to go to counseling."

"So when did Brent find out that you were sleeping with John?"

"Uh, while I was still living with John, I told him."

"So, he really found out about it then."

"Yes, and, uh, he and—he and . . . Brent would stay home from work because he was so upset about it."

When Altman asked Renee if she thought John was really in love with her she shook her head no. She said she thought he was probably getting attached, but he wasn't in love with her.

"How did you feel about him getting attached to you?"

Renee grew silent, then answered, "It bothered me."

"How come?"

"Because I'm . . . I was still married."

Detective Altman glanced at his partner, then rolled his eyes again. Kings sat quietly, without expression, and continued watching her.

"Did you ever think about getting divorced from Brent to go with John?"

"Not to be with John, no," she snapped back in a voice unbelievably cold and hateful.

"So you had thought about divorcing him."

Her face tensed suddenly, but her manner remained stern. "I had thought about it, yeah."

"And what was your reason?"

"Uh, because he didn't spend the time with us. That was the reason I left him. 'Cause he didn't spend the time with us."

Up until this point, no one at the MBPD, including Captain Hendrick, Detectives Joyce, King and Altman, as well as advocate Mary Stogner, had directly accused Renee Poole of any deliberate involvement in her husband's murder. But all that was about to change. Her clever attempt to confuse the detectives with a little bit of truth and a whole lot of lies was about to end. Detective Altman pulled his chair in closer, put on his boxing gloves, and went to work on his prima donna.

"Did you tell John Boyd Frazier that you were coming to Myrtle Beach?"

The sudden change in the detective's intonation startled Renee. She sat up in her seat, then responded nervously, "I don't think that I did tell him. Uh, I did tell him that it was our anniversary. I think the last time I talked to John was before we came to Myrtle Beach. Maybe the beginning or middle of last week. But he was all for us getting back together."

Altman nodded vigorously. Slowly and methodically he took her back over the last two days that she and her husband had spent at the beach and asked her to describe once again in detail how they had been robbed and her husband murdered.

Both Altman and King already had made up their minds what had happened, but they listened this time as Renee described the events and studied her carefully, noting every grimace and twitch in her face, diversion in her eyes, wrinkle in her brow, bite of her lip, hesitation in her voice and movement of her hands. They both bore into her with no other thoughts in mind, as if they had no single purpose in life or no other interests but this single homicide investigation.

It was an attitude Renee greatly resented. She had already been through several lengthy interviews. She wasn't involved in Brent's murder and she had nothing to fear, but it was late and she was exhausted. She had been as forthright and honest as she knew how to be—what more did they want from her? Her lips now trembling, she took a deep, shaky breath, and braced herself for the onslaught.

The detectives centered their attack on Renee's inability to remember certain fine points about the shooter and the particulars of how her husband had been executed. During their lengthy interview, Renee had added a few variations to her story, including the disclosures about the shooter. When asked, "Could you tell if the shooter was black or white?" Renee said she couldn't.

"What?" Altman shouted. "You mean to tell me you were a hundred feet from this guy, it was a full moon, and you couldn't tell?"

"I just . . . I—I glanced at him," Renee said sheepishly.

"I mean, you guys were pretty scared that this guy was starting to follow you. You didn't really take a good look around and see what he looked like?"

Renee said she thought the shooter must have put the mask on at this point. "He must have had it on before he turned around to come back in the opposite direction." It was when she and her husband turned around and saw that mask that they looked at each other and sped up.

"So, why didn't you start running?" Altman asked.

She said she didn't know why. They just sped up. But they didn't start running, even though they saw the man had a mask on.

"So, he's dressed all in black and he's got a ski mask on, and you didn't run away?" Altman asked, as if he and Detective King were the only ones who were speechless by that remark.

Renee admitted she just started walking fast.

"Then how did he catch up to you guys if you guys started walking real fast?"

She said she didn't know, the shooter must have run, obviously. She didn't know which side he came up or how he got in front of them, even though they were walking toward the lights in front of them and there was a full moon, but this guy got in front of them somehow. Said she didn't see him run by, she didn't hear him running, no thumping or kicking sand out, no little noise of squishing sand. But somehow he just caught up to them.

Altman imagined it must have been easy for Renee to visualize how all this had happened, but he was having a very hard time believing it had actually occurred as she said it did. Then Renee told him the shooter made a strange request in asking them to lie not on their stomachs, but on their backs. In fact, he believed it was so bizarre that he asked her to draw out on a piece of paper exactly how he had told them to lie down. She described how they were lying, Brent facing with his feet toward the hotel, feet close, two feet apart from each other. His feet toward the south and her feet toward the ocean. They instantly lay down when the shooter told them and then he proceeded to rob them of everything they had on them, including Brent's wallet. She gave him her wedding rings and a diamond engagement ring.

Altman glanced at Renee's neck and hand. He then pointed, as if her eyes had been shrouded by a blindfold, and asked, "But you still got a bracelet and another ring on?"

"Oh, uh, I didn't realize I had this on at the time," she replied. "I was just trying to do what he said and obviously didn't see it."

Detective King kept his eyes stuck on Renee.

"So, by this time," Altman continued, "you guys are a couple feet apart. This guy is right in between you and you're close to him. Now you're probably as close as the three of us are. Right?"

"Right," Renee said nonchalantly.

"And you're looking over at the suspect and he's all in black. And he's got a ski mask on. Can you tell if this guy is white or black?"

"No. I was scared to death." Renee said the man had a deep voice and that he had a ski mask covering his face. When she told Altman she didn't recall if it had anything covering the mouth or nose, he made her draw a picture of it on paper. "It looked like something cut out around the eyes," she mumbled as she sketched out the image. "Maybe at the top of the mask. One hole. Like one big eye." When asked to describe the shooter's eyes, Renee said she didn't see his eyes at all.

Altman was a man on fire, clearly obsessed with getting

at the truth. He knew he had grabbed a tigress by the tail, but this didn't stop him from going after her.

"And what was Brent doing all this time? Was he just lying there?" Altman leaned back in his chair. He started waving his hands again, pleading with her. "Didn't he tell this guy to leave you guys alone or anything like that? Didn't he make any comments to him at all? I mean, this guy is kneeling over him and he doesn't do anything. Nothing?"

"No," Renee told him quite calmly. She shook her head. The only thing she could remember were his words when the shooter asked why shouldn't he kill him. Brent begged for his life and said, "Because I have a daughter that I love very much."

Renee said she then heard a click that sounded like the gun was shot, but there was nothing in it. Said she knew a little about guns. She could see this one was black. It wasn't a revolver, but a semiautomatic. The shooter was holding it in his right hand, and it sounded to her like he was messing with the gun trying to get a bullet in the chamber.

Altman sat silent for a moment. He deliberately phrased his question so that it would be impossible for her to misinterpret his inference. "And you didn't decide at that time you needed to get out of there?"

"I was afraid he was gonna shoot me."

"I mean, he's already tried to shoot Brent once and it didn't go off," Altman countered. "Didn't it click in your mind that this is it? It's time to run or die? I mean, you're just gonna lay there and let him shoot you?"

"Well, I—I was scared. I didn't know what he would do."

She sounded frazzled and flighty, but Altman couldn't seem to break her. Like a heavyweight fighter who had suddenly tied his opponent against the ropes, he went in with the knockout punch.

"What about Brent? I mean, he's laying over there?" He jabbed at her again. "This guy's got a gun on him and it's misfired. He didn't decide, 'Hey, it's time to get the hell out of here'?"

Then, with his best one-two combination, Altman moved in closer.

"He never tried to fight this guy off? He just laid there? Where did this guy have this gun pointed?"

"I didn't see," Renee answered as a matter of fact. She looked beat, but was still determined to put on her best performance.

"You're only . . . ," Altman started, then backed up. "This space between us is maybe—what—four feet?"

"I . . . I—"

The detective cut her off. "I mean, across this table right here. That's how close you are and you don't see where he pointed that gun?"

"I had my eyes closed at that point."

Renee could feel the pressure building. Her head pounded every second like the hands on an old antique clock. Hot, dank air filled the room. She lowered her head and closed her eyes.

"So, you're just sitting there waiting for him to shoot you?"

"Pretty much."

Altman demanded to know what she had heard. Her stomach rumbled. For a moment, she felt sick. She closed, then slowly opened her eyes. She spoke without looking at him.

"I heard the gun misfire once and heard the shooter clicking it around again. I kept my eyes closed the whole time. When he got the gun cleared, he then shot my husband. I put my hands over my eyes and just started shaking. I didn't see what was going on. Just heard two shots. Didn't look over. Didn't look up to see what was going on. I did see the guy run away. I leaned up and looked at my husband, then looked up to see where the man was running."

"Then how come he didn't shoot you?" Altman barked. His voice sounded too harsh to be anything but a nightmare.

"I don't know," Renee said through trembling lips. "Maybe he saw somebody or heard something."

"Do you know where your husband got shot?"

Renee lowered her head again.

"In the head," she answered softly. "The blood was coming from the side of his head."

Altman leaned forward. He was only inches away from her face. She could feel his breath. It smelled like day-old cat food.

"Now, don't you think that's kind of unusual?" he began slowly, working his way to a fevered pitch. "That he shoots your husband, twice, and just lets you lay there and takes off. I mean, I don't know if you know about Myrtle Beach too well—you've probably only been here a couple of times—but this place . . . this residential area you're in is high-dollar district. We got nice, wealthy people living there."

Renee looked up and forced a smile. "Yes, my husband and I were noticing the houses."

Altman ignored her attempt to be cordial. He didn't hesitate. He was on a roll.

"These—these things don't happen up there, okay? We don't have robberies on the beach up in that area. You might have a few alternative-lifestyle people that hang up in the dunes, but we just don't have robbers pop out of the dunes with a gun and shoot somebody twice. Who shoots somebody and leaves that other person there. Can you see what I'm saying?"

"Yeah," Renee answered grimly.

"I mean, you see where none of this makes any sense?" the detective pleaded. "Or, why he would shoot your husband twice. Your husband, the father of your child, and leave you there. Doesn't say a word to you. I mean, can you explain this?"

"No, I can't," Renee responded curtly. What did he think she was? A fucking detective?

"Then let me ask you something. Do you know who shot your husband?"

"No," she answered emphatically.

"This is your time, right now, to come clean on this," Altman said in a patronizing voice. "Because your husband's dead."

Renee shook her head. "I know that."

Altman continued pressuring her.

"The father of your child is dead. These things don't happen in Myrtle Beach like this. Especially in that neighborhood. I've worked here for six years. Sergeant King has worked here going on about fifteen. And we can both tell you from our experiences, things just don't happen up there. You're sure not gonna get one person shot up there and leave a witness wide open. Without shooting at you once. Maybe trying to shoot you in the stomach. The way your husband was shot, it could almost be considered an execution. I think somebody intentionally shot your husband to get rid of him. Now, he's the father of your child. And you say you love him?"

"I do love him," Renee shot back.

Altman was merciless. "Then maybe you just loved him a little bit too much, where you couldn't decide which way you were gonna go?"

She shook her head. "No." That wasn't the way it was.

"Because, like I said, to leave somebody, a solid witness like that, without even taking a pop shot at them." Altman let that thought sink deep before driving a second stake. "You know your husband was shot point-blank. Twice. You know, somebody's gotta live with this the rest of their life."

Renee's stomach tightened. She felt scared and confused. Her stomach came up, but an hour without food or water hadn't changed anything. There was still nothing there left for her to throw up.

Altman didn't stop his relentless grilling. He believed he had her back against the wall. As he thought about it, she had never behaved like a woman who was struggling with dreadful emotional trauma. She had never acted like a woman who had just seen her husband brutally murdered. At least, she hadn't shown any signs of stress that in his experience he normally expected a woman would. He wanted to ask the question he had been holding back for the longest time, but before he asked it, he went on to say, "I mean, you say you've been going to church and stuff with Brent. Do you know anything about this murder? You know, we've been sitting here talking with you about a good forty-five minutes and you've talked to Sergeant King for about an hour before this, and you're really showing no emotion at all about this."

Renee heard her teeth grinding. She looked Altman straight in the eyes, then told him, "I've already done my crying." Her eyes told him to kiss off.

"I understand that, but to have somebody murdered, this is

some pretty serious stuff. We called Brent's parents and the first words out of their mouth were about all this fussing and fighting that's been going on between you two."

"Like I've told you, we had our arguments, but we had everything worked out before we even left. I took him shopping. I bought him all kinds of church clothes. I bought him brand-new clothes, underwear, socks. Because I wanted him to look nice."

If that was all true, Altman thought, it was understandable why she should be furious with his accusations. It was obvious in her face and in her razor speech that his name would not be included on her Christmas mailing list this year. But as he belatedly realized, it was impossible to miss that to which he was referring. Not once had he seen a tear mist in her eyes or trickle down her cheeks. The detective was determined not to let Renee off the hook.

"Yes, I understand," he continued. "I saw him at the hospital and I'll admit he looked like Tommy Hilfiger. But how are you gonna explain this to your daughter when she's old enough to understand this stuff?"

Altman immediately recognized the anxiety in her face. He had finally touched a sore spot in her heart and it burned.

"I been trying to think of that all night," Renee said, for the first time looking as if she were going to break down. "'Cause I know when I walk in that hotel room, she's gonna ask me, 'Where's my daddy?' I don't know what to tell her. I don't know what to tell her."

Altman leaned back in his chair and signaled for Sergeant King to jump in. He had pinned her to the canvas. It was time for his partner to take over.

It was time now to end this match.

CHAPTER 14

When Sergeant King pulled his chair in closer to Renee, it finally dawned on her what was happening. She had seen enough police shows on television and watched enough crime movies to recognize this was going to be a tag-team match. This oldest trick in the book. Good cop versus bad cop.

Sergeant King, the quiet and unassuming one, through his slow, easy style, had appeared sympathetic to Renee's unfortunate plight. He was tall and lean, a clean-cut black man who reminded her of Denzel Washington. She had thought the two of them had developed a good rapport. But now, she could see the world was his stage, and he, like Denzel, was just acting out the part of a good cop.

Sergeant Altman was the bad cop. Even though he, too, was clean-cut and handsome, with his closely cut dark black hair—the Ben Affleck type, she surmised—he came off as very arrogant and aggressive.

The way she saw it, Altman had been nothing like King. From the start, he had treated her like some child who had gotten caught with her hand in the cookie jar. He was rude, had yelled at her and, at times, had resorted to bullying her. There was a bead of sweat tracing his upper lip—why he kept insisting she knew more about Brent's murder than she was telling them, she never would know. She guessed he played the role of the bad cop admirably, and as well as anyone, but she'd be the first to tell him she didn't appreciate the way he was treating her. It was like she was some kind of common criminal.

At first, Renee had believed the Myrtle Beach police were as determined as she to find out who had killed her husband. But she now realized that had been her fatal error. In retrospect, she now felt like they had all been wearing blinders by focusing totally on her. There was a point during her first interrogation, when the police had told her they had used tracking dogs, that she had asked him to turn off the recorder for a second. She could then see it in their faces, that they were bound and determined to think she had something to do with Brent's murder. That she was going to offer them at that moment some incriminating information against John Boyd Frazier.

But she let them know she was good and tired of all their questions. Fed up with their bullshit. She was agitated at them for trying to implicate she was somehow involved in any of this. She made it clear it was time for them to stop *accusing* her and to start *giving* her some answers. After all, had it not been *her* husband who had been unexplainably murdered on their beach? And didn't she deserve the same consideration as any other victim whose husband had just been brutally murdered before her very eyes?

"Tell me, then," Renee said to the police with renewed courage, "if your dogs are supposed to be so goddamned good, why haven't they found anything yet?"

"We were hoping you could tell us that," she was told.

The tedious and tiring wrestling match between the interviewers and the interviewee continued for another hour or more, covering much of the same ground. Renee knew she was being double-teamed. The only problem was, when she had last looked in her corner, there was nobody there for her.

"Renee, do you understand the problems we are having with this?" Sergeant King began slowly. "The main problem I have is the ski mask and how you have drawn this design." He pointed at the sheet of paper lying in front of them on the table. "If that mask had that much of a gap in it around the eyes, you could see if that person's black or white." He pointed at

Renee's drawing again. "And if he's that close to you, and there was a full moon out there, then you could see that."

"I wasn't paying attention to him," Renee said, waiting to catch her breath. "I looked at his build; I looked at his height. I mean, that was obvious because he was, he was bigger than we were, but we're small people. He was taller than we were."

Detective King dug in again. When he asked Renee if John knew she and her husband were coming to Myrtle Beach, she said she hadn't told him—that she could recall. Then again, once she thought about it, she may have told him. But she was definitely sure she hadn't told John where they would be staying.

King was unimpressed, but inquired patiently, "John really didn't like this too much about you going back to your husband, did he? One thing you told me that stands out is when you told him that you were moving back, he said, 'Well, you need to get somebody else to help you pack.' He said he wasn't going to help. He helped you pack to move in with him, but he wasn't going to help you pack to move out."

Renee tried to focus harder. She squinted her eyes, but her pupils refused to cooperate. She didn't bother looking up at the detective.

King lifted his head condescendingly.

"You see, that is kind of odd there." He crossed his arms and leaned back against his chair as if he had just figured out the missing part to this riddle. "Something just ain't right here. It's just not adding up. Something's wrong."

The back of her neck suddenly turned red and her eyes looked as if they were ready to shoot fire. "Then, why don't you pick up the phone and call him?" she said gamely, shifting her gaze from King to Altman.

King arched a brow at her unexpected barb, then glanced at his partner. "Call who?" he said stiffly, squaring his shoulders.

"John," she answered calmly.

King shook his head, then gave her his best scowl. "Okay, what's his number?" He had called her bluff.

Renee's heart began beating rapidly. "I have his pager number, but I don't have his house number." A few volleys were launched between her and the detectives as to why she didn't have his home number. "Both numbers had been changed because John and I were both getting hang-ups. In all honesty, I really didn't want to have it anyway, because the month before I had gotten a three-hundred-dollar phone bill."

"Somebody's been doing a lot of talking," King couldn't resist saying.

When Renee finally scribbled the pager number on the paper with her drawings that still sat in front of them, the detective asked, "You think if we call this number right now, do you actually think he'll call back?"

"He may." Renee shrugged. Then, quickly changed her mind to: "No, I'm pretty sure he will. He always did his best to call me right back."

Sergeant King stared long and hard at Renee. He smiled wanly at her, then snorted. "Was it John that did this?"

"I don't know," she said quickly, glancing at the detectives to see if they believed her or not.

King shook his head, this time in disgust. "You don't know?"

Renee felt as if she had spoken too quickly. She fell silent, before offering, "I don't know if John was here or not."

"Did John do this?" King said abruptly.

"I don't know if John was here and I don't know if that was John," she said quietly.

King tapped the tip of his finger on the desk. He began to grin smugly. "Now, I really find that hard to believe."

"I don't know if he was here."

"Come on, Renee," he muttered fiercely. "Was this John?"

Frustration animated her body, bringing up her chin. "I don't know if that was John." She shrugged.

King looked away from Renee and nodded at his partner.

"Renee . . ." Altman leaned in, as if he were hurtling his full weight against her.

"I really don't know." Renee winced. When she looked at him, her eyes still shot fire.

"But John loves you so much," he supplied as an explanation.

"He's not that stupid," she said flatly.

"But he killed your husband 'cause he loves you!" Altman shouted, asking her to try that one on for size. When she didn't say anything, he thrust a finger at her and roared, "Now tell us what happened out there!"

"I told you what happened," Renee shouted, still seeing red. "I don't think that John could do that."

Altman backed off and King stepped back up to the plate. Renee noticed King always tried to console her when Altman got outraged and couldn't get anywhere with her. "Renee," he said her name gently but firmly, as a father would have, "he asked you if that was John."

She could feel her chest tighten again. "I don't know if it was John," she whimpered. "I don't know who it was."

"Now, you've talked with John plenty of times," King continued to coax in the voice of a loving parent. "You got a three-hundred-dollar phone bill to back that up. You could recognize John's voice in this room, but you're telling me you don't know if this was John or not."

"No," she swore again.

"So it could have been John?"

She shook her head lightly, then whispered at last, "Could have been."

"Ah, come on now. . . ."

"But I don't know if it was him."

King paled. "Renee, don't get yourself in big trouble here," he admonished.

She didn't say anything.

Altman leaned back in.

"You don't need to die in a death penalty case because of something that he did because he loves you," he growled. "We already know John's not home. We've already had the police go to his house and he's not there. Now tell us what happened on the beach tonight."

Renee closed her eyes. Everything started spinning sickeningly around her. Her brain suddenly felt pickled, like it had been sealed in a Mason jar and had sat on a dusty shelf in somebody's basement.

"I told you exactly what happened," she snapped. "I really don't know if it was him."

"Renee," King addressed her again, "why don't you know if it was him? Tell us, why don't you know if this was John?"

"Because I don't think John would be that stupid."

"You don't think John would be that stupid," the detective acknowledged. "But tell us, why you don't know that?"

Renee sat silent.

"Was it him? Or not?"

Renee took a deep breath. "John sounded like he was happy for my marriage to work. He was being that friend who . . . who was proud of me for going back to my husband and making my family work."

"But deep down, there was something else there," King chided her.

"He never portrayed it to me." She fell back against the chair and shook her head slowly. She felt the instinctive need to breathe. "I don't know."

"Here's your chance," King urged, trying to pin her with his bleary gaze. "The door is wide open."

Renee didn't hesitate. "I don't know."

"Don't let it close." King feigned reluctance. "Don't let the door close. Help yourself." Before she had a chance to respond, he reminded her again, "Don't let the door close, Renee."

"I don't know anything," she insisted. "I really don't."

For another hour, the homicide detectives grilled Renee, asking, time and time again, if the shooter had been John Boyd Frazier. But Renee's response was the same after each challenge: "It could have been, but I really don't know."

The detectives told her clearly and firmly they found it hard to believe that someone who had been around John as long as she had, and who had been involved with him sexually, would not have been able to recognize his voice, his build and his mannerisms, especially at that close of a range and in the full light of the moon.

Altman and King started pulling every rabbit out of the hat to try and discredit Renee's story. Utilizing almost every strategy in the training manual, they told her someone had recognized John's car at the beach last night; they talked with her about a gun, she said, she thought he owned; they debated with her all the good reasons—right or wrong—John Boyd Frazier had for killing her husband.

"I would say he had good reasons to," Sergeant King emphasized, trying to convince Renee that John had a strong motive to see her husband dead. To see her husband lying on the beach with his baby blue eyes wide open and chunks of his brain blown away.

King's statement didn't appear to shock Renee at all. She immediately blurted out, "Why? Because he was a friend of mine?"

"Because he was in love," King added, as if he were surprised that she didn't already know that.

Renee stared at the detective with an expression that struck him as if she thought that was the most ridiculous statement she had heard all morning. "I don't think John was in love with me. I didn't live with him but a week. I only slept with him a couple of times." She continued to look at King as if his questions were immaterial to her present situation.

"People fall in love overnight," he sneered.

"But he knew I loved my husband," she argued. "He knew that he couldn't have me—"

King cut her short. "But it happened. You take your husband out of the picture, there's nobody left in his way. You think we're making all this up. But the puzzle fits, Renee. It fits in every way."

Renee closed her eyes as she listened. "No. I don't know who killed my husband. There has to be fingerprints or something somewhere."

King glanced at Altman. He shook his head lightly, then turned back to Renee. "So, you had nothing to do with this. You have no knowledge whatsoever?"

"No," she drawled in her deep Southern accent.

Altman gestured to his partner to back off. Tossing a net over her was beginning to get as difficult as trying to squeeze an elephant into a pair of Spider-Man pajamas. It was something clearly within the realm of possibility, but tough to do. He'd give it another try.

Altman slowly and meticulously spelled it all out for Renee one last time. He provided her the motive, a timeline, and an opportunity. Applying everything, from God to fate, reason to conscience—and throwing everything in to boot, but the American flag—he officially accused Renee of knowing the time, place and how the murder had gone down.

But he still couldn't tie her to anything incriminating.

"You know, to take somebody's life is the worst thing you can do to somebody," Altman just had to say. "And people will do that to get things out of their way. To get things that they want. Maybe this wasn't planned, but somebody followed through with what they wanted to do. There are two people, right now, that know who was there."

Renee purposefully didn't respond.

"And what you're saying could be true," the detective continued, "but when we dig more and more into this, and we find out there's a boyfriend—an ex-boyfriend—who's not happy with you going back to your husband, then the ax is going to fall. And if you're not careful, it's going to fall right on your head."

Altman constructed one last-ditch effort to solicit a confession. Hoping this one would stick against the wall, he inched steadily toward her and threw out, "Are you sure you didn't shoot him and just make this thing up about this guy dressed in all black?"

"No," Renee said, never flinching. "I couldn't shoot my husband."

"Maybe you shot him and then threw the gun out in the ocean?"

She didn't fall for that one, either.

Altman finally backed off. He and Sergeant King were both done for the night. They guessed the gun and the answer as to who killed Brent had probably been tossed in the ocean and was resting on the bottom among the myriad of sea urchins by now.

In spite of the detectives' grueling and intense interrogation, "It could have been John Frazier, but I'm not sure" was as far as they could get with Renee. And that was certainly nothing to write home about. After Renee had been escorted out of the interview room and back to the victim's advocacy office, the two detectives emerged with faces of battle-laden warriors. Although they believed their witness wasn't a genius by any definition of the word, she was feisty. And tough. And they were convinced she was very savvy and had street smarts. A valiant effort against a stubborn opponent, but they had come up empty-handed, they informed Captain Hendrick and Lieutenant Frontz immediately afterward. If they were going to prove Renee Poole was involved in any way with this murder, they would have to do it the old-fashioned way. They'd have to go out and beat the bushes. Interview witnesses and find someone who had seen the couple or the killer on the beach. Talk to everyone who knew anything about their relationship and somehow prove she and her lover were involved, beyond a reasonable doubt.

But the day was young. And the investigation still fresh on the table.

Detective Altman believed, although he had not been able to tighten the noose around Renee this time, he knew they would do battle again. Before she left the interview room, he made himself a promise. If she had anything to do with her husband's murder, he swore, they would meet again.

And, the next time, he *would* take her down.

CHAPTER 15

Captain Hendrick walked into the interrogation room where Detectives King and Altman sat relaxing at the table. Renee was with Mary Stogner in the victim's advocacy office.

"John Boyd Frazier was at home when the WSPD checked his residence about five-thirty this morning," Captain Hendrick said with a bit of disappointment. "We received word of this while you both were in the interviewing room with Renee. It's best we not give her or anyone else that information at this time."

The detectives nodded their heads in unison.

Detective Altman reached over and grabbed a fresh bottle of water, twisted it open and poured the contents into a Styrofoam cup. He drew in a quick breath, then took a few hurried sips just as fast. Trying not to show his frustrations, he piped in, "I hope this doesn't mean we've lost John Frazier as a promising suspect and quickly erase him from suspicion."

Captain Hendrick assured him it had not. There were numerous ways to check on Frazier to determine if he had been home all night. There were phone records to check, friends and neighbors, who could have remembered him coming and going, and outside witnesses who might have seen him or his car at the beach that night. In addition, they could drive the route from the crime scene to his house and develop a timeline. Just because he was home at the precise moment the police checked his home didn't prove he wasn't involved in the murder. Even if he didn't kill Brent Poole, it was certainly possible he could have hired someone else to do it. Hendrick emphasized John Frazier was still the man with the greatest motive, thus their primary suspect. And he would remain so until proven otherwise.

Victim's advocate Stogner had offered Renee a ride from MBPD headquarters back to her hotel.

"My parents are coming to get me and take me and Katie back home," Renee told her, smiling for the first time.

Stogner could see there was a sense of relief in Renee that she finally had made it over this hurdle and was going home. It was 7:30 A.M. Renee told Stogner she felt like she had just been put through the wringer and was eager to see her parents.

Just as Renee and Stogner stepped out the door and were greeted by the first shafts of daylight, they heard the echoes of a man's hoarse voice from outside the building. The boisterous man was pointing at Renee, but yelling at Stogner in an unfriendly manner. "You best get her away from us," he shouted. "I'm telling you, you better take her away, and now!"

It was Brent Poole's father, his mother and his sister. This was not the warm reception Renee had hoped for. The homicide detectives saw what was happening, ran to the front door and got between Renee and the Pooles, then hurried the in-laws inside the building. They led them through the hall and into the interrogation room, where they had just finished almost seven hours interviewing Renee. The Pooles sat down at the table and tried to calm themselves.

Bill Poole was a small, thin man with gray hair combed across his balding head. With wrinkles stretched across his forehead and all around his blue eyes and graying mustached mouth, he was the picture of what Brent Poole would have looked like, had he lived to be an older man.

Brent's mother, Agnes, was much taller than her husband. She was thin, with pallid cheeks and an ashen complexion, and eyebrows that seemed permanently squinted, as if she had been straining all her life to see something more clearly. Her partially graying hair revealed she was a week or two past-due on her last coloring.

Brent's sister, Dee, looked to be in her late thirties. But with her short blond hair, a cute, round face and her trim figure, she could easily have been mistaken—under any other circumstances—for a high-school cheerleader. This time, a frown replaced a smile across her face.

"Are you folks the Pooles?" Hendrick asked as he introduced himself.

They nodded in unison. Bill politely stood up and introduced his family to the chief and Detectives King and Altman.

"We're sorry to meet you under these circumstances," Hendrick stated genuinely. "I know this is not a good time for you. Please believe we're going to do all we can to help solve Brent's murder and find the killer who did this."

As King and Altman took a seat across from the Pooles, Hendrick made his apologies and excused himself from the room. Bill Poole took a couple of quicksteps toward them, as if he were too angry to stand still. Altman invited him to take a seat and Poole finally sat down beside his wife.

"I hate to see you folks have to come down to Myrtle Beach for these circumstances," Altman began in his usual manner. "And it's unfortunate to meet you like this. But we're gonna be as honest as we can on most things. It's not that we're trying to hide anything from you; of course, some of the details we're not gonna be able to tell you—but there are certain things that our investigations are gonna be able to reveal to the person that we believe was involved in Brent's murder."

The Pooles nodded. They wanted Altman to know from the start that they would cooperate in any way.

Altman slowly blew out the breath he had been holding.

"I can tell you up front," he said, thinking they would want to know, "your son, and your brother, was shot. He died instantly and probably didn't feel a thing. Speaking with the physicians up at the emergency room tonight, it was very quick. From what they're saying and from the things they have dealt with, it was very painless because it just happened so fast."

Brent's mother gasped. "Was it in the head?" she asked. Her

bottom lip quivered as if she had been standing in subtemperature weather.

Altman arched a brow. "I can tell you it was a head shot. I can't tell you where in the head."

"Do you know if his face is disfigured?" Agnes needed to know.

"No," the detective answered flatly. He hesitated, then offered, "When I saw him, of course, there was blood. When you have a head wound, it does bleed a lot. So there was a lot of blood on him."

When Bill asked if his son was facing down or standing up, Altman declined to answer, for fear those details would somehow become public. That was information that would be privy to the killer and couldn't be leaked for obvious reasons. Altman quickly moved the grieving trio from questions concerning the details of Brent's murder to information regarding Renee and John Frazier's relationship. The family eagerly furnished dates, times and events from when Renee had moved in and out of John's home.

"She moved everything out, all of our granddaughter's clothes and furniture," Brent's parents said, almost in unison. Detective Altman noted how one would start a sentence, mainly Brent's father, then the other, routinely his mother, would always finish it. Brent's sister, Dee, sat quietly at the table, supporting her parents while they did most of the talking.

"She did it while our son was at work," Agnes said, cutting Bill off. "So, he had no idea she was moving out. We accidentally came across her with John at a service station that night, not knowing that she had moved out."

"So, there's not a joint relationship that had been worked out between John and Brent for Renee's affection every day?" Altman asked, believing he already knew the answer.

The Pooles looked back at him, stupefied, as if his inquiry had been telephoned from the planet Venus. They all three sat back in their seats, glanced at each other, shook their heads, then stared at Altman. Their blank faces conveyed to him this was a game Renee had been playing with him. They cautioned him when dealing with someone like Renee, her deceptive maneuvers and lies were as predictable as the rising and setting of the sun.

"Then, in your opinion, how was the relationship between Brent and Renee?"

"He loved her with all his heart," Agnes said through her tears. "But he also wanted this to stop. He just found out last week that she was having contact with John again on the Internet and through phone calls. It just about blew him away. And one night—"

"He called us one night," Bill said, this time finishing his wife's sentence, "one Saturday night, and said, 'Can I come home?' Said this is not working out, that she can't make up her mind who she wants. And in my mind, that's not an agreeable joint relationship."

Agnes picked up where Bill left off. "And the next day, she showed up. Dee had her little girls over that night, and Brent was just in a really low mood." She turned toward her daughter and tilted her head for confirmation. "Wasn't he?"

Dee agreed.

"He was very down," Agnes elaborated. "Just really like his heart was broken. But Renee was all cheery and everything, like nothing had happened. I kept saying, 'Brent, have I done something. Is everything all right?' And he said, 'Everything is not all right, but it will be.'"

Altman glanced at Sergeant King, who sat next to him, quietly taking notes.

"Renee was real smiley," Agnes continued, dabbing at her moist eyes with a crumpled tissue. "And he kept on being downcast, so I asked him, 'Brent, honey, what's wrong? What's wrong with you?' Renee then grabbed his arm and took him in the back bedroom and had a talk with him. And when he came back out, she said they were going to shoot pool and then they went home. I think something was going on that day between Renee and John, and Brent found out about it."

Dee cleared her throat then and everyone in the room turned toward her, waiting to hear what she had to say.

"When Brent called me that night on the phone, I had a long talk with him. And he said, 'Isn't this something? Renee wants to have another child with me, but she can't decide whether she wants to be with me or John.' When I asked Brent, 'I thought you were going to the beach,' he responded, 'Well, we're gonna go.' But he kept saying, 'Isn't that funny that she can't decide who she wants to be with?'"

The homicide sleuths were intrigued. It looked as if their hunches had been right all along.

Dee shared more of the same.

"I asked him if he wanted to come over and he put Renee on the phone. 'I'm trying to work on my feelings for Brent,' Renee told me. When I asked her, 'Are you telling me that John is interfering with your feelings for my brother?' she said, 'Yeah, it's confusing me.' I then asked Renee if she was seeing John. She denied it, of course, but did admit she was talking to him."

Agnes colored in the rest of the picture, connecting the dots.

"We found out later that was not true, because my son's best friend called up and told my husband that he had seen Renee and John at a shoe place right after they had had that conversation. Then, the first week after Renee came back home, Brent couldn't find her for about three hours and he called our house looking for her. She finally showed up at ten o'clock that night and said she had been at a shoe place that we knew closed at five-thirty or six. It was just that kind of thing all the time. And this is her second affair. He found out after he was married one month that she had started having an affair when she was pregnant with Katie. This one lasted for two years, so it just didn't start—"

Altman interrupted Agnes before she caught her breath. "Was that with John also, or somebody else?" She shook her head no.

"Well, when she moved out, Brent was working on getting an attorney and getting ready to get involved in the legal aspects of separation. I think a few things influenced her to come back. Her mother went over there and got the baby's clothes and said the baby is not living in this environment. So, I think she realized she didn't have anybody but her and John.

But to say this was an agreement between all three of them was the furthest thing from Brent's mind."

The detectives looked at each other, then shifted in their seats. The information Renee had given them did not jive with the Pooles'. They wanted to give her the benefit of the doubt, but it appeared as if there were far too many discrepancies between her and her in-laws' stories.

While the detectives compared impressions, the Pooles tried to deal the best they could with what had happened. But what they really wanted to know was how the murder had happened and if there were any other witnesses. Altman told them Renee had been the only witness, besides the shooter.

Bill Poole was curious as to why only Brent had been shot and why there was no blood on Renee's shirt and pants when Altman had told them there had been a lot of blood on Brent's head. The distraught father stated he was suspicious of the people that Renee had been associating with. He admitted he didn't personally know them, but he was still very suspicious of them.

Dee then suddenly turned to her mother and asked, "Who was the guy that sent you the videotape?" To which, Agnes replied, "Oh, that was the guy she had the first affair with."

Altman was stunned. "Wait a minute," he said, suddenly focusing on Agnes. "Somebody sent you a videotape?"

Agnes nodded.

"And what was on the videotape?"

She dropped her eyes, then answered disgustedly, "Them having sex."

Altman sat up in his seat and rolled his eyes toward the ceiling. "I can't believe it," he said incredulously. "He sent that to you folks?"

Agnes lifted her head, then slowly cut her eyes at her husband. Altman sensed this tape could have been a source of tension between the couple.

"Actually, the tape had been sent to Brent in care of his father," Agnes said, still looking at her red-faced husband. "Bill was out of town, and after looking at that package for three days, I decided I was going to open it." Agnes turned from her husband and looked at Altman. "I just knew if Brent saw this visual, it would devastate him."

Altman looked at Bill, then back at Agnes. His heart ached for them.

"But what really made up my mind was that one night Renee called me and *griped* for forty-five minutes about what Brent did and didn't do."

Agnes paused. She looked down nervously at her hands in her lap. Visibly upset, she bit down on her bottom lip, fighting back her tears, then continued weakly, almost apologetically.

"You know, I never came down on Renee for this, and when she called to gripe about Brent, I would sit with the phone held out and just listen. But it suddenly dawned on me that Renee had been coming by our house every day, about the same time the mailman came to deliver our mail. I remembered noticing Renee was always looking, checking the box and seeing what was in our mail. One day, I quickly ran out to the mailbox before she got there and saw that package. I put it under my arm and ran back to the house. Renee arrived a minute later. Too late to see what I had found."

Agnes sat at the table with her fists clenched. As she talked, she pounded them lightly on the table. Altman swallowed hard, gladly knowing Agnes was not his mother-in-law and mad at him.

"That night, she called again, about eleven-fifteen, and infuriated me with her complaints about my son. I was so angry at Renee that when we hung up, I got that package and immediately opened it. Inside was a videotape and I shoved it in the television."

Agnes slowed down. She lowered her eyes, then blew out a deep breath, as if expelling years of deeply buried pain. "It was a tape of Renee and a boy named Danny having sex," she said in a low voice, a little below a whisper.

Detective Altman leaned forward to hear her. Agnes cleared her voice, then looked up at him.

"In vivid color, I saw my daughter-in-law and a stranger having sex," she said, getting teary-eyed again. "I watched as she and this stranger demonstrated the finer techniques of a vibrator."

Brent's mother paused, then turned toward her husband, who had reached out and held her hand.

"There were also additional footage of Renee and this guy when she graduated from night class and received her GED. As I watched this, I hung my head in disbelief when Renee was presented an engagement ring. There, on the video, he gave her this ring and she accepted it."

Bill Poole shook his head in agony. Dee lowered her head and started to cry.

"There was a big poster board on the TV screen and it read, 'Renee, will you marry me? Will you be my wife?' Then Renee accepts the ring, looks into the camera and says, 'Yes, I'll marry you.'"

Altman was confused. He looked at Sergeant King for help. King shrugged.

"Wait a minute"—Altman held out his hand, palms up—"is this while she is still married to Brent?"

"Yes, this is while she is still married to our son," Agnes acknowledged.

Bill started squirming in his seat, as if he had just realized he had been sitting on a tack all this time. He looked at the detectives and shook his head.

"I didn't see this video," he protested, holding up both his hands.

Agnes turned and apologized to her husband that she had kept it from him for about a year. "I was just too ashamed to show it to you."

Bill tilted his head slightly, then said to Altman, "This girl is bad . . . bad news."

Altman thought about his own mother and how she would have reacted if she had received a tape like that. Stunned by the thought, he asked Agnes, "So, why would this guy send this tape to you, of all people?"

"Because he thought she was having an affair with some-body else and that was his way of getting back," Agnes said, without having to think about it. "Brent and Renee lived with us when they got married, and I think until Katie was about three months old. And she had been having an affair the whole time and we didn't know it. She was even bringing him into our home and having sex with him there. He called Brent at work and told him about it. 'I have been in your home,' he said. 'Your parents are remodeling.' He even described our home."

Altman rolled his eyes and smirked. Renee's in-laws were peeling away the layers of her life like an overripe banana. She was rotten to the core.

"We learned later Renee had met this guy Danny at the Home Depot when she was working there while she was pregnant." Agnes kept on exposing her daughter-in-law's unscrupulous behavior. "One time, when Katie had eye surgery, she told me not to come to the hospital unless I checked with her. But I went one morning anyway to carry her breakfast, and this guy was there. I was suspicious at the time, but I let it go, 'cause I didn't know anything. Then Brent started getting phone calls at work, and the guy would ask him, 'Do you want to know who your wife is screwing? She is screwing everybody in town.' And Brent would say, 'No, I don't want to know'; then he changed his mind and said, 'Yeah, go ahead and tell me.' 'Well, she is f-ing everybody in town,' the guy told him. And that is when Brent started coming home from work and checking on her."

Agnes wiped her eyes again, but there was nothing there. She was beyond the point of tears.

"Brent has really put up with a lot. And we have loved Renee, we have encouraged her. Brent just started back in church three Sundays ago. He'd been out for quite a while."

It was time for Dee to play the drums, and she didn't miss a beat.

"When Renee finally agreed to move back home," she chimed in, "Brent asked her if she would come over and help clean the house and get it ready for her return. She was supposed to have been back that Saturday night, but didn't show. But when we paged her, John called and cussed me out one side and down the other."

She made a contorted face. She pretended she was holding a phone away from her ear.

"He said, 'I mean you f-ing this and your family is f-ing this and you're a G.D. this and your f-ing brother is this.' When I asked to speak to Renee, that I understood she was on her way back, John screamed again, 'That's what you think. She's not coming back.' For about five minutes more, John rambled on until he finally put Renee on the phone. I asked her, 'Can you hear how he's talking to me?' 'Yeah, but I didn't hear what you said to him.'"

Dee said the hair on her head stood on end and she started spitting fire.

"'Renee, I asked to talk to you. Don't you understand, I'm here trying to get this house ready for you to come back home.' At that point, and after talking with Brent for an hour and a half, Renee finally said she would come, but she didn't. She called Brent the next day and admitted that she'd had sex again with John and wasn't coming back. And the sad thing is, her daughter was with us."

Altman thought he had heard it all, but apparently not. "Do you think it's possible she's still carrying on a relationship with this Danny guy?"

"I think it is possible she could be carrying on a relationship with three or four guys," Agnes said in sarcasm, before exclaiming, "And that's the truth!"

Bill shook his head, then jumped on the bandwagon. "Yes, I believe that based on a phone call that Brent received at work. And also based on the first affair . . . you know, she's married and she's having an affair, and this guy is jealous because she is having another affair . . . but that's what initiated this tape. So I don't think there is any limit to what Renee might be capable of when it comes to affairs."

Agnes agreed. "Her own mother will tell you." She sighed. "It sounds like we are coming down hard on her, but we have loved that girl. And I have. I have. I really have." She shook her head slowly, then glanced at her husband and daughter. "They have been upset with me for giving her as many chances as I did."

"The only thing we want," Bill pleaded, suddenly changing the subject, "and she may be as much a victim as Brent or we are. I don't know that. But if she has any part in this, she needs to pay for it."

"Yes," Agnes and Dee stated, almost at the same time. They looked at each other and would nod in agreement each time Bill said something significant they wanted to emphasize.

"And I don't want her to have a part in it. If she's a victim, then I'll apologize to her," Bill said more than once. He wanted the detectives to know exactly where they were coming from. "The hurt is real, and if she's a victim, it's real on her side. If it's not, then it's not real. But you need to turn over every stone you can to see if she had anything to do with it, because the kind of people she is involved with think they can do anything."

"Knowing Renee's past," Altman concluded, sensing he needed to wrap it up, "what is your gut feeling on what has happened tonight?"

Bill was the first to offer his opinion. "My gut feeling is that this is no coincidence. This is not an accident. This is not a random act. That is my first feeling."

"Do you think she played a part in it?" Altman asked him curiously.

"I don't want to be wrong, I mean, I'm judging and that's not for me to do. That's just my initial feeling. She could have been a victim, just like everybody else in this situation."

Agnes verbalized her husband's utmost fear. "That's what is so scary. What if we are wrong and judging her? That's where we're at. What if we are wrong?"

"But the way she has treated our son . . ." Bill argued his case with great fervor. "The way she respects herself—her marriage and her vows—and her daughter. I just wouldn't put it past her. I mean, I really wouldn't. You know he wouldn't give up and that maybe was the only out for John. He wouldn't give up, he wouldn't let go . . . I don't know. I just don't want to think she couldn't be involved, but justice has got to be done." Bill looked toward the detectives with hopeless eyes and begged them for justice. "Y'all just do everything you can," he said, wiping his eyes with the back of his hand.

"Just be assured that we're gonna look at everything we can on this," Altman promised him. He questioned the family about a life insurance policy on Brent and was told there was one with his employer. Brent had worked as a mechanic for a Mack Truck dealership in Charlotte, North Carolina, and had taken out a life insurance policy. They thought Renee was the sole beneficiary, but didn't know the face value of the policy, but thought it was around $100,000.

The Pooles suggested further that if Altman needed more information on Renee's scruples, he could contact Brent's good friend Brad Williams. As a favor to Brent, Brad had been spying on Renee and John, and the Pooles were confident he could provide additional insight into their affair.

"Well, the answers will come when she finally sees it in the picture," Bill encouraged the detectives. "I don't think Renee pulled the trigger. I don't believe it's in her nature. But there is an individual, I really believe, there's somebody else who did pull it."

"Do you think she would cover up for someone?" Altman asked, testing his theory. "I mean, would she be the type of person to continually stick to her story? Or do you think there's a breaking point?"

Bill provided a most helpful insight into Renee's character. "I think there's a breaking point," he advised truthfully. "Because when she got into the conversation about these affairs, there would be all kinds of discrepancies in her stories. If there were any discrepancies in her story about this, then they will eventually come out."

"And her mother will also tell you Renee's a liar," Agnes added. "She has told us this on many occasions. Her mother has said, 'Even as much as her dad loves her, he, too, will admit to you that Renee's a liar.'"

"I really think she doesn't know what the truth is," Bill said adamantly.

When the Pooles asked if there was a chance they could see Brent's body, Detective Altman deferred the question to the more experienced officer. Sergeant King spoke up, saying, "If that's something you truly want to do, we'll talk to the coroner. He has to approve it, but I want you to know it's not a pretty sight. I wouldn't want you to remember him that way, but if you insist."

Agnes clutched at her throat, then gasped. "What do you mean 'it's not a pretty sight'?"

King explained. "The injuries Brent sustained were from a large-caliber gun. Either a nine-millimeter or a three-eighty. He was shot twice. And in the head."

Dee leaned into her father, then clutched his arm. "Oh, God," she cried.

"Are you saying it messed up his face?" Agnes asked hesitantly.

King paused. "Yes, to see him the way he is right now. I think it would be safe to say that."

Bill looked at his wife and daughter. Both of them were already in tears. He shook his head and looked at the detective bravely. "No, I don't think we could handle it, 'cause I . . ." Brent's father stumbled on his words. His felt his heart drop to his feet. His lips started trembling and tears brimmed in his blue eyes. He put his arms around his wife and daughter. "Oh, my God, they wanted to be sure he didn't have an opportunity to say anything, didn't they? If . . . if you shoot a guy twice"—Bill tried to go on, his voice cracking—"If . . . if you shoot a guy twice in the head . . ." But he broke down, never finished his sentence.

The two hardened detectives were as tough as old hunting boots, but they, too, nearly broke down and cried with the family. It was as if they and the Pooles' lives had intertwined somehow and were now bonded in cement.

Before their conversation ended, the Pooles asked again what Renee had said about the murder. They wanted to know if she would be required to take a lie detector test, or was that just something seen on television?

"We'll certainly offer," King explained, "but we can't force her to take one. And even if she agreed, then we couldn't use it against her in court."

For one of the only times in her life, Agnes Poole was outside herself. For a woman who had always seemed to be pretty much in control of her life, she couldn't think of anything to ask. She drew in a deep, trembling breath. She didn't know what to ask, but, after all, this was her son's murder they were talking about. She had to ask something. Finally she blurted out, "Would you have to see something in your investigation to warrant any charges before anything like that could be done?"

"Well, we're looking at it from all aspects right now, and she is our key witness." King corrected himself and quickly substituted "key suspect" in place of "key witness." He continued, "She's the only one right now that can tell us something. Whether she's telling us the truth, we really don't know at this point. We have some concerns about what happened, how she said it happened, the whole nine yards. We've been talking with her seriously since about three this morning. As you can see, she just left, so we're not just taking her story at face value. We want you folks to know this will not be the last time we talk with her. We even gave her the residue test to make sure she didn't fire the gun."

"One more question," Bill said before he stood up. "What is the frequency of murders in Myrtle Beach?"

"Uh, this is actually our first murder this year," Altman told him. "We count them per year. I think last year we might have had . . . maybe five?"

"And last year, that was a whole lot for us," King added.

Bill stood up slowly, as if getting to his feet were difficult. "You know, it's my son here and I can get . . ." His voice broke again. He took a short breath, then said as he exhaled, "I'm trying not to be too emotional about this, but what happened here . . . This was no robbery; this was a murder. And I believe that with all my heart."

The detectives couldn't have agreed with him more. The greatest task they now faced was gathering enough evidence against Brent's killer, get him arrested, and off the street before he hurt anyone else.

"Could you show us where it happened?" Bill Poole asked

on the way out. Dee wanted to know if it was okay to put some flowers on the beach, while Agnes inquired as how to make contact with the coroner and get permission to view Bent's body.

"I want to go and see Katie," Dee said slowly, as if the thought of seeing her and knowing that she would ask for Brent suddenly pained her greatly.

Sergeant King volunteered to call the coroner and ask for a viewing of the body, and Sergeant Altman agreed to lead them to the crime scene. It was 8:24 A.M. when they walked out of the interview room with the Pooles. Both men had been up all night and their bodies were running on four cylinders.

However, seeing the soft, sticky brains of someone lying on the beach hardens a man and sends determination through his veins like very few things can. When a detective sees a family like the Pooles going through the pain and misery of losing a loved one, it changes something inside him. Grief runs through a man's soul like a small rabid animal and is as contagious as a virus. It causes a good cop to deny himself all necessities of life: sleep, food, nourishment and companionship. And if he's not careful about it, he can end up making it personal and spending every waking minute craving justice and seeking closure for the family. A homicide detective can at the drop of a hat become delusional and obsessed in thinking if only he could solve this murder, then somehow that would finally end the family's pain and suffering.

Men like that, Altman was well aware, who often find themselves bound by a silent inward promise, find themselves shot, through and through, with adrenaline at every turn in the case, regardless of how big or small, until the case is finally solved. He'd heard of men like that spending a lifetime, sacrificing all health, family, friends, sanity—whatever it took—in pursuit of cases that, for whatever reason, could never be solved.

Altman's stomach tightened in knots like tree roots from a large oak, tightly gnarled. He asked himself, *What if we never solve this case? What happens if we don't find out who murdered Brent Poole?* Then he quickly dismissed the thought.

The detective reached for his keys from the top of his

desk. He grabbed his water and his sunglasses, then headed out the door after the Pooles.

Altman knew better than to think negatively. It just wasn't his style.

CHAPTER 16

Renee Poole and the female police officer walked across the parking lot to the blue-and-white Myrtle Beach police squad car that was to take her back to her hotel. "As you may have detected, Brent's family isn't very fond of me," she said disappointed as she climbed into the backseat of the car.

The officer smiled and nodded, but didn't comment. She twisted the key in the ignition and the big engine roared. Before pulling out of the parking lot, she fastened her seat belt and reminded Renee to do the same.

"On my husband's senior-prom night," Renee began, erroneously thinking her driver was as eager to hear the rest of the story as she was to share it, "his parents walked in on us having sex."

She paused as if her relationship with Brent's parents had always been a taboo subject, then added, more so for her benefit than anyone else's, "I don't know what the fuss was all about. We'd been dating for over a year by that time. But obviously they were totally unaware of the intimacy between us." Another long pause before she concluded: "Since that day, my mother-in-law has never cared for me."

Renee laid her head against the back of the seat and closed her tired eyes. She snickered silently. The memory of Brent's parents catching them having sex was very funny, now that she thought about it.

Growing up in Winston-Salem, Renee's childhood hadn't been anything like Beaver Cleaver's, but it wasn't anything like Kelly Osbourne's either. Renee supposed it was something that fell in between the two. Her mother and father, Jack and Marie Summey, had met at Daytona Beach, Florida, in 1974, where Jack was working as a finish carpenter. The two started dating, eventually moved in together, then got married a year later. When Jack moved his family back to North Carolina in 1977, he and Marie were the proud parents of two little girls, Brandy and Renee.

The Summey girls grew into their own personalities. The oldest of the two, Brandy, was always content and never cried. While Renee was a loving and very smart child, she was feisty and independent. Renee was forever wanting to do everything for herself, but the two sisters developed a strong bond and fortunately never fought or argued. Brandy didn't mind being the quiet one and would always bow out to her younger, gregarious sister.

For some reason, Renee didn't remember a lot about her childhood other than her father was the permissive, easy-going and laid-back parent. Her mother was the one who had to discipline her and her sister. Jack was self-employed by then and owned his own paint-and-body shop, while Marie worked mostly in clerical positions for physicians and health clinics. In 1990, her parents bought land in Clemmons, North Carolina, and Jack built a new body shop, then constructed his family's log cabin home.

Renee's most vivid memories in her life began when she was twelve years old and had just gone through puberty. She was attending Wiley Junior High, in Winston-Salem, and always had been a motivated student who did very well when she applied herself. With a natural ability for drawing she had inherited from her father, she excelled in art. Several of Renee's art projects were sent off to art shows and to scholastic events and came back with high praise from the judges.

But Renee never felt comfortable around the other kids in her school. It was as if she never felt good enough, rich enough or privileged enough as the other children. She remembered other kids in the neighborhood began teasing her when she was in the fourth grade. Because she and her family lived in a mobile home, she said, her schoolmates would laugh at her for being poor. Said they'd call her and her sister, "white trailer trash."

Renee had always been thin and small, which gave her classmates even more fodder for jokes. The other kids in school called her "Ethiopian" and taunted her about being skinny with names like "beanpole" or "light pole."

After all this teasing, Renee started feeling insecure about who she was and where she lived. In order to compensate for her low self-esteem, she began hanging out with the wrong crowd—a bunch of misfits, just like her, from lower-class families and poor neighborhoods. She figured since her peers were already labeling her an outcast, she might as well be like them. Renee grew up thinking the rebellious crowd was where she really belonged.

One weekend, Renee was spending the night with a friend. She felt safe with this family, for they were friends with her parents, and one of their sons had visited Renee's dad at his auto body shop from time to time. She didn't know it, but the young man smoked pot, and since his sister was Renee's friend, she felt that if she didn't try it, then they would make fun of her. Renee smoked cigarettes, but this was the first time she had ever tried pot.

After they had smoked a joint, Renee's friend left to go to the bathroom and never came back. Being so high from the pot, Renee wasn't sure what was going on and ended up having sexual intercourse with her friend's brother. She knew she didn't like what was happening, but was confused. She couldn't think straight. He had hurt her, but she didn't know how to stop him. If she yelled, she might get into trouble for the pot they had just smoked, so she just let it happen. She prayed for it to be over with, but never said another word about it.

Renee was young and didn't have the interpersonal skills to get out of the situation with her girlfriend's brother. She thought she had done something wrong and she would ultimately get into trouble for it. A couple of times, the boy showed up at her dad's shop when he wasn't there, and he'd call for Renee to come out and he'd have sex with her. She was scared to say anything about it and afraid to tell on him, so she just went along with it.

It was then that Renee became very depressed and started skipping school. She started hanging out with the wrong crowd, drinking, smoking pot and sneaking out of the house to meet her friends. Usually she would ride around and get high or drunk with a few friends or meet her boyfriend in the park and make out for a little while.

Renee's parents had no idea what had happened to their daughter and attributed her bad grades and behavioral changes to "teenage problems" and her new set of friends. Renee said it was no big deal and claimed all the "cool kids" she knew were behaving the same. It was common to just hang out, rarely do any kind of homework and routinely fail tests. Renee never told her parents she did it because she didn't want to seem like a nerd and be an outcast from the in crowd.

Renee and her parents had many discussions about her behavior and they administered many types of discipline to try and correct the problems. Renee would always promise to do better, but never did. But never—by any stretch of the imagination—did she see herself as a bad girl. After all, it was the 1990s. There were much younger girls at her school that were already having sex and doing drugs. She only had smoked pot a few times and limited her sexual activities to only the boys she dated.

When Renee first met Brent seven years ago at RJ Reynolds High School in Winston-Salem, she was a thin, mousy fourteen-year-old. She and a friend needed a ride home from school, and they were bumming a ride for another student as well. At the last moment, their friend saw Brent getting into his blue-and-white S15 pickup truck and asked if he would give them all a ride. Brent agreed, and the four of them found themselves crammed inside the cab of Brent's pickup.

Renee thought Brent was cute and learned they had a lot in common. He, too, had grown up in a family whose men shared a love for motorcycles and cars and was obsessed with anything mechanical. The youngest of three children, he got along well with his older brother and sister. Renee thought he was adorable with his big, beautiful eyes, his full, soft lips and great smile. He had braces on his teeth and wore those little blue rubber bands on them. But all the kids did that; it was the popular thing to do. When Brent agreed to give them a ride home, she was as excited as a first grader with a new bicycle.

At age seventeen, Brent was so much more mature than the boys in her class and the next day he found her in the hall at school and asked her out. Their relationship took off like a rocket. They were so affectionate and drawn to each other that they couldn't keep their hands off one another. It took only a week of dating before they had engaged in their first sexual experience.

Renee recalled the first time she and Brent made love was kinda funny, because they were so nervous. It was Brent's first time and he was a little anxious about that. He had had a girlfriend prior to her and admitted they had attempted to have sexual intercourse, but had only gotten as far as oral sex.

Renee didn't care whom Brent had been with or what they had done. She was just excited about holding and kissing him. She had known from the very first kiss that she'd fall in love with him. And after they had made love the first time, she was convinced she'd met her soul mate for life. It was so perfect. No awkwardness at all. It was like their bodies just fit together perfectly.

Renee and Brent's first sexual experience actually occurred at the Pooles' home on Kerstmill Road. They lived in a ranch-style brick house across from the rock quarry and asphalt plant owned by Vulcan Materials, where Brent's dad was employed. Renee and Brent jokingly referred to him as "Barney Rubble." While Brent's parents were upstairs, they were downstairs in the basement, watching a movie they had rented. But before long, they started kissing and petting, until finally things got out of control and the movie was long forgotten.

For Renee, everything had been storybook perfect. She and Brent were young and made love every chance they got.

Their passion was so strong they never missed an opportunity to be together. Brent went to work after school, so he would have Renee meet him at his truck. He had tinted the windows in his truck so no one could see what they were doing. Before he went to work and she to her next class, they would disrobe in the cab and make love. When that got too cramped, Brent lined the bed of his truck with carpet and they'd climb back there and make love.

Sometime afterward, Brent's classmates started kidding him about the "rocking and knocking" truck in the parking lot. And when Renee started complaining about the carpet burns, he took some of his money he earned working at the bus station and rented a room at the Innkeeper Motel on Peter's Creek Parkway.

Renee confided to her friends that she didn't know why they always went to the same motel, but it sure beat doing it in the truck. Brent said he couldn't help but feel like Dustin Hoffman in *The Graduate*. All the employees at the Innkeeper Motel had grown accustomed to him, his blue-and-white pickup truck and his mysterious lover. But he didn't care. Some days he even went by early to pay for the room and pick up the key so he wouldn't have to waste time on the trivial things.

The in crowd Renee used to hang out with quickly became the out crowd after she started dating Brent. She abruptly ditched her old friends, believing he was all she ever needed to make her life complete. After Brent graduated from high school, he chose to attend diesel school in Tennessee. Renee saw no need to continue school if Brent wasn't going to be there and dropped out in the tenth grade. That year, she had a disagreement with the assistant principal and got expelled for using the "N" word. Her father found out what had happened and took her back to school to apologize, but the die had already been cast.

Renee had been working as a cashier in the cosmetics department at the Drug Emporium since she was fourteen. Living at home, and with no real expenses, she used most of her money to buy presents for Brent. While he was away at school, they maintained their relationship, calling one another regularly and writing letters. He came home every other weekend and would sometimes spend the night with Renee at her parents' home.

One day, out of the blue, Brent confessed to Renee that an ex-girlfriend of his lived in Tennessee and he had looked her up. Said she had wanted a ride back to North Carolina to visit her friends, and since Brent was coming home that weekend, he agreed to give her a lift. In return, she had given him a blow job.

Renee was furious. How could he let something like that happen? She decided the only way not to let that happen was to make sure Brent wasn't lonely and to find out what was going on at his school. She started visiting him in Tennessee, one time agreeing to stay with him for several months. While she was there, she found out about a girl he *claimed* he had taken to the hospital. Or, at least that was his story and he was sticking to it. He told Renee she had come to his door selling magazines and he innocently had given her a ride to the hospital, and that was why she had his leather jacket. Brent swore he loved Renee more than anything in the world and promised never to let anyone come between them again.

Like all relationships, Brent and Renee's always had its ups and downs. Although Renee continually seemed to be at odds with Brent's mother, she was beginning to feel somewhat comfortable around his family. She had forgiven his parents for calling her a "whore" and a "slut" the night they caught her and Brent naked, and she didn't put up a fuss whenever he asked her to do something for their sake. There were times when he would take her out for a date, then drive her back home to change clothes before she went to his house. Brent would never admit his mother had said anything about the way she dressed, but Renee knew she would always have to be mindful of what she wore around her.

Renee fondly remembered a particular day when Brent and his parents came to visit her dad at his shop next to their house. She was sick with a cold and went to Brent's truck to get her cough drops. When she reached in the door pocket of his truck, to her utter surprise, she found a little box with a diamond inside. She was so excited, she had to tell someone and later confided to Brandy that Brent had bought her a diamond. She swore her sister to secrecy, but Brandy let it slip out. Brent was angry at Brandy when she ruined his surprise, but not deterred. That night, he came back over to their house and phoned her from her dad's shop. He asked her to come out of the house, that he wanted to talk with her about something.

Renee said she still didn't feel well, but Brent wouldn't take no for an answer. When she finally came walking out the door, he told her to close her eyes and he got down on one knee, with a single yellow rose in his hand, and proposed. "Kimberly Renee Poole, would you marry me?" he said romantically. She started crying, but somehow managed to squeeze out an acceptance. After he handed her the yellow rose, she saw the diamond, fastened onto one of the leaves, sparkling in the light.

Brent had always been careful to use a condom when he and Renee were having sex. He knew if he got her pregnant, abortion would not be an option. But now that they were engaged, why worry? They had already decided to get married and knew they were going to be together for a lifetime, so what difference did it make?

But in the spring of 1995, Renee began craving pickles and other odd assortments of foods. A home pregnancy test confirmed she was pregnant, and when she called Brent to tell him, he said he had already figured it out. He told her it didn't matter; she was seventeen and he was twenty. He had already completed diesel school and was working for Mack Truck sales in Kernersville. She was working at Home Depot. If they needed any further help financially, he knew both their parents would help out.

Renee wanted to have this baby for Brent, but she found it difficult to concentrate at home. When she and her mother argued about her not following the rules of the house, she started spending nights over at her friend April's house. That didn't help to resolve the situation, and as a final ultimatum, Marie packed her daughter's stuff and left it outside on the porch.

With the usual obstinacy of an ox, Renee picked up her

things, drove back to April's house and moved in with her. April was only sixteen and living with her older sister, who ironically was one of Brent's ex-girlfriends. Her sister was working as an exotic dancer at a gentleman's club in Winston-Salem and making good enough money to let them stay as long as they liked. After a few phone calls, Renee's parents learned she was staying with April and that April had started dancing in the club as well. They were afraid Renee would follow suit.

Renee assured her parents that April's choices didn't really affect her either way. It was her life after all, and she had a right to live it as she pleased. She then revealed to them she was pregnant and that Brent was the father. With a baby on the way, there was no way she was going to be dancing naked.

Renee's parents always liked Brent. They thought of him as the son they never had. All they wanted for their daughter was to be happy. She didn't have to marry Brent, but if that was what she wanted, then they would accept her decision. They asked Renee to move back home.

Jack and Marie Summey found out they weren't the first parents—nor would they be the last—to hold their tongues and their breath over decisions their children had made. Renee and Brent had been together for seven years, and in spite of all the odds against them, they seemed to love each other. Brent assured Renee's parents that he loved Renee more than life itself, but he wasn't so sure how his parents would respond to the news of her being pregnant.

Brent told his future in-laws that his dad would probably take it okay, but it was his mother he was concerned about. Said she'd worry the warts off a toad over the smallest things. And he knew she wasn't going to like them having a baby out of wedlock. She'd be terrified of what the people in the church and the community were going to say. Lord how people love to talk.

Brent was right. His parents were upset when he first told them about the pregnancy, but eventually they got over it. One night, Bill brought out a jar of pickles and told Renee she would probably be wanting them soon and officially welcomed her into his family. Brent said his mother had finally accepted it, too, but was still worried about saving face with their friends. His mother insisted they get married before Renee started showing.

Renee's parents had wanted her to wait until she had gotten her GED and had saved enough money to have a decent wedding. But out of respect for the Pooles, they started planning and throwing things together as quickly as possible. They would have the wedding at their home and ask their friends to help prepare food and refreshments. Jack made a phone call to the minister who married him and Marie eighteen years ago and the reverend agreed to perform the ceremony.

On June 9, 1995, a perfect sunny day, Renee's and Brent's family and friends gathered at the Summey home in Clemmons to help them celebrate their wedding. Renee was beautiful in her long white gown. Her dark hair had been pulled up into a cascade of curls, laced with a matching white floral band, and she wore a corsage of her favorite flower, three yellow roses.

In front of the Summeys' gray stone fireplace, Brent turned to his bride for the first time in her wedding dress and a smile lit up his face. The minister read from the Bible, then asked if Brent took Renee to be his lawful and wedded wife until death did they part. He smiled at her nervously before replying, "I do." Renee had no problems with her vows, and after the minister asked for rings, she placed a small gold wedding band on his ring finger and pledged her love forever.

It was all over in about ten minutes. Renee and Brent were now husband and wife. Everyone raised a glass of apple cider— Brent's family had asked that no alcoholic beverages be at the wedding—toasted the bride and groom and wished them well on their honeymoon in the mountains at Gatlinburg, Tennessee.

Six months later, Renee gave birth to Katie Lynn Poole at Forsyth Memorial Hospital, in Winston-Salem. Brent's brother, Craig, and his wife, Amy, were also at the same hospital with their newborn. Bill and Agnes Poole were elated to have two little granddaughters at the hospital. It was probably the most special day of Agnes's life; that is, until she walked in Renee's room and saw a strange man standing by her bed. She noticed the suspicious red-faced man couldn't get out of the room fast enough after she had walked in. But Renee claimed Danny was just a coworker from Home Depot, somebody who just happened to be at the hospital and had stopped by to congratulate her.

"But from now on," Renee advised Agnes, "you need to call ahead before you make a surprise visit to my room."

CHAPTER 17

The idea for Renee to become an exotic dancer probably originated with her friend April Eason. In the fall of 1995, April dropped by to visit Renee at her mom's house. Renee was seven months pregnant at the time and she and Brent were sitting at the kitchen table talking with April when she started telling them about how much money she was making as a dancer in a topless club.

Renee's mouth dropped open. She found it strange having a friend in that type of business. She didn't know a lot about what all went on at the clubs, but what she had heard sounded like some weird stuff. But it didn't really affect her either way. She was just happy to hear April was doing well and making so much money.

Brent, on the other hand, thought it was awesome. He looked at Renee and told her after she had the baby, she could start dancing and making big money like April.

Renee couldn't believe her husband had said that. Her mom was standing behind her and she couldn't believe it, either. Marie kind of huffed and went on about her business, knowing that Renee would never do anything like that. But there was a lot going on in Renee's life that she never had told her mother.

From Renee and Brent's earlier days in high school, they had always been sexually attracted to each other. But for some reason, after Katie was born, Brent didn't want to have sexual relations with Renee. Renee was too ashamed to talk with anyone about it, but she believed the real reason their relationship had taken a nosedive was because Brent had gotten hooked on Internet porno sites. She said at first they would sit down and look through the sites together, hoping that it would add some spark to their spiraling sex life. But she soon got tired of that and wanted to do other things. She said she liked doing things with her daughter, like taking her to the park or visiting her or Brent's parents. Brent worked second shift, so they didn't see a lot of each other at night. And when he wasn't working, he was either riding four-wheelers, hanging out with his friends or on the computer pulling up more porno sites.

As long as Renee had known Brent, he had indulged in pornography. At home, he would hide his magazines in the drop-ceiling tiles of his room so his mom wouldn't find them. When they were dating, she said, he kept his magazines stashed under the driver's seat of his truck. And after they were married, he would hide them in their home under their water bed so that Katie wouldn't find them accidentally. Brent also kept other magazines under the driver's seat of his car and would look at them in the parking lot after he got off work.

What Brent didn't seem to understand was that Renee's appetite for sex easily equaled his. She wanted him to know that all the while she, too, craved the same sexual attention and pleasure he wanted for himself. She tried initiating sex with him several times, but each time he turned her down flat. Yet, in the early-morning hours, she would watch him from her empty bed go into the next room and masturbate while watching porno films. She couldn't understand Brent's logic. She was more than willing to please him and instead he chose to do that. For a while, she tried to satisfy herself by masturbating with a vibrator, until he asked to borrow it to pleasure himself. She told him he could have it, that she didn't want it anymore. After that incident, she vowed she would find herself someone who would spend time with her gladly.

Renee guessed she may have had that in the back of her

mind when she agreed with Brent to apply at the Silver Fox Gentleman's Club in Winston-Salem. She had always been an attractive woman and had gotten her share of hits from men, but she was a little apprehensive about competing with professional dancers for attention.

Brent was confident she could make as much money as any of those other dancers. One night, he had talked her into wearing a white patent-leather outfit. The costume consisted of a skirt and a jacket—all of twelve inches—that zipped up the front and only came down to the middle of her back, and she wore six-inch-heeled knee-high boots to match. Brent was standing behind the curtain, watching the delivery boy's face when Renee answered the door in her skimpy outfit, and nearly fell through the window laughing so hard.

Renee looked like a Playboy foldout. She had those large Bambi eyes and long, black-colored lashes that would mesmerize any man. As she prepared herself for her new career, she realized this was her strongest feature and would spend a lot of time searching for the perfect shades of eyeliner and mascara. She started experimenting with different brands of shadows, lipsticks and makeup. She had been wearing makeup since she was about fourteen, but she was going after a much different look and it took a different approach. Sultry, sweltering and sizzling was more the look she was now seeking.

Renee found she didn't need anything to highlight her lips. Just a little lipstick would always accent her pouting lips. She normally wore her hair pulled up in a ponytail or completely down. A bad hair day for her was any day when the humidity was high. Her hair was naturally curly and frizzed when there was moisture in the air. But now that she was making the transition from teenager to woman, she'd have to find a new hairdo. The big-hair thing was definitely out. She needed to let her hair grow to one length and straighten it a bit, start wearing barrettes and swing it across her face and shoulders.

All of Renee's old clothes would have to go, too. She told Brent she'd have to expand her closet and update the outfits she had. She started looking in fashion magazines and buying clothes with colors that would complement her hair, eyes, and skin tone. She tried different styles and wore things she had never thought of wearing before, like sandals, open-toed shoes and ankle-length dresses in reds, browns, slivers and greens. The more she worked at it, the more sophisticated she got. She knew she had finally arrived when total strangers would stop her in the street to tell her she looked like Ashley Judd, Jennifer Love Hewitt or Alyssa Milano.

Renee got hired as a dancer and she went to work right away. She hadn't ever taken any dance lessons, but she quickly picked up little moves from the other girls and incorporated them into her routine. She became more limber and, at times, even felt sexy. As she became less conscious of her nudity, it made things easier for her to adopt a sultry look and concentrate on making the customer feel as if he/she were the only person in the room. Before long, the money came in like it was falling from the sky.

At first, Brent was more interested in Renee making money. But he, too, became infatuated with the new Renee and began to show her some attention. He liked it when the green in her eyes was more predominant than the brown. He liked it when she started wearing her hair down and across her face. And he liked for her to wear short skirts, tight dresses and low-rise, tight jeans that showed off her stomach. Belly-baring jeans was his particular favorite, but for some reason, he still wouldn't allow her to wear them around his family. It didn't matter to Renee, for she was more comfortable in T-shirts, tank tops or sweaters, and loose-fitting jeans. When she dressed in ankle-length dresses, Brent said, she looked more like a schoolteacher and he didn't want her to wear them around him. She never protested to Brent about it, though, and did whatever he wanted just to avoid an argument.

What Renee did enjoy was their lovemaking. Brent was probably turned on to the fact that she was now willing to do whatever he wanted her to and was as vocal as he was about sex. Working at the club had given her the confidence she was seeking and allowed her to be more experimental at home.

Renee's dancing at the Silver Fox had definitely livened up their sex life at home. Brent would ask her to dance for him as foreplay, and she'd dress up in one of her sexy outfits and perform. She always had been shy growing up, not real sure of herself, and had struggled with low self-esteem. She still wrestled with it, but all the attention she had gotten from men at the club, the many compliments they paid her, helped to boost her confidence and reconstruct her ego. How could she not think she was anything but lavishly gorgeous when she was repeatedly told she was too beautiful to be working there. Deep down inside, she didn't believe it was true. But it sure helped to hear it and at least pretend it was true.

If Brent was intimidated by other men watching his wife dance naked and lusting after her, he didn't show it. He never complained about her closet expanding with the many show time outfits Renee had purchased specially from stores in Greensboro and Charlotte. There was also a seamstress who made outfits and came to the club to sell them, and Renee was soon designing her own clothing.

One of Renee's favorite outfits was a man's white, solid and button-down shirt, with a white satiny bra and thong underneath. The thigh-highs were white with lace at the tops of them. The shirt was oversize for Renee and was buttoned with one button about halfway down. She had bought the shirt after having seen one of the girls wear the button-down over a teddy and thought it'd look better with a simple bra and a standard thong.

Brent found it hard to believe his wife was making as much money dancing two nights a week as he was for working forty hours per week. He started inviting all his friends to visit the club and encouraging them to ask his wife to do a table dance for them. Some found it a little bizarre to see him sitting in the club and watching his wife dance naked. They knew his family and that his parents were very religious. Now they only could wonder what his parents must be thinking.

Renee admitted she had found it a little uncomfortable dancing naked at first, then didn't see what all the fuss was about. None of what she wore was any more revealing than what had been seen at the beach, except for her cheeks hanging out from the thong. She didn't have all the slick moves of the other dancers, but it was easy to close her eyes and get into the music. Fantasy names also weren't one of her strong points, but she remembered April had once used the stage name "Carlee" at a club where she was dancing and it had seemed to work for her. Renee adopted "Carlee" as her stage name. April had also gotten a theatrical mask tattooed on her shoulder blade and had talked Renee into getting one tattooed on her thigh.

One thing Renee hadn't thought about before working at the club was the large number of women who came into the club, usually with their boyfriends or husbands, who would pay the dancers to perform for them. She would soon learn from performing in the club that two women being intimate wasn't as big a deal as everyone made it out to be. There were ways women could pleasure other women that men knew absolutely nothing about and discovered from experience that women were much more patient and sensual than men. She realized women knew what felt good to a woman because they shared the same anatomy. Women took their time and did not focus on their own pleasure, as most men did.

As far as she knew, Brent had never actually seen her being sexual with another woman—other than kissing. He may have been looking through the crack in the door at the club, assuming every man she had ever known had a fantasy of making love to two women. Brent had tons of magazines and movies at home portraying this same subject.

Brent appreciated the fringe benefits that came with his wife's new job as much as she did. He loved for Renee to bring women home with her after work. He would purse his lips, pout like a baby and get mad at her for days until she finally agreed to his requests. Because she hated Brent being mad at her, she would usually give in and promise she'd try to talk one of the girls into coming home with her.

Two girls from the Silver Fox did come home with her on two separate occasions. It was late, around three or four in the morning, but Brent didn't mind. He said he felt like he had died and gone to heaven. He cooked for everyone and they all sat around, watched television and talked for a while, then went to bed. They had a spare bedroom upstairs, but Renee saw to it that the girls slept in the bed with her. While Brent slept on the couch downstairs, she and her friends were upstairs having more than a pajama party. They were intimate in every way—kissing, touching, tasting and exploring—but all she allowed her husband to do was fantasize about it.

Brent had always encouraged Renee to bring other women into their marriage. With his fetish for pornography, she believed he was one of those people that psychologists called "voyeurs." But, he told her, it went deeper than that. He begged Renee to let him join in, but she just couldn't bring herself to watch him be intimate with another woman. What he did away from her, she didn't know, but she wasn't going to sit back and watch him do it in her own home. He, on the other hand, wanted more than anything to watch Renee make love with another woman, but she just didn't feel comfortable with that, either. The next day, he'd always ask for details, but she kept them to herself. He had told her that just the thought of his wife being with another woman turned him on, so she thought it best to leave this to his imagination.

There was one certain waitress at the club who once spent the night with Renee that Brent had hoped he could turn into a threesome, but nothing ever transpired. She was very beautiful and Brent desperately wanted her, but she said she was not interested in any of his sex games. They all went out with her on a few occasions; then she quit the club and they never heard from her again.

Renee started to enjoy her liaisons with the women she brought home, but she never told Brent that. She didn't want him to feel inadequate as a lover. Renee knew a lot of people who preached that homosexual relationships were wrong, but since Brent had encouraged her to indulge and she had experimented with it, she didn't feel there was anything more wrong with that than the porn films people watched, the magazines they masturbated to or the premarital sex they engaged in.

Renee was particularly attracted to another dancer she had met at the club, Cynthia Hanson. They quickly became friends and after hours would go out dancing at regular clubs or she'd cook and they'd hang out at her apartment watching Walt

Disney movies with Katie. When they went out to regular clubs, they'd dance together, feed each other and do all the things that "girlfriends" would do. They would even kiss, but that was about it. Cynthia had a boyfriend, so they never had sex. She had already told Renee she had never indulged before and Renee didn't want to pressure her into it. Whenever she was ready, she said, she'd let Renee know.

The two dancers were so close that when Renee wanted another tattoo, she asked to have Cynthia's lip prints tattooed on her neck. She thought it would be sexy and different. She had chosen Cynthia's impressions because her lips were always fuller than hers. From an outside appearance, it looked as if Renee and Cynthia had done a lot more than they actually had. Inside the Silver Fox, Cynthia would tip Renee while she was on stage dancing and Renee would return the favor and pay Cynthia extra attention. It always seemed to raise the customers' curiosity and increase the numbers of dollars in their garters.

Renee's specialty at the Silver Fox was the shower dance, where she would shower behind a glass petition wearing only a thong. Using Pert shampoo—because it glowed under the black lights—and rinsing with a handheld nozzle, she did it alone, or with another girl behind the glass with her. She was a most desirable temptress, and received many offers for sex and private parties. Two deejays and another man, who always brought the dancers bouquets of flowers every night, had also propositioned her for sex. One of the dancers had also wanted Renee to join her and her girlfriend for a threesome. Other customers had offered to take her out to dinner, to vacation in Grand Cayman, and one even told her he would pay what she made in a week's salary to come and clean his house naked. He was married, but said his wife wouldn't mind her doing that.

Renee had gotten real friendly with the other dancers and developed a special attraction with another girl in the club. Courtney Wolford was a real knockout with long brunette hair, brown eyes, and her cherub face. Renee had seen Courtney's Web site featuring Courtney posing partially nude with adults toys for sale and the option to pay and see more. Her husband, Bruce, worked as a bartender in the club and said he was the one who had set the site up. He offered to do the same for any girl in the club. There were rumors circulating within the dancer's dressing room that Courtney was having some problems. Renee could see Courtney was getting as thin as fishing line.

Renee learned later that Bruce had a job working with computers in addition to his bartending at the club. Since Brent and Renee were now into computers, Bruce had promised to show them a few technical options. One night, they were all talking on the computer and Bruce hacked into their computer and pulled up everything they had on their hard drive. Suddenly all the Pooles information was staring at them from their monitor. Brent was amazed at the knowledge Bruce had acquired about computers and wanted to learn more.

Eventually the Pooles had a camera installed on their computer and would use it to IM the Wolfords while on the Internet. The two couples talked about others who had used the camera for the purpose of Internet sex and suggested they might try it. Renee really liked Courtney and they had talked of being intimate, but it never took place. Brent was also chomping at the bit for a threesome with Courtney, but he wasn't having much success, either. He was well-endowed and thought it would help their case if he e-mailed her a picture of himself nude and his shaven penis. But when she saw it, she e-mailed him back and said he was way too big for her.

Renee knew all about her husband's fantasies with Courtney. She wasn't sure how Courtney felt about it, but Bruce had told her he dated others in the club and participated in extramarital affairs on a regular basis. So, she wasn't surprised when he started making little sly remarks to her and making flirtatious advances toward her. She figured Brent and Bruce had secretly set up a "trade-off," an agreement to switch partners. When Courtney told Renee that Bruce had the hotel room all set up and was just waiting for her, she went along with it. She remembered seeing a camera facing the bed while she and Bruce were having sex, but she never saw the little red light flashing. She had no idea that Bruce would be filming it until he showed her the remote control afterward.

Renee and Bruce were determined not to allow what had happened between them to mar their friendship. The Pooles would remain friends with the Wolfords, continue to talk in the club and communicate over the computer. Bruce would occasionally make reference to their affair, just flirting or joking, but that was about all. Renee still believed Brent had set up her affair with Bruce so that he could have his wish to be with Courtney. The way she saw it, she was just basically "following orders," as she usually did when it came to Brent.

CHAPTER 18

It has been said that animals were a good representation of human character traits. The peacock, for example, is a vibrant example of pride, and whenever he senses he has an audience, he spreads his brightly colored feathers and struts about proudly for all to see. As if such strutting were not enough, he also makes a loud, almost screeching sound, seemingly to ensure that all eyes are turned his way. But unlike the peacock, people who proudly strut their stuff and seek complete adulation and fawning from others soon learn that such unadulterated displays of pride quickly lead to their doom and demise, and this inevitably becomes their ultimate undoing.

It was bound to have happened to the Pooles when Renee's mother kept calling their house at night, but there was no answer. Marie told Jack she knew their daughter was working as an exotic dancer. She could just feel it in her heart. When they rode by the Silver Fox and saw her car parked outside, she immediately called Brent's mother. "Guess where your son has my daughter working?"

"Oh, my, that is going to kill us!" Agnes exclaimed. "Especially Bill. He's a deacon in the church."

Even when Brent was working the second shift, he and Renee would drop Katie off at the Pooles' until late in the night or pick her up the next day. Marie cautioned Agnes about keeping Katie, allowing them to go off in directions she knew nothing about. Renee had admitted on the nights the Pooles had kept Katie, she had been dancing. On some nights, Katie had gone to an all-night day care and stayed there until after one in the morning.

Jack Summey was furious with his daughter and refused to speak with her as long as she continued dancing at the club. For weeks, when she walked in one door, he would walk out the other. Brent's sister, Dee, tried to talk with Renee about how being an exotic dancer would affect her marriage and about the example she would be setting for Katie, but Renee didn't like to talk about it. Dee could also tell from Brent's reaction to her questioning Renee that there was a line of questioning that she had not better cross. It was kind of like they were aggravated that anyone had found out about their being involved in this activity. Actually, some of Agnes's friends had seen a program on television about the strip clubs in Winston-Salem and had recognized Renee as she twirled around the brass pole at the Silver Fox. They told Agnes after the program aired that the news was probably spread all over town about her daughter-in-law.

But look at how much money I'm making was always Renee's response to those who confronted her. *Where could I find a job that pays that much money for so few days' work?* Renee ultimately did decide to stop dancing, but swore she wouldn't stop seeing her friends.

With Renee no longer working at the club, it seemed she and Brent had lost interest in each other again. One day in March 1998, when Renee was missing her old life, she called Cynthia and invited her out for dinner. It just so happened that her boyfriend, Thomas Pedersen, and his friend John Frazier arrived home just as they were leaving and asked to accompany them to dinner.

Although John had been a regular patron at the club, Renee said she didn't remember him. She was told he worked at Champion Products in Winston-Salem as a computer technician and lived about forty miles from her house. John was very witty, polite and very attentive to Renee. Before dinner was over, they had exchanged phone numbers and agreed to see each other again.

If Brent was pretending there was no one else in his life, Renee made no bones about the other man in hers. MBPD detectives were told by another dancer at the Silver Fox, Tonia Grubbs Atwood, that Renee had stopped dancing in the club for a while, but returned sometime in March. She had overheard Renee in the dressing room talking about how bad she hated being married. Renee was dating John Frazier at the time; she was the fourth stripper in the club he had dated.

Tonia knew that Renee hadn't told Brent about her relationship with John, that they had just started off talking, and seemed to hit it off perfectly. John was twenty-eight—four years older than Brent—but Renee didn't think he was any more mature. He just paid her a lot more attention.

Renee and John started out talking on the phone and then she started visiting him at his house. It was always while Brent was working in the evenings. She would take Katie with her to visit, and the three of them would watch Disney movies or run errands together. Renee liked John and found him very entertaining. He was always a big joker and enjoyed being the life of the party.

Renee continued seeing and communicating with John almost every day for the first four months of 1998. Tonia remembered John had been cheating on Renee with another dancer while she was absent from the club, but Renee found out about it and had it out with the girl. That night, Tonia said, she had heard Renee complaining in the dressing room about what had just happened with her and John's girlfriend.

"Renee was like, 'Oh, I need a vacation. I need a vacation.' Then someone, a redheaded girl—and I can't remember her name—entered the room. I guess Renee had a child, because this girl asked where her child was going to start play school, and Renee told her she wasn't going to play school. That she wasn't sure where she would be moving. So, the other girls asked if she and her husband were moving, and Renee's like, 'Well, my husband's not moving, but I'm definitely moving. I don't want to be with him anymore. He's driving me crazy.'"

During the three days in May 1998 that Renee had moved in with John, Tonia's roommate overheard her talking with Brent on the phone in the dressing room at the club. She was screaming at him, saying how bad she hated him, and that she was not coming home.

"I'm not coming home tonight, but I will be back tomorrow night," Renee had yelled out. Brent must not have liked her response, because she then told him, "Well, you're just gonna have to learn to live with stuff like this because I'm tired of being with you. And I don't want to be with you anymore."

Tonia said that the next day, Renee had come into work again; two days in a row was a rarity for her. But this night, she was with John Frazier, Cynthia Hanson and some other people. They were showing everyone the tattoo of Cynthia's lips on Renee's neck. She said Renee and John were acting like a couple, embarrassingly hanging all over each other. And when she and Cynthia went into the dressing room to fix their hair or do whatever they needed to do, Renee said, "I think that I really like John. He seems to be a nice guy and he knows the kind of things I like to do."

"Well, what are you going to do about Brent?" Cynthia had asked.

"I'm not really sure what to do with him," Renee then answered. "I do know that I would like to continue seeing John, but I'm sure if Brent finds out, he's not gonna be very happy at all."

Tonia went on to say that the next night when Renee was dancing at the Silver Fox, she had several messages stuck on the mirror above her stuff. One was from Brent and one was from John. She said she watched Renee call John first and heard her say to John over the phone, "I don't know how he got our number. What all did you say to him?" She stated she had to leave and go back on stage for two songs for about ten minutes. When she came back to the dressing room, she heard Renee then talking to someone else she believed was Brent. She remembered hearing Renee say, "I hate you. I wish you were dead. And I hope I never have to see you again."

Tonia told police she didn't see much of Renee after that. For some reason, she just quit working at the club. But that wasn't unusual. That sort of thing happened to entertainers all the time. "One day, they'll drop out and you just won't see them anymore," she said, guessing that was what had happened to Renee.

Like many couples who choose to dishonor their marital vows, Brent and Renee had come to a crossroads in their relationship. They discovered that unless they changed their lifestyles and rededicated themselves to one another, their two left-handed rings would never guarantee things would be right in their marriage. Their families had heard the grumblings way before now, but what they didn't know was that Brent and Renee's relationship was in deeper trouble than they had realized. They found out the night Brent came home from work and his house was empty. Renee had taken Katie and moved out.

Later, when Renee and Brent reconciled, it wasn't the money that had driven her back to Brent, she said. She had worked since she was fourteen, and was never accustomed to anyone supporting her completely. She was making good money as a dancer, was used to having her own spending money and could make a living if she had to. But she had come back to Brent because she truly loved him and wanted to make her marriage work.

"There was a time when I tried to overdose on pills right after I broke off with John," Renee would admit years later. "Brent and John were mad, but were taking it out on me. Brent was giving me hell about John and John about him. I went to John's house and told him, 'You have got to quit all this stuff. You're about to push me off the edge. If you don't quit, I'm going to kill myself.'"

Renee said she got a paring knife, put it to her wrist and cut herself. It bled, but didn't hurt. She was ready to quit, ready to give up. Frazier came back in and saw the blood, then told her he didn't think she had the balls to do it. She asked him why, if he wanted her so bad, was he doing this to her?

Brent was to be home at midnight. Renee had just put Katie to bed and was sad and depressed. She had a bunch of pills: Valium, uppers and downers. She took a handful of pills and tried to kill herself. She was very mad at herself for giving up, but had already made up her mind she wasn't going through this anymore. The next night, she went into work and thought about how it wasn't working with Brent because he didn't want to let the marriage go. He wouldn't give up and John wouldn't leave her alone.

"I felt like shit for putting my marriage through all that. I couldn't take it anymore. I wanted to take the easy way out, so I took pills for three days. I wasn't sure if I was awake or if I was dreaming. I never told Brent; he just thought I was depressed. A couple of weeks later, he took me to the emergency room for my depression, and when I was asked by the physician if I had any thought of suicide, I said yes. Brent was shocked to learn that. My purpose in leaving Brent and having an affair was to change his eyes and be sure that he was willing to change to help me keep our marriage together. And as we worked on things between us, my thoughts subsided and we talked of having a baby. It gave me hope and meant things were going to be okay. That was the sole intent and purpose of our beach trip—to put our marriage back together."

One night, John and Brent had gotten into an altercation at the Silver Fox over Renee. John had threatened Brent, called him a "pussy" and tried to get him out of the car and into a fight. Brent refused. A few hundred yards down the road, he stopped at a Mr. Waffle restaurant and told Renee he couldn't live like that anymore. She agreed, and they talked about getting a restraining order against John to make him leave them alone. But Brent cooled down and took a let's-just-wait-and-see attitude.

But when the Pooles got home around 2:00 A.M., the phone rang. They both knew who it would be on the phone. John talked with Brent and said he just wanted to know what was going on with Renee. Brent then handed the phone to Renee, and John asked her, "Are you going to stay with that asshole?"

As Renee stepped out of the police car at the Carolina Winds Hotel on the northern end of Myrtle Beach, she knew things for her were only going to get worse. Looking down at her hands, she hadn't realized it until then, but she had bitten at her fingers and shredded what little nails she had left. Her fingers were bleeding at the quicks. They looked awful.

Renee looked forward to seeing her daughter and taking her back to North Carolina. It had been a long night and she wondered what her little girl was doing just then. She was relieved to see her parents' car in the hotel parking lot. Hopefully, her mom had already gotten Katie up and out of bed and changed her flannel nightgown by now. Maybe she had already given Katie a bath, so Renee wouldn't have to.

She suddenly remembered she had left the stuffed animal Mary Stogner had given her. Katie would ask if she brought her something from the store and she wished now she hadn't left it at the police station. Perhaps the little stuffed animal would have kept Katie preoccupied, at least until she and her parents could figure how they were going to handle this delicate situation.

Renee clutched at her stomach. It felt so hollow. As she stepped off the elevator with the police officer, she turned toward the hall leading to room 604 and tried to pull herself together. Her feet felt like they were glued to the carpet that led to the hotel room and it took all the strength she could muster to move forward. She was terrified at the thought of having to tell her little girl that she was never going to see her father again.

The expression on Renee's face said it all.

Just how do you tell your child that there had been a terrible accident and that a bad man on the beach had murdered her father? How can you ask a child to say goodbye forever?

CHAPTER 19

Those persons vacationing and living in Myrtle Beach who happened to read about Brent Poole's murder in the newspaper or walk by the crime scene on the beach were perplexed. There was a sense of overwhelming disbelief that someone, especially a young husband and father taking a midnight stroll on the beach with his wife, could end up lying in a pool of blood. What explanation was there to justify killing a young man apparently filled with such life and love for his family? A bright wreath of red, yellow and white flowers, placed at the crime scene by Brent's family, stood like a beacon on stilts in about a foot of yellow sand. A banner emblazoned with OUR SON WAS MURDERED sliced across the memorial flowers, reminding the public to call the Myrtle Beach Police Department if they had any information on the killer.

Two young men from Charlotte, North Carolina, on their senior trip after graduation from high school, had been at the beach the night of the murder and remembered seeing Brent and Renee huddled up in the sand dunes around Eighty-second Avenue. Chris Hensley and his friend Tommy Hudnall told police they had also seen the mysterious man dressed in black walking along the public-access path that same night. Thirty minutes later, as they stood talking with a friend, they were told someone had been shot and killed on the beach.

Chris provided a description of the man to Myrtle Beach

detective Len Sloan. He said it was dark that night, and had he known it was going to be of great significance, he would have paid closer attention. But one thing that stood out about the man in black was that he had an irritated look on his face. As he walked north along the hurricane fences, he looked back at them like he was ignoring them or he was mad at something. Chris was certain the man in black was Caucasian and had a stocky build, about five feet ten, and thought he had medium-to-long, dark brown hair. There might have been some facial hair, maybe a slight mustache, and when they saw him, it was probably around 10:30 or 11:30 P.M.

Tommy confirmed Chris's story, but he told Sloan he couldn't tell if the guy was white or black, and if he had short hair, long hair or no hair.

Sloan attempted to generate a computerized composite of the suspect from what information they gave him, but both Hensley and Hudnall were adamant that the picture did not look like the person they had seen on the beach.

A second report from someone having seen the suspect on the beach was called into Myrtle Beach headquarters the day after Brent's murder. Mark and Donna Hobbs were from Bedford County, Virginia, and were staying at the same hotel as the Pooles. Ironically they, too, had also decided to take a walk on the beach that same night to celebrate their anniversary. Sometime around 11:00 P.M., the Hobbses came out of their hotel and stood near the outdoor pools, where they noticed a man dressed in black about forty to fifty feet away on the other side of the fencing. Not only was the man dressed inappropriately, but he had an odd look in his eyes that frightened them. After seeing him again on the beach, this time at a distance of twenty-five to thirty feet and in bright lights, the couple decided it was not in their best interest to be on the beach with this man around, and called it a night.

The Hobbses assisted police in completing a second computerized composite of the murder suspect, but they, too, were not pleased with the results. It wasn't difficult for them to recollect the face of the individual they had seen, but the real challenge was in looking through all those hundreds of eyes, mouths and noses and trying to put them together to make a face. It didn't matter how many times they adjusted the composite, nothing they saw resembled the individual on the beach.

The Myrtle Beach detectives still believed the answers to all their questions were harbored in Renee Poole. They were all convinced she was holding something back—not telling the truth—and needed to be interviewed again. Perhaps if they pushed her harder on the specific details of the murder and plunged even deeper into her relationship with Frazier, then she might fold. With a little luck, there was a real possibility they could shake her story. If Frazier was involved, they needed to get enough damaging information from her to implicate him and make the charges stick before they went after him.

Detective Altman had driven the Pooles out to the crime scene and conducted another lengthy conversation with them about their daughter-in-law. A complete forensic analysis had already been ordered for room 604 at the Carolina Winds, once Renee and her family vacated. He understood the Pooles to say they were going to meet Renee and her family at the hotel, then drive over to the hospital and view Brent's body.

Brent Poole's family had insisted against the detectives and Dr. Duffy's advice that they see their son in the morgue. But the Pooles had to do it for their own peace of mind. To lessen the shock, Duffy had pulled one of the nurses aside and asked her to do the best she could to prepare the victim's body for viewing.

The sorrowful mourners were led through a door into a smaller room, where Brent's body had been relocated. The blinds were closed and the lights turned down low. A stainless-steel gurney sat in the middle of the room. The outline of Brent's body could be seen underneath a white cover sheet. It was just like a scene from some murder mystery on television. The only problem was, this was their own true-to-life show they were watching.

Bill Poole's face grew tighter and redder as he waited with his family to see his son's body. Small white lines appeared at both corners of his mouth. Renee and her mother stood behind them, crying and holding on to each other. Out of the corner of her eye, Renee watched Brent's mother. Her jaw was set in permanent scorn and she was staring at her with a cold, hardened look. It was as if her eyes were saying that Renee was the reason they were all here.

Duffy waited until everyone had entered the dimly lit room, then shut the door behind them. When everyone was still and settled, he took a deep breath, then stepped up to the stainless-steel gurney and slowly uncovered Brent's naked body.

"Oh, my God," Duffy heard the family members behind him gasp, as if they had all whispered it at the same time.

The body of Brent Poole was lying on its side and on top of sheets covered in blood. He still had the tubes protruding from his mouth and his arm that Duffy and his team of nurses had used during surgery to help sustain him. The greater portions of his head on both the right and left sides were covered in dried and caked blood. Due to internal cranial pressure, his head was swollen and larger than its normal size.

As the family inched closer, they looked at Brent's face. It was titled backward, all swollen and puffy. The muzzle imprint of the gun was easily noticeable underneath his chin. Inside the imprint, there was a hole like a bull's-eye in a shooting target. Traces of black soot were recognizable above the hole in his left ear. Sticky, bright red blood had discharged from his mouth and both his ears.

Bill Poole fought hard to control his emotions. He took a closer look at the ample amount of blood still on Brent's body and the sheets underneath him. He remembered what the police had told him earlier and silently wondered if Brent had bled on the beach, bled on the operating table—and still had all this blood on him and the sheets—then why was there no blood on Renee, who had reached down and picked up his head? If she was that close to Brent and the robber, then why hadn't blood splatter gotten on her, too? For Christ's sake, she was wearing a white T-shirt. He looked at Renee, who was still wearing the same clothes she had on the night before, and felt a cold tremor crawl down his spine like a black widow spider.

Agnes stood limply beside her husband. She felt numb, no

longer capable of feeling anything in her body. It was as if someone had suddenly ripped her heart from her chest and all the blood had drained from her body. She stared at Brent's body, reflexively holding her hands out firmly in front of her, wishing she could somehow reach out and take all her son's pain away.

Dee took another look at her baby brother and turned her head. She couldn't stand to look at him in that condition for a second longer.

Renee and Marie stood behind the Pooles, looking at the body from over their shoulders. They held on to each other and continued crying, then slipped out and walked back into an adjoining conference room to wait on the Pooles.

As the Pooles stood silently together, the tears rolling off their cheeks and their gazes locked onto Brent's tattered body, Bill could see the darkness rolling upon them. Finally, in a brusque voice, he announced it was time for them to leave. Bunching the muscles in his neck and rounding his shoulders, he directed Agnes and Dee out of the room and to where Renee and Marie were waiting. As they stepped out of the dark room and into the larger one, the bright lights washed over their faces, but it couldn't penetrate the shuttered look masking their sentiments. Walking toward a corner in the room, they collapsed against each other and pleaded to God for the strength they needed to get through this terrible ordeal.

Renee watched from across the room. She was hurting, too. She had hoped she could have stayed with Brent's body a little longer, wanting so badly to reach out and touch her husband to see if he was as cold as he looked. She still couldn't believe he was dead and thought it would help if she touched his body. But she never got the chance. She believed the Pooles had deliberately stood in front of her and shut her out so she couldn't get a clear view of Brent's body.

Renee had been so careful in studying her mother-in-law's face while she looked for the sympathy that eluded her, but there was none. True, Agnes had lost her son. But did she not realize that Renee had lost her husband? Had it not dawned on her that she would be the one who would sleep alone tonight? Had she once asked Renee how she was holding up?

Ten minutes passed and the Pooles were still huddled in the corner. When Marie realized she and her daughter were not going to be invited, she told Renee it was time for them to leave.

"We don't have to put up with this," Marie had said crisply, suddenly beginning to feel out of place. She motioned for Renee to follow her. Didn't their feelings matter at all? Did anyone ever think they needed prayers, too? On the way out of the hospital, she told Renee she had seen how the Pooles had acted toward her and they had no clue as to what really had happened with Brent on the beach. The only thing they knew was what the police had told them and what they had told the police.

Jack Summey had wisely chosen to remain outside the hospital and stay with Katie. When the two families emerged from the emergency room a few minutes later, he could tell there had been words. It was disheartening for him to see how much pain everyone was in and their relationships had become so strained that they couldn't comfort each other.

The sky overhead was beginning to darken and turn black. The ambiance outside reflected the emotions of the two families as they stood and stared accusingly at each other in the parking lot. All their best-laid plans for Brent and Renee's marriage had now crumbled before their very eyes—whether they were victims of circumstance, fate, poor decisions or malicious evil remained to be seen. All that could be said and proven at this point and time was that the battle lines had been drawn by an unfortunate incident that would separate the two families and change their lives forever.

CHAPTER 20

Renee Poole had wanted to get herself and Katie back to Mocksville as soon as possible, back to their lives, to feel the safety of her home and their own beds. But the thought of returning to her home—once filled with such life and love—was too much for her. Besides, she was still in shock and in no shape to be caring for anyone. She and Katie would live in Clemmons with her parents until she was able to recover.

Renee knew how well-liked Brent was at his job and how much his friends cared for him. Like any thoughtful wife, as soon as she arrived home that day, she called Brent's employer and contacted many of his coworkers and friends just to let them know what had happened and to ask for their prayers and support.

If there had been some strains in the Pooles' marriage, Brent Poole had never let if affect his job as a diesel mechanic at Mack Trucks in Charlotte, North Carolina. Brent repaired tractor-trailer engines and electronics systems from 2:30 P.M. to 1:00 A.M., four days a week.

One of Brent's coworkers, who identified himself as Ronnie, told reporter Lauren Leach of the *Sun News* that whatever happened at the beach, Brent didn't deserve it. "The shooting has stunned us all," he said. "He was a supernice guy who would do anything in the world for you. He loved his child and he loved his wife."

Dealership owner Pat McMahon was saddened to hear the news about Brent, whom he called a "superior" employee. McMahon said when he had received the phone call from Renee, she had seemed like a grieving wife.

Renee may have been acting like the prototypical grieving widow, but Brent Poole's family was not buying it. From the first moment they spoke with the police about Brent's murder, they had begun doubting her story and feared she was somehow involved. When they tried to talk with her about what had happened, they said Renee wouldn't even look them in their eyes. They were hoping that it wasn't so, but they were afraid it was. They alerted the Myrtle Beach detectives, who had already found her statements full of inconsistencies and were way beyond suspicions.

That Wednesday afternoon, Renee had remembered the photos from their Myrtle Beach vacation were still in her bag. There were several good photos of Brent in the bunch and she thought the Pooles would appreciate her furnishing them with copies of those. When two friends of Brent's, Vincent Moore and Tony White, stopped by her mother's house to pay their respect, Renee asked if she could ride over with them and visit the Pooles.

Vincent and Tony were struggling with the same issues as the Pooles. "I just don't want to believe she could have something to do with this," Vincent confided to his friend. "I'm really trying not to think about it, but it keeps going through my mind."

Although Renee denied the incident ever occurred, Bill Poole told police that same day he had cornered his daughter-in-law in the bedroom and just asked her to tell him what happened. She told him the same story she had told the police, and when she got through, he asked her whether it was possible that anybody could have followed them to the beach.

Bill said he was trying to keep an open mind. Although he hadn't told Renee, he was thinking if somehow the evidence proved she wasn't involved in Brent's murder, then maybe some of her friends were. Maybe it was some of those men she had been having affairs with. That was why he asked her, "Is it possible anybody followed you guys to the beach?"

Renee chose her words carefully. "Well, on the way down, Katie got kinda irritable and we had to stop two or three times. But I never saw anything that would lead me to believe that."

"Do you think that John could have anything to do with this?" Bill asked candidly.

Renee shook her head. She didn't think so.

"Do you understand why I'm asking you these questions?" She said she did.

Bill wanted to let her know that he was concerned that some of the parties she had had an affair with could have been a part of this. "You know, Renee, when people get into relationships and in lust, all of this comes into play. They do crazy things."

"Yeah, I understand that," Renee answered.

Bill Poole didn't think she did. His family was suspicious and saw the worst-possible scenario. The way he saw it, Renee's behavior from the beginning was disturbingly out of kilter with someone who claimed to have loved her husband. Bill could look at Renee and see it in her face and in her fractured emotions. To him, there hadn't been much change in her emotions from when he had seen her the day before. Maybe a few tears had misted in her eyes and trickled down her cheeks, but it still appeared the motivation was the same. The only thing he saw in her was pure fear.

Renee would say later that she didn't remember any conversation with Bill. But she did recall the moment when his preacher asked everybody to sit in a circle that evening and asked them to say something about Brent.

"Nobody really knew what to say," she would comment afterward. "Everybody was just hurting so bad."

But that wasn't the way Bill perceived it. He said when they went around the circle, he looked at Renee and she reminded him of Susan Smith, that lady from Union, South Carolina, who had let her car slip into a murky lake with her two kids still inside.

"Everybody around my house, you know, was crying and

hugging each other. But she never looked up. Her eyes were down the entire time. Not once would she look you in the eye."

When asked if Renee cried at all, he replied, "She had brought over some pictures for us of her, Brent and Katie that they had taken at the beach. She cried some then, in the hall. But when my preacher asked her to say something, she said very calmly, 'I hope you know that—that we did love him, that Katie loved him, and I just hope that he knows that.'"

While Renee stood outside and smoked a cigarette, Vincent and Tony stood near the back porch and talked with Craig Poole. Craig was giving them the lowdown on Renee and John's affair and what he thought had happened in Myrtle Beach.

"I don't believe a word Renee's said about what happened," he said.

"She's the one who set this whole trip up. She called in the reservations, got the baby-sitter, and did everything she needed to get my brother there. At the same time, John had already asked for time off at work."

It was all a shock to Brent's friends. Brent had told them all about Renee's affairs, but they never imagined she would play a part in his murder.

"I don't even want to be in the same room as her," Craig said disgusted, glancing toward Renee. "I have no doubt that John did murder Brent and she had something to do with it."

After Renee finished her cigarette, she stepped back inside the Pooles' home and started looking for her two friends. She and Brent's parents had discussed what clothing they wanted him to be buried in. She asked Tony and Vincent if they would drive her to her house on Blue Bonnet Court to pick up his burial clothes.

As the Pooles became even more suspicious of Renee and her involvement in Brent's murder, their relationship with her and her parents, Jack and Marie, began to sour. At a time when families needed to make peace and draw strength from one another, the growing rift between the Pooles and the Summeys placed an even darker cloud over an already tragic and difficult situation.

Detective Terry Altman talked with Renee later that day. She told him she remembered the man's voice sounded black and that he used slang words that resembled a black man's speech.

Here we go again, Altman thought. In 1994, the description Susan Smith had used to describe the man who had supposedly kidnapped her children was a black man in a toboggan-type hat. It sounded as if Renee had taken a page right out of that crime story.

CHAPTER 21

The Myrtle Beach Homicide Division team was gathering momentum and obtaining a lot of incriminating information that pointed toward John Frazier as Brent Poole's killer. All their bells and whistles had been put in place. Rather than casting a wide net to see what they could haul in, the detectives were focusing on their most likely suspect—who had motive, means and opportunity—and working to eliminate him first. This made sense, of course, since it was the most time-efficient way of solving a murder.

Detective Altman had continued his steady pressure on Renee Poole and she was beginning to bend. In several phone calls from her home, she confessed Brent was not only insured for $100,000 but would receive a generous employee benefit package upon his death. She also had begun to soften on the idea that John Frazier had been the killer.

To help solve the case, Captain Hendrick had requested additional assistance from the North Carolina State Bureau of Investigations (SBI). Special Agents James R. Bowman and H. G. Pendergrass had interviewed Frazier at his home in Winston-Salem. He admitted he had borrowed his friend's gray 1990 Acura the week the Pooles had been at the beach. He also acknowledged ownership of a Glock, model 19, 9mm handgun, and that he had previously owned an Italian-made

TZ-75 9mm pistol. He had forgotten who had purchased the TZ-75.

John Boyd Frazier's dilemma was beginning to look dimmer by the moment. Thomas Pedersen, one of his best friends in Winston-Salem, told him the MBPD had been calling his house and were talking with his girlfriend about John. Cynthia knew all about John and Renee's affair and had spoken with them about it.

Thomas urged John to phone Detective Altman and try and straighten out the mess he had gotten himself into. John called the MBPD and spoke with Lieutenant Bill Frontz, who informed him that Brent Poole had been murdered and he was a suspect. John was not laughing when he called Thomas back to say his name was being mentioned in connection with Brent's murder. He had been Renee's most recent lover and came unglued after the police told him they were looking at him as a suspect.

When Thomas got home from work that night around six o'clock, John was waiting on him. He looked like death warmed over. Cynthia told her boyfriend John had only stayed awake for twenty minutes, then fell asleep on the couch. When he woke up, he looked kind of pale and sounded really rough—kind of like he was drunk. Said John wasn't clear and logical about everything that was going on, but she figured he probably had a lot to think about. Thomas didn't waste any time in asking him if he had anything to do with Brent's murder.

"Man, I swear I wasn't in Myrtle Beach," John assured his friend. He not only proclaimed his innocence, but insisted he had been sick and was at home in bed the entire time. "I was taking NyQuil all night just to get by."

"Well, did you talk to anybody?" Thomas asked in a panic. "Anybody that could verify you were at home?"

"No, nobody's seen me," John said in a low voice. "I worked that past weekend, so I was beat. Sick and pretty much asleep the whole time."

Even though John had been off from work the same three days the Pooles had vacationed at the beach, he still told

Thomas he had been too sick to go anywhere. Nobody had called him and nobody had come over to see him.

Thomas had been John's friend for almost a year and one of the things he appreciated about him was his not getting wild and into crazy stuff. He had never known John to do a lot of drinking or drugs—nothing like that—and he was very close to his family. Thomas's own gut feeling told him that John didn't have anything to do with Brent's death, but his lack of an alibi definitely caused him to question whether John was telling him the truth or not.

Thomas told the police all he ever knew about John and Renee's relationship was that they were sleeping together. Renee had planned on leaving her husband—and John had even gotten his lawyer to talk with her about it—but John never said he loved Renee and she was the girl that he really wanted to be with. Besides, John always had had a thing for strippers, taking them into his home like stray cats. Thomas admitted John was somewhat upset at first, wanting to know why Renee had moved in with him, then had moved back in with Brent. Said he was hurt and believed she had used him just to get back at her husband, but it wasn't like the biggest thing in his life.

Thomas said he didn't know Renee well, but she had been over to their house to visit Cynthia at least four or five times. In all those times, he had heard her talk about her husband only once.

"The first night I met her," he explained, "she and Cynthia were going out to play pool and I was going to watch her kid for her. It was kind of odd that I was sitting on the couch and she kind of up and said, 'Cynthia is really lucky to have a guy like you. It's been a month or more since I've had sex with my husband.'"

In those first five minutes of conversation, Thomas said he learned that Renee and Brent were having serious trouble in their marriage. Cynthia told him afterward that Renee said Brent had forced himself on her, they were having money problems and their relationship was rotten, and that she wanted to leave him but didn't know how to do it.

According to Thomas, John was scared and had already spoken with an attorney who had advised him to remove anything and everything in his house that had to do with Renee Poole and put it in a safe place. When Thomas asked John where he had put Renee's things, he wouldn't tell him. One of the items he specifically asked John about was his 9mm Glock. "John, why don't you take your gun down to the police department and let them check it out, so at least they could clarify it wasn't the gun that killed Brent." John said his gun had never been fired and that wouldn't be a problem, but when he talked to his lawyer, he had advised against it. The gun had been removed from John's house, but he wouldn't tell Thomas where it was hidden.

Cynthia told police Renee was acting as strange as John. She had called her the day she arrived home from the beach to break the news about Brent's murder. In their conversation, Cynthia had asked Renee if she thought John had murdered Brent. Renee told her the killer was bigger than John and his voice was deeper. Afterward, Cynthia called John and left him a message not to worry about the police, that Renee had said it wasn't him. John then telephoned her and asked if she would phone Renee to see if it was okay for him to call her.

"No, I'd rather not talk with him right now, "Renee said harshly. "I'd rather not see him. I'm with my family now and I have a friend of the family coming over. I really need to get off the phone."

Renee's snub had rubbed Cynthia the wrong way. Knowing that she and John were having an affair and were supposedly in love, it was strange for her not to want to see him. After all she had said about how much she loved him and then had left her husband for him, it just didn't sound like Renee.

"I haven't eaten and I haven't slept," Renee reminded her. "The only thing you can do for me is pray."

Cynthia couldn't believe her ears. *Pray? Has Renee forgotten who she is?* Before she could respond, Renee asked her if she would retrieve a ring she had left at John's house. Cynthia promised she would.

Renee's next-door neighbors Jim and Renee Bollow told the

police Renee had called them the day after Brent had been killed. Renee Bollow called her husband at work and Jim rushed home. He and Brent had not only been neighbors, but were good friends. The first words out of Jim's mouth were "Oh, my God, she did it. And she's going to try and get away with it."

The Bollows had also recognized some of Renee's inappropriate behavior the Wednesday she stopped by to pick up some things from her house. They had been the Pooles' neighbors on Blue Bonnet Court in Mocksville for 2½ years and were very much aware of their marital problems. They recalled for police many examples of the Pooles' troubled marriage and detailed the time Renee had moved out to live with John, then came back home to Brent.

While the Pooles had been on vacation in Myrtle Beach, the Bollows had volunteered to retrieve their mail. The first thing Renee had asked them on Wednesday was "Can I get the mail? There's supposed to be a check in there for Brent and I need it."

Renee Bollow gave Renee her mail, and she and her husband watched as she stood there and opened it. Jim could see in one envelope there was a check made out to Brent, but he couldn't see the amount. There was a little note with it thanking Brent for his work on a diesel engine.

Renee closed the letter and shoved it and the check back in the envelope. "Okay, this is what I needed, thank you," she said in a rush. Jim walked her back over to her house, where he saw two men waiting.

"There were two young guys sitting there on the front porch," Jim told his wife after Renee had left. "They looked like guard dogs."

Renee Bollow informed her husband that they were friends of Brent's and were there to make sure something didn't happen to Renee.

"Wow, they're really misdirected if they think that they are going to be protecting her," he said sarcastically. "Wait until they find out that she could have possibly been responsible for killing their friend. They'll think twice about protecting her then."

The next day, Renee came back over to her house with Vincent and Tony to get some pictures of Brent. She asked Renee Bollow if they could park in her driveway because they didn't want the press to see her.

Bollow would later tell the police that for about nine months she had seen a red car over at Renee's every night. The driver obviously knew Brent's working hours because he would wait around the corner, at the end of the neighborhood, until Brent left and would always leave a half hour before he returned. Frazier's Black Blazer had started showing up about three months ago. It was the same routine as the first one: Renee's lover inside the house with no lights on, then leaving just before Brent arrives.

Renee had told her neighbors quite a lot about her new boyfriend, John. Said she was still in love with him and had only moved back in with Brent because of the security. The Thursday before the Pooles left to go to the beach, Renee Bollow had overheard her saying to John, "I wish you'd come over, please, please come over. I love you, I don't really know what you want to know." A few days later, Poole had been talking on her cordless phone to John again, talking real low and telling him how much she loved and missed him. "And then she got her daughter, Katie, to tell him she loved him," Bollow added, saying that had really upset her and her husband.

Renee had boasted to Bollow that she liked John a lot because he babied her. He would paint her toenails, wash her hair and watch Katie while she took a nap. One evening, she said, they had made sure Katie was asleep, then videotaped themselves having sex.

"I'm no goddess of marriage or anything," Bollow had tried to tell Poole, "but things like that don't usually last. It's just good little nothings."

The Bollows had never seen Brent get physically abusive. But they had seen him get angry and then trash his house when he learned Renee had been having an affair with John. After she moved back in, he had caught her talking to John over the

Internet and pulled the phone cord out, then threw it against the wall.

Jim Bollow said he had talked with Renee several times after she returned home to Brent in May. Among other things, she told him she was still in love with John and that they had gone out and gotten their genitalia pierced. "Renee said it was really uncomfortable and she had wanted to take hers out, but John had kept his in for her. She said it was some kind of bond thing they had for each other."

After hearing about Renee's undying love for Frazier, Jim honestly asked why she had come back home.

"I don't know," she answered. "I guess it was the money. Brent can afford me."

Jim shook his head in disgust.

"Don't tell Brent, but I've talked with an attorney," Renee whispered, "but he told me that I could lose my daughter in custody because I just up and left one night. And that I had to get Brent to let me back in the house, and if he did that, then it means legally he accepts me and he can't sue. Now I'm back in, so here I am."

Jim had to turn away from her before he said something he would regret later. He started to walk away, but she grabbed him by the arm.

"Well, you know we're fighting again. He wants me to get a regular job and I told him there's no way."

"Why?" Jim asked. "What do you want to do?"

Renee informed him she had been working at the Silver Fox for about ten months. She was good at what she did, but a full-nudity bar had just opened in Winston-Salem that was going to compete with the Silver Fox and other gentleman's clubs for business. It would take some of their customers away.

"I want to work at that full strip joint," she said with a straight face. "I've been talking to the girls there and they've been making as much money in one night as what I make in a week."

"How does Brent feel about that?"

"He wants me to get a secretarial job or drive a truck, a courier for a junkyard delivering parts."

"Well, you ought to think about that," Jim advised earnestly.

"There is no way in hell I'm going to do that," Renee shot back.

Bollow also recalled for the police an incident Renee had shared with him about Brent and John getting into a fight at the Silver Fox. It had started the weekend before they went to the beach. John was at their house in his black Blazer when Brent suddenly popped into the driveway, looking real mad. Renee and Brent had gotten into a very big fight about John being there. Finally they decided they needed to chill out and rode over to the Silver Fox for a few drinks. John came in later and he and Brent wound up having words in the parking lot. Renee told him that John had threatened to kill Brent.

Above everything else, Bollow said, it was the nonchalant manner in which Renee was handling Brent's death that was eating him alive. "She walked over to my house on Thursday and handed me the keys to her house in case something happened while she was away. And when my wife told her again how sorry we were that Brent was dead, she said, 'We'd been fighting like cats and dogs. You know he was a shit, but I kind of feel sorry for him.'"

Bollow said that comment had made him so mad that he called Crimestoppers and told them, "Y'all don't know what she's done yet, but Renee Poole had her husband murdered."

Channel 45 ABC-news in Winston-Salem aired an exclusive interview with Renee that hot and humid Thursday evening. It would become a big story; the kind that would send their ratings through the roof. A polite, handsome and broad-shouldered Troy Harbison interviewed Renee and the two of them quickly developed a good rapport. He made light conversation by asking how she and Brent had met, and then a disheveled Renee, dressed in jeans and a long-sleeved cotton shirt, looked away from the camera and started crying. She could barely get the words out that a man had robbed them at gunpoint and shot and killed her husband after he begged for his life.

"Do you know why anyone would want to kill your husband?" Harbison asked her.

Looking away from both the camera and the reporter, as if

she were in shock, Renee shook her head, sniffed, then answered no. "He never did anything to anybody," she said in a nervous and apprehensive voice. "He never did anything. He was so kind."

Harbison wrapped up his part of the newscast and thanked Renee for her participation. Brent Poole's murder was definitely going to be a major news story that would demand their total attention until it was finally resolved. As he was putting the final touches on his lead story for the 4:30 P.M. news, anchors from other television stations were also attempting to be the first to interview Renee. Harbison's crosstown rival, Channel 12, could see it was going to be a killer story the moment word was out. Newshound Adam Shapiro drove out to the Summeys' house in search of an interview.

Marie Summey spotted Shapiro that afternoon standing on her front porch, peeking in her front window. She opened the door and greeted him. When Shapiro mistakenly assumed Brandy, the girl standing behind her, was Renee, he got excited and shouted, "Is that Renee? Does she have an attorney?"

Marie was livid. She told him they had an attorney and that he needed to leave, then slammed the door in his face. Shapiro's crew parked their car in the cul-de-sac near her house and waited for something to happen. Marie called the sheriff's office and then phoned Shapiro's boss at the television station. There was a prickly distrust that lingered between Marie and the reporter. When told she and Shapiro needed to make up, she snapped back, "Well, you and Adam can make up. But the next time he sticks a microphone in my face, I'm going to whip his ass."

CHAPTER 22

Captain Sam Hendrick believed it was time to move their investigation to Mocksville, North Carolina. The Pooles lived in Mocksville, a part of Davie County in the western section of North Carolina. Centrally located between the bustling metropolitan areas of Charlotte and Greensboro on I-40, Davie County, at that time, had a comfortable population of around thirty thousand. Detective Altman called SBI agent Steve Gregory and advised him they would be coming to Mocksville on Friday.

Detectives Altman and King got off to a late start and didn't arrive at the Davie County Sheriff's Office until around 8:30 P.M. Someone had already leaked the word to the press and reporters were crawling around the sheriff's office like ants at a Fourth of July picnic. As the detectives slipped in through the back door, they could see the media still crowded around the front of the police station, standing poised and ready to respond like a disassembled precision military unit. Once inside, Agent Gregory brought them up to speed on the information they had received relating to Frazier's background checks and his criminal history.

Detective Altman called Renee's parents' home and asked if Renee could come to the police station for an interview. Renee called back a short time later and told him they were coming, but needed to call their attorney first. At 9:00 P.M., she and her parents arrived with attorney Victor M. Leckowitz in tow. The entourage managed to park the car and get out unnoticed, but just as soon as the press recognized Renee, they bombarded them.

Marie Summey had been taking chemotherapy treatments to combat breast cancer, but it didn't slow her as she bravely led the way through the army of reporters and a barrage of cameras and microphones. The reporters were competing furiously, as if they were in a race vying for some kind of news Emmy. Tension mounted immediately as her little group walked together a few feet toward the police station. James Brown, reporter with News Channel 12, ran forward and closed in on them. In his quest for a story, he asked Renee, "Did the Myrtle Beach police ask you to come here?"

There wasn't much room to navigate with the crews in front of Marie and Renee and Jack and their lawyer behind them. "No questions and there will be no questions answered," Attorney Victor Leckowitz shouted from the rear. Marie looked like a raging bull, dragging her daughter behind her and changing directions when the reporters stood in her way. The camera didn't display her anxiety, but she struggled to maintain a cool, calm demeanor, while inside her heart was pounding away.

Renee was forced to keep moving forward, her focus intensely oblivious to everything and everybody. She looked worried. Never looking around at all the people pressing in on her, she thought about exactly what had happened to put her in this predicament, then glanced up at the police station and nearly broke into tears. They seemed to be moving in slow motion, barely inching their way through the crowd. She could hear her heart throbbing above everything. It seemed to take forever for them to get to the front door. They scampered through the crowd, and finally distanced themselves from the reporters and their television microphones.

Marie caught her breath, walked up to the front desk and stated, with a wry smile, "We're here to see Detective Altman." For the first time in her life, she didn't have to explain to the police who she was and what she was doing at the police station.

Perspiration dampened Renee's body and her nerves jangled. Her mouth felt like she had left it open while asleep during a sandstorm.

Before the interview started, the detectives spoke with attorney Leckowitz alone and explained the reason they wanted to interview Renee again was that her story did not seem consistent. He advised them that he didn't know the specifics of Brent's murder because the family had just called him and asked if he could attend the interview.

Renee was read her Miranda rights and was told the interview would be recorded. The detectives didn't want to risk losing a word of it and, to ensure there would be no mistakes, they had even brought their own recorder. As in their other interviews with Renee, they recorded it all for posterity.

"Maybe you're thinking that you'd be spending tonight somewhere else than home," Detective Altman began. "But let me tell you, you will be going home tonight."

Renee breathed easier, then nodded. "Thank you."

Altman had set the tone for the meeting. It was to be an interview, not an interrogation. They were in no way trying to bamboozle or pull a fast one over on her. Even though she had been read her rights, she was not going to be arrested. And for her protection, she had her attorney sitting beside her.

Altman began with an apology. "I'm sure you can tell by everything that's going on up here that people are taking your husband's murder very seriously. Things have been turned completely around and it's almost turned into a circus. Unfortunately, the news media takes things and they run with it."

Renee nodded. She was beginning to feel that pressure. Suddenly her life had been thrust under a microscope. She told them they would not like it, had it been their life the media had been spotlighting.

"You might feel like you've already been tried and convicted in the news," Altman sympathized. "But that is by no means true in our investigation. We're controlling this. It's just when the news media take things, they bend them way out of proportion."

"Uh, we've seen that," Renee said, rolling her eyes.

"This is probably the biggest thing that has happened around Mocksville in a long, long time. I just want you to know that we've been working twenty-four-hours per day on your husband's case."

Renee thanked him.

Altman then pulled off the kid gloves and got down to business. Brent Poole's murder, he assured her, had much the same impact on the community in Myrtle Beach as it did in Mocksville. And there were some explanations related to this incident she had given that just didn't seem possible. He and King were there to ask her a few questions, then they could tie up those loose ends.

"You probably feel like you're in an ocean right now, treading water," Altman began. It was a line the detective had used, over and over, in an attempt to sway her to tell the truth and take responsibility for what had happened. "And your life jacket is pretty much gone. I'm here tonight as if we're lifeguards in a rowboat and were throwing out a life preserver to you."

Renee didn't take the bait this time. If the detectives were truthful, then that was reassuring. But she'd heard it all before and, at this point, she no longer trusted them.

Altman reassured her, "All I'm trying to do is create a scenario for you and I don't want to see you go down for something—"

"That somebody else did," Renee mouthed in pursed lips.

"Yeah, it's not worth you going down just to help somebody," the detective said, ignoring her antics. "To protect somebody. It's not worth it in the long run. Look, this is the most serious crime anyone could ever be involved in. And that's why this circus is going around here. Because it is a big deal."

Altman had Renee go through the events of her husband's murder, over and over again. They covered much of the same ground—bit by bit and piece by piece—as they had the days before, but Renee was still adamant she had no idea how or why it had happened.

"Why were you dancing at the Silver Fox?" Altman asked, suddenly taking a nasty turn. "Wasn't Brent making enough money for you?"

"Well, we had a lot of bills," Renee said, giving him a what's-that-got-to-do-with-you stare. "We just wanted to pay some bills off."

Altman was not about to let her off the hook that easily. "What kind of lifestyle did the two of you live?"

"Uh, an occasional drink. He quit smoking. We didn't want to go out much. Just kinda so-so, you know."

"I mean, you didn't live the lavish lifestyle of fancy clothes and going out all the time?"

Renee had no idea where he was going with this line of questioning, but she had nothing to be ashamed of. "We had bought an entertainment center, television and stereo when we lived with his parents. He had put it on his credit card and we were trying to pay that off. We did go out and buy a new car from my brother-in-law, but it was a used car. A Grand Prix. Then we bought a 1984 Dodge Daytona Truck. Something for Brent to drive back and forth to work. And a new 1998 Dodge Dakota truck for me."

"Now tell me about Danny Shrewsbury," Altman asked, thinking he had caught her off-balance.

Renee rolled her eyes and took a deep breath. She and Danny had once worked together at Home Depot. After talking at work, the two of them had developed a friendship. She would go to his house for lunch sometimes and they would just do things together, as she would with other associates there. She said she had seen him for only a few months. (The truth was that their relationship had lasted almost two years.) Renee explained that she was confused about Brent just getting out of diesel school and then her getting pregnant. And then they had to tell their parents about getting pregnant. She had also enrolled in Forsyth Technical College and was trying to get her GED. There was just a lot going on in her life at the time.

"But why were you with Danny?" Altman asked. "Didn't Brent treat you okay?"

"Yeah, Brent treated me great. Danny was kinda jealous that we were married, but he was married also."

"Wasn't there another individual at the Home Depot, also named Shrewsbury, that you also had an affair with?"

"Yes, there was," Renee said like it was no big deal. "He was a friend of mine from school. I saw him about a month. I had broken it off with Danny and started seeing John. I had no intention of seeing him, but we were friends. It just happened."

"What happened with you and Danny?"

"Danny was the jealous type and he wanted me to leave Brent. But you see, I had just gotten married to him and I couldn't do that."

Altman looked over at his partner and tried to keep a straight face. "Did you ever film sex acts with Danny and he sent those to Brent's house when he was mad at you?"

"Yes."

"How did you feel about this?"

"It upset me. Brent was told about Danny after he found out about John. He didn't get upset. He was just disappointed." Renee said she never had an affair with anybody else after Danny until John Frazier came along.

"What would Brent have done if he had found out you were having an affair with John?" Renee said Brent would have been disappointed if he knew she was having an affair with John. Disappointed and hurt. But Altman told her the way he had heard it, Brent would have been a little more than hurt. He would have been totally pissed.

"From all the friends we talked to on Brent's side," he told her, "they say that's not true. That he was very angry that you'd been seeing John."

"Okay." Renee shrugged, as if to say *so what?*

"His family said that he worshiped the ground you walked on. And his friends are saying that he worshiped the ground you walked on."

Renee shook her head, then admitted, "He . . . he did."

"And I think he wanted to be with you so much that he didn't want you to be with anybody else. I think that kinda tightened

you up a little bit. Like I said, when you start dating somebody when you're fourteen years old and that's the only
person you have been with, you're gonna experiment. And obviously, that's what you did."

Renee didn't respond.

"But you were still with Brent. You still had a link with him."
Altman let it all sink in, then asked her, "Do you consider Brent
to be the possessive type?"

"No . . . no," she protested. "He'd let me do basically what
I wanted to do—if I wanted to go out with my friends."

"I understand going out with your friends, but seeing another guy is not part of what he wanted you to do." Altman
admonished her like a schoolgirl and got her to admit that she
had hidden her relationship with Frazier from her husband.

Renee said although John hadn't completely talked her
into leaving, he did have a lot of influence on her. "John
would say, well, you know. If it's not going well, then maybe
you need to get away from him."

That was the door Altman had been looking for. He leaned
in toward her and asked, "And what did you do about that?"

"Uh, I said, well, I don't have anywhere to go. My parents
have enough people staying with them. And I didn't really want
to burden them with it. And, uh, I told him I couldn't afford
to leave. To move out. And he offered to let me stay with him."

"You're saying you didn't move out just so you could be with
him?"

"No, no. I had told him I would eventually leave. As soon
as I could afford to move out. I would get my own place."

Altman didn't believe her. "But you moved everything
from your house out that belonged to you. Even though this
was not going to be a permanent relationship with John?"

"Right."

"Now, that seems a little strange. I want you to be honest
with me. Were you leaving Brent for John?"

Renee leaned backward. "No. No," she answered bluntly.

"You just decided to move in with him?"

"Right. I thought if I left anything at home, then I would
not be allowed to go back in and get it."

"How come?"

"If he were to get a divorce. If it would go to that, custody and things like that. I was afraid I would not be allowed to go back in and get my things."

"How do you think Brent felt when he came home from work that night and all your stuff was gone?"

"Devastated. Devastated."

"But you told us in the first interview that he was okay with it."

"After I talked with him. After he knew where I was, he was okay with it."

Altman paused, then stared hard at her. "That isn't what his friends and family are saying now."

"But he was okay with it," Renee said, trying to convince him of that. "Uh, he knew who I was staying with. He knew where I was at. Uh, I didn't tell him the address. But I did give him a phone number. I had a pager and I told him anytime he needed me he could page me. That Katie was safe." She locked eyes with him again. "I told him that I was with a friend. And he asked who and I told him and he said, 'Well, is he a friend?' I said, 'Yeah, he is a friend.' And at that time, he was okay with that."

"You're saying he just . . . He went along with that?"

"Right. 'Cause I talked to him every single day."

"The love of his life [and he] doesn't care if you're with somebody else and sleeping with 'em?" he asked incredulously.

"Well, at the time, he didn't know I was sleeping with him."

"But dealing with your past track record, with Danny and the other Shrewsbury, I find that hard to believe. That you would wait until you moved in with this guy to sleep with him? And you only slept with him twice in a week period?"

"No. No. I didn't sleep with him only twice."

Altman was confused. "But that's what you told us before?"

"I don't recall saying that."

"Well, you told us that you had slept with him twice. We've got that on tape-recorded statements. Somebody that gets married and starts an affair a couple of days later, it leads me to believe that you were sleeping with him a little more than just twice in a week's time."

She nodded her head, acknowledging she had said that. "But I wasn't there as much as it seems that I was there."

Altman continued to question Renee about her affair with John and the last time she had seen him. He also asked her about the confrontation John had had with Brent at the Silver Fox.

Renee grew bored with Altman's line of questions. To her, they were just a rehash of the same old things they had talked about last week. She was tired of this humdrum and said in an exasperated voice, when Detective King started in on her, "I thought I already answered these questions."

"You answered *his* questions," King corrected her, "but I'm asking the questions now and you're still not giving the answers to my satisfaction."

"The answers *you're* looking for," Renee said, befuddled.

"I'm looking for the logical answers," he responded.

Renee looked away, then blew out the breath she had been holding. "Look, I've been through a lot. I'm sure you both know that and I'm doing the best that I can to help you. Because I want to know who did this to my husband as well. And I'm willing to cooperate with you one hundred percent. I apologize if it's not to your satisfaction." She looked at Altman when she said it, then back at King. "Or yours. But I'm doing the best that I can."

Just as it appeared the investigators were not going to get what they were looking for from Renee, her lawyer, Leckowitz, began asking questions.

Renee had no idea what had happened, but felt suddenly as if she were fighting everyone. Leckowitz continued throughout the rest of the interview, interrupting the detectives' questioning at critical intervals with questions of his own.

As the detectives probed deeper into Renee and Brent's relationship, they insisted she knew very well who had killed her husband. They went, over and over, the details of the night Brent was murdered, constantly picking at her story like vultures would pick at a dead carcass. Leckowitz sat next to his client and seemingly continued to feed off their questions.

Finally, when Altman thought they had stripped Renee down to the bone, he went after her again: "You know, this is the time to come clean on this, Renee. Let's stop this circus that's going on."

"I'm telling you what I know," she pleaded.

"You know who murdered Brent." He pushed Renee.

In a weak voice, she answered, "No. No, I don't."

"The last time I asked you that question, you didn't have an answer for it."

"I—I don't know who did it," Renee said in desperation.

Altman sat back in his seat, then asked accusingly, "Was John on the beach that night?"

"No. Not that I know of. No."

"Well, the last time you answered that question, you said it could've been him."

Renee hesitated. "It—it very well could have been. But I don't know."

"That does not make sense. Don't sink with him."

She nodded. "I understand that."

Altman gestured toward Leckowitz, then said to her, "This man's an attorney. When somebody says it could have been . . ." He let her chew on that for a while before adding, "Like I said, don't go under with John. Don't try to protect him."

She assured him she wasn't protecting John.

"Because this is your lifeline right now, to catch on and get out of this ocean that keeps getting deep around you. You remember answering that question to that effect, though, the last time we talked to you?"

"Uh, I think I said it could have been John."

This time, it was Leckowitz who sat up in his seat. "What did you say?"

"Ah, that . . . It could have been," Renee answered softly.

After another round or two of questioning transpired about what Renee meant by her answer of "It could have been," Leckowitz requested a bathroom break. When they returned, the detectives posed a slightly different question to her, "Would it surprise you if it turns out to be John?"

As if Renee had a change of heart, she responded, "Not totally, no."

"Not totally?" Altman asked.

"No. I don't think that John would do something like that. But from the size of the person I saw, it wouldn't surprise me [if] it turned out to be him."

"Okay, I ask you again," Altman said slowly. "Why would it not surprise you?"

Leckowitz could see that his client was stepping out into deeper water and asked her to step outside. He wanted to talk with the detectives off the record. When Renee stepped outside, he verified that Renee would be free to go home tonight, then asked the detectives if the balance of their investigation would result in the drawing of a criminal warrant charging a homicide or something else in addition to that. Would they postpone any criminal process against Renee for ten days until he returned from his vacation in Europe? He was told that decision would be out of the detectives' hands and passed on to higher authorities above.

It was a little before 1:00 A.M. when Leckowitz moved out into the hall for a conversation with Renee and her parents. Her parents had been sitting outside the door and had heard some of what had been said during the interview. Renee's father advised her, "If you think it was John Frazier that shot Brent, then go ahead and tell them."

When they returned to the interview room, Leckowitz informed the detectives he had his own agenda and a new set of questions. He then turned to Renee.

"You were asked before if you know who pulled the trigger that killed your husband," he began. "And you said you didn't know. Is that correct?"

"Right."

"Do you have any further information or do you want to change the story as to who you believe pulled the trigger that killed your husband?"

"Yes, I do."

The detectives relaxed in their chairs. They had finally gotten the break they were looking for. With the help of

Renee's attorney, the interview had shifted dramatically toward their side. They hoped the next development in the interview was as promising for their case as the last.

"Well, who is it, if you know?" Leckowitz continued.

Renee looked straight ahead, then admitted for the first time, it was John who had murdered her husband. John Frazier.

Leckowitz then led Renee through a series of questions that required her to corroborate her identification of Frazier as Brent's killer. She said it was his voice she had heard that night and the size and shape of the man that had convinced her. There was no doubt whatsoever it was John. She said she had told the detectives previously she didn't know who it was because she really didn't believe that John could have done it.

Renee also substantiated John had at least one gun in his house when she lived there and believed it to be a 9mm Glock. Her account of the murder was that she didn't know it was John at first, but the more he spoke, the more it sounded like him. From then on, she had thought it was him and had never changed her mind to believe it was somebody else. That night, she assumed—particularly when she heard the *click-click* of the gun—John had been joking. Renee admitted further that she had never said anything to her husband that night, nor had she said anything to John. She had not screamed at John not to kill Brent, nor had she begged him to stop. She just prayed that he wouldn't shoot him.

The air hung heavy in the interview room as Renee provided the missing pieces to the puzzle.

"I don't know why Brent didn't run after the first, second and third misfires," she added. "I don't know if John was holding him down or what. I was watching, but thinking about how it couldn't be happening. That he couldn't be doing this." The reason she gave for not screaming for help after her husband was shot and mortally wounded was because she was in shock.

Renee told the detectives she didn't know how John had found out where they were at the beach. She had told no one but his and her parents and knew no one had called them to find out. She had told a few friends, like Cynthia Hanson, and maybe John could have heard about it from her, then followed them on the beach. But she wasn't sure.

Her theory was that John had probably killed Brent because he felt he couldn't have her. That he needed to get Brent out of the way. But she wanted the detectives to know that she did not conspire with John about coming to the beach, nor had she planned to have Brent at the beach at a certain time for John to kill him.

"It wasn't that I was trying to protect John," Renee said. "I just . . . I wanted to make sure that I knew that it was him. I mean, in my heart, I knew it was him. But in my mind, I just didn't want to accept the fact that he could have done that."

Altman was relieved to have heard Renee finally tell the truth. But just to be sure, he asked her, "So, why would you change your mind now after three hours of saying it wasn't?"

"My daughter," Renee answered solemnly. "I know my daughter loves her daddy. I love her daddy. I still don't want to accept the fact that he's gone. But when I really just start thinking about the fact that she could lose me as well. And the more and more I thought about it, I knew it was him."

Altman wanted to be sure he was hearing her right. "There's no doubt in your mind, then, that it was John Frazier?"

"It was him," Renee said firmly.

The detectives had what they'd come for, but they continued the interview until 1:53 P.M., gathering even more incriminating testimony against Renee and Frazier. As promised, they let Renee go home with her family to sleep in her own bed. This wouldn't, by any means, be the end of their investigation, but it had certainly turned the tide in their favor.

Before Renee left the room, she reached out to hug Detective Altman. This was a new one for him. Nowhere, in all of his police training, had he been instructed on how to respond when a suspect offered affection. He reached out and quickly grabbed Renee by her arms. Police officers weren't allowed to reciprocate.

It was early morning, but Captain Hendrick was standing by at Myrtle Beach police headquarters, waiting on Detective King's phone call. With the new information Renee had given them, warrants were drawn up against her and Frazier, signed by a judge in Myrtle Beach, and then faxed back to King at WSPD. Thinking John Frazier might want to run after having seen news of Renee's police interview on television, King and Altman teamed up with several WSPD officers and drove to John's residence, as well as to Kayle Schettler's residence looking for him. When Frazier was not found at either location, it suddenly dawned on them he was probably at work, but they didn't have that exact location. The arrest would have to wait another day.

The exhausted detectives checked in at the Marriott Courtyard and finally caught up on some well-deserved shut-eye. While they were having the benefit of their first good night's sleep in a week, they hoped John Frazier was enjoying his last night of freedom.

CHAPTER 23

MBPD lieutenant Bill Frontz and Detective Richard Beatty arrived in Winston-Salem the next day, June 13, to assist in the arrest of John Boyd Frazier and Kimberly Renee Poole. Frontz carried a copy of Thursday's *Sun News* with him to show the other detectives. It contained an article about Brent's murder and a quote from Renee about her dead husband.

"We all love him," she had said to reporter Lauren Leach. "This didn't have to happen to him . . . but we know he's with the Lord. We're still praying for him."

Detective Altman had made several calls throughout the day trying to alert the Pooles of the upcoming arrests, but had no luck. He finally learned they were with Renee and her family at the Hayworth-Miller Funeral Home in Winston-Salem for the viewing of Brent's body.

In all, much work remained before an arrest of Frazier could be made. He had worked his midnight shift at Champion Products and left that morning, but didn't go home. His whereabouts were still unknown. Working with the Federal Marshal Fugitive Task Force Team, WSPD finally located Frazier that evening at his parents' home. Just as he and his family were sitting down to a steak dinner, they heard a knock on the door. Frazier was served with the warrants and arrested without incident then transported to the WSPD. He was charged with murder and armed robbery and brought to the Investigative Division for an interview.

While Detectives Altman and Frontz were sitting there waiting on him, Frazier made a phone call to his lawyer and one to the Summey house to speak with Renee. Brandy answered the phone and told him Renee was at Brent's wake then hung up on him. She was given explicit explanations that John was not to call their house for any reason.

Twenty-eight-year-old John Boyd Frazier was a tremendous disappointment to Detective Altman. When he sat down to interview Frazier at 8:20 P.M., he could see there was something about his roly-poly body that would make everyone grin. His face was chubby and he had dark black, thinning hair and dark bug eyes. A real class clown. That is, until someone said something he didn't like and he turned on them. For a moment, the detective stared at him silently. He certainly was not the suave and debonair type he had imagined Renee would have had reason to leave her husband.

Frazier reacted as if he had nothing to hide. "I have an attorney," he said void of all emotion.

"Okay." Altman accepted that. "Do you want to make a statement at this time?"

"Not without an attorney," Frazier said, clasping his short beefy fingers together. Suddenly he became hostile and unruly. "I left a voice mail message for you that I had an attorney. I left his name and number on your voice mail. Then my attorney called and left it on your voice mail that he was representing me. When the SBI came to my house, I gave them his name and phone number several times. And they still refused to try and call him. They still insisted on trying to question me in my driveway."

Frazier was red in the face and breathing heavily. The detectives attempted to settle him and apologized for the inconvenience.

"I'm not trying to be rude or anything," Frazier growled, "but everybody's been rude to me." He made it clear he wouldn't be talking to anybody until he talked with his parents and his lawyer. A few minutes later, Robert Probst, his attorney, called the police station and talked with Altman. Probst wanted to know if Altman could share any information related to the arrest over the phone, but he declined. Probst then stated his client would not be cooperating with them in any way and was prepared to fight extradition back to South Carolina.

In the meantime, the combined forces of police officers from the MBPD, SBI and WSPD were all in place and headed toward the funeral home to arrest the witness who had identified Frazier as her husband's killer and put him in this precarious spot.

Even though three full days had passed since Brent had been murdered, that was still not enough time for many of his friends and relatives to at least grasp he had been murdered. Some shivered at the thought of an open casket, given that they had heard his head had been blown off. And the growing divide between the Summeys and the Pooles had already heightened the somber ceremony.

Renee arrived early at the funeral home that Saturday evening, believing she would have some time alone with her husband. Brent's family had picked out the casket and she had asked that two dozen white roses be placed on the top. The funeral home had done its best to make Brent look normal, but his face was still sunken and had that gray pallor look to it. Renee had selected for him a white dress shirt with a blue design down the front, black dress pants, a black leather belt with a silver buckle, Tommy Hilfiger underwear and socks and his black leather dress shoes. Just so he'd look more like himself, she had given the funeral home hair gel to put in his hair.

Earlier in the week, Renee had noticed a memory board of Brent at the Pooles' home, but it didn't have any pictures of her and Brent. Thinking that surely must have been an oversight, she stopped by her house and got some pictures for Dee to include in the collage. She had wanted everyone at the funeral to remember how happy she and Brent had been, and Dee had promised her she would bring the memory board with those of her on it to the viewing. But she didn't see any.

For the wake, Renee wore a dress her mother had purchased.

It was a very conservative, ankle-length, dark blue dress with short sleeves and a white square neckline trimmed in blue-and-white buttons down the front.

As is customary in the South, Brent's body lay fully exposed in the open casket. Renee stood by the casket for nearly two hours with her head bowed and attempted to greet those who had come to express their condolences. There were a few friends of her and her relatives, but mostly people from the Pooles' church, many of whom were reluctant to embrace her. She stood by and watched as her in-laws, dazed and unbelieving at what had happened, fell into the arms of those who were trying to comfort them by saying Brent was safe and happy with Jesus now. The Pooles would nod, and then break down again after being asked if anything could be done for them.

When the crowds slowed near the end of the service, Renee told Dee she was holding Brent's wedding ring and wanted him to be buried with it. She asked Dee if she would help put it back on his finger. While Agnes and Marie admired the flowers and decided which ones would be appropriate for the grave site, Dee positioned Brent's finger and Renee slid the gold band over it. Renee and Dee then embraced each other and cried again.

Just as Renee stepped outside to smoke a cigarette, several police cars drove up in the parking lot. She couldn't believe it. Couldn't they at least let her grieve in private? Did they have no heart? As Detective King and a group of officers got out and headed toward the front door, Marie walked over to them and asked, "You're not here to arrest my daughter, are you?"

Detective King had seen Renee standing outside the funeral home and noticed she had stepped back inside. His main objective was to speak with Brent's family and let them know what was going on. After taking the Pooles into a separate room, he informed them Frazier had been arrested and they were there to arrest Renee. He then spoke with Renee's parents and advised them Renee was being taken to the sheriff's department for the purpose of obtaining another statement about Frazier.

Thinking Renee was being transported to the police station

for additional information, Marie volunteered to the police, "Sometimes, in order to get Renee to tell the truth, you have to get down on her pretty hard. When she was a child, that was the only way I could get her to tell me the truth."

The Summeys did not know their daughter was being charged with obstruction of justice. They jumped in their car and followed the police to the large, three-story building. As soon as they got there, a warrant of obstruction of justice was sworn against Renee and she was entered in the system as a fugitive of justice from South Carolina.

Detective Altman and Lieutenant Frontz were waiting to interview Renee on the first floor, inside a small eight-by-nine cubicle in the detective's division. A long, narrow table and chairs on either side of the table were the only furniture in the room. Just before the interview, Renee had been asked and received a Mountain Dew.

The detectives explained why she had been arrested. She was told this time it would be just only the three of them in the room. When they attempted to Mirandize her, she asked if she could consult her parents. Altman said she couldn't do that; rules at the WSPD prohibited it. Besides, she was her own person now. She'd have to decide what was best to do. Renee signed a waiver of her rights and agreed to make a statement without the presence of her lawyer.

"I know you went over the incident several times with me and Detective King last night," Altman started in on her, "and we did get the truth of exactly what happened. In fact, that was the reason for John Frazier being arrested today."

Renee shifted in her chair. Her eyes were more rounded than usual. She looked scattered and distraught.

"But one of the things we were having a problem with last night is still a concern today," Altman continued. "And that's how John knew you were staying in Myrtle Beach. Okay, uh, I know Detective King and I were telling you that the door was closing on you last night though I think you pushed that door open pretty good to save yourself last night, but there's still that concern of how John knew where you and Brent were staying. Do you still maintain the stance that you don't know how he got down there?"

Renee shifted in her seat, then answered, "I don't know how he got there." Frazier may have followed her, but she didn't know that for a fact.

Altman's words surprised her when he accused Frazier of asking her to lure Brent to a secluded place so he could kill him.

Her mouth and eyes were wide open. "No," she insisted, "he's never done that. No, never." She was 100 percent positive the murderer was John, but she didn't have anything to do with killing Brent.

Altman threw the names of Cynthia Hanson and Thomas Pedersen at Renee. He told her what they had said about her and Frazier, that she had left her husband for him.

"You know we've arrested John," Altman said smugly. "And the lieutenant and I have talked with him. And what do you think he's telling us?"

"I don't know," she said, his words scaring her like a numbing explosion. "I don't know what he's saying."

"Okay, I want you to think about this real hard. I think you were about ninety-nine percent honest with us last night. There's still one percent left for you to tell us about how he knew you and Brent were at the beach. I'm telling you that this was preconceived or planned; right now, this is your only chance. Because once we leave Winston-Salem tonight, that's it. The solicitors are not gonna be willing to listen anymore. And remember when I told you that we threw that lifeline out to you last night and that big ocean was engulfing you?"

Renee began to panic. A sense of total helplessness swept over her as she tried to explain how John could have known where they were staying at the beach. There were many possibilities.

"So, why would John go to all the trouble to follow you to Myrtle Beach?" Altman asked. "Do you think he planned to kill Brent the whole time?"

"I can't say," she answered.

"Had he ever said to you, he wanted to kill Brent?"

"No. I know that he wasn't very happy with him. That

maybe he wanted to physically get in a fight with him. But I'm not sure if he meant to kill him."

"So, he never told you to try and get him someplace where he could try and kill him?"

"No," Renee stated without a need to explain.

As the interview continued, Sergeant King, who was monitoring it from the other side of the two-way glass, saw Renee was wound tighter than a drum. It was a long and tedious interview, but she remained steady in answering questions designed to trip her up. He remembered the advice Renee's mother had given him back at the funeral home and believed Altman could use it against her. He wrote the information on a piece of paper and slid it under the door.

The remainder of the interview took on a new dimension.

"Renee, you need to think real hard about what he said to you. At any time, has he told you, or did you guys plan in any way, even if you weren't taking it serious, about coming to Myrtle Beach or a secluded area, and getting you and Brent away from the public so he could kill him?"

She could feel the heat of Altman's rage. He kept needling her, telling her she and Frazier had conspired to murder Brent.

"Like I said, you need to be totally honest with us now." Altman came down hard on her. "Don't let him turn this around on you and you go down for the fall. If you planned it, it's a lot better to say it now than letting the solicitor get a hold of this whole package. Because let me tell you. They are pretty ruthless there. They don't care who's going up for the murder charge."

Then Altman's questions touched on what he had come to know as a very vulnerable area in her life.

"Okay, I want you to be totally honest on this," he said in a low voice. "If you conspired in any way to do this, I need you to tell me. So when I go to the solicitor and say, 'Look, Renee's done wrong. It took her a little bit to come clean with us, but she values her life, she's got a daughter she's gotta raise. You know, I want to help her out as much as I can.' I know I can't bring your husband back, but I don't want to see you go to jail for life or possibly the death penalty. Because that's what

John is looking at right now. He's looking at the death penalty, okay? I don't want to see you go down for that. You're too pretty of a girl for that."

She hesitated to look Altman in the eyes. She was shocked that he had kept pushing her buttons like he had.

"Even with a conspiracy charge into this, you're not going to be up there as much as he is. I just want you to help yourself, so I can help you. Uh, Lieutenant Frontz can tell you, we've got a good rapport with our solicitor's office. When I go to him—and I'm gonna put everything down we've talked about and he's gonna look at it—I'll say, 'But look over here. Here's where Renee's coming clean on everything. And John's trying to bring her down for it, but he's pushed her to this. He wanted her so bad, he had to get rid of Brent. And he twisted her mind so much that she didn't know what she was doing.' Okay?"

Renee looked up at him sheepishly, shook her head and nodded.

Altman leaned forward and looked her directly in her eyes. "That's what happened, isn't it?"

"Yeah."

Altman and Frontz glanced at each other. Altman took a deep breath, sat back in his chair and gave her some room. "Now I want you to tell me how he did this."

Renee began slowly. "The last time I went to his house"—she seemed distracted, as if she were looking for something, then began again—"I, uh, I uh—I, uh, you think I could get a cigarette?"

Altman told her she could get one when the interview ended. If he had to run to the store himself, he would get her a whole pack.

Renee apologized profusely and said repeatedly she didn't want to lose her daughter. She had already lost her husband, and was about to lose her freedom. She didn't want to lose her child, too.

"You're not going to lose your daughter," Altman assured her.

"I know it's not the right thing to do. I know it hasn't been all along, but I just don't want to lose my daughter," Renee said the third time.

"You're not gonna lose her," Altman assured her. He cranked her back up and redirected her toward her involvement with Frazier and the murder.

Renee stated John had brought it up at work one day. She thought he was playing and didn't take him seriously. Later on, she found out he had a tape recorder and was taping their conversation. He threatened to use it against her if she ever turned on him.

"But I told him, I said, 'No, don't do that, don't do it,' you know. I thought he was playing. I just kept on saying, 'Don't do it. Don't do it.' After that, that was pretty much the end of that conversation . . . but I thought he was playing. I didn't think he was serious about it. . . . One of the last times I talked to him, uh, I didn't know what he was talking about. He said he had gotten me and Brent an anniversary present. I said, 'Thank you.' Then he said, 'Where do you want it to happen?' And obviously that's what it was."

The detectives did not discount what Renee was saying, but they were not dissuaded into thinking she had not known Frazier was going to be in Myrtle Beach. She denied having any contact with him about being there the night of the murder, but Altman kept hammering away at her story until he had reconstructed what he thought was the truth. Then he posed several questions to her for what he believed summarized the entire incident. Wasn't this whole scenario in Myrtle Beach the result of him getting her involved in this conspiracy? Didn't he force her to get Brent to a secluded place so he could get rid of him?

"No, no, no," she protested. "I did not expect him to be there. Like I said, I felt the conversation was all a joke."

Still following the interview from behind the glass, Sergeant King perked up like a cat in a bowl of tuna. She had said, "I did not expect him to be there." He wrote Altman another note, advising him to return to that point, then slipped it under the door.

Seeds of doubt, which had long ago taken root in Altman's mind, now blossomed before him.

"And, lo and behold, when you come to Myrtle Beach, you guys end up in a secluded place—just like John asked you to," he said with renewed vigor. "You see what I'm saying? I'm just saying I don't want you to find yourself in a bind after what he's telling us. Because I'm telling you, he's saying it's all your idea."

Renee bit her nails; she had her back to the wall. There was no other way to go, but forward. She could make an easy truce, and began telling them everything they wanted to know. She and John had planned it all. The last time she had seen him was at her house, the Thursday before they left to go to the beach, and they had talked about it then.

"I know that one day he came back over to my house, he was still talking about killing him. And I told him, I said, 'You know, you don't have the balls to do something like that. Just don't talk about it.' And, uh, my daughter was there and I had to tend to her, so I don't think we ever really finished the conversation. But I do recall telling him, he didn't have the balls to do it, and to stop talking about it. . . . For all I know, he probably recorded that conversation, too."

Altman's suspicions had been validated; she remembered every detail of the conversation. And like almost every criminal he had known, when their plan faltered and plummeted straight down the earth, they wasted no time in blaming someone else. "And John's purpose for recording these was that when it did happen, you were going to go down with him?" he asked, just to make sure he understood her.

"Right," she answered calmly. "If it did happen."

Altman was pumped. He took her back through the wringer again, making certain he had an answer for every single question, then let it all hang out to dry. "Renee, you planned this. I know you did. But he pushed you into it. He pulled you so deep down into this pit, you couldn't get out. He's pushing you. He's threatening you. This is it. He's gotta get rid of Brent. But you had to get him there as bait for that hunter."

Sounding as if there were no point in wasting any more time or trying to hide it, she finally agreed. "Yeah," she whispered, looking down at the floor.

"Renee, we've gone round and round. I know you're going to tell me the truth. I'm ready for you to tell me the truth. I know you're ready to get this ton of bricks off your shoulder right now, because it's got to be killing you."

"Honestly, last night, I felt so much better after I talked to you," she said. Her words stunned even her. It was the last thing she had expected to say to him.

"Make yourself come clean of all this, Renee." Altman kept preaching to her. "This is the only thing you can do right now. Because I'm telling you, we've talked to him. We know the whole deal. But we've got to hear it from you. Save yourself. Don't make him come out smelling like a rose. Because he's a piece of shit."

She agreed. "Yep, he is."

"He's gonna come out smelling better out of this than you, because you're holding back. Tell me you guys planned this together, because he's saying you planned it together. It takes two people to come up with something like this."

"Right."

Renee then proceeded to tell Altman they had planned it, just like he had said. She had told him they were coming to the beach, and she and John had agreed to get Brent out on the beach around two or three o'clock in the morning.

"'Cause there's nobody gonna be out on the beach at that time,' John had told her. 'And you just get him away and I'll do whatever you want me to do.' I was like, you know, 'You're full of it. What are you going to do? You're full of it.' He said, 'You just don't worry about it.' That's why I thought he was full of it. 'Cause he wouldn't tell me."

She was suddenly aware of the humming in the room from the overhead lights.

"And I knew that it was early when we went out. That's why I didn't think that he was gonna be there. I was like, okay, it's early. We're gonna go back to the hotel and he's gonna be fine because he's not going to expect us out this early. Early being when we got to the beach. Which was around midnight. But apparently, he was already in Myrtle Beach. But I did not know he was there until that point where he walked up on us."

Altman and Frontz took Renee through her story a third and then a fourth time. When they believed it was complete, they asked Renee what she thought was the reason for Frazier killing her husband.

"Because he wanted me," she blurted out. "He wanted to be with me. And he knew that as long as I was with my husband, that I love my husband. That I was not going to leave him. 'Cause I went back to my husband because I loved him."

Altman asked a question for which he already had the answer and didn't need her to respond. "And he couldn't deal with that?"

Looking at Altman with an expression that struck him as almost utterly unbelievable, she said, "No. I didn't want my husband to die."

As if all the questions they had asked her were meaningless or immaterial, Renee would acclaim against all odds that she had not wanted her husband dead.

"If John was there . . . if he was following me . . . if he was watching us . . . he would have seen us making love together. He would have seen I did not want my husband to die. I mean, I was all over him. He was all over me—the time that our child was not between us. I mean, we were all over each other. He could have seen that."

Altman thought about what she said, but didn't fall for it. It was easy for him to believe John had killed Brent and to visualize everything she told them had happened. It was just hard imagining what Brent thought about it. Surely, he had to have known what was happening and why it was happening.

After spending half the night being incarcerated by the detectives and the other half of the night in a holding cell, Renee was finally allowed to take a shower and put on an orange jumpsuit. She asked the WSPD officers if they were going to allow her to go to Brent's funeral, but was told no.

Thinking about her arrest years later, Renee would say, "Had I not been arrested that night, I would have killed myself. I envisioned myself driving my truck off a bridge on the way home from the funeral home. I don't know that I would have done it sober, but I know there is no doubt that I would have hurt or killed myself under the influence of alcohol. I didn't want to live anymore. I wanted to see that Katie was safe and taken care of and then it was off to do what I felt I needed to do. There have been times over the years since then that I feel that way and I will hurt myself. Not to the point of doing a lot of serious damage, but just enough to feel the pain and try to get some of the emotional torment out. It doesn't always help, but I just don't know what else to do at those times when things get to me. I can't say that I would have gone back to school, dated or remarried eventually, because I didn't want to live anymore. And, more than likely, I would have succeeded in killing myself after Brent's wake."

While Renee was getting settled into her new accommodations and trying on her less fashionable prison wardrobe, Detective Altman sat alone in the interview room and listened to the stillness around him.

For the first time, he could almost hear Brent talking to him.

Earlier that night, Craig Poole had spoken to the press about his family's feelings after having watched Renee being arrested at the funeral home, where his brother's body lay.

"It's devastating," Craig said. "It magnifies so much the evilness of the entire situation. She had just got through hugging my sister when the police came and took her away. It has always been in the back of our minds, but we were just hoping it wasn't so. There are no winners in this."

CHAPTER 24

Early Sunday morning, Bill Poole phoned Jack Summey and asked if he wanted the funeral home to send the family limousine to his house for them. It was a nice gesture and Jack appreciated the fact they were still considered part of Brent's family, but he declined the offer. He and Marie had been up all night worried sick over Renee's arrest and would not be attending. What family he had that were planning on attending would be driving their own cars.

Of course, Katie would not be among those attending her father's funeral.

At 2:00 P.M., more than five hundred people assembled together at the Pooles' home church, the Calvary Baptist Church, to celebrate the assurance of Brent's eternal life. The arrest of Renee and Frazier gave some semblance of peace to the ceremony. Ordinarily, it would have taken place on Friday or Saturday, but the church was holding a statewide conference then. With the timing of the arrests, the family was glad the funeral had been delayed.

The afternoon was cloudy and crisp. Way before the services began, people were already crowded into the pews. Restrained sobs broke the quiet as the family members filed inside the church and sat in a special area. The sobbing returned when the preacher stood up to address the congregation.

Senior pastor Mark Corts emphasized the positive things in Brent's life.

"I've been Brent's minister since he was born," Corts said from the pulpit. "He was an eternal optimist, a happy-go-lucky guy who just loved life. He had a deep love for his family and a very forgiving nature. God had begun to do new things in Brent's life in the days before he was killed. He was going through a real spiritual renewal. It's all a very tragic thing."

In his brief remarks, Corts talked of hope beyond the grave. Virtually everyone was in tears when he ended by admitting that they all would greatly miss Brent. At this time, Brent was with the Lord. "[God's] with him, he's safe and there's no more pain and sorrow for him."

The mournful silence seemed prolonged as the six pallbearers followed the casket out of the church and lifted it into the hearse. The Pooles gripped each other's hands and wept, slowly walking down the long aisle and behind the casket. Just as they reached the door, Agnes Poole collapsed into her family's arms. A cameraman from News Channel 12 was standing outside the church and purposefully captured the moment. They also filmed Brandy Summey stopping at the family vehicle to express her deep-felt sorrow and the Poole's all filing out to embrace her. Both were very gut-wrenching moments.

"The service reflected the goodness in Brent Poole," Craig Poole said afterward. "It was great. It honored Brent and talked about the many great things in his life. He was a neat, giving person. He was filled with hope and continued on when other people would have given up."

Now the Pooles were the ones who had to struggle not to give up. The funeral was hard—knowing all that had gone on. Everyone talked about Renee at the funeral and how could she have been involved in this. Everyone felt better about the arrests that were made, but no one could ever feel any better about what had happened. While coping with their loss, the family was still pondering how to tell Katie about their father's murder. Most upsetting was the fact that Katie would have to grow up without a mom or a dad—the way things were looking. And that wasn't fair to her.

"That is going to be a tough, tough thing," Craig admitted. "He was a very, very devoted father. His daughter is missing him. She has gone to the door several times looking for him and thinks he is in his shop or has gone to get pizza."

Craig held up a picture of Brent and Katie taken on the beach by Renee, five hours before the shooting. "This [photo] brings to light what was really going on in his mind. It shows in his face. It makes you reevaluate the whole last day and the farce of the trip."

Katie had been dividing her time between the Pooles and the Summeys. Craig said his father was keeping in touch with Renee's family.

"Dad is very gracious in reaching out to them," Craig said. "They're pretty devastated."

Television stations throughout the North Carolina Piedmont area broadcast film clips of the funeral and press that day, along with the older one of Renee dancing around the brass pole at the Silver Fox in a very seductive, black, skintight halter top and slacks.

That Sunday evening, the Pooles called the Summeys and asked if Katie could come over to their house for her cousin's sleep-over and birthday party. When Dee came and got her, she and Marie talked about the awkward situation.

"She's wanting both her mommy and her daddy," Marie said. "But I think we have enough people between all of us we can take care of her."

Dee agreed. Everyone should be looking after Katie's best interest from now on.

The next day, the flags at Mack Trucks in Charlotte were lowered to half-mast, in memory of Brent. Craig and Dee scheduled a news conference at their parents' home in Clemmons that evening and spoke to reporters about their brother's death.

Dee held up the photograph Renee had given her the minute before she had been arrested. Pointing at the picture of Brent and Katie on the bench, she said, "This is how I want everybody to remember Brent; he's kneeling down on her level. . . . Please remember Katie in your prayers. She is the real victim in all of this." Before the news conference started, Katie had been filmed in her bathing suit, running in the yard, blowing and chasing bubbles along with her cousins.

Craig said that Katie had been told of her father's death and taken to his grave site. At first, she thought that he had gone to get a pizza, but now she was saying that he was in heaven and was with Jesus. "Brent loved Renee and Katie very much and would have died for them," he added. "And obviously did."

Craig said his family was not angry with Renee's parents. "They are hurting. They are grieving. They personally loved Brent a lot and now they are dealing with the separation of their daughter." When asked who would keep Katie now that Renee had been arrested, he stated his parents planned on adopting Katie.

The Summeys learned of the Pooles' plans to adopt their granddaughter the Monday night of the broadcast. The next day, they received a letter in the mail that the Pooles' attorneys were filing a custody complaint and petitioning the court to make Bill the executor of Brent's estate. Brent had named Renee as his beneficiary. The Summeys protested both petitions, but the courts eventually upheld the Pooles' requests.

The public got their first look at the suspects in an extradition hearing on Tuesday, June 16, 1998. It had been a full week after Brent had been murdered. Poole and Frazier walked into the hearing room in the Forsyth County Jail wearing matching orange jumpsuits and rubber sandals. They both spoke to the judge via a closed-circuit video link to the courthouse. Frazier came in first, ignoring a horde of television cameras banked within feet of him. He answered several questions posed to him.

"I have my own lawyer," he said, unblinking, as he stared at the face of magistrate judge Nancy Phelps on the video screen. She asked him whether he knew what the warrant was and he replied rather nonchalantly, "Sorta, yeah." He also informed the judge that he planned to fight against extradition every step of the way.

Renee looked very worried and nervous when she walked in and sat down in front of the video screen. She told Phelps she also wished to hire her own lawyer, but agreed to extradition.

When the MBPD came to transport Renee to South Carolina the following Wednesday afternoon, she had a lot more on her mind than celebrating a return trip to the beach. She never raised her head as police officers walked her to the squad car, with her hands cuffed behind her back. Dressed in the same ankle-length blue-and-white dress she had worn at her husband's wake, she never looked up and never spoke to anyone.

Chris Horne from News Channel 12 was there waiting and tried to get her to talk with him. He walked alongside her, pushing a microphone in her face, asking her a series of questions he knew would remain unanswered in front of the camera. "Renee, what really happened to Brent? Are you sorry your husband is dead? Did you arrange to have your husband killed?"

Renee kept her head down and lumbered toward the police car, where Detective Altman stood waiting at the open rear door of the passenger side to help her in the backseat.

After the vehicle had pulled away, Forsyth County sheriff Ron Barker told reporters the words "crying and staring" best described Renee's demeanor while in jail. "She has run the gamut somewhere between crying and staring," he said.

That night, Channel 12 profiled Renee's arrest with the catchy lead-in:

"Renee Poole is on her way back to Horry County for the first time since someone killed her husband, but this time she is making the trip in handcuffs."

The feature followed with an update on the investigation and an exclusive interview with Dee and Craig. Dee said her family was still numb from her brother's death and Renee's arrest; they were just getting by, day to day.

"I was just over with my dad, and he's struggling very much, knowing what Brent was doing now a week ago. He was happy, he was at the beach and he thought his life was everything he wanted it to be. He was with his wife and his two-and-a-half-year-old, and to think this was basically his last few days has been very difficult."

Dee said the only positive thing about all of this was knowing that Brent had rededicated his life to God about a month before he died.

"He was back in church, and like the pastor said at his funeral, it was like God was preparing his heart to be in His presence again. Knowing that my brother is in heaven, is about the only thing that has gotten us through it."

Craig talked about Katie and how she was a daddy's girl. He said Brent had loved every minute of it.

When the reporter asked how Katie was handling all that had happened, Dee said she believed Katie had no impression whatsoever of what was going on.

"The phone rings and she asks, 'Is that my daddy?' We went downstairs to where we had some of my brother's belongings and she asked, 'Are those my daddy's shoes? I want my daddy to put those on.' And I say to her, 'So do I, Katie. I really wish he could.'"

A little eight-year-old girl from Yadkinville, North Carolina, had watched Brent's story unfold on television and told her mother her heart was breaking for his little girl. She wanted to know if she could do something for Katie, and together they picked out a white teddy bear with angel wings. They sent this to the Pooles, along with a bag of guardian angel pins.

"All your life you watch TV and hear these stories and you say, 'Oh, how sad,' and turn it off and go to bed. Now it's my life, my parents' life, and it's Katie's life. It's like I am in a dream. This is a movie script—it's really not happening to us."

Dee choked back her tears, then talked about what lay ahead for her family.

"As bad as this weekend began, we are already prepared that this is the very beginning in terms of how bad it is going to be . . . because people will be fighting for their lives and we understand that. We feel like truth and justice will prevail, but it's going to be a long process."

The first week of Renee's arrest, she told her parents she was being treated like a common criminal. "Everyone's looking at me and whispering, 'That's her, she killed her husband,' and things of that nature. I am being treated worse than I would, had I been a mange animal."

CHAPTER 25

MBPD detectives Altman, King and Frontz met with WSPD detectives Mike Rowe and Penny Kearns to prepare search warrants for the Pooles' and Frazier's residence. Detective Rowe would spearhead all police efforts in Winston-Salem and coordinate both searches on June 14.

The Pooles' home at Blue Bonnet Court was turned upside down and inside out as police searched for evidence that would expose Renee's part in the plot. Renee's Daytona Datsun two-door red truck was also searched. Police confiscated, among other things, several minicassette recordings, floppy disks, CD-Rom disks, an IBM computer and two cards in a dresser drawer signed by John.

One of the letters written from Renee to John was penned on Champion Products stationery:

> I know now you're wondering exactly what is going [on]. Am I interested? Do I like you? Am I crazy? Well, I'll be honest. At first, when we "first" went out I enjoyed myself so much, but I just felt like, "nope, it's not time to let loose and see anyone." But the more we hang out the more I enjoy your company and appreciate you. I guess I am weird in that I just can't dive into this, because, just as most people have been I've been devastated. See, I don't even trust my own father as I

*should. But I see in you a heart of gold and I appreci-
ate it and I don't want to see you any other way. Funny
or not, the way we are seems so very romantic to me.
It's exciting and mysterious and with time it could get
better, but for now, I don't need any physical relations,
just a best friend to spend time with and sip wine with
in front of a "blazing" fire (haha). You fit my description. Don't quit now—don't change a thing. My heart
is coming around. I love the flowers, all flowers and lots
of 'em.*

*John you came around at the perfect time—and I
wish you only could know. Thanks for your help last
night. See ya @6pm sharp—time to do clothes (hahaha)!
Let me know!*

The lawn at Frazier's home on Kingswell Drive had been
neatly manicured and a banner of Snoopy hung from the
front porch when police arrived. Neighbors remembered first
seeing the striking dark-haired Poole at his house as early as
last summer and as recently as last week. Robert Probst, Frazier's attorney, was there to challenge the police's entrance at
his client's home, stating Frazier's home could not be searched
unless he was present. When he was presented with a copy
of the signed search warrant giving them the authorization to
execute the search, he took a set of keys out of his pocket and
opened the door.

The police seized notebooks, photographs, a holster, two
cellular telephones, videocassettes and players—anything
they believed would provide a link to the suspect and Poole's
murder. Detective Altman had not been surprised to find numerous pornographic materials in Frazier's residence and a
Sony 8mm camera set up in his bedroom and pointed directly
toward the bed.

In June 1997, Thomas Mitchell Parnell, senior manager of
employee relations at Champion Products Incorporated, began
an internal investigation regarding the theft of a Macintosh computer, a monitor and other computer products from their corporate offices located in Winston-Salem. The system alone was

valued in excess of $8,500. During Parnell's investigation, he developed leads identifying John Boyd Frazier Jr., a computer operator with their company, as a possible suspect.

Frazier was questioned the following month about the stolen equipment, but he denied any knowledge or involvement in the theft. He even took a polygraph and his residence was searched with his consent, but the equipment was not found at his home. But during the search at Frazier's home, the police observed a Macintosh computer, a Macintosh monitor and a graphics software program inside an interior room. The next day, Detective Rowe called Champion Products and learned that all of the equipment and software seen at Frazier's home matched the identification of the equipment that had been stolen from their corporate headquarters. A second search warrant was executed and the merchandise was recovered and held until it could be returned to its previous owner. Rowe was informed by the district attorney's office that there would be no local state charges regarding Frazier's embezzlement investigation pending the outcome of his murder trial in Myrtle Beach.

As the investigation progressed, MBPD quickly found out John Boyd Frazier had also left behind quite a collection of bad relationships. One of Frazier's former girlfriends, Wendy Collins, told Detective Altman, "The motherfucker is crazy!" She said about eight years ago, he had beaten her up on several occasions. In one incident, she had received medical treatment for injuries sustained by his actions and that he had pointed a pistol at her. She also said that she had filed charges against Frazier for this incident, but did not follow through with it and the charges were eventually dropped.

Megan Dayton Gilliam had dated Frazier in 1993 and 1994, and said he ran hot and cold. "He could go from the nicest person in the world to screaming and ranting and raving. He could just snap like that." Near the end of their relationship, Megan said she and Frazier got into an argument while sitting in his car, and when she opened the door to get out, he pushed her out and then came around the car and pushed her down again. She got into her car and drove away and Frazier came after her. She had to call 911 to get him to leave her alone.

Frazier was charged with assault on a female, but the charges were dropped when he begged Megan to forgive him. He was ordered into twenty sessions of a local abuse-counseling program as a result of the charge, but Jenny Hemmrick, a counselor at a domestic-violence-counseling center called Time Out In, reported to police that Frazier had been in counseling there, but had been thrown out of the program. Three months later, Megan filed a misdemeanor stalking charge against Frazier for harassing her, but the judge found him not guilty.

Before their investigation was complete, the police would hear from several other victims of John Frazier, male and female, who would tell similar stories to those of Wendy Collins and Megan Dayton Gilliam.

The MBPD met with Kayle Schettler, the owner of the gray Acura that Frazier had borrowed the week of Brent's murder, and he agreed to have his vehicle searched and processed for any possible evidence in the case. Kayle was a close friend of Frazier's, but he was upset that his car may have been used in the incident. He said he would help in any way.

A real neat freak, Kayle stated he had cleaned the car after Frazier returned it, because there had been cigarette ashes and gravel on the floor mat. He didn't know if Frazier had cleaned it or not, and had not looked at the odometer to see how far it had been driven. An SBI crime technician, Jerry Webster, processed the car, both inside and out, and checked for blood, hair and fibers, using an ultraviolet light. All areas of the car were checked thoroughly, including the doors, trunk and windows, but the only possible bit of evidence found was a lip print located on the outside of the windshield on the passenger side. The police got very excited when Webster advised they could match this print with one of Renee's lip prints and possibly tie the two suspects together. If the two prints matched, then it would be probable to conclude that Renee had kissed the windshield as a signal to Frazier their plan was still on. It could be the most damaging and diabolical evidence they'd have against her to prove she had conspired to murder her husband.

Renee was asked and agreed to provide samples of her lip imprints, but the SBI could not lift a suitable print from the windshield for comparison. Other than the lip print, that was all Webster could find in or on the car. There was no visible blood droplets, no beach sand in the floor mats, seats, underneath the car, on the wheel wells or inside the wheel rims. In spite of the distance the car was alleged to have traveled from Winston-Salem to Myrtle Beach and back, there was no significant evidence to indicate that.

A check had also been run by the Davie County Sheriff's Office to determine if Frazier had been stopped the night of June 9 or June 10, either in the 1990 Acura or his 1996 Chevy Blazer. When the results of that search produced nothing, it occurred to the MBPD that their only hope for placing Frazier at the crime scene the night of the murder were the eyewitness accounts. On June 16, at the request of MBPD, Detective Rowe was asked to complete a photographic lineup of Frazier and five other subjects.

With the photographic lineup in hand, MBPD contacted their eyewitnesses in North Carolina and Virginia and asked them to pick out the suspect. All but one of the four immediately identified John Frazier as the man they saw dressed in black on the beach that night.

CHAPTER 26

The arrest of the two suspects greatly calmed safety concerns in Myrtle Beach. It was obvious to everyone now that Brent Poole's murder was not a random act of violence, but rather a deliberate and planned act of murder. The city of Myrtle Beach and the Chamber of Commerce assured all tourists vacationing in the Grand Strand they were safe, and there was nothing to fear.

Renee had already waived extradition to South Carolina and her first court appearance in Horry County came quicker than the Pooles expected. On Friday, June 26, 1998, she was herded through the courthouse lawn dressed in prison-issued clothing and shoes and chained to four other inmates. She looked very tired and weary from her short week's stay at the J. Reuben Long Detention Center, in Conway. In her hands, she clutched a fistful of legal papers.

Reporter Adam Shapiro greeted her at the courthouse's front steps, hoping to get his exclusive interview finally.

"Renee, did you lure your husband to the beach?" Shapiro asked, moving in closer as the human train slowed.

Renee looked past Shapiro and smirked, before answering, "All I want to say is I love my daughter."

The scuttlebutt in the courtroom was that solicitor Ralph Wilson had already been talking about seeking the death penalty in this case. Voters in Horry County had elected

Wilson chief prosecutor in 1990 and they had great confidence in the judgment and abilities of the first black prosecutor elected in South Carolina since Reconstruction.

Renee's parents were there to support her, sitting nervously on the end in the front row of the gallery. Renee appeared calm and smiled frequently at them during the proceedings. She had already told her attorneys that rarely did forty-eight hours go by without her thinking about her dead husband. Even worse were the nightmares. Sometimes she got so scared, she would just start crying and shaking. She needed to be around someone who laughed, someone who had hope, but it was impossible inside a jail cell. At night, she would phone her parents and cry incessantly: "Oh, Mom, I thought you were always too strict on me. If I'd only listened and did what you said, I wouldn't be in this mess."

Randy Mullins, her court-appointed attorney, did not ask for bond, knowing the judge would order a mental competency to determine if Renee was fit to stand trial. He knew the interview and complete psychiatric assessment could take up to as long as six weeks.

Bill and Agnes Poole were also present in the courtroom, making certain those who were responsible for their son's death would be punished. After the judge suspended his daughter-in-law's bond hearing, Bill Poole walked directly toward Renee and looked her in the eye. On the way out of the courtroom, he spoke to reporters about his feelings toward her.

"We just want those responsible for Brent's death to be punished to the fullest extent of the law. With each day bringing new information to light, it keeps the pain right up front. Renee's arrest kind of finalized what we hoped was not true. It has just added tragedy to tragedy. What the police say they have done is the coldest premeditated act that could have ever been committed. In television, you don't see this degree of premeditation and coldness."

Renee's attorney overheard Poole's comment and warned, "The public should always be skeptical about any prerelease of information. The police may not be telling the whole story."

If the truth were known, the police *didn't* know the whole

story. Their investigation was still ongoing and they still had uncovered no physical evidence linking Frazier to Poole's murder. Investigators were busy interviewing acquaintances and friends, hoping to generate enough information to build a solid case beyond Renee's confession to the police. Forensic teams had been issued search warrants a second time to enter both Renee's and Frazier's homes again and they searched for any connections the two suspects may have had with the murder. They had already seized computer equipment, photographs, negatives, a videocassette, notebooks and miscellaneous papers.

"That's why I am not sending him down to be tried for his life based on the testimony of Renee Poole's word," Robert Probst, Frazier's attorney, said in his extradition hearing in the Forsyth Superior Court. Probst's contention was that Frazier was not involved in any way and he planned to contest the warrant that called for extraditing him to Conway to stand trial.

Probst already knew there was little chance that his fight against extradition would succeed. It was inevitable. All the MBPD had to do was get South Carolina governor David Beasley to sign the warrant and file it with Governor Jim Hunt, in North Carolina. Finally the papers were served and Frazier appeared with his attorneys in Forsyth County Courthouse for his last court hearing relating to his extradition on July 1, 1998.

Frazier came swaggering into the courtroom, smiling and nodding, with Probst and his newly acquired South Carolina attorney, Morgan Martin. Even though nothing stood in his way to be extradited to South Carolina and face murder charges against him, his defense team was hardly throwing in the towel. They were confident any evidence against him was rather flimsy, and those kind of cases were always tough for the prosecution to win. Dressed in a tiny white-and-black checked sportcoat and a white shirt with an open collar, Frazier wanted everyone to know his attorneys were gaining steam and were eager to prove he had been wrongly accused.

"It's time we go down to South Carolina and start to prove his innocence," Probst announced. "Even though we think there is a defect in this warrant, we waive his extradition."

Probst stated the reason they had fought the extradition in the first place was to have the time to hire a defense attorney. They had found that person in Morgan Martin. Martin and his partner, Tommy Brittain, had a reputation as one of the best defense teams in South Carolina and they came highly recommended. Martin quickly revealed to the press how he had earned that reputation.

"John is adamant about the fact he's not guilty. The only reason he's been arrested is because of the statements made by the lady, who is an established schemer and an admitted liar."

Martin said he came to his conclusion about Renee Poole because of what he had read in the police report. She had changed her story repeatedly.

"I think if you read the warrants and you put together the facts that she has told several different stories to the police about what had happened, it leads you to the inevitable conclusion that she is capable of telling a lie and she has lied to the police."

Martin made it clear there were no plans for any plea arrangement with the prosecutor to testify against Renee. John was an innocent man, who had been wrongly accused, and was going to South Carolina, hoping for better things. Hoping to win his freedom there.

Frazier's attorneys said it best when they hoped for better things for their client. The press was having a field day with his case, giving it twenty-four-hour coverage, and they were ruthless in their reports on him. Nearly every day, there was a newspaper article or television broadcast that portrayed John as a violent and volatile person, a real Jekyll and Hyde personality. Those who had any dealings with John were saying he was not a peaceful man. Stories of Frazier having assaulted, threatened, harassed or shot at others made the news nightly, attesting to his violent nature.

Tony Allen, of the MBPD, had taken a phone call from an anonymous caller before Frazier had been arrested, which later turned out to be the bartender at the Silver Fox Gentleman's Club, Bruce Wolford. Wolford said he didn't want to give information and the person (Frazier) turn out to be innocent: "I don't want one of my friends really pissed-off at me. You know,

In 1977, Jack and Marie Summey lived with their two daughters, Brandy and Renee.

Even as a child, their youngest daughter, Renee, had the looks of a fashion model.
(Marie Summey)

The Summeys vacationed together, visited Disney World, and enjoyed hiking in the mountains. *(Jack Summey)*

The Summeys lived in a mobile home until Jack could finish construction on their 3,000-square-foot log home in Clemmons, North Carolina. *(Jack Summey)*

At age nine, Renee loved school and earned good grades until the other children started making fun of her, calling her "white trailer trash."

When Renee was eleven, she started to slim down. Her classmates teased her, saying she was "as skinny as an Ethiopian."

The Summey girls were only
a year apart in age, yet
very different in personality
and temperament. Brandy,
the older one, was reserved
and shy, while Renee was
independent and feisty.

Renee was a freshman at
R.J. Reynolds High School
when she started dating a
senior, Brent Poole. The two
became inseparable.

By the time Renee was seventeen, she was bored with school and chose to work instead. She and Brent had been romantically involved for almost three years. They planned on getting married when she discovered she was pregnant. *(Marie Summey)*

Already expecting their first child, Brent and Renee were married at the Summeys' home on June 9, 1995. *(Marie Summey)*

Jack and Marie Summey loved Brent and welcomed him into their family as "the son they never had." *(Brandy Summey)*

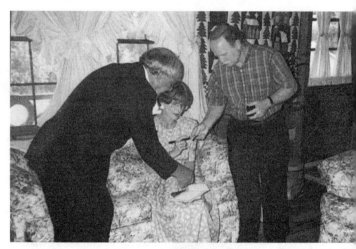

Bill and Agnes Poole wondered if their son, Brent, was making the right decision. Yet they respected him for wanting to do the honorable thing. *(Marie Summey)*

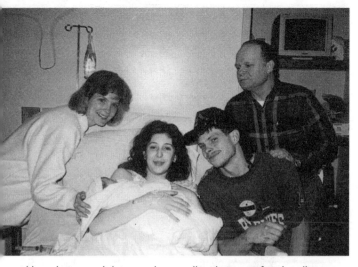

Although Renee didn't get along well with Brent's family, all was forgiven when she gave birth to Katie in December, 1995.
(Marie Summey)

In less than two years, the Pooles' marriage was in serious trouble. They hoped a June 1998 vacation in Myrtle Beach, South Carolina would help salvage it.

Brent Poole loved his daughter, Katie, more than anything in the world. While she slept in an oceanfront hotel only a few hundred yards away, he was gunned down on the beach. *(Renee Poole)*

Myrtle Beach Captain of Investigations Sam Hendrick led a multi-department investigation into the murder of Brent Poole. Renee Poole and her lover, John Boyd Frazier, were arrested for the crime four days later. *(Dale Hudson)*

Chief Homicide Detective Terry Altman sought justice for Brent's murder. *(Dale Hudson)*

Homicide Detective John King was Altman's partner. Renee was no match for these two skilled interviewers. *(Dale Hudson)*

In 1998, Ralph Wilson was the Horry County Solicitor who decided Renee Poole would face the death penalty for her part in her husband's murder. *(Dale Hudson)*

When Wilson lost the general election to Greg Hembree *(left)*, Renee's lawyers then had to face him and Deputy Solicitor Fran Humphries *(right)*. *(Dale Hudson)*

On trial for conspiracy to murder her husband, Renee Poole looked nothing like "Carlee," the stage name she used as an exotic dancer. *(Dale Hudson)*

Renee had a very capable defense team in William Isaac Diggs and Orrie West, but they could not overcome Renee's confession and her shady past. *(Dale Hudson)*

Renee showed little emotion while seated at the defense table.
However, she was brought to tears when she talked with family
and friends. *(Dale Hudson)*

Renee was convicted of conspiracy to murder her husband and
sentenced to life imprisonment without the possibility of parole.
(Dale Hudson)

Renee's lover, John Boyd Frazier, also stood trial for Brent's murder. His mother, Jane Lovett, said she knew her son didn't kill Brent, especially for "that" woman. *(Dale Hudson)*

John Boyd Frazier was represented by two of the best defense lawyers in South Carolina, Morgan Martin and Tommy Brittain. *(Dale Hudson)*

John Boyd Frazier's family held hands and prayed the jury would find him innocent. *(Dale Hudson)*

Finally, justice was served for Brent Poole's family when Frazier was found guilty. *(Dale Hudson)*

Now, Renee spends her time at Leath Correctional Institute in Greenwood, South Carolina.
(Marie Summey)

Although they seldom see one another, Renee and her sister, Brandy, are still very close.
(Marie Summey)

Jack and Marie Summey still believe their daughter is innocent. They see her regularly on weekends. (Brandy Summey)

Brent's grave marker reads, "Beloved son, brother, father, uncle, and friend." There is no mention of the word "husband." (Marie Summey)

thinking I'm trying to do something against him. I wouldn't want to be killed like Brent. You know, if this person done it, then I'm actually nervous about being around him."

Wolford claimed to be one of John's best friends, but the word was out about a $50,000 reward, and that was a lot of money to him. Real money. Enough to consider turning in his own mother—so, why not his best friend?

Even though John knew Wolford also had had an affair with Renee, he did not let what had happened in the past affect his friendship with Bruce. All the time he was under suspicion, he was counting on Wolford and his wife to standup for him in court. Wolford's wife would later tell police that John had hinted to her he needed an alibi and she could provide that.

Wolford told Allen he no longer trusted Frazier.

"As a matter of fact, I'm sitting here with my shotgun laying beside me on the couch, because I'm afraid if that person done it once, then he'll do it again," he said.

Wolford informed Detective Allen that he was friends with all three people involved. At one time or another, he had talked with Brent, Renee, and John via the Internet. Said he worked at the Silver Fox, where Renee worked, and that John was a customer there—and that's how he had met him.

"I work with John's computer. He comes around my house. He and Renee came together to see my wife when she was in the hospital. Renee was supposed to have been with her husband. I got e-mails to prove all that."

"Uh-huh," Allen said, in an easygoing manner.

"They are actually what you call carbon copies. You know, where you can send an original to one person, then make a carbon copy to a second person. I got one of them printed out right here. It talks about where John is pissed-off because she moved out from living with her husband to move in with him and then went back home to her husband. It also says Renee went back to her husband because he was threatening to take her kid away from her for leaving him. I can read it to you, if you want me to."

"Sure, go right ahead," Allen encouraged him.

Wolford read the entire May 31 e-mail. Parts of it, Allen jotted down:

> *I don't know who is the dumber of the two of us. One, for me trying to believe she really wanted me. Or, two, for you being so stupid that you really want her to be your wife and actually trust that she won't keep doing this again and again like she has done so many times in the past and that you don't know about it.*

Frazier told Poole he had seen some of the video footage of Bruce and Renee. He said he felt sorry for him believing they could make their "so-called marriage" work. "She's cheated on you with me and others, and me with you, so what makes you think she is still going to be faithful to you?" he posed the question, then answered it with, "She never did stop coming over to my house for the past three weeks."

At the bottom of the e-mail was an invitation:

> *"If you want to talk about a few things that I know, send me an e-mail. I don't think Renee would ever tell you all. I told you, Renee, not to cross me."*

A threat.

"Wow!" Allen said in an elevated voice. "Now, you have all this on hard copy?"

"I have this printed in front of me," Wolford said, like it was the winning ticket in the million-dollar lottery. "I have it still on my hard drive in my computer. I've actually made copies on floppy disks."

Wolford said he had been conversing with his friends on an Internet program called ICQ. Whenever one of his friends logged in, their name appeared on his buddy list. He admitted he was a do-it-yourself hacker and had confiscated some of John's e-mails. Those messages he had saved on floppy disks and volunteered to send copies to Allen for review.

"Let me boot my computer up and I'll read that dialogue to you where John's saying he's not worried. That he has a gun and tried to talk Renee into meeting him somewhere, but Renee was afraid he was going to kill Brent. I mean, I have that actual dialogue set up, too. To where it's obvious you know who said what."

"We're definitely interested in what you have," Allen said.

"I seen Brent last week," Wolford continued. "Him and Renee came into the club. John was also there. I do know for a fact that Brent and Renee came into the club one night and John walked with a pair of Renee's underwear in his back pocket hanging out, just to sort of tease Brent along."

"Was May thirty-first the last e-mail that you received?" Allen asked.

"That was the last e-mail that I received from John along this line. I do know John called into work Monday night, June 8, the night before Brent was murdered, and was taking a couple of days off from work."

"Were you there when the call was made?"

Wolford said he wasn't there when the call was made. "But I do know he called into work and didn't work those two nights. He usually calls me like every day or every other day for help with his computer. He didn't call me those few days, which I found was unusual. And he's made several calls here to my answering machine lately. I haven't been able to actually answer the phone, but it seems like he's wanting to talk to me or my wife about something very important."

Allen asked him, "How long has this problem been going on between these three people?"

"I'd say at least a month or so. My wife was in the hospital and had her gallbladder taken out. Renee and John came to see her. My mother was there when they showed up and met them. She thought John was Renee's husband."

Wolford also related an incident where Brent and John had a disagreement at the club. He said it was about two weeks ago that Brent and Renee came into the Silver Fox.

"They had just gotten back together and Brent was really pissed-off. He wasn't talking to anybody. He wasn't even talking to me. When he left, he just happened to run into John in the parking lot. I was being kind of nosy and just asked him what had happened."

Wolford just happened to have a copy of the conversation and read it to Detective Allen. The e-mail was from John, dated June 4, 1998, at 2:50 A.M. Bruce had asked John if he was worried about Brent, and he replied:

> *I ain't worried about shit. I just [think] it's funny as Hell. He told Renee he was going to kill me or at least beat my ass if he ever saw me out in public again.*

In that same e-mail, John also wrote:

> *I was trying to get Renee to show up somewhere preplanned with him but she wouldn't do it. She's afraid I'd kill him just for the hell of it.*

"Wait a minute." Allen stopped him. "Back up. John e-mailed you and said, 'I was trying to get Renee to show up somewhere preplanned, but she . . .'" Allen was writing it all down as fast as he could.

Wolford volunteered to e-mail him a copy. "'Somewhere preplanned with him . . .'" He filled in the blanks. "'But she wouldn't do it. She's afraid I'd kill him just for the hell of it.'"

Allen cupped his hand over the phone, called Chief Hendrick to his desk, and spoke with Hendrick about what Wolford had just shared with him. They agreed it was a good idea to get this information from Wolford before he changed his mind. "We've got some investigators up there now," Allen informed Wolford. "Can I get one of them face-to-face with you so you can show him that e-mail and talk with him about it?"

Wolford agreed and gave Allen directions to his house and his telephone number. "Like I said, I don't want everybody knowing what's going on with me. Because I know everybody in this situation, and if something turns out and they are innocent, I don't want to lose my friends over it. Like I said, I want to remain anonymous on this if possible to where I don't get myself in the middle of something. You see, I just called the club earlier today trying to find out my schedule and was told by one of the managers that there were some people up there asking questions about me and my wife and John Frazier and our relationship with the Pooles. Said his name was Frontz."

Allen informed him that was Lieutenant Frontz. One of the MBPD in Winston-Salem who was investigating the case.

"Well, I'll need to talk with him," Wolford insisted. "There's some other things in here he'll want to know. Something about a gun."

The detective's heart raced. "About a gun?"

"Yes. Where I left off it says: 'She's afraid I'd kill him just for the hell of it, 'and I said, 'Tell her a cop will be watching and get his [Brent's] ass arrested.' He goes, 'Hell no. They might try to arrest me too. Do you really think that scrawny little fucker could take me? Besides, I've got too many guns with me all the time.'"

"Well, that's stuff we need to know," Allen assured Wolford. "I'll have one of the detectives give you a call."

Wolford said he had it all on floppy disks and the police could take it with them if they wanted. He later mailed thirty-seven pages of copies from chat room conversations with John Boyd Frazier and Renee Poole and a videotape of him and Renee having sex. Police learned from the copies of Wolford's chat room conversations that Wolford and his wife were involved in computer sex with the Pooles.

Lieutenant Frontz visited Bruce Wolford after Frazier had been arrested and was delighted that he was still willing to assist in the investigation.

"Like I said, I don't mind cooperating with you," he assured Frontz. "A crazy asshole like him needs to be put away somewhere. The way I see it, I can understand situations with disagreements and arguments and fighting. And, you know, occasionally you do get into a fistfight, but I don't see no reason to take a gun out and kill somebody over some shit like that.

"And I damn sure don't want to even consider myself to be a friend of somebody like that. Before I found this out, I considered him to be a friend, but after thinking about all this shit, I don't care if he sits there and they electrocute him on the spot.

If you can prove him guilty, go for it. In my personal opinion, he is guilty."

If Bruce would have been a solid witness, the prosecution could have counted on him to help convince a jury that Frazier was the only man in the world that had reason to kill Brent Poole. The only problem was, there were dozens of men, including Bruce, who had had sex with Renee and could have wanted Brent out of the way.

Darrell Wilson, a private investigator from North Carolina hired by Frazier's mother, had investigated the case thoroughly and concluded Wolford to be as strong a suspect as John Frazier. The savvy ex–police officer had tracked down and interviewed not only Wolford, but many of the witnesses. During his interview with Chris Hensley, Wilson showed him the computer-generated composite completed by the MBPD, along with color photos of Wolford. When asked if Wolford could have been the person he passed on the beach, Hensley replied, "Yes, that could possibly have been him."

"Does he most favor that composite?" Wilson needed to know.

It was the first time Hensley had ever seen a photo of Wolford along with the composite. He told Wilson from what he remembered of the man's body—the height, the hair and face—everything in the photos clearly resembled the composite.

Wilson had also spoken with another of Wolford's girlfriends, Amy Marie Dudas. She had dated Wolford until she found out he was married to Courtney. When she broke up with him, he wouldn't leave her alone and eventually threatened to kill her. Dudas had seen several of Wolford's weapons, including a semiautomatic pistol with a slide on the top. She was so afraid he would make good on his threats that she had reported him to the Forsyth County Sheriff's Department. She also informed Wilson that he had several CDs with e-mails he had exchanged with John and Brent on it and had buried them in the woods in his backyard. Wolford had told her he was scared someone was after him.

Dudas said that she and Courtney had gotten Wolford committed to Charter Mandala in 1997 because he told them he was crazy. He said he loved Dudas and Courtney, but didn't know whom he wanted to be with.

But the MBPD were not that concerned about Wolford's screwed-up love life. Their investigation had led them to believe he was just one of only God-knows-how-many scheming bartenders preying on innocent women. The way they saw it, Wolford didn't care whom he hurt or used as long as they gave him the sexual attention and pleasure he desperately craved. The thirty-minute videotape of him and Renee having sex he had mailed to police was indicative of that fact. It was enlightening, to say the least, but the detectives didn't believe after having seen that tape that Wolford was so enthralled with Renee he would want to kill Brent to be with her. To Wolford, Renee was just another piece of ass.

The detectives were also aware that Wolford was hurting for money. They had been told that Courtney had been admitted to Charter Hills in Greensboro for drug addiction, and the weekend after she was released, she got into a nasty car accident and was rushed to the hospital. In late June, he told the police she was in her Miata and had rolled it after taking down a light pole. Said she was now in intensive care, suffering from multiple fractures in her skull, a crushed shoulder and a punctured lung.

"I'd heard one of the girls at work, Cynthia Hanson, is supposed to be a character witness for John," he told Lieutenant Frontz. "She came to ask me and Courtney if we would talk to his attorney. I really don't want to. I have no reason to, you know. Why should I talk to his defense when I'm dead sure he's the one that done it and I'm not gonna help the damn defense at all. The last thing in the world I'm gonna. . . . Well, it's just that they will try and turn my words around."

Wolford was about as paranoid as a woman who sat in the stadium at a football game and claimed the players in the huddle were talking about her. Said there had been some strange things happening at his house: somebody tampering with and setting his alarm system off and disconnecting his phone lines.

"I mean, there is some weird shit going on," he said, looking around him to see if anyone was listening, "And I just got nervous about some things. . . . [But] I've kept my ears open. Like I said, me working in the bar, everybody comes in and tells me everything. [And] I wanted to ask you if I was eligible for any part of that reward at all? I know they offered it up at one time, and I know they said something about they were keeping it for their little girl."

"Yeah, and they still are, Bruce," Frontz told him. "It's the family's discretion of what or how much they are gonna pay. But they have assured us they still have the reward money. It's still there."

Wolford was pleased to hear it was still a possibility. "Uh-huh. I didn't know if I was eligible for anything like that or not. Because right now, it would really help my hospital bills."

Frontz hated to rain on his parade, but told him the Pooles were holding the money now because arrests had already been made. "They are holding the money for what they think is gonna be helpful in the courtroom proceeding and in the trial. Again, it's gonna be up to them, but it is our understanding that this money is not gonna be disbursed until the trial."

Wolford said he understood that completely. He was just asking a question, and hoped the detective understood that was not the real reason he was helping out.

Another ex-lover of Renee's had contacted the police, but not for the reward money. He just wanted to make sure he wasn't being singled out as a murder suspect. Robert Cummings had been brushing his teeth when he heard the news about Brent's murder. Said he nearly swallowed his toothbrush. While Brent was at work, he had driven his red Eagle Talon over to her house many times and even gone to the park with Renee and Katie.

"I stop[ped] seeing Renee three weeks before the murder," Robert told Detective Beatty over the telephone. "I seen this coming on and I just barreled out pretty much. It was such a strange relationship. I don't mind a love triangle, but not a love square. I couldn't cope with her other boyfriend."

"Did you ever think something like this would happen?" Beatty asked.

"No. I was shocked out of my mind, especially when she got arrested. Running around on your husband is one thing, but killing somebody that's a whole lot different."

"So, did you ever talk with John?"

"Well, one time I paged her and got a callback, but it wasn't her. I recognized John's voice, but I didn't say anything. I could tell he was always a nutcase. I guess he figured out it was me, because he said 'hello' three times and then just went to cussing."

"Did you say anything to him?"

"No, I wasn't gonna listen to his bullshit over a married woman. I'll just go and find somebody else."

"How long did you actually see Renee?"

Robert thought a second, then responded, "About seven months." A lot longer than Frazier did.

"When was the last time you saw her?"

Robert told Beatty the last time he saw Renee was over at her house, probably about a month ago. "I tried to push her off. You know, like 'I don't want to see you no more,' but she wouldn't get the picture. I even called Brent at Charlotte Mack Truck and just asked him straight-up, 'Do you know how many people your wife's sleeping with while you're at work?' And he said, 'I don't have a clue.' I told him if he only knew."

"Then what happened?" Beatty asked.

"I didn't see her for two days and I thought it was over and done with. Then the next day, she pulls in my damn driveway. I couldn't believe it. I'm like 'Are you out of your fucking mind?' She tells me that she was leaving Brent, but, see, she had that Dodge truck she was paying like four hundred thirty a month in payments and a horrendous phone bill. So, I thought the way it was going to work out was she'd find out life wasn't too sweet on the other side of the fence and go back home to Brent. And when she did, this must have pissed this dude named John off. But now, it's looking like she stood right over him and watched him pull the trigger."

CHAPTER 27

Release bond hearings for Kimberly Renee Poole and John Boyd Frazier were held until September 11, 1998, in the Horry County Courthouse. In a bizarre incident, the two murder suspects were transported from the jail to the courthouse in the same vehicle.

"Are you going to testify against me?" John hurriedly asked when the vehicle stopped and the officers stepped outside. Renee shook her head no. She had nothing more to tell the police or the prosecution about him.

Once inside the courtroom, circuit court judge John Breeden was to decide whether they could post a bond to be released until their trials and set the amount of money that must be put up to guarantee the defendants would appear in court. Breeden also was to consider if either Poole or Frazier was likely to run or be a danger to the community. But during the hearing, requests for both defendants to be released on bond were withdrawn by their attorneys.

Bill and Agnes Poole were in court. They were glad bond had been withdrawn and celebrated the small victory of justice for their son. It was also their thirty-eighth wedding anniversary, and afterward, they drove to the spot on the beach where Brent had been shot and placed three roses—one for each of their children—on a fence, near where he had died.

"There are so many hundreds of times I've sat and visualized

Brent laying there and wonder how long did he suffer?" Agnes said softly to her husband.

Chief public defender Orrie West, Renee's attorney, said she did not want to comment on the proceedings. She had taken over the case from Randy Mullins. West had once worked with solicitor Wilson briefly when he was in the Legal Aid office, then followed his footsteps into the public defender's office. She was a South Carolina native who had graduated from law school and Northwestern University, and had retained her passion for those who needed her help.

Wilson couldn't say enough good things about West. "She's quiet and soft-spoken a little, but she knows how to get at the essence of a question and frame it to get the correct response. And she does it in a nonflamboyant way that can be really treacherous for a witness. She's so quiet and matter-of-fact that they don't realize they are giving away the kitchen, and they are giving it away and the sink, and everything, too."

West had represented clients in the past who had been charged with murder. She was a fighter and always put an enormous amount of energy into her cases. She knew she was going to have to poke holes in the state's case and create enough reasonable doubt by proving there was a lack of evidence to convict.

In order to fortify Wilson's theory of conspiracy, he had to go after the source itself—Renee Poole. There were no famed forensic experts to testify in this case, nor was there a smoking gun that had led the police to the killer. Wilson would have to fit all the pieces of the puzzle together and show them how easily the evidence fit against Poole and Frazier.

Wilson also had a lot of respect for Morgan Martin, Frazier's attorney, who had said he didn't think the timing was right to ask for Frazier's bond. "I thought I had reviewed all the evidence," Martin told the press after the proceedings, "but I learned later that I needed to check additional evidence and documents to maximize the opportunity for granting of bail."

Wilson and Martin had squared off against each other many times in their careers. Both had great respect for each other and maintained a close friendship. Wilson was not surprised by

Martin's actions. "Morgan pretends to be a country lawyer, but don't let him fool you. Behind the drawl and the smile, a lot of wheels are turning."

Martin had always credited his success as a top-notch defense attorney to luck, good trial partners and knowing when to try a case and when to make a plea bargain. This included bond hearings as well.

A month later, Frazier's attorneys had him back in front of a judge, again to request bond. This time, Judge James Williams set Frazier's bail at $200,000 and ordered him not to leave South Carolina or contact Brent Poole's family once he was released.

The thought of Frazier walking out of jail to freedom upset Brent and Renee's families. Agnes Poole said she was not only disappointed, but was terrified. "We are afraid. My grandchildren are afraid of him. They said if John Frazier gets out . . . they are afraid he would come back and murder them."

Agnes said having had to stand in the courtroom four feet away from the man who had been charged with murdering her son unnerved her and her husband.

"This was not just a murder," Bill Poole had told the judge. "It was a well-planned execution and well-orchestrated. Our family is fearful of him coming back. We do not think we could live knowing he was in the community."

Frazier was released from jail on Wednesday, October 21, 1998, and moved into a family-owned condo in North Myrtle Beach. Morgan Martin, his attorney, had helped him secure employment with his brother-in-law, who owned a large construction company in Horry County. Before John vacated the J. Reuben Long Detention Center, the guards thought he would be amused to know what his ex-lover Renee had been up to all this time. They showed him a stack of love letters Renee had written another prison inmate she'd met. The letters revealed the two lovebirds had concocted a feral scheme they thought would help her escape the death penalty. The guy would masturbate into a rubber glove, smuggle it underneath the door to Renee, where she, with a little help from her friends, would attempt to impregnate herself in the shower. The speculation was the state would be more sympathetic toward an expectant mother.

News the next day of Frazier's release added to an already upsetting day for Agnes. She told *Sun News* reporter Lauren Leach that her family was fearful of Frazier's next move. They had planned to keep their eyes open and not go out at night in case Frazier decided to return to North Carolina, despite the judge's order.

Agnes also related to the reporter how she had picked up three rolls of pictures she had developed, not realizing that one roll had been taken several years ago and contained photos of Brent when he was seven or eight. The sight of the pictures was bittersweet.

"I was thrilled," she said. "I found the pictures. I sat here and cried. But I believe finding the pictures of my son on the same day Frazier was released is more like a sign than a coincidence."

Pictures of Brent were a precious commodity indeed. Dee Mishler drove over to Marie Summey's house to ask for some more photographs of her brother. When Marie told her she did not have the photographs ready, Dee grew angry and began shoving and clawing at her.

"I hope your daughter rots in jail," Dee screamed, arms flailing.

"Don't you ever come back to my house again," Marie yelled back.

"You do the same," Dee answered.

Marie filed assault charges against Dee in the magistrate's court and showed them the scratch marks on her face and neck. Dee said she planned on filing her own charges. It was truly a black day for both families.

Renee was beginning to believe she would remain in jail forever, until finally it was announced her bond hearing would take place on Tuesday, December 1. Just to make certain Renee was not being treated unfairly by the prosecution, Jack and Marie Summey mortgaged their home and hired Myrtle Beach attorney William Isaac Diggs.

Diggs had a solid reputation around Horry County as

someone who was tough and would not be bullied by the police or prosecution. He was confident Renee would be granted bail.

"Renee is willing to cooperate," Diggs told the *Sun News*. "She wants the killer to go to jail, but the problem is, they won't work with her at all unless she is willing to plead guilty to murder. And why should she plead guilty to something she didn't do?" Diggs stated he wanted a trial in January or February. "In this case, I don't believe they have the evidence, and I don't believe they will ever prove it beyond a reasonable doubt."

During Frazier's bond hearing in October, Wilson had heard Morgan Martin say Frazier was adamant in the fact he was not guilty. That meant Frazier would be less inclined to plead guilty, but the prosecution had more evidence against Poole anyway. Since she had already confessed to participating with Frazier in a plot to kill her husband, he believed her attorneys would be receptive to a plea bargain. In exchange for Renee's testimony against John Frazier, the state offered a reduced sentence.

"A non capital murder conviction in South Carolina carries a sentence of thirty years to life," Wilson reminded Renee and her attorneys. "And that means life. You are in there until you're dead."

Renee rejected the state's offer, stating she was not about to confess to something she did not do. The police half-expected Renee would have accepted the plea bargain and a reduced sentence, try to pin it all on John and make him the fall guy. It would have been so easy for her to concoct a new story, claiming that it was all John's idea and that he had planned it without her knowledge. It wouldn't be out of character for her.

But that didn't happen. Bill Diggs warned Renee's parents they were in for a fight. The decision not to seek the death penalty against Renee was conditioned upon her full cooperation in terms of testifying against Frazier and pleading guilty to a substantial prison sentence of fifteen to twenty years.

"It appears that the Poole family is extremely bitter towards Renee," Diggs wrote to the Summeys. "So much so that they would rather Frazier go free than to see the state enter into a negotiated agreement with Renee wherein she is spared a lengthy prison sentence. Indeed, the Poole family would rather see the opposite: a deal extended to Frazier in exchange for his testimony against Renee. If Renee wants to plead not guilty, the state will seek the death penalty against her."

Even though the police and prosecution thought Renee would turn, she surprisingly continued to protect John. They may have had their own special reasons for killing Brent—John to have Renee, and Renee to have Katie, the insurance money, and everything else that Brent had—but she was stubbornly playing hardball by indicating she had no interest in cutting a deal against John. Renee and John were showing more loyalty and more stand-up toughness than originally suspected.

During Renee's bond hearing, Ralph Wilson announced he was seeking the death penalty against Renee. Renee grew teary-eyed as she sat in court and watched Wilson hand her attorney a copy of the death penalty notice.

"Her part was to lure him down to a certain location, knowing beforehand he was going to be killed," Wilson announced to circuit judge John Breeden. After listening to Wilson's argument, he denied bond, despite Diggs's request that it be set at $100,000.

Diggs told reporters outside the courtroom that the solicitor invoked the death penalty against Renee to pressure her into a deal. Wilson said he intended to seek the death penalty all along. The only problem was, Wilson would not be there when it came up. In November, Wilson had been locked in a dogfight with North Myrtle Beach lawyer Greg Hembree for his third term as prosecutor, and he lost his bid for reelection.

"I had hoped to leave the call to my successor," Wilson added. "He takes office January thirteenth. But Diggs had forced my hand by asking a judge to consider releasing Poole on bond. Bond can't be considered in a death penalty case, so either I had to act or let her out of jail. But I didn't do it just to keep her in jail."

Diggs said that Wilson was just bluffing because he had no real evidence and the tapes that police made of Renee's interrogation showed that police bullied and threatened her into agreeing with their propositions rather than confessing.

"It is inappropriate for me or Diggs to discuss the evidence in this case in a public forum prior to trial," Wilson responded, "but what I will say is that I have heard most of the tapes, too. And I am convinced there is substantial evidence on which to base a conviction and a death penalty.

"The evidence against Poole is much stronger than what I believe the evidence against Frazier is at this time," he said. "But that does not mean we will not serve the death penalty on him at some time, either."

Outside the courtroom, Bill Poole said he was disappointed Frazier was released on bond and thought his case qualified for the death penalty, along with Renee's. It had been almost twenty-five weeks since their son had been shot. December 1 was also Katie's third birthday.

"What makes it so difficult is the role she played," Bill said to the press. "She deserves the punishment for the crime she committed, even if that means death."

While they talked, Jack Summey walked across the courtyard with Marie and toward the Pooles. "I hope you're happy!" he shouted at them. "You got what you asked for? Is this Katie's birthday present?"

Bill did not respond. Jack was quickly ushered away by officials. As he and Marie were walking away, a reporter stuck a camera in her face and she swung her pocketbook and knocked it away. "Get that goddamned camera out of my face and you get the hell out of my face," she said angrily.

Wearing an aqua dress with a floral print, Renee was led out of the courtroom and to a waiting patrol car, handcuffed with chains around her waist. Once alone, and inside the partitioned backseat, she looked down at her lap and bit her lower lip as TV cameras surrounded the car.

A week later, Renee told Lauren Leach of the *Sun News* in an exclusive interview, she had expected the death penalty. "I expected the worst," she said in an interview room at the J. Reuben Long Detention Center in Conway, where she was accompanied by attorney Diggs and C. E. Martin, a private investigator Diggs had hired for the case.

Poole still insisted she was innocent. Although she admitted having affairs during their marriage, she told Leach she loved Brent, did not kill him and did not plot to have him killed. She said she would rather risk receiving the death sentence by going to trial than plead guilty.

In a lengthy, front-page feature complete with photo spreads of Renee, Leach wrote that Renee planned on testifying at her trial. "I'm not scared to die as long as my daughter knows her mommy is innocent. I don't want to die for something I did not do."

Renee had said one of the few highlights in her life was talking with Katie on the phone. She was fully aware that Brent's parents had gained temporary custody of Katie and was brokenhearted she couldn't be with Katie on her third birthday. She had sent Katie a birthday card, a letter and drawings she had drawn of a clown, a unicorn and a cake.

"I cried," Renee said.

But more than anything, Poole hoped she would be at home with her daughter on Katie's next birthday. She told Leach that if she was found not guilty, she planned to return home, go to school and study computers. "I'm not going to have negativity run me out of the town I was brought up in," she said.

Even if Diggs had filed a motion for a speedy trial before a judge, it would have been impossible to pull together a trial in January or February, most likely early summer. At last, Renee's and Brent Poole's families agreed on something in that they both thought it was not fair that Frazier was free while Renee was still in jail. Her parents said that Renee should have been released on bond, too, while Brent's family wanted them both in jail until their trials started.

In November, the estate of William Brent Poole filed a civil suit against Kimberly Renee Poole and John Boyd Frazier for the wrongful death of Brent Poole. But it never moved forward and was eventually dropped.

As the holidays approached, Renee reminisced about her favorite Christmas.

"It was in 1997, when Katie was two. She was fascinated with the lights and decorations, and got excited about ripping into her presents. I bought Brent several model Mack Trucks from Danbury Mint and Franklin Mint. I ended up spending twenty-five hundred altogether on him. Just the look on his face was enough to make me happy. That was our first Christmas in our new house and our first tree. We went tree shopping and found a six-foot tree that was fat. Brent wanted colored lights, so I let him have his way with that and let him handle decorating the porch and bushes while I decorated the tree. I'd been busy buying Disney collectibles ornaments and a Winnie the Pooh tree topper. I didn't receive any gifts from Brent that year, but it didn't matter to me. Just seeing his and Katie's excitement was my gift."

But now, in the worst Christmas of all, she'd lost Brent, missed Katie and was away from her whole family. She was lonely and in a jailhouse, surrounded by people she didn't know and she didn't care to know. The jail was filthy and cold; stinky and unsanitary. She had been there long enough to see some people come and go, and it unnerved her to think that these people had freedom but chose to keep coming back to jail. She had no choice but to stay in her private hell hole, but she just wanted to go home. Brent was gone and it hurt. But it also hurt her that Katie was without both of them. Katie was a part of him, and if she could just be with her, it would make things a little easier.

Perhaps that was what had motivated Renee's parents to sneak Katie into the prison to see her mother. The Pooles were furious when they learned what had happened and threatened to cut off all ties completely. For Renee, it didn't matter what they did. One day, she would get out of prison and get her daughter back from them.

CHAPTER 28

The new year promised hope for John Boyd Frazier's defense team. In a press conference held on February 12, 1999, Jane Lovett's voice was filled with emotion as she stood before the Winston-Salem press and declared her son's innocence. Reading from a prepared statement from her attorneys, she announced, "My son, John Frazier, has been arrested and charged with [the] murder of Brent Poole, but he is not guilty."

Lovett and one of her Myrtle Beach attorneys, Tommy Brittain, described another possible suspect who may have gunned down Brent Poole and presented a police sketch of a white man of average build with light-colored, shoulder-length hair.

"There is evidence of an identifiable suspect," Lovett proposed. "He was observed at or near the crime scene and was dressed in all black."

Lovett and her son's attorney wouldn't elaborate about the man they were searching for, but said the information was recently developed by their private investigator, Darrell Wilson. Wilson would tell reporters the next day that he discovered the key suspect that the Myrtle Beach police had ignored.

Referring to the composite of the blond-haired man police had constructed after talking with Christopher Hensley, Wilson said they had "just sort of deep-sixed it and lost it. They didn't want to pursue it. But I've found two witnesses who put a blond-haired man dressed in black in the area of the slaying, within ten to fifteen minutes of the time it occurred. He doesn't have a name and I need help finding him, but he's out there somewhere." Frazier's family was offering a $10,000 reward for additional information leading to the arrest and conviction of the person who shot Brent Poole and resulting in the dismissal of the charges against John.

Solicitor Greg Hembree scoffed at the idea. "The way this was handled (I received a fax after the news conference) is a whole lot more Barnum and Bailey than it is law and order. But finding another suspect near the crime scene at the time of the killing is not that impressive. For heaven's sake, it was summertime at the beach."

Myrtle Beach police supported Hembree's summation. In a written statement, they stated that no new information had been developed that would lessen their belief that John Frazier was the true perpetrator in this murder.

Renee was running her own public-relations campaign from prison, still insisting that John Frazier was her husband's killer. In a jailhouse interview with Christopher Guinn, of the *Winston-Salem Journal,* in early March, she described her time with Frazier as a fling and not a relationship.

"Sex really didn't happen before I knew him at least for a month," she said. "It was a fling and that was all. There is a difference between a relationship and a fling."

Renee told Guinn she never had any intention of a permanent relationship with Frazier. There had been other affairs before him and she had sought Frazier for sex and attention because she was lonely and Brent was not paying her or Katie the daily attention she thought they deserved. After she had moved in briefly with Frazier, Brent had pleaded with her to return, but was feeling awful. She told Frazier she thought about killing herself and that was when he made the remarks about finding another solution.

"He said, 'Well, why don't you kill him?' He brought up a couple of ways. . . . I said, 'What are you talking about?' That is when he brought up the beach trip. He said, 'Your anniversary is coming up. Where is he taking you?' I told him we were going to the Carolina Winds. He said, 'that's a nice hotel. I have family near there.' And he said, 'What if someone approached you?' And I can't recall, he said kill him, or hurt him, or injure him. But it was to the effect of doing harm to him. I said, 'What are you talking about?' He said, 'What if somebody robbed you and did this?' I told him he was crazy and don't do it. 'Don't do anything like that.'"

Renee said after police questioned her, she had thought about the proposal Frazier had made to her several weeks before, but she didn't tell police. "But the thought ran through my mind, yeah, but I didn't want to say that it was, because I wasn't sure." When police asked her again whether she and Frazier ever planned or conspired, or whether Frazier ever planned or said anything about killing Brent Poole, she recalled thinking about something Frazier had said that she hadn't taken seriously. That's when she had told them yes. When she answered that question, she said she was thinking of the what-if question Frazier had asked her weeks before, but was not admitting that she had conspired with him to do so.

Renee admitted she had told police she had taken part in her husband's killing, but said she had made those admissions because the police had interrogated her for hours without a break, threatened and screamed at her. They had pressured her and wore her down until she was willing to make those admissions, knowing full well they were not true and that they would get her into trouble.

"I know now that what I told the police wasn't true and made under duress. I don't know whether the man in black was John. If it was, he was acting alone." She said she loved her husband and didn't want to leave him. "We were going to go home and renew our vows and have another baby."

Guinn had also talked with Renee's former next-door neighbor Renee Bollow, who said that was not the Renee Poole she had remembered. "Renee told me that it was Brent Poole who wanted to have another baby, not her. She said, 'No way in hell.' That is what she told me. She also told me that she loved Frazier. That she had already talked to a lawyer about leaving her husband. If she were intent on staying with Brent, why would she do that?"

Dee Mishler was angry when Guinn told her what her sister-in-law had said. "Renee has already made her confession. Now that she is down to having to spend the rest of her life in jail or face death, she is going to renege on it. Like the prodigal son, Brent had returned to church during his last months of life. That may have caused more tension between Brent and Renee. I would love to believe that Renee had nothing to do with his death, but I think otherwise."

Agnes Poole said she believed that Renee had been a manipulator from the very beginning. "She manipulated Brent. We raised Brent to go to church, but after he started dating Renee, he stopped going to church. He started bringing home R-rated movies to watch with Renee until we asked him to stop. Anytime you have someone that goes against the beliefs you know they were raised with, it is disappointing."

Marie Summey was livid when she read in the newspaper what Dee and Agnes had said about her daughter. "Let those of us who are without sin throw the first stone. But if you're talking about going against someone's beliefs, have they forgotten that Dee had an affair with a Baptist deacon in their church? Don't they know that people who live in glass houses shouldn't throw stones?"

Things were really beginning to heat up in North Carolina.

The first-year anniversary of Brent Poole's death passed and the state had still not set a trial date for either Renee Poole or John Frazier. Renee and her family still hung all their hopes on Bill Diggs. Diggs had told them they had a defendable case. In fact, he had won a similar murder case in Myrtle Beach just last year, where there was a confession and inconsistencies in the confession. The client in that case admitted he had used a .25-caliber pistol to shoot a store clerk during a robbery, but the police's investigation later showed that the gun used was a .22-caliber pistol and he was acquitted.

Prosecutors had shown Diggs the evidence they had, and he saw immediately the case against Renee was weak and had a lot of problems. He was so confident in his ability to win this case, he went so far as to offer Renee a job with him when she was released from prison. She took him at his word.

Diggs also believed the change in the solicitor's office had helped their case. He cited the length of time it was taking for the state to prosecute Renee's case as an example of their difficulty to formulate enough evidence to get a conviction.

Although the newly elected solicitor Greg Hembree had never worked on a death penalty or a murder case, he had gained experience while working as an assistant solicitor in the largest solicitor's office in the state of South Carolina, the Fifth Judicial Circuit, in Richland County. "I prosecuted thousands of cases working in an office of twenty-plus lawyers," the North Myrtle Beach city attorney boasted. "In that atmosphere, I absorbed the methodology to run a big office. My number one responsibility is to be not only a good trial lawyer and chief operating officer, but to be a leader. You have to set a tone and give your soldiers marching orders."

Hembree was fortunate enough to have hired at the beginning of the year Fran Humphries as one of his deputy solicitors. Considered one of the most honest and honorable lawyers Hembree had ever worked with, Humphries' experience in the Lexington County prosecutor's office would be of great help to familiarize Hembree more with the case. Once those two lawyers were into it, they would first have to decide whether to try the two suspects together or separately.

Myrtle Beach captain Sam Hendrick said even if the trial doesn't start anytime soon, he didn't know that time would have any bearing on whether the state got a conviction or not.

"Certainly, we have a very good case against them," Hendrick said to the press. "You've seen the affidavits and warrants. There's plenty of evidence to support the charges. We have a good case against them. We've continued to work on the case, and certainly as time wears on, it gives us the opportunity to gain some additional evidence. We still are investigating, although the charges have already been made. All we're after is the truth."

The Pooles were supportive of the police and the prosecution.

They said they just wanted justice done—whether here on earth, or in the hereafter.

"I cannot imagine these two not being convicted," Dee Mishler stated. "I can't even think like that. They're just evil people. I hope the jury can see that."

It would be another five months before the jury would get their first look at either Renee or John. After an Horry County grand jury indicted the two defendants on August 26 for murder, conspiracy to commit murder and armed robbery, the prosecution asked they be tried separately. Renee would be the first to get her day in court on Monday, November 8, 1999.

CHAPTER 29

The trial Court TV had already dubbed the "Love Triangle Murder" was to be held at the Horry County Courthouse in Conway. The town of Conway, Horry County's seat, is exactly fifteen miles west of Myrtle Beach. Conway's population in 1998 was elven thousand, as compared to Myrtle Beach's 165,000. There are no high-rise hotels, fast-paced lifestyle, or adult entertainment clubs in Conway. People talk and move at a slower pace, and there are as many churches as there are businesses in this small Southern town. Bill Diggs wondered if his client could get a fair trial in Conway.

Renee missed her daughter greatly and was eager to be able to tell her side of the story finally. Renee's parents still had visitation rights, but it was very unlikely that Katie would spend any time with her mother at the Horry County Jail or at her trial. Oddly enough, Renee would celebrate her twenty-third birthday on her first day in court.

When Dee Mishler was asked before court began how Katie was doing, she answered, "Katie is wonderful and is doing great. She has held up well. Raising Katie has kept our family strong."

Renee's road to justice, however, would take a short detour.

Two days before Renee's trial was to begin, solicitor Hembree announced he was dropping the death penalty against Renee Poole. The solicitor believed a jury would agree with him that Renee had not only witnessed the entire scenario of Brent's murder, but had also willingly participated in the planning of it. And most jurors would probably understand, after having been explained the legal definition of "one hand is the hand of all," that she was just as culpable under the law as John Frazier. But would they feel comfortable enough to hand down a verdict of death? Renee was young, had no previous history of any crime and was still, after all, the mother of a 3½-year-old daughter. That had to mean something.

Brent Poole's family was not taken aback by the prosecution's decision not to seek the death penalty. "It's not an issue for us," Dee Mishler said. "This does not change the proof and the evidence. Our family has never said we wanted the death penalty for Renee. Brent's life cannot be brought back, regardless of what Renee's penalty is. We do not want revenge; we just want Renee and John to pay for what they did. We want justice."

Renee's mother, Marie Summey, said she was happy with the decision, but still believed that the call for the death penalty was only made to keep Renee in jail and away from Katie. If the prosecutors had not sought the death penalty, she may have been released on bond and could have been with her daughter all this time. Marie wondered what took the prosecution so long in deciding this.

"We have put it all in God's hands and Bill's hands and let it go," she said. "I know Renee is innocent and this just goes to prove how weak the prosecution's case really is."

But as the opening of the trial drew closer, the prosecution had actually grown much more confident in its case. They firmly believed they could weave a basket of physical and circumstantial evidence that could convince a jury that Renee Poole and John Frazier were lovers and they had conspired to murder her husband. It wasn't a matter of John just acting off his cuff because he wanted to have Renee. They could prove by her own admissions that they had had more than just a conversation about it. After all, she had, in the presence of her lawyer, admitted John had killed her husband, then later confessed she had helped him plan it.

The prosecution planned on playing Renee's taped interviews with the police and let her own statements be her own undoing. Even though they couldn't produce the murder weapon, they were convinced they could string enough facts and technical information together to prove Brent had been killed with a gun that John previously had owned. And because she and John had acted in concert, she was just as guilty as if she had pulled the trigger.

Of course, problematic for the defense were the statements Renee had made to the police. Her attorneys would have no alternative but to try and construct a defense around the age-old scenario that she had been coerced by the police into a confession. Diggs admitted before the trial that Renee's life was a tangled tale, but claimed her case was a classic example of false confession. Tight-lipped John Frazier had said nothing to the police and they had not one iota of physical evidence linking him to the crime scene. Outside of Renee's confession and a possible eyewitness, who looked shaky, Diggs thought their case against Renee was based solely on speculation and innuendo. What motive did Renee have for killing her husband? And if she had wanted to, couldn't she have easily blamed it on Frazier and walked away?

Although Court TV had already announced it would televise the Renee Poole trial at a later date, all the major-network news reporters still planned to cover the trial. Horry County's judicial junkies predicted a lackluster event. The interest in the case stirred heavily from western North Carolina, but produced little-to-no interest from Horry County. Horry County's biggest trial of the century had already taken place six years earlier in 1993 with the conviction of Ken Register. Nineteen-year-old Register had been arrested and tried for the murder of Conway High School senior Crystal Todd, a friend. Crowds of two-hundred or more spectators stood in line every day for a seat at the controversial two-week death penalty trial. In a courtroom overflowing and bursting at its seams, solicitor Ralph Wilson convinced the jury that Register was the only person in the world who could have killed Todd. Working against Register was his own admission to the crime and a collected DNA sample identifying him as the killer. The jury found him guilty, but thanks to the efforts of defense counsel Morgan Martin and Tommy Brittain, the jurors showed mercy and spared his life.

The Poole case, so sensational in the "Tar Heel State," raced on toward a trial in South Carolina with much work for both sides still needing to be done. The prosecution wanted to make sure they had tied up all loose ends and had all their evidence and presentation materials ready for trial. The defense would argue then—and throughout the trial—that they felt rushed and had not been given enough time to prepare their case and schedule their expert witnesses.

Nevertheless, when the Honorable Edward B. Cottingham called the court to order on Monday morning, nearly two hundred jurors-to-be were ready and seated in the second-floor auditorium. The old courthouse resembled a refurbished schoolhouse auditorium. The seats squeaked and squawked every time someone stood up and sat down, but it didn't seem to bother Cottingham.

Judge Cottingham had a reputation for maintaining firm control of his courtroom. Cottingham's forty-five years of experience as a former defense lawyer and trial judge was nearly twice as long as Renee Poole had lived. Short and broad, with ghost-pale skin and thinning white hair, he was a tough, nononsense judge with a wit as dry and quick as a late-night comedian. Throughout his trials, especially when he got excited, he would stumble through his words or refer to people by the wrong name, prompting his clerks or the attorneys to respectfully "remind" him of his error. But lawyers from both sides of the law who had challenged and bantered with Cottingham on legal issues would be the first to say he got their respect. As predictable as a summer storm that followed a formation of dark clouds, he was known to lean across his desk and gaze down at the trial participants before issuing one of his scathing reprimands, "That'll never happen in Judge Cottingham's courtroom." However, lawyers appreciated him for his consistency. They always knew there would be no monkey business of any kind in his courtroom.

Prosecution and defense attorneys sat in comfortable leather chairs at the large, rectangular wooden tables at the front of the courtroom facing the judge and the court reporter. Family members took their seats behind the prosecution or defense, while potential jurors sat behind them in less comfortable chairs.

Renee had been brought in from the back of the courthouse, up the elevator and escorted in chains to the second-floor auditorium. She had traded her shackles and prison-issued orange jumpsuit, worn during her preliminary hearings, for a conservative, dark blue pantsuit. She donned a pair of gold-rimmed eyeglasses and silver earrings. Her long, dark hair had been cut, pulled back and adorned with a gold hair bow. She wore a little eye shadow, a touch of rouge and a bit of red lipstick. It was obvious she had been "toned" down for trial, looking nothing like the sultry stripper Carlee who had once danced and trolled the stage floor at the Silver Fox Gentleman's Club, collecting dollar bills like they were rose petals.

Cottingham began the trial by explaining the charges. He then asked Renee to stand and face the jury panel. She seemed nervous as the judge reminded them this was not a death penalty case. It took only one day for Cottingham to whittle down a jury from more than 225 perspective jurors to a panel of twelve jurors and two alternates, evenly divided between men and women.

The defense gave a hint as to what cards they were playing in their hand when Diggs excused the first eight male candidates. In order to give a fair and impartial rendering to his client, Diggs believed it required a jury of *her* peers. He thought he had struck pay dirt when one female candidate revealed she worked at a bar from 7:00 P.M. to about 3:00 A.M. in the morning. When she asked to be dismissed due to a hardship it would place on her child, Diggs protested heavily.

"Your Honor, just for the record, and not singling out this particular juror," he pleaded, "but this is the objection that we've made before in these types of cases. When you've got a general exclusion of young women from the jury just because of their children, it impacts on the cross-sectional representation of the jury."

Cottingham listened to Diggs's objection, but did not bend. "I understand what you're saying. But if a mother comes to me and says that there's nobody to take care of that child at night but her, what do you think this court ought to do?"

Diggs offered a knee-jerk response that the county should provide some type of child care in those situations, but Cottingham made light of it.

Where some trials take days, even weeks, for the voir dire, Judge Cottingham had his jurors already selected, had given them their instructions and dismissed them, along with the other potential jurors, shortly after lunch. By 3:45 P.M., he announced to the lawyers he was ready to hear their motions.

It was obvious the defense still had a bee in its bonnet over their client's previous death penalty charge. When assistant solicitor Humphries reported they had not received any of the expert witness reports from the defense, Diggs stated evasively that a biographical sketch and the subject matter of their testimony had been forwarded. And he believed, under the discovery rules, that was all they were entitled to.

Cottingham wouldn't hear of it. He expected a report from every one of these witnesses regardless of what excuse they had for not providing it. He asked Diggs to send them this message: "You telephone those witnesses and tell them that before they are permitted to testify, a written report will be required. Or they will not be permitted and they certainly won't be paid."

Diggs stirred the pot again with the death penalty issue. The problem, he insisted, was when the solicitor dropped the death penalty, it sped everything up. It had thrown a wrench in his spokes and screwed up his schedule for expert witnesses, who had already agreed to be there the following week. Furthermore, Diggs squabbled, the notice of the death penalty against their client had generated a lot of pretrial publicity and they were concerned as to what extent it would have on the outcome of this case.

"For the record," Diggs submitted, "among other things, I

believe when the death penalty was served at the bond hearing in December of 1998, it was done for one purpose. And that was to prevent this defendant from being admitted to bail and released on bond."

Diggs pointed out that the indictment against Renee Poole didn't come until August 1999, and then the withdrawal of the bond notice came after that—two working days before the call of the case for the trial. Renee had sat in jail all that time from June 1998, while her codefendant, John Frazier, had already been released on bond.

"The shooter in this case was released on bond under the state's theory of the case and she wasn't," Diggs went on to say. "And the only reason for that was because they wanted to squeeze her, as we put in the motion. To testify, provide evidence and certain testimony, and when that didn't happen, they served a death notice in the case just to keep her in jail—to prevent her from being released on bond. The fact that her codefendant, who is not under a death penalty notice, was released on bond—and the fact that he was the shooter—is strong evidence that she would have been admitted to bail and released on bond, and she's had a constitutional right deprived for seventeen months because of that action by the state. What other remedy do we have in that situation other than to dismiss the charge?"

It took Cottingham all of five minutes to assure Diggs that Judge Breeden had the right to refuse his client bond—even if the death penalty notice had not been there. He denied him the motion to dismiss the trial and told him in no uncertain terms that if he didn't agree, then take his arguments to another forum.

Diggs gave it one last shot. Shifting anxiously at his table, he warned, "The confidence the general public is gonna have in the procedure that was used in this case [is at stake]. And that's not where we want to go when we've got a young person's life at stake in terms of spending the rest of her life in jail. We've already got a tragic situation in the death of Brent Poole. There's no doubt about it. We've got another potentially tragic situation by having an innocent person in jail. Our point is that it undermines the confidence in the system to which Your Honor has a chance to show—"

Cottingham cut him off. He let Diggs know right away the monkey was not on his back. "It is expressed in the verdict of the jury, who will hear the testimony, and I have full confidence that the jury will do what they perceive to be right and what the evidence suggests, and in my view, that's where the confidence is in the court."

And with that being said, a little housekeeping was done, and with nothing more from the prosecution and defense, court was adjourned at 4:30 P.M. On the way out of the courtroom, reporter Adam Shapiro, with News Channel 12, announced he was taking bets that Renee Poole would walk. Nobody offered to side against him.

CHAPTER 30

The trial of the *State of South Carolina* v. *Kimberly Renee Poole* reconvened Wednesday, November 10, at 9:30 A.M. Adam Shapiro and his television crew was there to film it. He talked with Marie Summey before the trial started and told her not to worry, he wouldn't be around to question her when the verdict was handed down. "Well, don't you worry," she told him. "John and Renee are coming home."

As a courtesy to the defense, Judge Cottingham had given them an extra day to prepare and meet with their witnesses. The jurors now sat in much more comfortable chairs to the left of the prosecution's table, and adjacent to the camera crew from Court TV. Cottingham made it clear to the jury a second time that the state was not seeking the death penalty against Renee Poole. The burden of proof, however, was on the state to prove her guilty beyond a reasonable doubt. The indictment was for murder and criminal conspiracy.

Greg Hembree and Fran Humphries, both dressed in dark blue suits, sat at the prosecution table beside Bill Diggs, his attorney son Parnell Diggs and co-counsel Orrie West. At the end of the defense table private investigator C. E. Martin sat to the right of Renee and helped with the workload. His presence would be explained later by the defense in detail.

The victim's and defendant's families sat directly behind their respective attorneys, along with their supportive staff members. As normally occurs in a trial, the lawyers and staff members continually exchanged whispers and shuffled paperwork throughout the proceedings. For some odd reason, there was one large wooden chair in the courtroom—directly behind and in the middle of the prosecution and defense tables—that was elevated approximately twelve inches off the floor. Unbeknownst to anyone but himself, Detective Terry Altman made this his special seat. It gave him the appearance of being in an elevated position, and he sat there, grinning like a Cheshire cat who had finally caught his songbird. A small, insignificant matter, yet it seemed to give the prosecution a large boost in the courtroom.

Sitting to the right of the defense table in the gallery reserved for newsprint reporters was John Hinton, of the *Winston-Salem Journal*. For several days, Hinton would be the lone wolf covering the trial, writing dozens of articles about the Poole murder case. North Carolina television reporters and their cameramen were positioned in the balcony, appreciative of having been granted a bird's-eye view of the proceedings. Outside the courtroom, their parked satellite vans beamed the news back daily to their affiliates, just in time to share with their interested viewers. Judge Cottingham had given permission for the use of cameras and tape recorders in the courtroom, but disallowed the use of any strobes or camera flashes. The handful of spectators sitting in the gallery behind the families believed from what they had read in the newspaper that the prosecution and his team already had the upper hand. There seemed to be no unreasonable doubt the suspects were lovers and that love or jealously was always motive enough for murder.

Renee looked straight ahead when the judge read Count 1 of the indictment:

> *Kimberly Renee Poole along with John Boyd Frazier did in Horry County on or about June the 9th of 1998, willfully, feloniously, and intentionally, with malice aforethought, kill the victim, William Brent Poole, by means of shooting the victim twice in the head, and the*

victim did die as a proximate result thereof in Horry County on or about June the 9th, 1998.

Count 2 involved criminal conspiracy in that:

Kimberly Renee Poole did in Horry County on or about June the 9th of 1998, and dates preceding, unlawfully, knowingly, willfully, and feloniously, unite, combine, conspire, confederate, agree, and have tacit understanding with John Boyd Frazier and/or with other Persons, whose names are unknown to the Grand Jurors, for the purposes of committing the offense of murder of William Brent Poole.

Bill Diggs glanced at his client and took a deep breath, knowing he was about to begin a tough battle against the state. He had already filed his motions to try and stop the onslaught, arguing with the judge that Renee had been slighted from the day she had been arrested. But it had fallen on deaf ears.

Diggs was also about to discover that solicitor Hembree and deputy solicitor Humphries were meticulous lawyers who had done their homework. They had crossed all their t's and dotted all their i's. Not only would he have to play a near-perfect game of defense to get Renee acquitted, throughout the course of the trial, he also would have to defend the prosecution's accusations against John Frazier. It was not an enviable position. With Court TV airing the event in its entirety, and other news crews taping for nightly broadcasts, Diggs found himself in the battle of his career with the prosecution pulling out all the stops.

Fran Humphries was the first to draw blood. He kept his opening statement brief, telling the jury what he was going to prove to them and how he would present witnesses to substantiate his opening statement. He stood directly in front of the jurors and never broke eye contact. In a soft and low voice, he laid out the prosecution's case.

"In late April or so of 1998, Kimberly Renee Poole became

so confined by the walls which were her ordinary life—you know the life that I talk about, the life that most of us aspire to—those walls became so confining to her that she developed a plan, a plan with a lover that she had had for about three months at the time. And on May 1, 1998, Kimberly Renee Poole, this defendant, took her two-and-a-half-year-old daughter, boxed up her belongings and, in the dead of night while her husband was at work, moved out of the marital residence and moved in with a fellow named John Boyd Frazier.

"Now, folks, if that were the end of it, it would be an age-old sad story, divorce and moving on, but Mrs. Poole got some good advice. She got some good advice which told her, 'Mrs. Poole, if you believe that based on your circumstances, having left the marital residence, having no reputable and steady employment, and in the midst of an adulterous affair, you think you're gonna keep this child, you are sorely mistaken.'

"On May fifteenth, Kimberly Renee Poole moved back in with her husband, our victim, William Brent Poole. Now, was she happy about it? No, ma'am. No, sir. And the evidence will show you. What did she do about it? She treated this situation just as she had treated each and every situation in her life. What Kimberly Renee Poole wanted, Kimberly Renee Poole got.

"That home was not the place for her, but she wanted it all. And, folks, there was only one way to have it all. Oh, she wanted the home, but she didn't want the husband. And in the first week of June, after having moved back in with her long-suffering husband, she meets with her lover and a number of others, and over the course of an evening, plans a trap which will ultimately gain her that one thing she wants, which, folks, is everything.

"They planned it in meticulous detail, leaving absolutely nothing to chance. They set the trap, folks, with the one bait that this man, William Brent Poole, could not resist, and that was this: William Brent Poole, hoping against hope, hoped for a meaningful reunion with his wife. A reuniting of his family. Father, mother and daughter. Kimberly Renee Poole proposed to William Brent Poole that they take a vacation, that they celebrate their third anniversary, that they do that in Myrtle

Beach, and on June 9, 1998, in the very late evening hours, on their anniversary, Kimberly Renee Poole walked her husband of three years, the father of her daughter, down an Horry County beach, away from the lights, to her lover, John Boyd Frazier. And there in the darkness, ladies and gentlemen, John Boyd Frazier shot and killed William Brent Poole.

"Folks, this is a murder case. Now I've already told you that Kimberly Renee Poole didn't pull the trigger. This case is founded upon a legal principle called the law of parties. Now the judge is gonna charge you about the law in this case, but as a preface to that, let me tell you this: The law of parties basically is this; it's more commonly called the hand of one is the hand of all, and what it means is this. If one is present, if one is aiding and abetting or participating, even though that person does not have the finger on the trigger, that person is equally— folks, equally—as guilty as the person who pulls the trigger and fires the fatal shots.

"That principle is founded in common sense because I tell you this, ladies and gentlemen, but for the conduct of Kimberly Renee Poole in this instance, William Brent Poole, husband, father and son, would not be dead.

"Over the course of the next few days, the state will present to you a number of witnesses, maybe as much as thirty-five or forty. We'll start at the crime scene. From there, we'll go back, because that is really where the story is.

"Now, you may ask me, 'Mr. Solicitor, how do you know all of this? How do you know all of this?' She told us. Kimberly Renee Poole. She talked to law enforcement immediately after, and in her first contact with law enforcement, she described an armed robbery and murder by an unknown male assailant in dark clothing. That's where she starts, but, folks, over the course of the next four days, Kimberly Renee Poole, predator, becomes prey, and as walls, which she absolutely abhors, when they come in and start to enclose her, then and only then does she begin to trickle out the truth.

"You'll have the opportunity to hear all those statements and, more importantly, folks, you'll hear the evidence which supports those statements, at least in the portions that are true, by a number of witnesses whose credibility you'll judge.

"This is a murder case. This is a case based on a conspiracy and this is a case in which our victim, William Brent Poole, but for the actions of his wife of three years, a woman who wanted it all, would be alive today. Folks, it will require your absolute certain attention to detail, because, folks, it is the details. . . .

"But I tell you, folks, today and the next few days are maybe some of the most important days you'll breathe on this earth because you have a unique opportunity in this trial to speak the truth when you render your verdict because that's that—that means, to speak the truth."

Humphries thanked the jurors for their service in his closing remarks, then gave way to the defense.

Bill Diggs rose to make his opening statement and addressed the jurors.

"Having staked out what the state's position is in this case," he began, "I want you to think for just a minute about this: what if he is wrong? I want you to think a minute about what this young girl, this young woman, has been through herself for the last year and a half.

"They are public servants. They are doing their jobs, but they better hope that they're right, because if they are wrong we've compounded a tragedy. The tragedy of Brent Poole's death with another tragedy, and that is forcing her to go through an accusation of the most terrible kind that we could make in our society. I want you to think about this. What if they are wrong?

"Now, the state has the burden of proof in this case. Your job is to hold him to that burden of proof, which he says he's gonna make and meet. He's already told you my client"—Diggs asked Renee to stand, then introduced her to the jury—"This is Kimberly Renee Poole. She's the only one you're sitting in judgment of. That's her."

Renee sat back down and Diggs continued.

"He's already told you she didn't pull the trigger. She didn't kill her husband. You don't have to worry about that. That's not an issue in this case. Somebody pulled the trigger. He told you it was John Frazier, and so the only issue that you have to decide, was she conspiring with him to bring that about? And I'm gonna tell you right now, and you can take this to the bank, he's not gonna be able to prove it. He's not gonna be able to prove it, because it didn't happen.

"Fortunately, and thank heavens for technology, he tells you she told them she did this. Gonna have a chance not to just take his word for that. You're gonna have a chance to listen to her own words. After eleven or twelve hours of interrogation, on and on and on, to see what she said, look at the conditions under which she said those things, and you make a decision right there as to whether or not we've got a reliable statement here that we can take to the bank and convict this young girl on. That's a decision you're gonna have to make and it's not gonna get the state where it wants to go, because it didn't happen."

Diggs cautioned them not to make up their mind until all the facts were in. "You talk about reasonable doubt, you're gonna have two, at least two. Very strong and overpowering doubts that compel a not guilty verdict. You're gonna have doubts in this case for two basic fundamental reasons, completely disassociated from one another, based on the evidence in this case. They are gonna be completely unrelated, either one of which is gonna require a verdict of not guilty.

"It's a tragedy that brings us here, and we don't apologize for that. That's tragic. This family is entitled to justice, but I will bet you they're the first ones who would say, 'We want the killer of our son brought to justice. We don't want an innocent person instead or in lieu of that person,' and that's your job. Not only to determine who the killer was, but to make sure an innocent person doesn't stand in lieu of that killer.

"This is a hard, demanding job that you're gonna have. Hold me to my representations. I don't mind you doing that. You just hold the solicitor to the representations that he made.

"We appreciate your participation in this case. Without you, simply pointing the finger or using the state to point the finger at Renee, and that would do it for her. Thank heavens we don't live in that society."

Across the courtroom, Renee sat uncomfortably. She grimaced at Diggs when he sat down. In a methodical, concise, step-by-step manner, the prosecution called its witnesses one at a time to relate to the jurors a horrific sequence of events that led to Brent's murder. Rather than using high-tech resources, such as PowerPoint, 3-D computer displays or an array of expensive audiovisual equipment, they made their case the old-fashioned way and kept everything straight by presenting facts, dates, timelines and maps mounted on Styrofoam boards. Renee followed along nervously, her eyes darting between the prosecution and defense attorneys as they revealed her complicated, tangled life.

The prosecution would build its case with a parade of twenty-nine witnesses over the span of six days. The majority of those testifying were professional people and employed by law enforcement agencies. It was a progressive revelation as to why Renee Poole had wanted her husband dead. There was so much information that the prosecution had to painstakingly construct their full deck, one card at a time. At certain moments during the trial, some of the jurors displayed incredulous looks at what they were seeing and hearing. It was apparent that a few of them, especially the female jurors, had led lives where they had never been exposed to things from Renee's life that were being discussed in the courtroom.

In the two days the defense were scheduled to call its witnesses, it would be unlikely they could gather enough steam to do even the slightest damage to the prosecution's case. And it appeared a very weak challenge if they intended to use only ten called witnesses. Of the ten, only two were expert witnesses, while the remainder were either Renee's family or her friends.

CHAPTER 31

The first witness of the trial was Myrtle Beach patrol officer Scott Brown, who had been patrolling the beach the night Brent Poole had been murdered. Renee had flagged him down to say her husband had been murdered. He would testify about the incident and her demeanor when he first made contact with her on the beach.

"'In shock' is about the best way I could put it," he stated. "She was not screaming and flailing around, but she was extremely upset." He would later describe how she had reacted when he found her on the beach. She had fallen to her knees and knelt down beside her husband. She remained trembling and crying the entire time. She had picked up his hand, crying, and had started rubbing his hand.

At one point, Hembree asked Brown, "What if anything did she tell you about the instructions by the killer?"

Brown stated that the suspect had told them to lay down on the beach. "She told me that she had done so, and as soon as she laid down, she heard two shots. And at that time, the shooter ran toward the sand dunes."

Hembree asked at the end of his testimony, "I have one more question for you. What was the condition of the defendant's T-shirt? Did it have anything on it?"

Brown testified that he got a good look at her shirt and there was nothing on it. There was no sand on the back of it. There was sand in the front seat where he had placed her in the driver's side, but there was no sand on the back of the seat. He said his seats had had regular cloth seats on them.

On cross-examination, Diggs pointed out the sand in the vehicle had to come from somewhere. And the fact that she flagged the officer down had to imply she was trying to get emergency help for her husband, that she was in shock.

"Shock . . . meandering." Diggs emphasized the buzz-words before asking Brown, "Given your understanding of what was taking place, was that pretty normal of what you would expect in that situation?"

Brown said that it would depend on the person. He'd seen both sides.

"But she *was* in shock?" The level of Diggs's voice rose in indignation.

"Yes, sir, she was," Brown answered.

Diggs painted a portrait of a woman who was crying and extremely upset. He made Brown admit she was trembling when he first talked with her and was still trembling when she picked up her husband's hand and held it.

"Officer Brown, do you recall it being just a general conversation that you were having with her, or was she still in shock and was she still trembling while you were speaking to her?"

"Yes, she was still trembling and forcefully crying. She kept her hands cupped over her mouth and nose."

Diggs got Brown to consider that Renee was "noticeably crying with force, even to say it might have been controlled panic to some extent."

"Could say that," Brown interjected.

"One last question, Officer Brown," Diggs promised. "When you saw her, did it appear to you that she was seeking you out as opposed to maybe trying to evade being seen by you at that time?"

"Neither," he answered. "She appeared to be a normal beach walker, just walking toward me."

"Toward you?" Diggs repeated. "But you never got any—any indication that she might be trying to hide from you?"

"No."

If the spectators were keeping score, Diggs would have won that round on points. But the next three witnesses would have been scored as a draw.

Private First Class A. L. "Lewis" Aiossa, second shift in the beach patrol, was on duty that same night Brent was killed and had responded to the scene. With the help of a previously drawn diagram of the crime scene mounted on the Styrofoam poster, he highlighted and described the area from the high-rise hotel at Seventy-sixth Avenue, the Carolina Winds, up to Eighty-second Avenue, and beyond the northern end of Myrtle Beach. He concluded with the response of the officers and emergency personnel and how they sealed the area and protected the crime scene.

Diggs did little on cross, except accuse the officers of interrogating Renee from the very beginning.

The second witness, Karole Jensen, identified her home on the diagram and stated she heard a series of firecracker noises at 11:45 P.M. and a man's voice coming from the beach and in front of her next-door neighbor's house. Jensen didn't see a lot, but what she had heard was significant. Her testimony had pinned down the time of the shooting. Officer Brown had testified earlier he had placed his first call at 11:51 P.M., that was six minutes after Brent had been shot. Jensen had also said she had heard no one screaming, only the sound of a man's voice. The prosecution hoped the jurors would speculate that some of the six minutes it took for Renee to flag down Officer Brown she had spent talking with John Frazier.

Corporal David Grazioso, crime scene witness, reported what had been found at the crime scene, documented and marked as evidence. Of note was a photograph shown to the jury documenting the empty 9mm cartridges at the scene and where they were found. Four live 9mm cartridges and two fired 9mm casings had been found in the immediate crime scene area. They were presented and introduced, along with twenty-one other state exhibits. Humphries had Grazioso hold each photo exhibit up and identify its found location on the Styrofoam board.

The prosecution had placed valuable property at the scene,

especially the wedding rings of both Renee and Brent. If this was a robbery, they contended, why would these items still be there? Had the robber gotten spooked and spilled his loot? Or, as the prosecution wanted the jury to conclude, the robbery had never occurred at all.

Orrie West needed to offer an explanation of how all that stuff got there. On cross-examination, she got Grazioso to say that any of the evidence—i.e. cigarette pack, change and a towel found at the crime scene—would not be uncommon to find at the beach. As far as the wedding band and the unspent 9mm cartridges, who was to say that the robber didn't get spooked, was in a hurry, fumbled with the stuff and found it difficult to find in the sand? It could have happened exactly like that.

The prosecution laid rest to this theory, however, with their fourth witness, seventy-five-year-old Howard Sirles. Sirles lived in Richmond, Virginia, but had been visiting his beach house on Myrtle Beach Drive when he found Brent's wallet in his yard. He told the jury about the condition of the wallet when he found it and how his yard had a brick-and-wooden fence that enclosed it, along with four-foot-high shrubbery. It had to have been purposely thrown into his yard. He said at the time he didn't know anything about Brent Poole or his murder, and didn't realize the importance of his finding the wallet. The prosecution made it clear there was no other explanation for the wallet being in Sirles's yard other than the robber himself had tossed it over the fence during his getaway.

"When I opened it up and saw the nine dollars inside [the credit cards and driver's license], it became a different thing," Sirles said, believing at the time the wallet had not been stolen. "Had it been empty, I would have probably put it in an envelope and mailed [it] to North Carolina. If it had eight thousand dollars in it, I don't know what I'd have done."

A roar of laugher erupted in the courtroom.

All Diggs could do in cross was to have Sirles concede it had probably been thrown over the fence from the street.

Sirles was clearly enjoying his fifteen minutes of fame. It

took Judge Cottingham a few extra minutes to persuade him his services would no longer be necessary. While the courtroom enjoyed a much needed comic relief, several members of the jury experienced a lightbulb moment. The finding of Brent's wallet—with his credit cards, driver's license and money still inside—could possibly disprove the motive was robbery. Why would a robber throw a wallet away with money and credit cards in it?

The fifth witness, David Blubaugh, was the officer on duty who drove to Sirles's house and confiscated the stolen wallet. With his testimony, the pendulum had begun to swing toward the prosecution. And with their next witness, pathologist Dr. Edward L. Proctor, they moved forward to deliver a crushing blow.

Dr. Proctor lived in Myrtle Beach and was engaged in the practice of clinical and anatomic pathology, as well as forensic pathology. He had the normal four years of college and four years of medical school, then finished another four years of pathology training and additional studies to become a forensic pathologist. His credentials in and around Horry County were well-known in the field of anatomic pathology, clinical pathology and forensic pathology, and he was certified by the American Board of Pathology. No one from the defense rose to challenge his qualifications as an expert witness in forensic pathology.

Before the casually dressed doctor began his testimony concerning Brent Poole's wounds, the prosecution asked the court to pause so that the Pooles could exit. Craig Poole, his wife, Amy, and his sister, Dee, chose to remain in the courtroom during Proctor's testimony and had to bite a lot of bottom lip to keep from choking up. Renee looked straight ahead while the doctor testified, but she was able to hold her composure. The usual widening of the eyes, gasping and lowering of the eyes from the jurors occurred during Proctor's lengthy explanation of Brent's wounds and demonstration of how they occurred. One huge point of contention for the defense took place when he stated that Brent Poole was shot standing up, and not while lying down as Renee had claimed.

The surreal moment in the trial came when Humphries asked Proctor to demonstrate the wounds using his face as a prop. Proctor pointed to the points of entry and explained to the jurors that both projectiles had passed through the brain, tearing apart vital brain tissue. Either projectile was fatal and would have rendered him unconscious in a matter of seconds. His testimony was certainly not for the weak-kneed.

Diggs tried to counterpunch by getting the doctor to agree that it was possible if the angles were the same, Brent could have been shot in a kneeling or squatting position. Standing two feet from Proctor, Diggs also wanted him to concede that Renee could have held Brent's head without getting any blood on her clothing, but he never could make that connection.

After watching Diggs dance around the issue for about five minutes, Humphries rose to his feet and responded, "Your Honor, if there's some evidence of that, I'll be glad for him to ask that question."

"Well, I'll let the doctor respond," Cottingham ruled.

Proctor searched for the right words, before finally giving up, "Well, I certainly wasn't there. I don't know how he was handled or if he was or was not touched. But had someone grabbed his head, or both sides of the head, or about the ears, or under the chin, in all likelihood there would have been some blood present. But how much? I have no idea, sir."

Diggs had hit a snag. All he could do was add, "But certainly this is not a situation where an artery had been severed and you had a massive amount of blood spewing out of that particular wound?"

"No, sir, there would not," Proctor conceded. "I do not think there would have been a spurting artery, no, sir."

"All right, that's all I'm trying to get at," Diggs concluded. "Thank you very much, Doctor."

CHAPTER 32

It had been a long morning of testimony on the first day of trial and the jurors were tired and hungry. The defense had gone nowhere with their cross and recross of the pathologist and the courtroom was getting restless. Judge Cottingham decided it was a good time to break for lunch.

The Horry County Courthouse is nestled among towering oak trees in downtown Conway. Mostly lawyers and accounting offices face the courthouse on the front and sides of the streets. On the corner, not even a block away, sits Wayne's Restaurant, where most of the court participants enjoyed Southern fried cooking at its finest. Their menu featured a hearty selection of vegetables, salads, desserts, breads and an array of meats, including fried chicken, pork chops, quail, barbecue and shrimp. The meal and a beverage could be purchased at a reasonable price, but the hospitality and trial commentary from Wayne's owner, Linda Hucks, was always free.

After lunch, all the spectators and participants in the trial took their seats and waited on Judge Cottingham. The first witness called to the stand by the prosecution was Winston-Salem investigative officer Mike Rowe, who had put together the photographic lineup package for Myrtle Beach police on June 16, 1998. The jury was shown the five photographs chosen from a computer database that were similar in physical characteristics to Frazier. The prosecution introduced this to them for the purpose of familiarity. Their plan was to recall this same document on another day, with witnesses who had identified John Frazier as the man dressed in black on the beach the night Brent was killed.

The prosecution continued its presentation of evidence with Detective Terry Altman and crime scene specialists from both Myrtle Beach police and SLED. In their slow and deliberate style of questioning, Hembree and Humphries took turns asking each officer their connection with the personal effects and clothing of Brent Poole after his death and what involvement did they have in collection of those items and turning them into property and evidence. Again, the judge paused, as before, to excuse Brent Poole's family before the evidence was produced.

The defense had no questions to ask of these witnesses but one. Lieutenant Ira Jeffcoat, a fifteen-year-veteran forensic evidence technician with SLED, testified that among the evidence submitted to him to be tested for body fluids was Brent's underwear. They tested for blood on his blue jeans and striped shirt, white towel, right shoe—all of those cuttings contained human blood belonging to Brent. One particular item swab tested for human semen came from Brent's pair of white underwear. After a chemical test, it was determined there was, in fact, human semen on the underwear of William Brent Poole. It had given the appearance that Renee had had sex with Brent in an effort to stall so that John could get in place to deliver the fatal blast.

The trial had pretty much lost its emotional edge with the late-afternoon witnesses, but it quickly returned to a higher intensity when sex was mentioned. Dressed fashionably in a bright red suit, Orrie West questioned Jeffcoat in relation to his findings. "Did they ask you to determine whose semen that was in his underwear?" she asked.

"No, I did not. I was never submitted a sample of blood from the victim to compare to the unknown stain. I would have to have that sample to make that comparison."

"So you don't know that it was Mr. Poole's?"

"All I know is there was semen on his underwear," Jeffcoat stated.

"Now, you said how long have you been doing this for SLED?"

"Fifteen years."

Hembree asked for permission to redirect and with one question he asked what everyone already knew was the answer: "How would you expect it to get there?"

"Through ejaculation after sex," Jeffcoat replied.

The unspoken affirmation on the jury's face was significant. Had Renee Poole really made love to her husband on the night he was shot, thus luring him right into a death trap?

After a brief sidebar and a few remarks from the judge to the jury, the court called for a break.

During the break, Diggs rallied his troops. He anticipated the prosecution was about to make one of its biggest strategic moves. They were preparing to bring on the big boys, Detectives John King and Terry Altman. In addition, they would introduce and play the tapes of Renee's interviews. This, he believed, was where the game would be won or lost.

Diggs wasn't worried. He had promised the jury in his opening remarks they would hear Renee's testimony in her own words. After the tapes were played, his plan was to launch a ruthless attack against the detectives and accuse them of coercing Renee into a confession. This would later on lead the jury straight to his strongest defensive claim when he introduced his expert witness and his testimony relating to false confessions. Renee was in shock after the murder of her husband and suffered from post-traumatic stress disorder (PTSD). She was in a vulnerable position while she was being interviewed by the police and was coerced into giving a confession. This tactic would put the defense back where they wanted to be in this trial and give them a strong defensive foothold.

But, first things first. He had to contend with the prosecution's witnesses.

Humphries' questioning of the mild-mannered and gentle—dressed to the nines—Detective King led into Renee's confession that she and John had conspired to murder. For the jury, it was hard to imagine this soft-spoken detective forcing Renee into a confession. King implied it was as plain as the nose on his face, she was not under any undue duress and was more than willing to talk with the police. And at no time had she been threatened or had she been promised any hope of reward or hope of leniency for her statements. She had not only agreed to provide a statement voluntarily, but had allowed them to tape it as well. King had no concerns whatsoever regarding whether or not Renee understood what she was saying to him.

Humphries took his time and through King's examination methodically presented to the jury the circumstances of and conversations from Renee's interviews. During this process, he introduced and explained in a lengthy discourse with King the Miranda warnings and Waiver of Rights forms that Renee had signed, indicating she had been advised of her rights. He then addressed her interview in Davie County, where she was represented by counsel.

"Specifically, in regard to that particular interview," Humphries asked, "was the defendant asked directly by law enforcement whether or not John Boyd Frazier had shot William Brent Poole?"

"Yes, she was," King answered softly.

"And during the interview, the first part of that interview, what was her answer to law enforcement?"

"She said no," King responded. "She said [that] it could have been. Then she said it could have been anyone. But she didn't give a direct answer and say, 'Yes, it was.'" He then revealed that during the interview process her attorney had requested a fifteen-minute recess.

Humphries approached the witness. "What new, specific information did you receive, if any, in this second portion of the interview which occurred on the twelfth of June at Davie County?"

"She told us it was John Frazier that shot and killed her husband."

"And did she indicate to you how she was sure of that information?"

"She said she knew it was John from his voice, from his build, from his mannerism and just from being around him."

Humphries then asked King to explain for the jury Renee's arrest the night of her husband's wake at the funeral home. Why it was necessary to arrest her that evening?

King explained the fugitive task force had located and arrested John Frazier and they had some concern Renee might flee. He admitted his concern was not just specific to Renee, but as it would have been under any other circumstance when a codefendant was arrested prior to another codefendant.

The prosecution held nothing back. "What if anything," Humphries began, throwing everything out but the kitchen sink, "was said by the mother of the defendant to "Butch," a member of the fugitive task force, regarding interview techniques, if you will, regarding her daughter."

King didn't bat an eye. He looked straight at the jury and responded, "It was relayed that you have to really get on Renee real hard to get the truth out of her."

Diggs rose to his feet and offered a boisterous objection on the basis of hearsay. The prosecution had insinuated that even the mother couldn't trust her daughter to tell the truth. Cottingham sustained.

"Your Honor, I understand," Humphries countered. "Just as a basis, I submit to the court this is not offered for the truth of the matter asserted, but to support the technique used by law enforcement in the interview of the defendant, which will be relevant clearly on cross-examination."

"All right," the judge accepted the explanation. "I charge the jury that the assertion by the mother at that time may not be used as any evidence other than it is for the truth asserted. It is merely solicited for the purposes of his further technique in discussing with the defendant. Is that correct?"

"That is correct, Your Honor," Humphries assured the judge.

Cottingham explained his decision to the jurors again and cleared it with Diggs before he allowed King to continue.

"Once I was in possession of that information," King stated, "as a result of that information, I wrote that down on a piece of paper and slipped it under the door during her interview."

"Now, after giving this note that you've spoken of to Detective Altman," Humphries went on to say, "what, if anything, did you note regarding his interview technique with the defendant?"

"Once I gave him that information, his technique did change," King answered.

"Was it more assertive?"

"Yes, it was."

"Did there come another point during the interview where you heard something that you wished to then convey back to the interviewers?"

"Yes, I did."

Several of the jurors leaned forward or sat up in their chairs. Humphries smiled, then instructed King to tell the jury about that.

"During the course of the interview, I heard Renee tell Detective Altman and Lieutenant Frontz that she didn't think John was gonna be there because the time was too soon. I then wrote that information down on another piece of paper and slipped it under the door to bring that to their attention."

Humphries took a step toward Sergeant King. "And after giving them that information, did those detectives then go back to that point—that they thought John would be there too soon?"

"Yes, they did."

Humphries then moved to publish to the court typed transcripts and the first recorded interview between Detective King and Renee on the night of Brent's murder at 3:37 in the morning. He wanted the jury to hear how much her story changed from this interview to her later ones, and that the most incriminating evidence against her would come not in this interview but in a subsequent one when she was in the presence of her attorney.

Before the jury heard the tape, Judge Cottingham wanted to make certain Renee got a fair shake. For fifteen minutes, he instructed the jury on the Miranda warnings and the law as it related to Renee's alleged voluntary statements. It was an impressive history lesson concerning constitutional rights. As the judge went through it all, Renee stared at King from across the courtroom.

The jury listened to the taped interview and followed along with their typed transcript copies for exactly one hour and two minutes. They heard a very calm and collected Renee Poole being interviewed by the polite Detective King. At 6:27 P.M., Judge Cottingham asked the defense if they desired to cross-examine the witness or break for the evening.

Diggs wisely chose to break and begin with King in the morning.

The prosecution believed they had delivered a tremendous blow to the defense's case that Renee had been coerced into making a confession, in allowing them to listen to the taped interview. They had wanted them to see that even the not-so-bright persons could figure out a fallback position after they had said something they regretted and claim they had been pressured—when it had never happened. The prosecution was convinced Renee was sophisticated enough to do just that when she saw her statement was going to be used against her.

The defense had their work cut out for them. The jury would want to know why it was that Renee hadn't been able to keep quiet and kept talking to the police until she finally confessed? Had she helped to plan it, but thought she could get away with it simply because she hadn't pulled the trigger?

Sergeant King was a very believable witness. If the defense was going to discredit him, then Diggs was going to have to show up in court tomorrow with his boxing gloves on.

CHAPTER 33

Bill Diggs must have lain awake all night thinking about damage control, for his first question of the day was so intimidating that it set the tone for the remainder of his cross-examination.

"Is it, *Detective* King?" he asked slyly.

Deputy solicitor Humphries' gentle questioning the day before suddenly gave way to a blistering cross-examination from the defense. Diggs came out of his corner swinging and went after King with a vengeance. In a loud, sometimes sarcastic voice, he pounced on the detective from the get-go. With a series of questions he asked with his back turned toward the witness, he began accusing King of having a role in purposely staging the times and places of Renee's interviews that put her at an unfair disadvantage.

It was a valiant effort—but, somehow, somewhere—Diggs got sidetracked. When King bucked up and refused to answer questions regarding simple information, to his satisfaction, Diggs lost his focus and King's cross-examination turned into an ugly slugfest. He kept firing his questions at King so fast and furious, often on insignificant matters, that they overlapped his answers, prompting Judge Cottingham to issue several harsh warnings.

"Are you gonna let me finish my answer?" King would shoot back at Diggs throughout his testimony when he tried to snowball him with rapid questions. A frustrated Diggs would respond with: "All I'm trying to ask you is . . . that's all I'm trying to get to." Back and forth it went each time, until Diggs made the statement to King, "I understand how limited your knowledge is with respect to this case."

Humphries jumped to his feet in a strong prosecution objection. "(He's) characterizing the testimony, Your Honor. That's improper and he knows it."

Diggs didn't fare any better after that, and seemed to get deeper and deeper into a pissing contest with Sergeant King. But he never could land a solid punch. King led him around in circles, time and time again, until he was totally frustrated. Diggs took on the face of a law student who had just been told there was a pop quiz and he had studied the wrong chapter the night before.

"How many interviews did you conduct?" Diggs asked.

King looked at him as though he were confused. "How many interviews? Interviews that I had personally conducted?"

"Well, when I say you, in that sense, I mean the detective unit that was working on this case? However many detectives that may have been?"

"There were several interviews conducted," King answered.

"Okay, could you tell me the individuals who were interviewed?"

"I don't have the names. No, I don't."

"Do you know . . . ," Diggs said, wagging his head like a dog. "Is there anybody in the Myrtle Beach Police Department that would have a list of the names of people who were interviewed by that investigative unit prior to your going to North Carolina?"

"Yes, it would be documented which investigator talked to who."

"And who . . . who would have that documentation?"

"Whichever investigator was assisting in, in talking with these different people."

Diggs took a deep breath. "All right. Did the investigators talk among themselves or did they construct this wall of silence between themselves?"

"I don't understand what you're talking about," King responded. "'A wall of silence'?"

"Did the . . . Did the detectives discuss this case among themselves and share information?"

"That's correct."

"And did they share it with you?"

"I may have some of it. Yes."

"And they may have shared it with you, but you just forgot it. Is that what you're saying?"

"No, that's not what I'm saying," King shot back.

"Did they share it with you or not?"

"Like I said, I may have got some of the information. Yes."

Diggs kept his back turned toward King. "Either you did or you did not, or you forgot it. Now which one is it? Did you get information from them or not?"

"No, sir," the judge admonished Diggs. "You're not gonna limit him that way. He may explain his answer."

"All right, certainly, I wish he would do that, Your Honor."

King still wouldn't answer. After several questions, and getting the runaround, Diggs asked him again, with sarcasm as thick as karo syrup: "Did you get it or not? That's all I am asking. Can you tell us for sure if you got the information?"

"I'm telling you, Mr. Diggs. I may have got some of the information."

"All right. And I—I . . . I concede that. You're doing the best you can. Is that correct?"

"Is that a question you're asking me?" King asked, catching his drift.

"Yes, sir. You're doing your best?"

King didn't respond, but the judge did. "That's a question for the jury," Cottingham admonished the counselor. "Go ahead."

Diggs grilled King further about how they determined John was a suspect. At one point, he asked, "Well, did you base your analysis on anything other than evidence that you were collecting? I mean, when you talk about this, was it like crystal balls or something?"

Eyes in the jury widened. The judge boomed, "That would be an improper question."

"Well, I apologize for that," Diggs conceded.

"That's totally improper," Cottingham reminded him.

The jury's body language indicated Diggs had hit a sour note. His banter with Sergeant King did more to turn the jury off to his line of questioning than to turn them on. And to make matters worse, the remainder of his time would be spent in hurling spitballs at King, getting objections from the prosecution and then sparring with the judge. Cottingham even lost his patience with Diggs and his antics. After Diggs's persistent protest that King wasn't cooperating with him, Cottingham shouted, "No, sir, that's not true. The jury will determine that. Now don't argue with me. Get on with the question."

Finally Diggs threw up his hands in despair and called it quits. "I don't have anything else. I'm gonna bring him back as a defense witness, Your Honor. At this point—"

Judge Cottingham wouldn't let him off the hook. "No, wait a minute." He called Diggs back to the front of the courtroom. "Let this record reflect that I'm giving you unlimited opportunity to cross-examine this witness. I only say to you that question was answered, and the record will reflect it, on three separate occasions, and that's sufficient as to that question. Now, if you've got any more, have at it."

"Your Honor, I don't have any more at this time," a totally perturbed Diggs answered.

On redirect, Humphries again had no problem soliciting information from King. In questions about Renee and John's relationship, he worked the sergeant like a well-oiled machine. They were obviously on the same team, but more important, he knew what buttons of his to push and what buttons not to push.

Finally, after about five minutes of smooth sailing, Humphries asked King, "Did [Renee] later explain to you what she meant by her statement [of] 'I kind of changed in that relationship'?"

"Yes."

"How did she explain that change? Was it a change in her, the relationship or the character of the relationship?"

"It was a change in the relationship," King answered.

Diggs objected, but the judge allowed it.

When King stated, "It became a sexual relationship," Humphries made him repeat it again.

The prosecution was racking up big time, as Humphries and King continued to work off each other. The average juror had watched enough court cases on television and at the movies to know so many conspirators were inept at keeping their story straight and normally became very sloppy in their schemes. They were very surprised to hear Renee's lawyer Victor Leckowitz had allowed her to confess, unless he mistakenly thought she was innocent. Jurors were smart enough to understand the police can be overbearing, but not to the point where she would confess to an incriminating statement that could be used against her. She was obviously not the brightest bulb in the chandelier for not keeping her mouth shut, but it was a hard sale to say she invented a story because she was tired and wanted to go home.

Diggs's rhythm had been broken by King, and it clearly showed. When he had questioned the detective on the stand, it was like playing tennis with no one to return his serves. It wasn't fair to the defense. Diggs objected several times to the prosecution's line of questions related to Renee and John's relationship, but it didn't take root. King was a key witness, but every step Diggs took to go after him, he had been hammered. Finally, in desperation, he asked for a sidebar. The judge dismissed the jury.

"Your Honor," Diggs stated candidly, "the question I have is I don't understand how the witness can testify that through his investigation he learned that the defendant supposedly was lying about a relationship [with Frazier] and the time limit or the length of it when the court will not permit him to tell me what he learned about the position of the body of Brent Poole when he was shot."

"Well, you examined him exhaustively on that subject, Mr. Diggs. He told you and this jury at least three times, and perhaps five times, that he got his information only on the position of the body from the doctor."

Diggs continued to protest for several minutes. "My objection is we've got a two . . . we're not . . . The solicitor can bring in information based on what the detective learned in his investigation, but I can't. And that's what I object to."

When Diggs had exhausted his argument, Orrie West, his co-counselor, attempted to come to his aid. She didn't fare any better.

"No, ma'am. I'm gonna take one lawyer at a time now," Cottingham advised her. West retreated to her seat at the defense table.

But Diggs stood his ground, arguing back and forth with the judge for another five minutes about how King was responding to his questions. "But, Your Honor," he had said, "with all due respect, he didn't answer. . . . He gave an answer, but it wasn't responsive. I would ask Your Honor to direct him to answer the question."

"He did," Cottingham said impatiently. "The record is clear on that. . . . He answered it. Three times. No, sir. I'm through with that issue now, through with it."

The morning had been a disaster for Renee Poole's defense. If it wasn't a revelation to her, it was to nearly everyone who mattered. The defense had never anticipated King's strength on the witness stand, and, as a result, they had been completely derailed.

CHAPTER 34

In the second half of the morning's proceedings, the prosecution called another of its key witnesses, Detective Terry Altman. Just as the defense had finally settled their stomachs from their fiasco with King, another formidable opponent was taking the stand.

Solicitor Hembree began Altman's testimony by having him provide a detailed account of the night of Brent Poole's murder, what had taken place at the hospital between him and Dr. Duffy and his view of Renee's demeanor after she had been told her husband was dead.

"The first time I saw her [on the beach], she was just sitting there like this, with her hands clasped." Altman mimicked her position. "She looked a little pale, but very nonemotional, not upset. . . ."

A few questions later, Hembree then asked Altman about her demeanor and her condition at 5:10 A.M. when he went in to speak with her?

"She was very nonemotional and very calm," Altman answered. "Her voice was just a steady monotone. She was just really sitting there. Just very nonemotional and calm."

"Did it strike you as odd? Did her demeanor strike you as strange?"

Altman pulled at his tie. "Yeah, it really caught my attention." He told the jury the impression he got was that it didn't really seem to make sense why she was calm and collected about what had happened. Her husband had just been shot, and she wasn't crying. Just calm. "Just like the jurors are sitting right now is how she was sitting. Just sitting there," he marveled.

"Did you question her about that?" Hembree inquired.

"Yes, I did. I asked her . . . I told her that it seemed very strange that she was nonemotional and that she was not crying."

"What was her response to you?"

Altman paused, then turned toward the jurors. "Her reply was that she had already done her crying."

"How long had this been after the killing of her husband?"

Both West and Diggs rose in unison in protest. Cottingham agreed the question was improper. He advised the jury to disregard the question and that the phraseology of that question was totally improper. "Dismiss it from your mind," he said.

In Altman's testimony, Hembree carried the jurors through the details of each of his interviews with Renee. The first time he had talked with her on June 10, she had told him it "could have been" John Frazier who shot her husband; then when he called her on June 11, she said, "When the suspect talked, it sounded like he was using black slang words." Altman said he asked her if it was a black person who had robbed them, she said she didn't know.

Hembree had Altman step down from the witness stand and add six more pictures to the Styrofoam board resting on a tripod in front of the jurors, describing each place that Renee and Brent had visited the night before and where he had been killed.

Altman testified he heard from Renee again, on June 11, that she had called him to see how the investigation was going. Said she had brought up the fact that Brent had insurance, and when questioned as to the amount, she had said, $100,000. She also had indicated during that conversation there was going to be some other financial resources available to her in the way of a benefits package with Brent's employer, Mack Trucks.

The prosecution in this case never had to prove motive. But they had just supplied the jury with one: money!

Hembree then asked Altman to describe his meeting at the Davie County Sheriff's Office in Mocksville on June 12. Since his story coincided with Sergeant King's, the prosecution had planned on the jury listening to portions of the tape, rather than reviewing all of the testimony. Again they furnished headphones and typed transcripts for the jury and the press.

Altman was asked to set the stage for the taped interview. He stated that when she presented herself at Davie County, she was once again very calm and collected, and a little bit more confident and assertive in her answers. He clarified what had been going on with Renee's lawyers and what happened after the break. Prior to the break, she had been very vague with specifics as to the identity of the shooter. But after the break, she confessed that the shooter was John Frazier. It was then Sergeant King had called back to Myrtle Beach and a warrant was issued for John Frazier for murder and armed robbery and obstruction of justice for Renee.

Hembree wanted the jury to understand Renee had been charged and arrested at the wake for "obstruction of justice," but not for "conspiracy to commit murder." The conspiracy charge came about after Renee had been placed under arrest and interviewed in custody at the Winston-Salem Police Department on June 13.

"Again, what was her demeanor on this occasion?" Hembree asked in equally measured and precise tones.

"Very calm and collected still," Altman said. "I think she was a little upset that she had been arrested, but very calm and very coherent of what was going on around her and where she was."

The taped interview Hembree had planned on publishing was almost two hours long. Because it was nearly noon, Judge Cottingham offered Diggs the opportunity to interview Altman before the jury heard the tape.

On cross-examination, Diggs found the going much easier with Altman than he had with King. He reviewed Altman's involvement in Renee's interviews and discussed his motive. "Were you aware that officers in the police department had described Mrs. Poole as being in shock?" he asked.

Altman said he wasn't aware of that.

"Were you aware that they had described her as crying, uncontrollably so?"

"I don't remember anybody saying that, no."

Diggs dug deeper. "All right. Do you remember them telling you that she had been trembling?" As with Detective King, he kept his back turned toward the witness, looking at the jurors for a nod of affirmation.

"Like I said, I don't remember anybody telling me that specifically."

"Now, you're the lead detective in this case, are you not?" Diggs asked. Altman acknowledged he was. "And so you've seen those reports, have you not?"

"I've seen those reports, yes."

Diggs then challenged if Altman had seen those references and characteristics in those reports, and that he had been in the courtroom for the trial and listened to the testimony of Officer Brown, then he should have known she was in shock. Altman claimed he had not read them and they were not fresh in his memory.

The defense scored on this point, but it was a moot point. And Diggs wanted something more. When he began questioning Altman about his method of interview, everyone in the courtroom recognized that he was going for the knockout.

"Are you telling the jury there was no intent on the part of the police department to kind of tag-team Renee at this point?"

Altman looked surprised. "I don't understand what you mean by that."

"With first Detective King and then you?"

"I don't really understand what you mean by 'tag team.'"

Diggs narrowed his eyes. "I mean him interviewing her at length and then you coming in and going over the same stuff again at length. Was there an intent and a design to bring that about?"

"No," Altman quickly answered. "Like I said before, I didn't know all the facts of the case and I had to become educated, so to speak, of what was going on." He stated John Frazier was not the primary suspect until after Renee's interview.

That he wasn't convinced of that until after the one interview and the two telephone calls with her.

Diggs asked the detective how many times had Renee told him John Frazier was not the shooter. Altman said he didn't know, he had never counted them. Diggs also brought out the fact that Renee had had ineffective counsel during that interview. "Even on the tape itself that we just heard, he says, 'Renee, that doesn't make sense.' Remember that?"

Altman had remembered him saying that.

"At one point, you have a conversation with Victor Leckowitz. At the conclusion of the interview. And he says something about having to go out of the country?"

Altman had heard him say that, too.

"Yeah, [and he said,] 'Go ahead, and if you want to talk to Renee, you just go ahead and do whatever you want to do to wrap this thing up,' in effect. That's what he tells you, right?"

Altman had not heard that part, and told Diggs so. "No. He specifically told Renee that if we had any more questions, that he directed her to answer them."

"All right," Diggs said, "in effect to what I just said, 'Go ahead and have at it. Wrap it up and get whatever you need from her and be done with it.'"

"Well, those are your words," Altman returned. "His words were, if you have any more questions, he gave her permission to answer them."

"The bottom line, there is no difference, is there?"

Altman said the way he saw it Leckowitz was telling her that if the police had any more questions, to answer them.

"And so with his blessings, you go ahead and do that?"

Altman agreed he had.

Diggs got through much of Renee's testimony and had Altman read a great deal of it back to the jury. But with all the different interviews she had had with the police, it was difficult for both Diggs and the jury to keep straight what was said in what interview. One point Diggs did make was when he got Altman to agree that it was vague, how Frazier had gotten in front of them, and that it was vague now.

"It was always vague," Diggs added. "And what do we know

any more today about how Brent was killed than we knew the first night that she talked to you about it?"

"Well, we know he was shot," Altman quipped.

"Well, yes," Diggs came back, "But on the vagueness issue, she's pretty much told the same—relayed the same events from the very first day until the last day she ever spoke about the case?"

Altman had to agree.

Renee had sat still during Altman's entire testimony. She looked straight at him, glaring, as if to say it was all his fault that she was sitting in this courtroom today.

After lunch, Hembree entered into evidence Renee's taped interview conducted on June 13, 1998. Again, as the prior day, Judge Cottingham issued a lengthy discourse to the jury in regard to the alleged statements of the defendant contained in the 148 pages of the transcript. Renee slumped in her chair at the defense table, listening to her life pass by as the drama played out before her. For the first time in her trial, she visibly broke down. As she listened to the detectives chisel away at her story until she finally laid out the entire scenario of how she had set up her husband's murder, she lowered her head and mopped her eyes with a white handkerchief. She had confessed no less than eight different times on tape of having conspired to her husband's murder. Some jurors wondered why she was crying at that point. Upon hearing the tape again in the courtroom, had it suddenly dawned upon her just how much trouble she had gotten herself into?

Another difficult problem the defense had was that key aspects against their client was in the form of taped interviews and they couldn't cross-examine the audiotapes. All they could do was cross-examine the officers who took the interviews. Diggs's recross of Altman was tough, as expected, though considerably different from King's. While in King's, Diggs had come out swinging, he paced himself with Altman, at times being nice to him and at times grilling him hard. The line of defense with which he had chosen to do battle against Altman was to discredit him as a professional for allowing her interviews to continue on the night of her husband's murder without Mirandizing her until he got what he wanted.

Altman said his position with Renee was treating her both as a victim and a witness at that time and he had no responsibility to Mirandize until she had become a suspect.

Continuing to play pit bull, Diggs went after Altman's experience and background. He got him to admit he had only been a detective two years when he had been assigned lead to the case and that he had never been to a specific homicide class, not even the first class on investigative techniques. Altman had attended a couple of interview classes on how to interview witnesses and suspects, but failed to identify any of the big names in interview techniques.

Diggs kept gnawing away. "Have you ever had any training or discussion with your superiors on how to play one co-defendant against another?"

"No," Altman answered.

"Have you ever had a class or any training or any seminar or any in-house instruction that tells you when you interview defendants, that you can lie to them?"

Altman frowned. "I don't remember any specific training on that. I think it's just a common knowledge that you can tell them certain things."

"Who in your department has told you that you can lie to a defendant or a suspect or a witness?"

Altman shrugged. "Nobody has told me that."

"All right, you have just assumed on your own that you could do that as part of proper police technique?"

"I don't think I've assumed it. I know I've heard it somewhere and I know that the technique has been used before."

Diggs chewed on that a little longer, then asked him, "Do you remember where you heard it?"

"No. I sure don't."

"All right, but you acknowledge to this jury now that you did lie to Renee during the interview that they just heard?"

Altman admitted he had told her some things that were not true.

"You lied to her," Diggs growled.

"I did tell her some things that were not true" was all Altman was going to admit.

"And you knew they weren't true," Diggs added.

"That's correct."

Now that Diggs finally had a bite into him, he wasn't about to let up. "And you knew that she did not know that they weren't true?"

"That's correct."

"All right. And why did you do that? Why did you . . . I say lie . . . Why did you tell her certain things you know that were not true?"

"Because what we were looking for with the defendant was the truth—"

Diggs didn't let him finish, and inserted the words "a confession."

The prosecution protested. "Whoa, Judge. Whoa, whoa, whoa. He's got to be allowed to answer his question."

"Yes, sir," Cottingham agreed. "You didn't permit him to finish his answer."

"Like I said," Altman continued, "what we were trying to find from the defendant was the truth, and telling her certain things would make her feel more comfortable, and if she thought we knew things that were true, then she would tell us the truth."

When Diggs accused Altman of staging all the interviews for late at night, he said that it wasn't true. He stated there were no promises made to Renee. It was just the way it happened. They hadn't specifically set up times to talk to her. It was just when she was brought to the police department. Just the way the facts of the day panned out.

Diggs kept at him. "You knew it would be the weakest, the most vulnerable time for her, did you not?" When Altman disagreed, he quickly shot back, "And you would not have done that, had it entered into your mind? You would not have wanted to take advantage of her?"

"I would not have taken advantage of her if I [had] interviewed her at seven o'clock in the morning," Altman insisted. "It might have been too early and she wasn't awake.

It's just that's the time she got there. That's the time we interviewed her."

"Okay, so your testimony is these late-night—three in a row—interviews with Renee were not done by design?"

"No, they were not."

"And they were not done to get a tactical advantage over her?"

"No," Altman said again.

Altman then told Diggs the reason why Renee was interviewed again—even though she had told who the shooter was and told all the details she could remember. What bothered them the most was how John Frazier knew they were in Myrtle Beach and at what hotel they were staying. They speculated she knew more and was withholding that information. They felt she knew how he got there, and when and where he was supposed to appear on the beach.

Diggs attempted to trip him up. "Okay, and so you were thinking, 'She knows Frazier might have acquired knowledge of this trip through some source,' and so you had her there from ten-thirty until midnight, raising your voice at her. I'm not gonna say screaming, but forcing her to go ahead and tell you the truth about the case, even though she wasn't a murder suspect."

"We did raise our voices at her," Altman agreed, "but to get her to tell us the truth, which she did."

"And your testimony is that you did that because Renee's parents, of all people, told you you'd have to do that, earlier the previous day; is that correct?"

Altman said it was the information they had received.

"Who told you you had to be rough with Renee to get her to tell you the truth?"

"Well, nobody told me to be rough," Altman confessed. "They just said you had to be more assertive with her."

At this point, Diggs got everyone confused, including himself, as to during which interview the note had been passed from Sergeant King with that information from her mother on it. It had been a long day for everyone.

Diggs then tried a new approach he hadn't used, but

probably wished he had, especially during King's testimony. He had Altman read from several excerpts of the transcript and comment on them. Each question he asked was directed at Altman's intent to coerce Renee into a confession.

"'I'm just saying I don't want you to find yourself in a bind from what he's telling us, because I'm telling you he's saying it's all your idea,'" Diggs had Altman read his own words to Renee. He then asked, "That is an absolute false representation, isn't it?"

Altman admitted John Frazier had never told them that. And that he had told Renee something that wasn't true.

A few questions later, Diggs fell into the same trap as he had with King, when the answers didn't come out quite as he had hoped, prompting the judge to call him down again. "Wait a minute, now," Cottingham warned. "You can't require him to answer the way you want him to answer. He's entitled to answer you and you can ask the next question."

"He's entitled to answer and explain," Diggs stated.

"No, sir," Cottingham corrected him. "He can answer and explain, but not yes or no if he doesn't care to. There's no rule that says he's got to say yes or no."

Diggs was able to bounce back and get Altman to admit a second time to where he hadn't told her the truth. Reading again from the transcript, "'We've talked with him. We know the whole deal. But make yourself come clean of all this, Renee. This is the only thing you can do right now, because I'm telling you, we've talked with him. We know the whole deal. But we've got to hear it from you. Save yourself, don't make him come out smelling like a rose, because he's a piece of shit.'"

Diggs jumped on Altman with both feet. "The fact of the matter is, again you hadn't talked to Frazier on the first instance about this shooting, had you?"

"No, but I had talked to him before she was in there," Altman tried to explain.

"But he certainly hadn't come clean, according to your statement here, had he?"

"No. He had not told us anything about the incident."

"He didn't tell you anything?"

"That's correct," Altman answered.

Diggs thought he had him up against the ropes again. "And you were telling another untruth to Renee to get her to do what?"

"To make her feel more uncomfortable and to make her think that we knew what he had told us and, therefore, then she would tell us the truth."

Diggs then accused Altman of making promises to Renee in order to get her to confess. In a succession of readings, he pointed out six different incidents perceived to be promises made by Altman to help her out if she confessed.

Altman said he knew he couldn't help her, but he wanted her to feel comfortable enough to tell him the truth.

"You told her you were gonna help her," Diggs admonished, "but you admit, not only is that another lie, but you didn't want to help her. You wanted to put her in either the electric chair or prison for life?"

Altman insisted all he wanted was the truth.

Diggs took another stab at him. "You wanted her to feel comfortable by lying to her and making promises to her; isn't that correct?"

"I made no promises to her," Altman defended himself. "I wanted to talk to her so she would talk to us and tell us the truth."

"I'm not gonna beat a horse to death at this point over it," Diggs concluded. "But you did say, 'I want to help you,' in your testimony, and is that not a promise?"

"I don't perceive it as a promise," Altman said. "There's nowhere in here that I said that I would promise her anything."

Before he was finished with Altman, Diggs would accuse him and Lieutenant Frontz of playing good cop and bad cop, too. He also claimed Altman had used Renee's daughter as a trump card: "You're not gonna lose your daughter if you're honest," Altman had said to Renee in her last interview before she was charged with murder.

"You gave her your version of the truth and that was he planned it," Diggs attempted to point out to the jurors in his last questions to Altman. "And that was the only way that she was not going to lose her daughter was to admit that?"

At first, it appeared Diggs was striking a chord pleasing to the jurors. While they had seemed restless during King's tedious chiding, they seemed reenergized during his document-filled cross-examination of Altman, in spite that it was nearly 6:00 P.M. It looked as though Diggs had finally found a style that worked.

However, would the jurors actually believe that an adult like Renee, the mother of a 2½-year-old then, was so naive as to believe that if she confessed to conspiring to murder her husband, then the police would see to it she wouldn't lose custody of her daughter, or that they were there to help her construct her story so as not to go to jail? It was not unconstitutional for police to trick the defendants into a confession. Surely, every juror had seen, read or heard about bail jumpers being rounded up by police with the promise of being sweepstakes winners?

The next witness of the evening was Mike Fultz, who had lived with John Frazier's friends Bruce and Courtney Wolford. Fultz testified that in March or April 1998, John and Renee had been over at Bruce's home with a 9mm pistol and he had overheard a conversation between them after dinner about Brent and Renee going to the beach. He was asked to pen the date on the Styrofoam board.

Other witnesses called to the stand were Calvin Harris, a senior manager at Champion who supervised John Frazier, who testified to Frazier's asking for and then not working the days of June 8 through June 10, and Kayle Schettler, the friend/mechanic who had loaned John his 1990 Model Acura Integra those same dates. Schettler was most damaging in that he revealed John had never asked to borrow his car overnight before; John also had not asked if Kayle had fixed or checked out his vehicle when he had brought it back to him prematurely the morning police had visited him. In addition, Schettler also told the jury he knew John to have two guns. One was a TZ-75 and the other was a 9mm Glock. He had been present with John when he shot the TZ-75, and John had experienced difficulties with that handgun jamming and failing to chamber the round.

Both testimonies from Harris and Schettler provided the prosecution's opportunity for John Frazier to kill Brent Poole.

Diggs countered Schettler by asking him if there was anything unusual about John borrowing his car. He admitted John had done that before. Diggs also asked if there was anything out of the ordinary about his car when he got it back from Frazier.

"No beach sand, no bug splatters on the front, no trash or anything in it," Schettler told the jury. "Nothing to indicate it had been driven a long way."

Officer Darrell Mills, of the WSPD, would testify about having responded to John's house the morning of Brent's murder, and how he had been detained by a car that ran a red light in front of him and narrowly hit him. Mills said he saw only the Acura Integra parked in the backyard at 5:25 A.M. on June 10. And it was within a closed fence, so that was why he had not checked it.

Through it all, Renee continued to show little emotion. During breaks, she would huddle with her family and friends, then start to tear up. She sensed her defense team was having problems, but she didn't know how to get herself out of this bind. Her lawyers' efforts had been fully eviscerated before her at times, but all she knew how to do was make mental notes and answer questions asked of her. She didn't think the problem with her trial was lack of time and effort spent on her case. It was just so complicated and involved a lot of witnesses who, for some unknown reason, seemed to have it in for her.

It was 7:30 P.M. The judge apologized for keeping the jury so long, but he stated that under the circumstances, since they were sequestered, he thought it was in their best interest to move the case along expeditiously. They had accomplished a lot in two days—and with any luck, they would be finished by the weekend.

CHAPTER 35

There were additional witnesses and issues the prosecution would introduce on Friday that Renee wasn't even aware of. The state had a lot more information to present to the jury and the trial would become even more complicated than she had ever imagined.

The crowd had picked up in the gallery, mostly from people who had already testified and decided to hang around. Kathy Ropp, editor of the *Horry Independent*, in Conway, and reporter Tanya Root, from the *Sun News*, in Myrtle Beach, had joined reporter John Hinton in the press box. As the prosecution began to push through the last days of Renee's trial, everyone in the courtroom knew, sooner or later, it would eventually come to a head. The big question was: how would it all end?

Dawn Albumani, the night office manager at the Carolina Winds, was the prosecution's first witness of the day. She told the jury she had received a phone call in late May 1998 from someone identifying herself as Kimberly Renee Poole for the purpose of inquiring about the motel and then later making reservations. She remembered Mrs. Poole because she had made an inquiry regarding baby-sitting. She had told Dawn it was her and her husband's anniversary and she inquired if there was a way she could have an evening alone with her husband. She had given Renee the number for the baby-sitting service and she had called back later that evening and made the reservations.

Carolyn Murphy, the baby-sitter for the Pooles on the night of the murder, next took the stand. She testified it had been Renee Poole who had called her in early June asking about baby-sitting. She specifically remembered Renee had asked for someone from ten until two in the morning.

"Well, I said the sitters won't start a job after eight-thirty, if I got a sitter. She seemed kind of disappointed and I said, 'The only one that would go out that late is myself, but I couldn't stay until two in the morning, because I get up at five in the morning. . . .' And she said, 'From nine till twelve then.' And I said, 'That would be fine.'" Murphy said she agreed to baby-sit for the Pooles and that Renee had called back on Tuesday, June 9, to tell her she had changed the time from eight-thirty to twelve.

Murphy said she had gotten lost that evening and didn't arrive at the hotel until almost 8:40 P.M. Renee had opened the door and Brent was sitting on the couch holding the little girl. She said when the couple got ready to go, the little girl started crying and he went over to her and said, "That's okay, Daddy will be back. Daddy will take you to the big sandbox tomorrow."

It was an emotional moment for nearly everyone in the courtroom. Brent's family was in tears; Murphy even found it difficult to talk about it. She had to fight to control her emotions. She cut her eyes toward Renee several times, but Renee never looked up. Renee never expressed any emotion.

"Did the little girl say anything when she woke up the next morning?" Humphries would ask several questions later.

"Yes, she did," Murphy said, holding back her tears. "She kind of sat up in the little beanbag chair and she was sleeping. I could tell she was kind of sleeping, but all she said was 'I want my daddy to hold me. I want my daddy to hold me.' So I went over there, and I knew she was asleep, and I thought, 'I can't handle this.' So I just laid her down and rubbed her back and she went back to sleep. So when Renee came, she was still sleeping. And I told Renee's parents and they said, 'Yes, she is a daddy's girl.'"

Brent's mother and sister were bent over, crying softly.

Renee's co-counsel, Orrie West, attempted to downplay Murphy's emotion-packed statements on cross-examination. "Is it unusual that one parent will be more than likely the one that will be able to calm them down more so than another? Is that unusual?"

"Not unusual, right," Murphy agreed.

"So, their whole conduct at the time you were there, there just really wasn't anything that struck you as odd, was there?"

"Right," Murphy answered, without further explanation.

Following the baby-sitter's testimony, the prosecution then launched a series of key witnesses they believed would drive the final nails into Renee's coffin. The damaging information from these witnesses would be a gigantic midtrial boost to the prosecution's case and leave the defense dancing on a tightrope.

The two young men who were visiting Myrtle Beach on a senior trip, Christopher Hensley and Thomas Hudnall, told the police they had seen Renee and Brent Poole having sex on the beach the night of the murder, as well as the man dressed in black. Hensley had agreed to testify in court.

Diggs did his best to rattle Hensley on cross-examination. Using his usual tough tactics and some very suggestive questions, he asked Hensley how they could identify someone they had only seen for two or three seconds as he walked by? Didn't the police repeatedly go over their story until they finally picked out the right one? Didn't the police tell them they knew who the murderer was? Didn't they tell them that pretty much the crime had been solved? And didn't the police tell them that they were simply trying to use them to corroborate what they already knew about this case?

But the young man never backed down, answering no on all accounts.

The jury also heard from Lieutenant Kent Robey, police officer with the Bedford County Sheriff's Office, in Virginia. In late June, he had assisted the Myrtle Beach Police Department in showing a lineup to a couple that was on the beach at the time of the murder, Mark and Donna Hobbs.

Normally, there's a great deal of skepticism about eyewitness testimony. But the prosecution had the good fortune to have two of the most reliable witnesses they could have ever hoped for dropped into their laps like a gift from above. The Hobbses *were* the state's star witnesses. Nicknamed "Andy and Helen of Mayberry" by the police and prosecution, the good-natured couple were also celebrating their honeymoon in Myrtle Beach at the same time as the Pooles. The night of the murder, they had seen the man in black, and several circumstances had caused them to be more observant than usual. The man had frightened them as he hung around the hotel, and they felt as if their own safety was at risk, enough to cancel their own walk on the beach. The man had stood out so much in their minds that even after all this time, there was no question it was John Boyd Frazier.

Diggs had even less luck with the Hobbses on cross-examination than he had had earlier with Hensley. He insisted it was near impossible to identify someone at a distance of approximately eighty feet. "How could someone get a good look at his eyes and his forehead?" he suggested to both of them.

Diggs had asked Mark Hobbs to read from the transcript of his earlier testimony when he identified John Frazier as the man they had seen on the beach. "You say there's like a ponytail down his [back], or something? You remember that?"

Mark titled his head. "No, sir, it was hard to tell," he said in his deep Southern drawl. "I mean, there was something behind his head. It was hard to tell the way the light was shining. You could see his face plain, but behind him was dark and there was something there. I couldn't see what it was. It was kind of flapping really when he was walking fast, or something was."

From the transcript, Diggs read Mark's testimony when he had been asked what he actually most remembered that would make the suspect stick out in his mind. His response had been: "[He] had a ponytail down his hair; high forehead stood out.

His eyes were big and round. His eyes and his forehead really is what I remember the most."

Diggs asked, "At that time or thereafter, did anybody ever ask you to expound on this ponytail?"

"No, sir," Mark answered politely. "I don't remember. I don't recall, but they might have. Uh, I mean, I don't recall that anyhow."

"Your testimony is today, though, you're not sure he had a ponytail?"

"Well, there was something behind his head when he was running fast. You could see something back there kind of flapping."

"And it looked like a ponytail to you?"

"Well, it was something," Mark said, squirming in the witness seat. "I'm not . . . I really couldn't see exactly what it was."

The thrust of the cross-examination was the contention that the suspect the Hobbses had seen on the beach had a ponytail. John Frazier had never had a ponytail, but Bruce Wolford had.

On redirect by Humphries, Hobbs was asked, "Could it just as easily have been a hood on a sweatshirt?" To which, he replied, "Yes, sir."

That seemed to have taken care of the situation in the mind of the jurors, but not with Diggs. Raising his voice, he boomed out, "Mr. Hobbs, why didn't you say that, that it could have been a hood on a sweatshirt?"

"When?"

"In September of 1998?"

"I probably wasn't asked. I mean, I—"

Diggs cut him off. He told Hobbs he *had been* asked and then accused him of changing his story. Diggs grabbed the picture from the photographic lineup, and handed it to Hobbs. "Now, where in that photograph do you see a ponytail?"

"I don't see one at all."

"You don't see anything approaching that, do you?"

"You can't see the back of the head, either," Mark said softly.

Diggs tried his best, but never could get Hobbs to admit he had seen a ponytail. All he would say was there was something behind his head. Spectators in the courtroom would later refer to the moment as the "case of the missing ponytail."

The defense had missed its chance to keep itself afloat in relation to the eyewitness testimonies. The first half of the Hobbses seemed to be very solid, and if they had become irritated with Mark's stubbornness for not saying what they thought he should have said, then Donna should have pushed them way beyond their boiling point. The impression was that Diggs would have continued his aggressive defense, but it seemed he had lost some of his firepower on Mark.

Donna Hobbs was very confident. She had clearly seen the suspect on the beach and immediately picked him out of the photographic lineup. As her husband had also stated, there was no question in her mind. No doubt about it, the man on the beach dressed in black was John Boyd Frazier.

Diggs did ask Donna during cross-examination, "Do you recall specifically what it is about the facial features of the individual depicted in that photo?"

"I just recall the man I seen that night," she assured him. When he asked her about all the trouble she was having constructing the composite, she replied, "If you've ever seen somebody and you see a picture of them, you recognize it. But it's hard to make up the face if you're trying to do it by a computer. And if you've seen how many sets of eyes and eyebrows and you're trying to go through and pick out facial structures and that kind of thing, I mean [there are] millions of them. It took forever to put that composite together and we still couldn't get it right."

Diggs had toned down his usual impatience for the prosecution's witness and let Donna slide without a lot of questioning. Both she and her husband had been unshakable witnesses. The prosecution had succeeded in undermining the defense's whole theory that Brent's murder had been a random robbery. That some wild, crazy man had bumped into this loving couple on the beach and impulsively decided to rob them. If that were so, then why hadn't he robbed the Hobbses when he had confronted them in isolation?

The prosecution brought out in Donna's testimony that the

man in black was looking for somebody else when he had seen the Hobbses and that's why he had moved on down the beach until he found the Pooles. They applauded the Hobbses for being very observant and a bit more suspicious than the normal person, for they had kept a close eye on someone up to no good and had the fortitude to report it after hearing about the murder the next day. They would have no reason to lie.

The defense had little to work with after the Hobbses testified, as the jury was then subjected to a tedious technical testimony from David Collins of the South Carolina Law Enforcement Division. Collins was a certified firearms and tool marks examiner and had performed forensics analysis on the two fired 9mm Luger-caliber cartridge cases and four unfired cartridges submitted by the Myrtle Beach Police Department. He was there to provide a list of what possible makes and manufacturers of firearms matched with the caliber of those projectiles.

Collins opined after examining both projectiles under a comparison microscope that they had indeed been fired by the same gun and explained in ballistics terms how he had come to that conclusion. Based on the weight and the design features on those particular projectiles, he was able to determine they were most consistent with bullets commonly found in 9mm Luger-caliber ammunition, usually intended for use in semiautomatic pistols. Looking at the four unfired cartridges, he was able to determine that three of them had also been cycled through or loaded into and extracted from the same gun.

Collins produced a list of thirty-eight possible makes or manufacturers in the 9mm Luger category that could have been the murder weapon. One of those on the list was an Italian-made TZ-75, the same type and model gun witnesses in court had testified that John Frazier once had owned.

Diggs did an excellent job in getting Collins to state there were probably sixty-five to seventy different types of weapons that could have fired those bullets. And, without the weapon, it was really hard to tell what kind of murder weapon actually had been used in this case.

"Yes, if I had an actual firearm in the laboratory," Collins told the jury, "I would test-fire that gun and then compare those tests with those items of evidence and would potentially reach a positive conclusion of that to be able to determine if that gun fired those items of evidence." And since he had never received a firearm in this case, he couldn't do that, he said.

The prosecution continued to hammer away that Kimberly Renee Poole was a cold-blooded murderer who had plotted the murder of her husband with her lover, and was not the grieving widow she had pretended to be. They called Kevin Todd Fain, an acquaintance of her lover's, and asked him to talk about a gun he had sold him. Kevin had met Frazier in mid-1992 and had sold him a 9mm semiautomatic TZ-75.

"I sold it to him in 1994 or 1995," the long-haired, portly Fain stated. "I didn't shoot it a lot, but when I did, the gun jammed once." He said when he sold the gun to John, he had given him two magazines full of Black Talons. It was a simple transaction: Fain needed the money and John wanted the gun.

Even more damaging testimony came when Fain said he had taken a small vacation with John and the others to the Myrtle Beach area. Said he had remembered it was in July, three weeks after he had sold him the gun. Oddly enough, the place they went to eat was in Barefoot Landing and called Dick's Last Resort. It was the same restaurant Brent and Renee had planned on visiting. John was related to the bartender who was working there at the time, Michael Frazier.

Both Fain and the witness to follow, Cynthia Hanson, were sure reminders that one must be not only careful of who your friends are, but also careful of what you say and do in front of them.

Cynthia Hanson and Renee had worked together as exotic dancers at the gentleman's club, the Silver Fox, in Winston-Salem. Cynthia and her boyfriend/now husband, Thomas Pedersen, had also been friends with John. She spoke of Renee's marital strife and her tumultuous relationship with John, all the time continuing to bury Renee with her testimony.

"She was having marital problems," the attractive blonde related. "She was very unhappy, to the point that she wanted a divorce, and financially she wasn't able to, I guess, get out on her own. So John agreed to have her move in until she was financially able to get a place of her own, and at this time, they contacted a lawyer."

Cynthia never glanced over at Renee to see how she was reacting, but Renee stared angrily at Cynthia. On her face was the look of *You are my friend and I can't believe you are doing this*.

The prosecution asked Cynthia how she would describe John Frazier's feelings in relation to Kimberly Renee Poole, and she stated, "I think that he was very [much] in love with her." When asked how she would describe Brent Poole's feelings for Renee, she repeated, "I think that he was very [much] in love with her as well."

In a very deliberate but soft voice, Hembree asked, "How would you describe the relationship as you observed it between the defendant and her husband, from your personal observations?"

"When I would talk to her on the phone, they were a lot . . . Well, most of the time, they were at each other's throats."

Cynthia further described in detail the conversations she had had with John on the phone and at her house the morning of the murder. She also talked about her conversations with Renee on the phone.

"I was relieved to hear Renee say John wasn't a suspect," she said. "I had called John and had told him that. He asked to speak with Renee, if he could talk to her or if he could see her. If there was anything he could do."

Said she had called Renee to say John wanted to see her.

"She said no right away. That this wasn't a good time. She wasn't crying. She was a totally different person. She was acting like the perfect wife, like 'I haven't eaten. I haven't slept. The only thing that you can do is pray.'"

"Did this strike you as strange?" Hembree asked.

"Totally," Cynthia said. "Because I knew her. I knew where she worked. I knew that she wasn't 'Little Miss Christian.'"

It was important for the defense to blow this witness off the stand. He needed to prove she had believed John was innocent, but the police had manipulated her into believing he was guilty. But before Diggs cross-examined the witness, he asked to take up a matter of law with the judge. Cottingham dismissed the jury and called a fifteen-minute recess so he could hear the pleadings.

Diggs proffered that Cynthia's testimony had been unduly influenced by the fact that Renee had not been granted bond and John Frazier had, and the police had used this against her in their interviews. "I would submit that this might shade or influence or color her testimony in a certain way," he argued, "especially given the fact that she knew, this witness knew that this defendant was under the notice of a death penalty while Frazier was not."

"No, sir," Cottingham stated, "I'm gonna tell you right now two things are not gonna happen. We're not going into the fact that they withdrew the death penalty. That has nothing to do with guilt or innocence. We've said that about ten different times. Now, Judge John Breeden, in his discretion, refused her bond, gave him two hundred thousand dollars. That has nothing to do with any issue in this case."

Diggs kept beating his chest, stating the police had influenced Cynthia to change her mind. "She starts out in this interview as a friendly witness for the defense, and now all of a sudden, at the end of about eight pages of transcript, she's totally against the defendant. And it's all based on what those detectives told her in that interview. She's changing her testimony and there are a lot of things, including the bond question that went into . . . that was told to his witness before she took the stand. I'm just saying I have a right to go into all of those things."

The judge was losing his patience again with Diggs and wanted to know what relevance it had to the credibility of the witness on the stand. In typical fashion, he leaned across his desk, raised his eyebrows and scolded Diggs. After a fairly heated exchange, the judge did agree for Diggs to cross-examine the witness on interviews that she had with agents of the prosecution, but nothing about the bond or the death penalty notice.

"It's got nothing to do with any issue in this case," Cottingham said. "Nothing to do with the guilt and innocence of this client—

and you're not going to do that. That's a matter of law. . . . No, sir, not going to get into the bond, not gonna—we're definitely not gonna get into any death penalty notice."

"I won't bring it up again," Diggs said heavily. "Please note my exception."

When the courtroom filled, Diggs's first question to Cynthia was "Do you remember telling one of the interviewers that you didn't believe John Frazier could do something like this because [he was]—and I apologize, but this came off of your interview tape—chickenshit?"

"Yes."

"And why did you tell him that?"

"Because the way he always treated us; he was like a big teddy bear. He was very gentle, had a very big heart, and I, up to this point, could never believe that he would do something like that."

"And when you say, 'Up to this point,' what do you mean?"

Cynthia said the evidence showed differently. Based on what the detectives had told her, she changed her mind about John's innocence. They had told her John was guilty and that they could prove he'd done it.

Diggs brought out other statements where police unduly influenced Cynthia. With a lot of passion and protest to the judge, he fought—like he'd never fought before—just to get this in.

"This young lady is on trial for murder, and if she's convicted, she's gonna be sentenced probably for the rest of her life in prison." Diggs thought it would help to remind Cottingham of that. "I'm trying to go through this and I understand the time constraints that we have, but the point is we're simply not being able to defend her the way that she needs and deserves to be." He insisted it was appropriate to be able to go into the detailed examination of this witness as to the interview that she had with the police.

Diggs won the argument for the opportunity to beat up on the police for what they had said to Cynthia. "Did not the police say to you, 'I'm going to tell you something, believe it or not, John shot Brent'? In reference to what you had heard, did they not say, 'I'm going to tell you that's not the truth because Renee has confessed to us and told us exactly what's happened from Plan A to Plan B'? Didn't they say, 'But like you know the path that you're heading down right now, don't you know you're only gonna be in the courtroom in the defense corner for a murder suspect?'"

And after each question, Diggs asked Cynthia in some form of another, "Now, did that type of information that was relayed to you by the police detectives tend to make you change your mind about the innocence of John Frazier?"

"Yes, it did," Cynthia admitted. She told they jury it had made her feel like she had to choose between siding with the police or siding with a murderer.

"And did that influence your opinion in the way you feel about the possible guilt of Mr. Frazier?" Diggs asked.

She said it had.

It was a small victory for the defense team and came just in the nick of time. One of the witnesses coming from Winston-Salem was going to arrive late, so the prosecution had asked if they could call Brent's mother, Agnes Poole, to the stand. After taking the oath, and sitting down in the witness chair, she looked as if she would have given her life not to be in that position. She wore a white dress trimmed with a black collar. Pinned to her dress was her angel pin.

Agnes began by telling the court that Brent was very crazy about Renee and that he loved her very, very much. "They moved in with us and everything seemed to be fine until January 1997," she said in a raspy voice. "That was the time she was a dancer at the Silver Fox. Renee was always complaining that Brent didn't do enough for her. She just never seemed to be happy."

Renee stared straight ahead at her mother-in-law and never batted an eye. Occasionally Agnes would dart her eyes in Renee's direction.

Agnes related an incident after Renee and Brent had just gotten back from their Chicago trip. She and her husband had kept Katie, and on May 1 (it was her daughter Dee's birthday), she and Bill had driven to a local pantry-type store, the

Texaco Mart. They pulled in and immediately saw Renee's red truck. Renee was pumping gas and on the opposite side was John Boyd Frazier and his black Blazer. Two young boys sat in his front seat.

Agnes said she didn't know John at the time, but they were whispering back and forth. It looked so suspicious that she went up to Renee and asked who that man was. She said it was a friend of her dad's who had just followed her up there to make sure she didn't run out of gas. The next morning, she said, May 2, at three, Brent called hysterically. Renee had moved out on him and taken Katie and all of their furniture, except for his bed and a chest of drawers, a few other items.

Witnesses in the trial were allowed to stay in the courtroom throughout all the proceedings. Many of them had a connection with Brent Poole or the Poole family. When Agnes aired their dirty laundry, there was a collective breath taken in the courtroom. It would get worse.

"May tenth was Mother's Day," Agnes continued, "and Brent went to church and heard a very moving message. And it really meant a lot to him. I told him later that I would get the tape for that service if he would like. And I did. I got two, one for Renee and one for Brent, and we gave them to them on the thirteenth. She moved back in on the fourteenth.

"They came over to our home on May thirtieth and they discussed going to the beach to celebrate their anniversary. They wanted to borrow some money and we loaned them three hundred dollars to make this trip to the beach. Sort of an anniversary present. We said it was a loan, but we later told him he didn't have to pay it back. He picked it up on the seventh, the day before they left."

Hembree watched the jurors. They were hanging on Agnes's every word. "Did you have occasion to speak with the defendant and your son after they got to the beach?" he asked gingerly.

"Yes, I did," she answered softly. "We had asked them that morning to call us when they got in and give us a phone number, and they called late that afternoon or evening and Renee came on the phone first."

"And what did she say?"

"She immediately started complaining. She said she had a bad headache, Brent was sunburned and Katie was up her butt."

"Kind of a bad mood?" Hembree snapped, his question dripping with sarcasm like nectar from a honeycomb.

"Yeah," Agnes said weakly.

"Did you speak with your son?"

"Yes . . . I normally . . . for three years." Agnes searched for words. "I would speak to Renee and try to encourage her and ask her questions, but I don't . . . I really don't to this day know why I just . . . I said, 'Let me speak to Brent,' and that's . . . We [then] got on the phone with him."

"Did you talk to him?"

"Yes," Agnes choked back. "He was having a great time."

"Did you ever speak with him again?"

This time, she couldn't get the words out. All she could do was shake her head no. It was the last time she had spoken to her son.

It seemed the prosecution would have pulled up stakes and quit while they were way ahead, but they kept piling it on. Renee's neighbors of two years, Jim and Renee Bollow, were two more of her acquaintances called to testify against her.

Jim Bollow had said he'd seen it all: John's black Blazer at the Pooles' house every evening Brent was working; John helping Renee move out on May 1; Renee moving back in a week later and him offering to move the boxes on her front porch, only to be told they weren't gonna be there for long.

When Bollow asked if he had had any other conversations with the defendant, his testimony became a sideshow. In Jerry Springer fashion, he related to the jury a conversation with Renee about her wanting to dance fully nude at another nightclub. That brought the defense to its feet and a strike from the judge. Strike one! Jim Bollow then spoke of another incident, where Renee and John had their genitals pierced. Both the defense and the judge were furious at that remark. Strike two! Cottingham ruled these issues were not relevant and ordered that his answers be stricken by the court. But were they forgotten? They had to have shaded Renee's character. It was yet another lesson in how to guard your privacy, lest it comes back to haunt you.

Bollow further testified the Saturday before the trip at the beach, he had seen the black Blazer at the house on that day for a couple of hours somewhere around nine in the morning. He also made a big deal about a check Brent had received in the mail the day after he had been murdered.

Renee never took notes, nor did she whisper anything to her defense team. She just sat there and looked straight ahead as Bollow continued dropping his pearls of wisdom.

"Renee was really concerned about finding a check in the mail. She was standing there rifling through the mail looking for this check, and when she came across it, she was very delighted. She immediately opened it up. I saw that there was a handwritten note with the check in the envelope, and she kind of crumpled everything up and took the check."

Under cross-examination by West, Jim Bollow said the check was, he thought, in the amount of $750. He believed it had been one of the side jobs Brent had done repairing an eighteen-wheeler. For some reason, the truth was never published to the jury that the check was not written for $750, as Bollow had estimated, but for $110. This incident supported the prosecution's theory that Renee was using Brent and his money to support her wicked lifestyle.

Renee Bollow followed her husband to the stand and testified that she had talked with Renee Poole two weeks before they had gone to the beach and the topic of the conversation was John Boyd Frazier.

"She told me that she was in a relationship with John. She was having an affair, and that . . . she was real, real head over heels over him. She said he treated her real nice, that he would paint her nails and he would let her lie down while he watched Katie."

"Just generally speaking," Hembree advised, "we don't have to go into all the blow by blow."

Renee Bollow shook her head. "Every time, I'd talk about something else, usually it wound back to being about John."

"Did she indicate to you that she was teaching her daughter something?"

"Yeah," Renee Bollow answered. "She was teaching her daughter to say, 'I love you' to John."

Bollow also explained that she had purchased her kids a blow-up swimming pool for the backyard during the summer. Renee Poole had brought Katie and her portable phone over to their backyard. She had heard her trying to call the babysitting service in Myrtle Beach. It was maybe eight to ten times, and she was upset when she couldn't get through.

"Did she receive any calls?" Hembree asked.

"Yes, she did. John called her while she was sitting on my deck with me."

"And she's the one who told you this?"

"Yes. She said that was John, when she got off the phone."

Bollow said Poole had had a discussion with John sitting on her back porch. She didn't hear any of that conversation, that she was holding her hand over the phone and talking real low. But toward the very end she had said, "I love you. I miss you. Won't you please come over?"

Bollow talked about speaking with Poole after her husband had been killed and when she came over to get her mail on Wednesday night and again on Thursday.

Hembree looked toward the jury, then asked, "And did you have a conversation with her out on your front porch?"

"Yes, sir."

Hembree took a few steps in line with the jury so the witness would be looking directly at them when she answered. "What did she say? Tell this jury what the defendant said."

Renee Bollow paused, then looked directly in the eyes of the jurors. "She said, 'He was a shit. But I feel bad anyhow.'"

An ominous feeling crept across the floors of the courtroom. Once again, Renee's words had come back to haunt her. Only this time, the prosecution used them to drive the final wooden stake through what they wanted the jury to believe was a calloused heart.

On cross-examination, the defense attempted to downplay Renee Bollow's last statement by asking if this was the only time she had ever heard Renee Poole say anything derogatory about her husband.

"No," Bollow simply replied. "She griped a lot. That wasn't the only time I had ever heard it." For good reason, West didn't get into any further discussion with Bollow about what else Poole had said about her husband.

After three days of testimony, solicitor Hembree announced to the judge, "The prosecution rests." The television news reporter Adam Shapiro, who had jokingly bet at the beginning of the trial that Renee would be found innocent, had now changed his mind. He admitted that the defense had to present a very strong case if they were going to overcome the odds.

No one in the courtroom wanted Bill Diggs's job. What hat trick could he possibly score that would refute the damning testimony against his client—the most damaging, perhaps, being her own words?

CHAPTER 36

With the jury out of the courtroom, Bill Diggs entered a motion for a directed verdict on the charge of murder. Diggs carefully led the judge through what he thought was the prosecution's problems. He was adamant that the state had failed to establish their theory that John Boyd Frazier was Brent's killer and Renee conspired to accomplish that, and at this point, a decision from the judge would set Renee free.

"There's not any evidence in the record that shows that this defendant had the intent or shared the intent with Frazier to carry out that murder," Diggs insisted. "Over and over again, she indicates that she didn't believe [him]. Even if there was some discussion by him of that act, she didn't ever take him seriously. It never entered her mind that he was actually gonna do it. . . ."

Renee sat stone-faced and listened as her attorney presented a detailed explanation of her actions the night of her husband's murder.

"She may have known. He may have asked her to take him down on the beach. He may have asked her to take him to Fast Eddie's, to do those things earlier in the evening, but how does it relate to this case? Even doing those things, she didn't take him seriously and understand that he was gonna be out there to take Brent Poole's life. There's not any evidence that she took her husband out to the beach for that purpose."

Judge Cottingham was not sympathetic. His white hair fell across his forehead and he stared down from the bench in small-framed glasses with an annoyed expression.

"Well, he told her he was gonna give her an anniversary present, and he killed him," the judge said wearily. "I mean, that's the assertion by the state."

Diggs was getting nowhere, but he wouldn't give up.

The judge finally had to put an end to his argument. "Let me put this to rest very quickly. I don't say it's true or not true—that's for the jury to determine—but the jury well may, as finders of the facts, conclude that they conspired to kill him, that she took him to an isolated spot, that she, in fact, killed her [husband], that she's guilty of it under the doctrine of the hand of one is the hand of all. . . ."

The judge had already denied many of Diggs's motions, and was about to deny this one, but never without a reasonable explanation.

"And let me say one further thing under the doctrine of the hand of one is the hand of all," he added. "Use of a deadly weapon in a violent crime gives rise to an inference of malice, which the jury may accept or reject."

"Your Honor," Diggs had more to say. "I don't recall there being evidence about a discussion [relating to the] use of a deadly weapon. Even in the state's exhibits that were introduced yesterday, there wasn't any indication."

"You're telling me . . . the man is dead. He was shot twice. Surely, there was a use of a deadly weapon."

"But there's not any evidence," Diggs countered. "There's no evidence that the defendant shot him."

"Under the hand of one, the hand of all, it may well be," Cottingham ruled. Diggs offered up a protest, but he cut him off. He was ready to move forward with the trial. "No need in me and you arguing. The evidence is just simply overwhelming. The testimony is for the jury to decide. One, the hand of one, the hand of all. Two, the jury may well conclude they conspired together to take him to an isolated spot and kill him. I don't say that occurred. I'm saying that it's testimony for the jury."

Diggs again argued there was uncontradicted evidence in the record that Renee asked Frazier not to do it, which would serve as her withdrawal from any kind of conspiracy.

The judge was not swayed by Diggs's argument and he let him know it. "Under the state's theory of the case, she took him to an isolated spot by a prearranged plan and he was there, waiting to accomplish the deadly deed. That's the state's version and there's some evidence that the jury can consider on that."

Cottingham quashed the defense's motion, further stating, "This is a classic case involving the hand of one, hand of all."

Diggs had fought an uphill battle all week. He seemed to stumble with nearly every move he made. His back was up against the wall and he needed to put on a good show for the jury. His first witness for the defense was Dr. James Thrasher, with a specialty in psychiatry and subspecialty in forensic psychiatry.

Thrasher had interviewed Renee six months after Brent's murder on December 15, 1998, at the J. Reuben Long Detention Center. He had been asked by the facility to visit her because she was having psychiatric problems. His was a standard-intake psychiatric interview with Renee's chief complaints being headaches, depression and a form of anxiety disorder he labeled post-traumatic stress disorder.

"She had some emotional complaints and was on medication," he testified, "and probably needed more of the same or a change of medication. She was in prison because of some very serious charges."

Diggs wanted the doctor to address a question that had been raised by the prosecution and something that many people in the courtroom wondered. Was Renee Poole as nonemotional and cold-blooded as the opposition had painted her?

Thrasher revealed Renee's past medical history and her physical illnesses. He talked about her social history, her background and development, where she grew up and those circumstances, and discussed a mental-status examination he had given her. Among those issues discussed was Renee having been raped by a friend of her father's when she was twelve years old and some history of her using marijuana at the time. The psychiatrist said he and Renee chatted about some possibilities for medication, he prescribed her some medications, and that was about it. The oral examination had related to her depression and her anxiety disorders, and he later determined she suffered from post-traumatic stress disorder.

"She wasn't sleeping well, she was sad and had despondent fatigue, low interest, low drive and energy, and a poor appetite," Thrasher related in clinical terms. "Despondency and crying spells—all criteria for depression."

Although Thrasher related to the jury that Renee suffered from adjustment disorder with depression, it didn't make as much of an impact as Diggs had hoped when he stated that condition had to be attributed to her response of "being in prison at the time and being under charges and being quite depressed in relationship to that."

"The other condition," he went on to say, "was post-traumatic stress disorder. She had a familiar tremor that has been there most of her life that makes her hands jitter. And she also had what amounted to migraine headaches. I gave her medication to address those issues and devise a suitable treatment plan."

Diggs asked the psychiatrist to explain what he thought was the source of those conditions.

"Hyperalert and fearful," he stated in his opinion. "She was reliving the event of the shooting. She was having nightmares of the blood on her deceased husband's face as she found him immediately after the shooting. All clearly symptoms of PTSD. She was prescribed Celexa and Doxepin—very safe, very well-tolerated and very effective. Celexa is taken during the day and the Doxepin is taken at night, which is very sedating. It allows her to sleep, which improves her condition significantly."

"Doctor, is there any way that you would have of being able to determine the cause of depression to the context you would separate out her confinement from the traumatic events that had occurred in June of 1998?" Diggs asked.

"Well, I think they run together so much. The description

of what happened is a tragic thing, was an awful thing. She was a witness at the scene, and as she couched it, she was intimidated by the shooter. Very frightening. Very depressing. You know, she heard her husband beg for his life, those sort of things, and there with the ultimate outcome—it's just shocking."

"Do you have a medical opinion as to when this depression that she suffered might have commenced?" Diggs asked.

"Oh, I think it began at the unfolding of this whole event. There were troubles in the marriage and alleged paramour, things like that. Those are very troubling things and disturbing things and people can certainly get anxious and upset and depressed over those, but the majority of her symptoms seemed to have appeared after the shooting."

Diggs wanted to make sure he hit all the defense's key points.

"If I wanted to be cynical about this," he continued, "could it reasonably be said that all she's doing is suffering depression because she's locked up?"

"The diagnosis was an adjustment disorder with a very serious crime," Thrasher responded. "Serious potential outcomes on these things, being locked away, away from her child. They're all depressing events." In relation to Renee's incarceration as a source of her post-traumatic stress disorder, he said it could have been. "I think people who lead very protective lives in very genteel settings, suddenly thrown into a prison setting where things can be pretty bleak, with a lot of noise, there's a lot of turmoil. They're out from their families, that sort of thing."

Diggs wanted to nail it down for the jury. "Do you have an opinion as to what the source of a post-traumatic stress disorder is with this particular defendant?"

Looking straight at the jury, Thrasher answered, "In this particular instance, I think it was the shooting of her husband."

"And why is that, Doctor?" Diggs asked further.

"Because that's when she began to have the symptomatology."

For the benefit of the jury, Diggs asked Doctor Thrasher to explain why PTSD was a mental disorder.

"It falls in the general category of an anxiety disorder and it's manifest by specific symptoms, hyperalertness, jumpiness, jitteriness, having nightmares of a traumatic event and reliving the traumatic event." Thrasher stated Renee had all those symptoms and testified they were linked to the shooting and not merely the incarceration. "They oftentimes have nightmares and relive the traumatic event rather vividly as very disturbing. They get lost in it. They have the whole emotional response well enough in them again and they oftentimes believe in exactly the same way as it's being repeated on the spot." Renee had told him she had those symptoms, but the symptoms were diminishing because she was under treatment.

Thrasher added that he had varied experiences with men in combat doing bad things and suffering from PTSD, and his experience had led him to believe it would be less common for someone to be suffering from post-traumatic stress disorder because of an intentional act that they had committed. He didn't believe Renee Poole's was the result of an intentional act. He thought the post-traumatic stress disorder started in this particular defendant at the time of the shooting, the exposure to that trauma.

Diggs never could get a definite answer on whether the doctor believed Renee's trauma was a delayed onset of the post-traumatic stress disorder or something that would have occurred under a normal time sequence. But Thrasher did conclude that by the time he saw her in December 1998, she had had an acute reaction or an acute illness that was partially treated and lingering.

Fran Humphries wanted the jury to know that Renee had reasons enough to be depressed and that all information the psychiatrist had received was "self-reported."

"The majority of the information provided from which you ultimately have to make a diagnosis is self-reported from the defendant?" he asked. "And that is the only source, other than your observations and your assessment of what she had told you and what you have seen in the interview?"

Thrasher answered yes to both questions.

Humphries also got Thrasher to admit that most of the folks, outside of the psychopathic and antisocial personality, if they're in prison, they're depressed.

"It's a depressing place," Thrasher acknowledged.

"Well, it certainly is to me and you," Humphries divulged. "I wouldn't want to be there and I would be depressed over it. There is, however, no way, Doctor, to a degree of medical certainty that you can tell this jury that these diagnoses, post-traumatic stress disorder and this adjustment disorder, depression, were not the result of one, her intentional act, and two, her subsequent incarceration, is there?"

"I've already answered that," Thrasher owned up. "I think it was a result of her being present at the time of the shooting of her husband."

"You cannot acknowledge the possibility that, in fact, it's just as I described it?" Humphries posed the question.

"The only picture that I have of it is as she described it and it was not couched in a willful-act terminology. [I] haven't heard the other side of that, no. I don't have the material in which to go make a different conclusion."

Humphries pressed harder. "And, in fact, you haven't had the benefit of all the other information in regard to her guilt in this case, have you, Doctor?"

"No, I haven't."

"You've had, just as you told this jury," Humphries concluded, "things as she described it."

"That's right," Thrasher agreed.

In an effort to prove the police had misinterpreted Renee's demeanor, and that someone would make incriminating statements against themselves when those statements weren't true, the defense called Dr. Bernard A. "Tony" Albiniak, a psychology professor, to the stand.

Albiniak had an impressive curriculum vitae. He had been employed with Coastal Carolina University for twenty-three years and had been studying about false confessions since they appeared in literature about twelve to fifteen years ago. He had completed fifty or so scientific reports relating to false confessions, attended three conferences of forensic psychology in which that was a major topic and taught this in "Psychology in the Law." He had taught two classes on that subject for five years, with false confessions as a major component. His premise was, given certain circumstantial arrangements, a third of the population would probably admit to something that they hadn't done because of the various pressures and psychological coercion that could be brought to bear.

But would the jury buy into it?

When asked by Diggs what were those pressures, Albiniak explained, "When an interrogation purposely leaves out some element of the case, having evidence, having fingerprints, as to a psychologist, that would be coercive because it will create the tendency in the person's mind that, 'Maybe, in fact, they do have evidence and maybe they are gonna find me guilty,' even if you may not be."

In regard to Renee's case, Albiniak had studied the tapes and transcripts of her interviews extensively and concluded there were fifteen incidents that troubled him about police tactics. Diggs passed out transcripts to the jurors again and asked the professor to point them out, then elaborate.

Albiniak told the jury there were more incidents of police pressure and psychological coercion when Renee didn't have an attorney. He said they were milder, were fewer, and were more subtle in other circumstances. With the aid of the transcripts, he identified where the police had, through their statements, put Renee in a more vulnerable state of mind. He was convinced their status as a law officer, as an authority and especially a male made a huge difference.

"The fact that he's an authority figure," Albiniak stated confidently, "the fact he's an older male makes a difference. He carries a certain degree of authority due to these characteristics. As a younger woman, she would be more vulnerable to cooperate. They gave her the impression they were gonna be truthful, and that's not the case. Law enforcement officers can lie legally and that's allowable under the law."

Albiniak termed the tactics by the detectives as the "lifeguard phenomenon." He then read and explained several of those from the transcript. For example, he chose Detective Altman's statement to Renee, "I'm right here tonight. If you want me to look at it as if we were lifeguards in a rowboat and we're throwing you out a life preserver."

Several jurors raised their eyebrows.

Albiniak discussed Victor Leckowitz, Renee's lawyer, and how his questioning and interrogating during her interview was inappropriate. "Her attorney actually contributed to her dilemma. That she had lost her counsel and gained a third interrogator. It isolated her more, lost her support psychologically and legally."

Nearly everyone in the courtroom, including the prosecution attorneys, truly agreed with him on that point.

Albiniak identified police statements in the transcripts that referred to Renee losing her daughter. He testified that tactic was very significant in getting her to become incredibly cooperative.

"Given that Renee had just lost her husband, 'If I'm taken out of the picture, my daughter is left by herself,' that could be a devastating scenario for her young daughter. It would lead her to try all kinds of attempts to satisfy the authorities to keep her daughter. If she wanted to keep her daughter, she's got to figure out now, 'What do I have to say in order to enable me to keep my daughter?' She's gonna attempt all kinds of, I think, exercises in order to gain that end result."

It all made good sense to the jury.

"The fact that they were taking place late at night," Albiniak continued. "Interrogations are done in a usually small, barren room, no distractions present. It's on police grounds. In other words, everything is done to make you as isolated as possible and as cooperative as possible, and from their point of view. I can understand that, from a psychological point of view, you can get all kinds of distorted information from that person because of that kind of situation, late at night. All those things play into that vulnerability.

"In the short term, you want out of that place. You'll do whatever you can sometimes to get out. There have been cases where people have admitted to crimes just to get out of the interrogation situation. They weren't as severe as this crime, but there were cases where people have acknowledged wrongdoing just to get out of the interrogation process because it is very unpleasant.

"Falsifications given by the detectives which led her to make statements that are not true. Deceptions, ploys of typical interrogation, subtle suggestions, misstatement of facts, police strategies and tactics, that can wreak havoc with a person who is under a lot of stress at the time they hear that statement." All that would contribute ultimately to making what Albiniak described as the false confession.

"You've got to remember in this situation, this woman at least witnessed a murder. Most of us will never have to do that. [It's] very traumatizing. She is being interviewed within a week's time for that terrible event. Memory fails when people are under tremendous stress. Like Dr. Thrasher mentioned, she was probably suffering from PTSD at this time. You don't recall things accurately. Sometimes you say things that are inaccurate under those conditions. It's fairly common for that to happen."

Albiniak cited those incidents that supported his theory.

"Some people are so vulnerable, that if you constantly insist that something is correct, which they know is not correct, they will eventually succumb and agree. [They] minimize the gravity of the situation so that you may agree with that statement; so if you minimize how serious the act is, the person may then agree with you, even if they know it not to be true. Blaming the accomplice and minimizing her direct involvement. To maneuver the person into a comfortable position where they're likely to make an admission that may or may not be true, but you have the admission.

"The whole point of any interrogation is to limit the respondent's ability to contradict their accusations. That's the whole point. You don't let the person make statements, you don't want them making those statements. You want to prevent them, you want to guide them gradually into making affirmative statements, and you can do that very slowly. But over the course of a four- or five-hour interrogation, you've got the person to the point where they're agreeing with a lot of statements they wouldn't have agreed with two hours ago. They've been gradually drawn in that direction. It's an artistic event."

"And are those techniques developed by psychologists?" Diggs asked.

"To a degree," Albiniak acknowledged. "But more police officers than psychologists. I think psychologists would tend to find this coercive, whereas law enforcement people might find them beneficial."

Near the end of Albiniak's testimony, Diggs posed a disturbing scenario. "From a psychological standpoint, given the fact you've got a twenty-one-year-old mother who's just witnessed the murder of her husband, you've gone through the interrogation scenarios for two days . . . from the psychological standpoint, did Mrs. Poole have any other viable option at that point other than to agree with what Detective Altman was either telling her or demanding of her?"

Albiniak didn't hesitate to say, "I don't think so, not at the very end of this process. Early on, there was lots of resistance, which there always is, but near the end of the interview process, you run out of resources. You are fatigued; you're sleepy; you're distressed and you don't see many options. You tend, then, to say things that you wouldn't otherwise have said."

Diggs wanted to be certain the jury understood what he was contending. "From a psychological standpoint, what would have been the consequences for Mrs. Poole to continue to assert her innocence?"

"She would have simply stayed in that unpleasant situation for days thereafter. There's no option. There's no out. . . . She will continue to be accused of the murder and possibly lose her daughter. . . . Those were the options that she perceived."

"And were they acceptable options for most normal human beings?" Diggs asked.

"Not for her," Albiniak assured the jurors.

It appeared to be a solid line of defense, but it was all smoke and mirrors to the prosecution. They asserted the defense had proved nothing with its theory that Renee had confessed to police there was a plan and she knew about it, because she was afraid she would lose her daughter—and the likelihood of police creating that scenario resulted in a false confession. Did they really believe she had confessed to what the police basically wanted to hear and falsely confessed to something she did not participate in? Did she admit to being a part of it, once police had "their foot in the door" generally, and agree to a much larger statement as they pushed her farther out? Did she admit to murder just to extricate herself from a situation that was unpleasant?

On cross, Fran Humphries would dispute that these issues may have been psychologically problematic, but they weren't *legal* ones. He started by getting Albiniak to admit he did not know Mrs. Poole, had not met with her and had not had the opportunity to perform psychological testing on her.

"So, you're left with hearing the words, reading the words, but not knowing the person," he delivered the accusation. "And you would do much better to access her vulnerability, had you had the opportunity to test her psychologically and conduct a thorough interview?"

Albiniak agreed. He further acknowledged that two-thirds— as opposed to one-third—of those interviewed *get caught* in a false confession. And that when a person in Renee Poole's position has been arrested on a criminal offense, a heinous charge, that there was adamant denial at the beginning. That it was all part of a self-protection strategy.

Diggs attempted to strengthen his position on redirect when he asked Albiniak, "Is a false confession likely to be more quickly retracted than a genuine confession?" But his answer wasn't particularly to his liking when it came back, "Not typically. They'll be persistent usually; they'll be persistent."

* * *

The evening was growing late, past the normal quitting time for the jury. Judge Cottingham gave them the option to retire or order sandwiches and keep on working. The jurors voted to keep on going.

The defense then called Mark Hobbs to the stand for the purpose of leading the jury through the ponytail scenario again. It made no sense to Hobbs, and even less sense when Diggs requested that one of the witnesses in the courtroom, Bruce Wolford, sit outside during his testimony. Hobbs didn't know anything about Wolford and had no way of knowing the person whom he now saw with a clean-shaven head and face had once sported a ponytail and sparse facial hair. Renee's supporters sitting in the gallery behind the defense table knew Bruce and were quick to say his new cue-ball look was a diversion to cast off any suspicions of him as the murderer.

When Mark Hobbs testified he was referring to a sweatshirt hood by alluding to the ponytail reference, Diggs went after him. What had made him change his statement now? Hobbs calmly told him he hadn't changed his statement. There was something behind the suspect's head, flopping when he was running, and it appeared to be a ponytail. But it was more than likely a hood on a jacket.

On cross-examination, Humphries had Hobbs confirm in the transcript the word "ponytail" was never used.

"No, sir," Hobbs added. "It just says it's hard to tell about his hair."

Hobbs's statement brought an avalanche of protests from the defense. For twenty minutes the debate continued about which was the correct transcript and if the taped interview with Hobbs had included the word "ponytail." The judge proposed the only fair thing to do was to replay the tape. The defense accused the prosecution of switching transcripts, but, in the end, they lost.

Diggs collected his bearings then called Detective Terry Altman back to the stand for a lengthy discussion on the

composite drawn of the suspect with information provided by
Chris Hensley. The composite was entered by Diggs as defendant's exhibit number two and shown to the jury. When he attempted to question Altman as to where it had been proven
that John Frazier still had the TZ-75 handgun in his possession, the judge dismissed the jury.

The question posed before the judge was whether or not
Altman could testify as to what Kevin Todd Fain had told him
about the transaction of the gun. The prosecution objected on
the basis of hearsay, and the defense argued all they wanted
Altman to do was testify to what was in his notes.

While the jury was out, Diggs questioned Altman concerning information from his notes. His line of questions asserted that the police were aware that Frazier no longer owned
the TZ-75 and had sold it to someone he worked with around
the winter of 1998.

The prosecution rose to their feet to let the cat out of the bag.
"This may be a touch anticipatory," Fran Humphries interjected, "but I know exactly where this is going and that's
third-party guilt. He's gonna try and point out somebody else.
In fact, he's gonna point out Bruce Wolford."

"No, sir, we're not going into third-party guilt," Cottingham declared strongly. Diggs intervened, saying he hadn't
planned on going into that tonight. "Well, when you get
ready to do that, let's excuse the jury before you do it, so I can
make sure that you comply with the various rules," the judge
told him.

The judge's decision must have rattled the defense, for
when the jury returned and Diggs stepped up to finish questioning Altman, he had misplaced his notes. A third-party suspect would not be mentioned again until Diggs's closing
remarks.

Diggs had just enough time to get in the testimonies of
Renee's great-aunt Rebecca Sexton and family friend Tammy
Blackwell before the jury's sandwiches arrived at 8:30 P.M. The
jury took a quick twenty-minute break and reentered the

courtroom for the testimony of Renee's grandmother Frances Bostick.

"Renee was like a zombie." Bostick testified to Renee's demeanor the day she arrived home from the beach. "Her eyes were real large and sunk back in her head. She had been crying. We left her alone, with her arms wrapped around her body. She said she was freezing. . . . She didn't sleep. . . . She was shivering. It was hot outside, but she was acting like a cocoon. . . . She didn't eat anything that I saw."

Bostick said she had asked Renee what had happened, that they had always been close, and she believed Renee would have told her, being her grandmother, more things than she would have told her parents. "And she said, 'I just don't know who done it.' When I asked what he looked like, she said, 'Well, he was dressed all in black.'"

A family friend, Joel Clampitt, testified next, followed by Renee's father, Jack Summey.

Jack recapped for the jury Renee's interview at the Davie County Courthouse. He said they had waited until 9:00 P.M. so that they could get a lawyer. Renee had also been getting Brent's affairs together for the funeral. He and his wife had sat outside the room, where they did the interview, right outside the door, and had heard quite a bit of it. He admitted they were trying to listen and to hear what was going on.

Jack recalled there was a break in the interview, somewhere around 12:30 or 1:00 A.M. In the hallway, he had access to his daughter and an opportunity to speak with her and her lawyer at that time. "I told Renee, 'If you know who it was, you tell them. If you don't know who it was, you tell them.'" He said this had gone on for about ten minutes. "I was holding her hand. I can take my hands and squeeze someone's hands very hard and I was doing that to her. And I don't know if I just realized what I was doing or what, but I realized later that my hand was hurting, so I know I had to have been hurting her. I think she said she had taken all she could take and she said, 'Let's go back in.' She goes back in and immediately identifies Mr. Frazier as the suspect."

Upon further examination, Jack told the jury he didn't intend to convey to Renee that she should identify John Frazier. "I don't think I implied that. I was just wanting her to either tell them she knew who it was or she didn't know who it was. Just tell them the truth."

In cross-examination from Hembree, Jack stated he hadn't suspected John Frazier as the killer. When he was asked what it was he wanted his daughter to do the night he talked with her and Victor Leckowitz during the break, he answered, "To either say she knew who did it or she didn't know who did it."

"Did you tell her to tell the truth?" Hembree asked.

"Yes."

"Repeatedly?"

"I asked her to tell either she did know who did it or she didn't know who did it."

"Did you tell her to say it was John Frazier?"

"No."

"Did you tell her to say she planned it?"

"No."

"Did you tell her to say that they were gonna go to Dick's Last Resort; then they were gonna go down to the beach in a secluded area and kill him?"

"I did not know anything about that."

"You didn't tell her that, did you?"

"No, I didn't."

Hembree shifted his question slightly. "Sir, I believe you're a male; is that true?"

"I hope so." Jack smiled.

"And you're older than your daughter."

"Right."

"And you're an authority figure to her, are you not?"

"I hope so."

"She's going to trust your advice, isn't that fair to say?"

"I should hope so."

"You even told Mr. Diggs a moment ago that subconsciously you were squeezing her hand to the point that it hurt your own hand. For what purpose?"

"I wanted to know if she knew who did it or she didn't know who did it."

"You wanted her to tell the truth?" Hembree continued to play the heavy.

"Right."

"And you conveyed that to her?"

"Yes, either she knew or she didn't know."

"Did you put pressure on her to tell the truth?"

"Yes."

"And she did tell the truth, didn't she?"

"That I don't know."

Marie Summey followed her husband to the stand, telling the jury that Renee was shopping and buying clothing for Brent shortly before his death. Brent needed new clothes for church and she was buying him new jeans, shirts, socks and underwear. She would bring it by her house and ask what she thought about the clothes she had picked out. Three days before their trip, Renee had bought him a new pair of tennis shoes, stuff from Kinney and Dillard's, two pairs of Tommy jeans, two pairs of Levi's jeans, socks, underwear and belts. Marie had saved and produced receipts of all those purchases for the court.

Diggs questioned Marie about each receipt and then introduced all of them as defense exhibits. He wanted the jury to consider that if Renee knew her husband was going to be murdered, why would she have gone to all the trouble to buy him such expensive clothes?

On cross-examination, Humphries asked her if she knew Renee had been shopping with Courtney and Bruce Wolford at any time? And did she know that on at least one of these trips, she had met John Frazier at the mall?

She said she did not know anything about those trips, nor did she know Renee had been seeing John after her return home.

Humphries then asked Marie about her statement made to the fugitive task force the night her daughter had been arrested. "Mrs. Summey, do you recall having told Butch that in the case of Renee, sometimes you have to be hard on her to get her to tell the truth?"

"I told him that I was hard on Renee and my hardness— for me to be hard on Renee, I would give her two chances to tell me the truth and that was it."

"Yes, ma'am, and I didn't mean to imply anything else," Humphries added.

But what other implication could the jury perceive than her own mother had to come down hard on her before she told the truth?

As the defense tried to build their case, it became increasingly clear what was happening. The fact was no matter how hard Diggs attacked the police, no matter how fervently he argued Renee's confession was false and had been coerced, there was no other way to get around the fact that she had confessed to conspiring with John Frazier to murder her husband. Of course, he believed there was no direct evidence other than her confession to support that. The police and prosecutors were able to question and to speculate as to Frazier, but as it turned out, all they had against her was circumstantial evidence. So, why wouldn't the jury find it so implausible to believe Bruce Wolford—another of Renee's lovers who had as much motive to kill Brent as John—had killed her husband?

"Your Honor, the defense calls C. E. Martin to the stand." Hembree was up and on his feet before the called witness took a step from his chair. A bench conference was held and then the judge dismissed the jury.

Hembree fired the first shot. "Your Honor, I submit that Mr. Diggs is proposed to call C. E. Martin, who is his paid investigator that's been working on this case with him since December or January. He proposes to qualify in what field, some sort of investigatory expert, to essentially challenge the police."

"Well, I haven't heard what Mr. Diggs . . ." The judge stared down at the defense table with a pensive expression. "Why are you calling him, Mr. Diggs?"

"I'm gonna call him because he's an investigative expert. He has twenty-one years' experience with the Army Criminal Investigative Division. He is an expert in criminal investigative technique. He has worked on this case. I'm going to ask him what he would have done to investigate this case, what he would have done. We're not going to go into anything the Myrtle Beach police did. We're not going to be critical of them in any way. We're gonna ask him what he would have done and how he would have handled this case, if there are any leads he's aware of that in his opinion are still available to—"

The judge's expression turned solemn. "Oh, no. You're talking about third-party guilt. We're not going into any leads that he's talking about." Cottingham didn't need any time to think about his decision and wasn't afraid of being overturned by a higher court. His mind was made up. "I'm not going into any third-party guilt," he admonished in specific tones. "I'm talking about leads that are . . . No. You want to do what you saw done in [the] O. J. Simpson [trial] and I'm not gonna let you try the investigating officers in this courtroom. Now, I'm not gonna do that."

"Judge, I'm not gonna do that," Diggs pleaded.

"Well, I'll let you get him on the stand and see where you're going," the judge quickly ruled. "The jury is outside. Go ahead. We're not going into that sort of stuff in South Carolina, [particularly] in Judge Cottingham's court."

There was a huge issue at stake for the defense, so Diggs appealed, "Let me say this, if you're not gonna let him testify—"

"Well, no, I'm not saying that," the judge reminded him. "I'm hearing where you think you're going and I'll see where you're going and then I'll rule on it."

Diggs acknowledged with a nod. "Well, for the purpose of this examination, let's go with the qualifications of an expert."

Rebuffed, Cottingham went on to state, "Well, you can tell me again now for the record and maybe we can save some time. Where is it you want to go with this witness? Perhaps I can save you some time."

"I'm going to ask him how [does] one go about investigating [in] a case of this type."

The judge wasn't exactly sure as to what issue. Diggs told him it was to solve the identity of the perpetrator of the murder, to which he asked, "As to what issue, that it was somebody else?"

"As to the issue, Your Honor, of creating a reliable, probative inquiry as to who the identity or as to the identity of the assailant in any kind of murder case. Not necessarily this one, but after we establish that, then we'll go into what he's done and what he's discovered in this case and go into other leads that still may not be fully developed in this case that maybe point somewhere other than to John Frazier."

The judge returned looking solemn. "All right, now, let me tell you something. Evidence offered by an accused as to the commission of a crime by another person must be limited to such facts as are inconsistent with his own guilt and to such facts as raise a reasonable inference or presumption as to his own innocence. Evidence which can have no other effect than to cast a bare suspicion under another or to raise conjectural inferences is not admissible."

"And I . . . Let me tell you what," Diggs postured, "I'm following that to the letter and let me tell you why, because John Frazier's photograph, and, of course, they tied their case—lock, stock and barrel—to John Frazier." He grabbed two sheets of paper up with his large hands. "Here's a photograph of John Frazier. Now, look, we have a composite drawing that's in evidence that was generated by one of the state's own witnesses, okay, and look at that composite." He pointed to the composite. "Look at the hairdo on that."

"What will this witness testify as to that issue?" Cottingham asked, trying to reconsider all the arguments and evidence of counsel.

"He's gonna testify about this being one factor in this case that hasn't been fully investigated," Diggs related.

"Your Honor," Hembree interrupted his argument, "he can

argue that all day to the jury, but to have him get up and say, 'Well, this is the way it ought to be done.'"

The judge had read arguments on this issue for weeks and was ready to side with the prosecution. "No, sir. No, sir. I'm not going to permit that. We're not going to get into third-party guilt unless you specifically follow the rule as enunciated in *Gregory,* in *Beckham,* in *Williams,* and I can name ten others. And you can, too."

"Well, I'm not gonna try to violate any of the rules in those cases, Your Honor," Diggs responded firmly. "I'm just not doing it."

"Well, you want to say, as I understand it, you want your paid investigator to get up and indicate any specificity that exculpates (*sic*) Mr. Frazier."

"Your Honor, it's right there," Diggs snapped back. "Defense exhibit two"

"No, sir. No, sir. That witness who furnished that information specifically said something . . ."

"No, no, this is from Mr. Hensley," Diggs reminded him.

"No, sir, the eyewitness, the information from Donna, did not meet what she saw."

Diggs shook his head. "No, sir. No, sir. No, sir."

The judge leaned forward over his desk. "Yes, sir. Wait a minute now."

"That's the other composite," Diggs protested. "This is the composite that was generated by Mr. Hensley."

"Well, we are not going down that road to let you indicate, to cast suspicions on a third party, on that picture. If you've got some evidence, [then] go ahead."

Diggs was nearly beaten back. "I mean, [the] only additional evidence I could have would be a name tag under it, but what we have obviously is a person who does not fit the description of John Frazier, okay. He has hair and he has a mustache. . . ."

As much as Diggs tried to get the judge to accept Martin's testimony, the prosecution argued against it. "I certainly don't have any objection to him being called as a witness," Hembree said to the judge, "but to have him come in and be qualified as an expert? I don't know of a case held by our supreme court that says you can call your own private investigator, qualify him as an expert and then put him up there to critique the efforts by the police department. And how he would do it different back where he came from, so that's something brand-new for South Carolina."

"No, it's not," Cottingham assured him. "It's not gonna happen in South Carolina in my court." After a fifteen-minute discussion on the matter, the judge offered his final words. "The thrust of your discussion is to put the guilt on somebody else. Well, sir, you're not entitled to it under the rule for your hired investigators to say that somebody else may have committed it instead of John Boyd Frazier. You simply can't do that. I specifically reject that and I decline to let him testify: one, as an expert; two, I'm not gonna let him get into any third-party guilt in his investigation. Clearly, that's what you want to show. I think as an officer of the court, you've got to admit that . . . If I'm wrong, the supreme court can tell me so. I'm not going to permit that, don't think our rules provide for it, and I'm certainly not going into a situation where the investigating officers are put on trial rather than the alleged defendant."

Shortly before 10:00 P.M., the court foreman was asked to bring the jury back in. They stayed long enough to hear defense counsel say there would be no more witnesses, that at this time they were gonna rest.

With the jury dismissed and most of the galleries nearly emptied, the judge asked to hear any motions. Since it had been a long day, Diggs asked to postpone any motions until the morning, and the prosecution agreed with one minor exception. The prosecution wanted to know if the state was going to be required to open on the law in regard to the general charges of murder. Cottingham informed that he intended to give the charge on murder, the definition of murder, the definition of malice and to charge the law as to conspiracy. He would also address the jury as to expert witnesses, the hand of one is the hand of all, mere presence and the voluntariness of the statement, identification charge with the testimony of John Boyd Frazier and charge with reference to failure to take the stand.

The judge then asked Renee to come forward as he questioned her about her absolute right to testify. "I do not wish to testify," she said softly after acknowledging she understood all her rights to testify. Given the evidence of Renee's many sexual affairs, her promiscuous lifestyle, her confessions to the police and her fragile state of mind, it was a wise decision. The prosecutors could have easily disemboweled her like a wounded deer in front of the jury.

The court finally recessed at 10:15 P.M. On the way out, those who had sat through the entire day's affairs pondered tomorrow's outcome. With the case now resting on the final arguments, the odds were in neither counsel's favor at this point. Even though the prosecution had presented a powerful case against Renee, its case could easily fail with the jurors. No matter what the jurors had seen and heard, it was still hard for some people to believe they would ever convict this young mother of conspiracy to commit murder. The jury had to have had doubts about her guilt, so how could they vote to send her to prison for the rest of her life without being absolutely positive she was guilty?

Although Renee looked worried, even she wholeheartedly believed the jury would have many reasonable doubts in mind.

CHAPTER 37

Throughout the trial, only a handful of seats were occupied on either side of the courtroom, and that changed only slightly the last day of court. Renee looked confident and was dressed in a dark blue business suit with a plain white button-down blouse. For good luck, she wore on the front of her dress a gold angel with a halo made of pearls. Her mother had given it to her the first day of court as a reminder of her support. Both she and her mother had prayed this would be her final day to think about wearing a prison jumpsuit again.

After the panel of jurors was escorted in and seated in the jury box, the morning began as promised with the normal motions for dismissal and charges to the jury. The state would have the honor of first and last final arguments and the defense would have just the one offered between.

Fran Humphries began summation in praise of the jurors, then explained the legal terms of murder, conspiracy to commit murder, responsibility of the police and Renee's voluntary confession, withdrawal from conspiracy, and the principle of the hand of one is the hand of all.

He reminded the jurors, "If Renee Poole had said, 'I'm not going through with it. You better not, either,' if and only if both of those predicate situations exist, then and only then does Kimberly Renee Poole escape responsibility in this matter.

"Even an intent to withdraw, and it is not suggested by this evidence, but even an intent to withdraw, if not communicated or if not done entirely, is insufficient and she is responsible, equally responsible for the murder of William Brent Poole. That is the law.

"Now, that is to say this: how do you communicate your entire and complete withdrawal from a conspiracy such as this? We can do it any number of ways: not just by word, but by action. Was there a withdrawal communicated entirely by this defendant, Kimberly Renee Poole, to John Boyd Frazier by her conduct? No, ma'am. No, sir. It is not enough to get the train off the tracks and then say, 'shouldn't have done that.' The law requires a derailing of that train, and in this case, there is absolutely no evidence to suggest that."

Humphries then turned the jurors' attention to logic. "Common sense, folks, is in the details, and there is one central, inescapable truth that is situated within the facts of this case: the conduct of Kimberly Renee Poole was intentional. It was goal oriented. It was purposeful, and it was knowing, and as a result, William Brent Poole lost his life by virtue of two gunshots to his head on an Horry County beach."

The prosecutor's words had been chosen carefully and were well-rehearsed. His delivery as smooth as any of the trial lawyers from television's *Law & Order*. He never broke eye contact with the jury.

"Her conduct was not by chance," Humphries concluded in a low voice. "It was not bad luck and it was not miscalculation. If there are two agreeing with one gun, each is as guilty as the other. Kimberly Renee Poole is as guilty as the other slayer, and in this case, almost entirely responsible."

Bill Diggs took his place in front of the jury and began the defense's position by presenting a scathing attack against the police. Going straight for the jugular, he accused them all of lying. "We have major problems about the reliability and the believability of Renee's statement. . . . There are major problems considering the lies and the deceit that went into the production of that statement. You're gonna have to have a doubt about her guilt simply because of that process."

Diggs's voice became louder as he then attacked the evidence presented by the prosecution. "The state doesn't have any evidence available to them that's certainly been introduced into this trial, any physical evidence to show you that John Frazier was at the beach that night. In a year and a half, they should have been able to find something, a piece of beach sand, a bug on the windshield, other than an eyewitness identification at twelve o'clock at night with somebody fifty to eighty feet away."

So, as to let them know he had not been grabbing at straws, Diggs talked again about the composite and missing ponytail.

"That guy has got a lot of hair, okay?" Diggs stressed as he held the composite up before the jury. "This man has got a mustache. Where did that detail come from? . . . They (the police) generated that, and I would submit that's the kind of lead [they received] from Mr. Hensley who said he was only five feet away from the fellow, as opposed to eighty feet, and he got a good look. . . . Why wasn't this followed up on, and why didn't you hear any testimony from the prosecution about why this wasn't? Well, obviously, they got a confession out of Renee early on in the case and they had their blinders on, and when they had this stuff like this out there, they didn't pursue it. You know, they didn't pursue it."

Diggs confessed he had been frustrated and in a bad mood last night when the judge ruled against him. He told the jurors that he had been mad at the prosecutors, the judge, and Detective King, but had apologized to everyone. Diggs's summation sounded fragmented and choppy, and he wasn't as sure of his words as Humphries had been. He strolled back and forth from his notes and fumbled awkwardly with his glasses, nervously putting them on, then taking them off again. His voice was weak and he seemed tired.

"I was thinking, 'this whole case is just in a mess,' and I was trying to put my finger on why it is so, and I think that it's so in this situation simply because of the sheer volume and amount of deception and lying that went on in this case by the prosecution in the interview, when Renee was being interviewed. . . ."

Diggs wasn't through with the detectives quite yet. He stepped away from his notes at the lectern and told the jurors how he thought the greatest fault was the detectives' interview techniques and how inappropriate he believed they truly were. "And the state failed, for whatever reasons, to correct that in their case. In some respects, that's on trial. I'm not condemning it in every case, but in this case, it's inappropriate, I submit, because it was done to her. Based on the deceit and the deception and the lack of physical evidence in this case connecting John Frazier to the murder, Renee is innocent. She carved out an admission that was designed to save her child and because she had ineffective counsel in Mr. Leckowitz."

Diggs reminded the jury of his expert, Dr. Tony Albiniak, who had singled out two dozen instances where she had been coerced into a confession. "She had been pushed into a corner and had no option available to her either to extricate herself from that very unnerving situation in the middle of the night with police detectives hovering around her, this twenty-one-year-old little girl, who turned twenty-three this week, she had no method or no means of getting out of that situation other than telling them what they wanted to say or wanted her to say. And, secondly, she had no way that was presented to her; she had no option. If she wanted to save her relationship with her child, she had no option except to tell them what they wanted to hear and get out of there."

Having disposed of this matter, Diggs then listed—in a "let's chase a few rabbits" fashion—those things he believed were known and unknown in the case. He addressed each of these issues and attempted to provide an explanation. The list also included Renee's problematic demeanor.

"She was crying. And she was physically upset. Emotionally upset, physically sick. According to the testimony prior to Detective Altman's arrival on the scene when she was down at the police station."

Diggs wanted the jury to believe the police had railroaded Renee into a confession. Then he attacked head-on the lesion that had infected Renee's defense throughout the entire case.

"Let's talk about Frazier and let's be done with it, okay? Because now the issue at hand is Renee, not Frazier, and that's another thing. Her conviction is superfluous to justice being done in this case because convicting or acquitting her, either way, Brent Poole's murderer is still out there on the street. We know that. Why are we here? Why isn't Frazier on trial? Have you thought about that during the course of this trial? I'll tell you why. One reason that might come to your mind is they don't have any evidence. I don't think there could be a louder admission than that by the prosecution than this trial, and I think—I would submit that those blinders need to come off the prosecution and they need to solve this case."

Diggs devoted the rest of his final argument to refuting Renee's "confession" and the physical evidence in the case.

"Justice in this case would require a complete acquittal of Renee on both of these charges, okay?" Diggs summed it up for the jury. "I would submit there's not any evidence at all. Without the use of her statement, there's no evidence to convict her of either offense. This case and the law cries out for an acquittal. This family cannot—cannot—under any circumstances receive justice today. That's gonna have to come when the trial is had for the murderer of their son."

Diggs paused briefly, then gave the jurors a most intense look.

". . . His Honor charged you a few minutes ago that mere presence at the crime scene—Renee was there; she was there. Over and over in her interview, she insisted, 'I didn't know it was gonna happen,' but she was there when it did, and His Honor has already instructed you that's not guilt; that's not evidence of guilt—it doesn't make her guilty in the eyes of the law. It doesn't make her guilty. Even—he said something even beyond that. Even knowledge that this was gonna happen doesn't make her guilty, you know, and that's not sufficient to convict her."

Solicitor Greg Hembree didn't mince any words with the jury in his opening statement of his closing arguments. "For the defense to suggest in its closing remarks that the conviction of Kimberly Renee Poole is superfluous, is insignificant to them, to the Poole family, it's offensive. This was a cold-blooded, premeditated, diabolical murder of their son and their brother."

With lots of dramatic flair and enthusiasm, Hembree told the jury this case had a lot of evidence. Using the three Styrofoam charts like a college professor would to help keep his summation organized, he assured the jurors, "There are a lot of exhibits. You've heard from a lot of witnesses, but when you boil it down, the case is actually quite straightforward. The motive is clear, the means is clear, the opportunity is clear, and the steps undertaken to cover the crime is clear. I ask you to do one thing, to use your good judgment and common sense to evaluate this evidence and render a verdict that speaks the truth."

The evidence supported a conviction, Hembree assured the jurors, as he reminded them of the facts from the beginning to the end of this case. He scoffed at the defense's suggestion of no motive.

"Several weeks before May first, defendant and John Boyd Frazier make a plan. They're gonna move in together. They're gonna set up housekeeping. She's gonna leave her husband for John Boyd Frazier, and she didn't cancel the trip with her husband to Chicago; she wants to get that in, but once she's finished with that, on Friday night, she leaves home, packs up in the dead of night, while her husband is out working the graveyard shift at Mack Trucks, trying to provide for their family. She boxes it up—bag and baggage, baby in the car—and disappears. He comes home to an empty house; no warnings; no clue, distraught.

"Now, this rocks along for a little while, but at some point, Mrs. Poole goes to see a lawyer. She says that in her statement. She went to see a lawyer about this family situation she finds herself in and he said, 'Well, maybe it wasn't such a good idea.' What's the story here? We've got a lady without a job—we know what her previous job was—who has abandoned the marital home in the dead of night. . . . I expect the lawyer did tell her that was kind of a bad idea. Ladies and gentlemen, where is the custody of that child going? It's a problem. She also figures out that maybe John Boyd Frazier isn't all he's cracked up to be. He's kind of a loser. He doesn't really have any money. He's kind of a loser."

Hembree picked up a copy of the transcript and held it out in front of the jurors. He read the parts as well as any amateur actor. "Let's see what Mrs. Poole tells us about John Frazier. We'll just read it right out of her statement."

The jury listened to Renee's own incriminating words relating to her feelings for her husband and her lover, and the insurance policy she was to receive.

"See how the stakes are building up on the table? Custody, the house, the truck, over a hundred thousand dollars; that's a lot of money, even for a loser. That's a lot of money, and I think the last important piece of evidence that has to go into this motive, which sets the stage for what's about to happen, is Mr. Bollow. He saw Renee the Saturday after she moved back in, on the sixteenth, and he said she smoked a cigarette, lit up a cigarette, and kind of leaned against the truck and she said, 'Brent will never make me do what I don't want to do.'

"So, we've got problems. We can't get custody; don't have any money, but we want to live together. What are we gonna do about it? And that is the plan. That's when they started making plans.

"First, they came on a couple of plans. The first plan was poison."

Hembree read from the transcript where Renee had said that John kept talking to her about killing her husband: "I think that was his main thing—me poisoning him. I was like, 'No, I'm not gonna do that.' He said something about he was gonna do one thing, then he was gonna do another thing. I said, 'Well, do it. I don't think you have the balls to do it.'"

Hembree elaborated, then reminded the jury, "The poisoning plan wasn't gonna work, so they came up with another plan, a second plan." He read excerpts from her statement that included John's instructions for murder:

Get out to the beach. Be there as late as possible, two, two-thirty, three, real late in the morning so there would be no one out on the beach and that he would take care of it from there.
Poole: I didn't know if he was gonna shoot him or if he was gonna use a knife, because John had knives at home, too.

Altman: But you knew he was gonna be killed?
Poole: Right.

"She volunteered this information about poison. She volunteered this information about a knife. These weren't questions that were put to her in a manner where she had no choice. They were open-ended questions and she just starts talking."

Hembree held the jury spellbound with his theatrical performance:

Poole: He never said that he was gonna do it.
Altman: But he said . . .
Poole: He said whoever would—whoever was gonna do it would know what to do. They would keep a close eye on us and they would take care of it. He said, "Walk north," because it gets away from all the hotels.
Altman: What was your plan after it happened?
Poole: He didn't . . . He didn't say anything.
Altman: You had to have rehearsed something. You knew you were gonna have to come up with a story.
Poole: He just told me, "Remember what I said."
Altman: And what did he say?
Poole: And stick to it.
Altman: What did he say?
Poole: He didn't say anything. He said, "You just have to remember what you've said and you have to let me know."
Altman: Now, you've said that—remember—so he told you . . .
Poole: No, he just said, "Remember what you say." He said, "Be careful what you say. Just answer the questions short. Don't go into any detail, but remember what you say because I have to know, because if my story conflicts with yours, then they are gonna know."

Brent Poole's family followed every word of Hembree's presentation. Their ashen faces and swollen red eyes testified to the many sleepless nights they had experienced since first hearing of Brent's murder.

"The plan, ladies and gentlemen, was laid out, not only the plan to commit the murder, but the plan to cover the murder after it was committed." Hembree delivered his fiery argument, using an elongated pointer to tap on the floor and the exhibits for emphasis when he wanted to make a point.

Hembree contended there were certain tasks Frazier had to do in preparation. "The plan goes into action, John Boyd Frazier first: One, got off work the eighth, nineth, and tenth. Two, got to have a car that nobody recognizes. Borrows car from his friend Kayle Schettler. Three, got to have a gun. 'I need a weapon. I can afford to get rid of that TZ-75 because it has a tendency to misfire.'

"Then, Renee's got to prepare. One, got to get the hotel. Gives John the room number at Carolina Winds. Room six-oh-four. Two, got to get him alone in a secluded area. They know of a secluded place in Myrtle Beach, where it's dark and no lights. Three, got to get a baby-sitter. Needed a baby-sitter from ten until two.

"That was all part of the plan. Renee and John had at least one conversation during the course of the week when she was trying to call the baby-sitter. And he was over at her house on the Saturday before they left for the beach. The plan is in——the train now is on the track. The plan is rolling, the execution of the plan."

Hembree waited for the jurors to digest it. His voice then turned soft and sympathetic.

"As you recall, little Katie was sitting on her daddy's lap. She begins crying when he gets up to leave. He's kind of trying to console her. 'Let me get you something to eat. Are you hungry?' And as Carolyn Murphy described it, Renee Poole was like, 'Get on out.' Go. Go. She was shooing him. It was sort of push . . . shooing him: 'Get on out. We've got to move. We've got to get moving.' And is this somebody on vacation or is this somebody that has a deadline to meet?"

The prosecutor continued to lay out the agenda: Dick's Last

Resort, Fast Eddie's, the withdrawal of fifty dollars at the ATM and the Wings Beachstore to get a towel.

"Now, ladies and gentlemen, I'm gonna submit to you that this starts one of the most diabolical aspects of this whole plan," he stressed. "This young man, his anniversary at the beach, [he's] excited . . . he's enthusiastic. They're going to get a towel, for one reason, and one reason only. . . ."

Hembree continued to build the suspense. "They began walking north. Brent Poole was happy. They get past Eighty-second Avenue and at some point there, Kimberly Renee Poole engages Brent Poole in . . . sex. . . . " His voice became even softer and he looked as if he were almost to the point of tears. "To give her lover time to get to the killing field. We know that, and the SLED officer testified that there was semen in his underwear on his anniversary."

Expressions on the juror's faces seemed to change, as if they, too, believed that was the most despicable act they'd ever heard.

"John Frazier. She's held up her end of the deal. She's got him secluded. She's got him vulnerable. She's got him right where she said she'd have him. North of the hotel, walk away from the lights, just like the plan, twelve o'clock, end of the baby-sitter's shift. Late as she could possibly do it. Have him right there. She's held up her end of the deal."

The jury was spellbound.

"After listening to all the testimony," Hembree concluded, "it is clear as to what Renee's plan was."

He then turned his comments toward Renee's lover and ridiculed him for his role in the murder.

"John Boyd Frazier, his execution of the plan. Now, John Boyd Frazier is certainly not a professional assassin. He has demonstrated that through his handling of this murder, the way he acted. He's hanging out at the hotel. He thinks he's pretty clever, all black. He must have seen this on *Hogan's Heroes,* or something. He's all dressed up in black—you know, black pants, long pants, in the middle of the summer, for heaven's sake. What's gonna draw someone's attention to you more than this—who is this yo-yo wearing, you know, a long-sleeved, hooded sweatshirt in the middle of the night, when it's warm, and long black pants? It drew their attention.

"The Hobbses, the first thing they [saw] when they came down for a midnight walk. You consider the credibility of those two witnesses, ladies and gentlemen. You consider the credibility of the Hobbses. It's their anniversary, too. It's kind of ironic. They come down here, they're gonna go for a walk on the beach, and they see this guy and he looks suspicious, and Mr. Hobbs said he had that kind of funny look in his eyes."

Hembree defended the Hobbses' description and identification of Frazier: "I'll tell you folks, that photo-lineup procedure that was followed in this case is outstanding. . . . Immediately, [they said] 'That's the guy. No problem. . . . No question about it.' Lo and behold, what a coincidence, they identified John Boyd Frazier."

Hembree paused to take a poke at the defense's ponytail theory.

". . . And this whole bit, I have to clear this up. It's not that important. This whole ponytail business, don't get sidetracked by that. You listen to the tape. There's no mention of a ponytail on that tape. . . . He never said anything about a ponytail. That was something Mr. Diggs kind of asked him about."

Hembree told the jurors that Renee and John had planned to cover up the murder with a robbery. But the found wallet with credit cards and money still in it—pitched twenty-five feet into a yard—had to dispel that notion.

Furthermore, why would a robber kill Brent and not Renee?

"He shot him, execution style, two bullets to the head. Now, again, not the best professional assassin in the world. [Frazier says,] 'We're gonna cover this thing with a robbery. That's the plan' . . . Well, if you're gonna commit a robbery and kill the witnesses, because there's no other reason in the world if you believe it's just a straight-out stranger robbery—and you're gonna kill the witnesses. You're gonna kill some, but not all? So now, you've got a witness not only to a robbery, but to a murder? It doesn't make sense. It's crazy. If you're gonna do that, you're gonna shoot one, and then you're not gonna shoot the other? It's not a robbery; it's a murder. It's an execution."

As related to Frazier's drive home after the murder, Hembree speculated he had 5½, almost 6 hours from the time he committed the murder until the officer knocked on his door to get back. "He had not only time to get back, he had time to wash the car, wax the car, take his clothes and drive out in the country and burn them. I mean, he had all kinds of time. That's not the problem."

The jurors were getting much more from Hembree than they had ever expected. He attacked the defense's perception of Renee's demeanor and told them Renee had waited five minutes before she acted. And that her vague story was part of the plan to protect herself and her lover. He reminded the jurors that her demeanor was calm and confident at times, looking for a check next door. It was the same type of masquerade she had worn while pretending to be "Miss Christian" with her friend Cynthia Hanson, but the statement to her next-door neighbors of, "I know he was a shit, but I still feel sorry for him" belied her true feelings.

"What possibly could be going through her mind and her heart?" Hembree dangled the question before the jurors. He then discussed her "supposedly" coercive testimony that the defense had made a lot of hoopla over. The prosecutor reminded the jury she had a lawyer. "She agrees to talk. It's just that simple. She made voluntary, knowing, and intelligent waiver, and she signed it, agreed to it. She made a choice."

Hembree disputed the testimony of the defense's key expert witness, Dr. Tony Albiniak. He alleged the expert witness did not give accurate information and had made assumptions that were outside his area of expertise.

"These statements are a tremendous problem for the defense in this case," he redirected the juror's attention in a loud voice. "Because they said, 'I did it.' They say, 'I'm guilty. I planned the murder with my boyfriend and I went out and I did it. I killed him,' and now here we are. [If] they don't deal with those, there's no reason to be here, okay? They've gotta do something about it. They can't just let them lay there, so they drag in ol' Dr. Albiniak from Coastal Carolina, a paid defense witness. 'Tell us what you know, Doctor. Give us your opinion on all this,' and he says, 'You know I don't like it.' You know, he doesn't like it. Well, folks, he's not the boss, all right? He's not the one that gets to decide these things. He's a psychologist, for heaven's sake. He's not—and he says—he admits this has nothing to do with the law. This is a legal problem. There's no legal problems with this, 'But as a psychologist, I have problems with it.'

"Well, you know, if he's on trial, then we can talk about that. But he's not, right? This isn't a court of psychology. Thank heavens we haven't moved to that yet in our country. It's a court of law. We deal with law, and he admits that that's not his thing, that's not what he's looking at. What's particularly troubling, though, about his testimony, which was really interesting, when he said, 'Well, there may have been actual cases where people have admitted to things that they didn't do, but nothing as serious as this now.' Those were his words, folks, 'But nothing as serious as this.' Now, I guess this would be the first reported case of its kind in his mind in the world. I find that kind of a stretch."

Hembree pointed out further that Albiniak failed to interview the defendant and even failed to listen to [Renee's] last interview tape [with the police]. "He just didn't take the time to do it. He had the tapes. He just didn't say, 'I didn't have the opportunity to,' [he] just didn't take the time, and that's poppycock. That's junk science, and it ought to be treated just like that."

The prosecutor then addressed what the defense had termed as being "unfair and dishonest" police interviews.

"It's no secret that they lied to her. That's no big revelation or smoking gun. They did it. They misled her to try to get her to confess. Now, you may not like that. I mean, personally you may feel like that's unfair or it's distasteful, but I'm gonna tell you it's legal. It's legal. Not only is it legal, it's effective in reaching the truth."

Jack and Marie Summey looked at each other and rolled their eyes.

Finally, the last issue Hembree chose to contest was the defense's contention regarding Renee's withdrawal from conspiracy.

"She could have canceled the trip, changed the hotel, or canceled the baby-sitter. At any point along here, she can get off that train. She doesn't do that. She can save her husband's life [at] any point. So many ways. 'Let's not go out tonight. Let's stay in the hotel. Let's not go to Dick's Last Resort. Why don't we go to the south end? I'm sorry, I don't feel like going out on the beach tonight. I have a headache. Why don't we put the kids [*sic*] to sleep and go out on the balcony? Or why don't we change hotels?' Or take your pick, all these opportunities to withdraw from this—this diabolical conspiracy—and every single time is consistent with one goal, one result. The death of Brent Poole."

It must have occurred to the jurors by now that the prosecution had already painted a portrait of inconsistency in Renee's testimony and her actions. Just in case, the solicitor provided them another plausible motive.

"She did not withdraw for a reason. And that reason was she wanted it all. She wanted the money, the hundred thousand plus; she wanted the house; she wanted the truck; she wanted sole custody of her daughter; she wanted her lover; she wanted to do what she wanted to do. That's why she didn't stop this thing. That's why she didn't withdraw. She not only didn't withdraw, she continued on after the crime had been committed, lying to protect herself and her lover. That's not withdrawal, ladies and gentlemen, that's not even close. That's not even a second thought."

Several of the jurors stared at Renee. She sat placidly at the defense table, looking straight ahead, listening to Hembree, who never missed a beat.

"Kimberly Renee Poole committed many sins. She lied and was unfaithful to her husband. She tried to turn the affection of her daughter to another man, teaching [her] to say, 'I love you, John.' She deserted her family. She planned a brutal murder, and she carried it out. She lured her husband, like prey, down to the beach, with the promise of sex to provide an opportunity for the murder, and she lied to protect herself and her lover. But, ladies and gentlemen, I submit to you that there is no sin that is more depraved, more diabolical in this case, than the robbery. And I don't mean the robbery, the false robbery, the fake robbery they did to cover their tracks. I'm talking about the robbery of Katie Poole's father, because Katie Poole was a daddy's girl. She was crying when he left, the last time she saw him, and thank God, she's got four grandparents that love her."

Hembree paused for the jury to consider that thought. He gave them his last piercing look.

"Because of the planning and execution of that plan by Kimberly Renee Poole," he started again in a soft and sorrowful voice, "Brent Poole will not be there for her. Because of the planning and execution of that plan by this defendant, Kimberly Renee Poole, Brent Poole will not be there when she starts kindergarten on her first day. Because of the planning and execution of that plan by Kimberly Renee Poole, he will not get the chance to walk her down the aisle when another man puts a ring like that on her finger, a ring like the one that was left next to the dying body of Brent Poole by this defendant and her lover."

Hembree's closing arguments had been filled with sincerity and humility, and when he finished, the courtroom was as silent as a Sunday-morning prayer meeting. Now the focus was on the jury and the one question that had brought them all together: *Had Renee Poole conspired with her lover to murder her husband?*

Judge Cottingham issued the charge of the court. He suggested the jury not start their deliberation until after they had had their lunch. The panel that would decide Renee Poole's fate retired at 12:54 P.M. There was a rustle in the courtroom and everyone rushed off to lunch.

At 4:40 P.M., the jury forelady asked and then received a communication from the judge. She had sent a note with the words "Laws in writing" at the top, and then asked for explanations of the legal terms: 1) weight of circumstantial evidence; 2) law of conspiracy, oral and written. The jury wanted those charges to be given to them by the judge in writing.

Cottingham quickly answered both questions for them. "The law makes absolutely no distinction between the weight or value to be given to either direct or circumstantial evidence, nor is a greater degree of certainty required of circumstantial evidence than of direct evidence. A conspiracy is a combination of two or more persons by concerted action to accomplish some unlawful purpose or to accomplish a lawful purpose by unlawful means." He handed them a copy of the instructions from which he read.

It seemed as if the jury was taking forever. However, four hours later, at 8:45 P.M., a juror rapped lightly on the door of the deliberation room. His signal indicated they had reached a verdict.

Word quickly spread in the courtroom that a verdict had been reached, and as if someone had pushed an imaginary panic button in the courtroom, people scampered for their seats. Slowly the jurors took their places while all eyes in the courtroom searched their faces for clues. The prosecution team was looking for justice, while Brent Poole's family needed closure and sought resolution and peace. The defense searched for a reasonable doubt in the faces of jurors. All they needed for a hung jury was one dissenting vote. Renee and her family prayed for that one juror who would give her the opportunity to get her life and her daughter back. In her hands, Renee clutched her daughter's beaded birth bracelet.

The judge turned toward the jury and asked, "Madam Forelady, has the jury reached a unanimous verdict?"

"Yes, we have, Your Honor," Gail Whitehead answered.

He asked for all the jurors to raise their hands, then directed, "Publish the verdict."

"This is indictment 99-GS-26-2250," the court clerk read aloud.

Both the victim's and the defendant's families were holding hands and trying to keep their composure. The jury felt sorry for them. This case was about one family losing their son and now another family risked losing their daughter. Regardless of the verdict, the two families would never be the same again.

"The *State of South Carolina* versus *Kimberly Renee Poole*," the clerk continued. "Indicted for count one, murder, the verdict is guilty."

Renee's family and friends looked completely stunned. Jack and Marie stared at each other in disbelief as the tears began to swell and fall on their cheeks.

All eyes were on Renee Poole, who had lowered her head into her hands.

"As to count two, criminal conspiracy," the clerk read again from the sheet of paper, "the verdict is guilty."

There was a collective groan heard throughout the courtroom. Members of the Poole family reached out and embraced one another. The prosecution team smiled and graciously nodded.

It wasn't difficult to determine if Renee Poole was acting or reacting to the decision of the jurors. Her face was beet red and washed with tears. She was bent over across the table and never once looked up when Diggs asked that the jury be polled. One by one, each juror stood up and confirmed the collective decision.

The judge asked to address the jury before he imposed sentence. After a brief show of appreciation, he stated, "I apologize for the inconvenience of having sequestered [you] from your loved ones and from your family. But I tell you that I've been on the bench now for sixteen years and was a trial lawyer for some thirty-two years prior to that, and in my experience, I don't know that I've ever seen a more dedicated jury, sworn to find the truth as you have. I observed you very carefully since Monday morning of last week. You were intent at all times in the pursuit of the truth, and that's what we were assembled for. And by your verdict, you have told me where the truth lies and we are in your debt."

The judge excused the jurors, but invited them to stay if they wished. Only two remained seated in the jury box: forelady Gail Whitehead and juror Jarid Hardee. When he asked for the defendant to approach the bench, her counsel had to embrace her physically and lead her to the front.

The judge gave the victim's family an opportunity to speak.

Agnes Poole had waited so long for this opportunity, but it was of little consolation in comparison to what she had lost.

"On January 24, 1974," she began, "a little baby boy was born to me after eleven years of not having a child. He was very, very special to us. We had wanted another baby for many, many years, and God so gave him to us. He was so special. He had the most beautiful smile you could ever envision.

"Our Thanksgiving that first year was absolutely horrible without him. Christmas without Brent, Katie's birthday without Brent . . . there were so many occasions. Mother's Day without my son. His birthday, we had to go to the cemetery instead of seeing him and wishing him 'Happy Birthday.' We had to put flowers on his grave. . . . "

Agnes's emotions got the best of her and she couldn't continue. Her daughter Dee stepped up to take her place.

"I wish that you had had a chance to know him," Dee said, fighting her tears all the time. "I wish that everyone working on the case had seen someone other than the person they saw lying in the sand. Brent was my baby. He was ten years younger, and I helped raise him, and when we got this news seventeen months ago, nothing prepared me. I absolutely felt like our family would never go through something like this. There was trust in our family, there was love; [this] was something that happened to other people, and nothing prepared me for this news. I pray that no one in this courtroom has to go through what our family has gone through.

"When I went to my parents' house in the middle of the morning, the sounds that came from my mom and dad were not even human. The pain that has rippled through our family is like there's a puzzle and the big piece that went right in the middle is missing, and the only thing that I can say is that I will not have to see my brother in pain anymore. I know that he is in heaven and I know that he is not begging to be loved." She cut her eyes toward Renee. "He is in heaven and I know he is not begging to be loved. He is not begging for anything. He is well taken care of."

Dressed in a dark blue suit with his angel wings on the front lapel, Bill Poole stood silently by, holding on to Agnes. She urged him to speak to the judge, to say something about Brent, but he shook his head. He was in too much pain and just couldn't bring himself to get the words out.

For most of her life, Renee had suffered from a familial tremor in her hands, which was known to be benign. As she stood propped up between attorney Diggs and Detective Martin, the tremor in her left hand was so pronounced it resembled a severe case of palsy. She couldn't stop crying, and her sniffles and snorts were so loud they were heard above the testimonies of her in-laws.

Diggs reached over and pulled out a few tissues from the clerk's desk, then handed them to Renee. He stood there, holding Renee up, with his head down, and a twisted smile across his face. In his eyes, it looked as if he, at that moment, had the whole weight of the trial on his shoulders.

"My client doesn't have a previous record," Orrie West reminded the judge. "I think the court is aware of that, and she's twenty-two, turned twenty three in the past week. Your Honor, I understand the court doesn't have much leeway in this matter, but any consideration you could give in this matter would be appreciated, particularly the possibility of running the sentences concurrent, since there are two charges, and we would ask the court to consider being as merciful as possible to our client."

All the color had gone out of Diggs's face. His sullen look was indicative of the weariness from the hellacious battle he had fought in this trial. Regardless of what the jury had determined, he still believed in her innocence.

"I would submit you heard the facts of this case," Diggs stated, "the evidence of the case, and certainly this defendant is, I would submit, deserving of mercy of the court at this point. It's never been asserted by the state that she was the person who murdered her husband. Your Honor knows, based on the evidence in this case, it is a rational verdict, that she had a minimal amount of involvement in this crime that would qualify her or put her in that area where the jury could reach that verdict, and I would ask Your Honor to be as merciful to her as you can."

Without a doubt, Renee Poole was in the most uncomfortable position she would ever know in her lifetime. Her soul was in the hands of God, but right now, all life—as she knew it—was in the hands of this man dressed in black who was about to pronounce sentence. She trembled profusely, with an obvious jerk in her left arm, as if she might break and fly apart in pieces at any moment. Cottingham's comments were scathing.

"Mrs. Poole, I have sat here very patiently listening to some horrible testimony during the past five [days] and the jury has found that you deliberately planned the killing of your husband and the father of a three-year-old child. That you led your lover to a site in Myrtle Beach, deliberately set [your husband] up to have him killed, planned it with him, and are just as guilty as the one as if you had pulled the fatal trigger that took the life of that young man and the father of your child. It is a horrible set of facts."

Renee could barely stand up straight. Crying steadily and the tremor in her left hand shaking uncontrollably, it was as if she were still in the midst of a bad dream. She glanced up at the judge with sad, puppy-dog eyes, begging for mercy, then looked down again.

"You have had the advantage of two distinguished attorneys, who have given you the benefit of every defense to which you are entitled, and then some, and yet a jury of your peers have found you guilty of this horrendous crime by evidence beyond a reasonable doubt. I see no basis in this world of showing you any mercy in the handing down of a sentence in this case."

Renee's whole body cringed at the judge's statement and collapsed against her supporters' outstretched arms. She struggled to breathe through subdued whimpers and cries.

The tone of the judge's voice would never change. The courtroom remained silent. The only sound heard was Cottingham's voice.

The judge cleared his throat.

"It is therefore, Kimberly Renee Poole, that the judgment and sentence of this court is that you be confined in the state penitentiary for the balance of your life. With regard to the charge of conspiracy, I sentence you to five years concurrent."

And with those last words, Renee collapsed and was literally dragged out of the courtroom by the bailiffs. She was handed over to the police, where she was handcuffed and transported back to the J. Reuben Long Detention Center. Knowing Renee would never taste freedom outside a jail cell again, it was a shocking event to witness.

CHAPTER 38

Posttrial motions to Judge Cottingham were presented the following Wednesday, November 17. In this hearing, Renee's defense team asked for a new trial because they believed trial errors had led to her conviction. Bill Diggs told the judge that Renee's confession should never had been admitted in court and Detective C. E. Martin should have been allowed to testify as a witness as to why and how he believed the composite pointed to another suspect other than Frazier.

Cottingham denied the first argument with little explanation and squashed the second motion on the basis that the composite drawing fell short of the standard required by the case law in regard to third-party guilt.

"A composite drawing that does not look like the alleged co-conspirator standing alone is not sufficient to raise the issue of third-party guilt, particularly when the individual who gave the information giving rise to the composite drawing says that 'it does not look like the individual I saw,'" the judge dutifully informed Diggs.

Diggs submitted a third motion for a new trial on the grounds that deputy solicitor Humphries had switched transcripts in relation to the ponytail incident.

"It made me appear to have a lack of command of the facts in the case in the presence of the jury," he complained to the judge. But after much discussion, it finally came out in the wash that the fault was not Humphries' at all but Diggs's. Diggs had never asked for a copy of the transcript from Mark Hobbs's testimony—only a copy of the taped interview—and thus had mistakenly assumed Hobbs had referred to a "pony-tail" when he listened to it. Hobbs and the prosecution both denied the statement was ever made.

Two additional motions for retrial submitted by Diggs were in regard to certain information he had received about the jury. Juror Jarid Hardee had called Diggs at home the day after the trial to complain he had not received an answer to his inquiry about the admittance of Renee's confession during the trial. Cottingham explained in great length how clear he had been in his instructions to the jury about Renee's confession and this particular juror had every chance during court to ask for further explanation, but did not. Motion denied.

The second tidbit of information passed on to Diggs was that the jury's forelady, Gail Whitehead, attended Humphries' church and failed to reflect that in jury selection. But once the judge heard the prosecutor's position on the incident, he was confident there had been no wrongdoing and denied the fifth motion.

In Diggs's last motion for a retrial, he cited the lack of ade-quate time to properly present Renee's case and cross-examine many of the witnesses.

"I felt like when this case was being tried last week, that we were under a tremendous amount of pressure to get that case finished so that [we'd be out of the way] of all those jurors coming in here for the next case Monday morning. . . . The defense attorneys were tired; we were exhausted; and the impression that we both had [was] to conclude that case that night and we didn't really have a full opportunity to do what could have been to represent this defendant."

Cottingham stated there was never a set time for the Poole case to conclude. The choice to continue working late on Friday night was not his choice, but had been the jury's. And that the record would reflect that he had never told the defense to hurry up in its cross-examinations. They had been given all the time they needed and had asked for. Diggs's last motion was denied as well.

As expected, Diggs would later file those same arguments with the South Carolina Court of Appeals in yet another effort to get a new trial for Renee.

Several weeks after the hearing of Renee's posttrial motions, solicitor Greg Hembree turned his attention toward John Boyd Frazier and filed a motion in the Fifteenth Judicial Court that his bond be revoked. In a hearing on December 9 at the Horry County Courthouse in front of the circuit court, Hembree and defense attorney Morgan Martin debated the issues in the presence of Judge John Breeden.

"Now that Renee Poole has been convicted and a jury convinced she and John had planned Brent Poole's killing, John Frazier might decide to flee," Hembree cautioned the judge. "Her trial became very much a trial of not only Kimberly Renee Poole, but also John Boyd Frazier. If Frazier had not done it, then Poole would have been exonerated."

Martin disagreed wholeheartedly. John had followed all the conditions of his bond established fourteen months ago and wasn't planning on going anywhere. "If he was going to run, it would have been before today," he argued. "John looks forward to answering these charges and getting on with his life. The fact that a jury has convicted Renee Poole doesn't mean that a jury will convict Mr. Frazier."

Morgan Martin had been practicing law in Horry County for nearly twenty years. In South Carolina, he and trial partner Tommy Brittain's reputations as criminal defense attorneys were legendary. Anyone who had ever looked at their track record would agree with that assessment. They had represented many clients who had been charged with murder and they excelled in that area. They both loved a challenge, were fierce competitors and always were a class act in court.

Martin and Brittain had defended some very high-profile clients with great success, getting many of their clients either acquitted or their charges reduced. Their most recent case was one that immediately followed Renee's and preceded the solicitor's request to revoke Frazier's bond. It involved a capital-murder charge where a man had supposedly killed his girlfriend by pushing her down a stairwell. In this case, Martin and Brittain amazingly got the jury to acquit their client of all charges. In another case, probably one of the most horrendous murders ever to occur in Horry County, their client had strangled his girlfriend and had set her body on fire; he should have faced the death penalty. But somehow the legal duo was so convincing they got a jury to reduce his charges from murder to voluntary manslaughter.

John Frazier's mother, Jane Lovett, had spent nearly $500,000 on her son's case since he had been arrested. And she was confident the flamboyant and dramatic team of Martin and Brittain were capable of winning her son's freedom.

After hearing from both sides, Judge Breeden issued a ruling that John Frazier would remain free until his trial began. "You can make me look real smart, Mr. Frazier," he told him, "or you can make me look real stupid. I suggest you make me look real smart."

Frazier did not comment during or after the hearing, but accepted the judge's order that he contact the solicitor's office weekly until his trial date, set for February 14. Judge Rodney A. Peeples, of Barnwell, already had been appointed to preside over the trial and his first show of authority was to impose a gag order. The prosecutors and defense attorneys were asked that they not comment on the trial.

CHAPTER 39

On Monday, Valentine's Day, 2000, Judge Peeples asked the one hundred prospective jurors seated in the Horry County Courthouse whether they had seen, heard or read news accounts of the case. Thirty-three potential jurors indicated they had. Three said they had formed an opinion about Frazier's guilt or innocence. Defense counsel believed jurors from Horry County had been swayed by the extensive media coverage were prejudiced and their client would not get a fair trial if these jurors heard the evidence. Martin had requested a change of venue or that jurors from another county be brought in to decide the case. Peeples declined Martin's request, saying to one juror who said she had read stories about the slaying, "None of us live in a vacuum. We all are creatures." He believed the jurors selected could give Frazier a fair trial. It took until nine o'clock that night, but seven women and five men were finally chosen as jurors and two alternates selected.

The same witnesses that testified at Renee's trial were expected to testify at Frazier's. Peeples had not decided yet if the prosecutors would be allowed to use Renee's statements to the police where she identified him as the killer. If convicted, Frazier would be looking at the same sentence as Renee's.

Renee had also been subpoenaed to testify at John's trial, but her attorneys told the press not to expect anything from her because it could jeopardize her appeal. "Poole will not testify at Frazier's trial because prosecutors have no authority to compel her to testify," Diggs told reporters before she appeared in court. "She doesn't know who the shooter is anyway. . . . She will not take a position that is inconsistent with [the] position she took at trial."

Renee's testimony could have flattened Frazier's case like roadkill.

John Frazier walked into the courtroom smiling, with his head held high. He was already a large man, but he looked as if he had added an additional forty pounds since his bond hearing.

As in Renee's trial, there was no rush of crowds from Myrtle Beach or any large media events at the beginning of this trial. Court prognosticators took in consideration a jury had already believed Frazier was guilty after hearing testimony in Renee's trial and were giving him only a faint hope for an acquittal.

Deputy solicitor Fran Humphries was the leadoff hitter again for the prosecution and used many of the same buzzwords he had used in Renee's trial. The prosecutor, by now, had put this case to memory and knew it better than he knew the back of his hand. He revealed to jurors that the two defendants in this case had given misleading statements to investigators after the shooting to cover up their plot and then summed up the facts proving that John Boyd Frazier certainly had the motive, reason, and ability to kill Brent Poole. And the evidence in this case would substantiate that Renee's confession to a plot of murder with Frazier was much more than the innocent panic of a woman suffering from post-traumatic stress disorder at having witnessed her husband's shooting on the beach.

"It is absolutely horrific what John Boyd Frazier has done for the love of a bad woman, Kimberly Renee Poole." Humphries outlined the motivations behind this. "People get divorced all the time. . . . In this case, Kimberly Poole wanted the house and home. John Boyd Frazier wanted Kimberly Renee Poole. Kimberly Renee Poole wanted her child. John Boyd Frazier wanted Kimberly Renee Poole. In order for

Kimberly Renee Poole to have what she wanted, William Brent Poole had to die. . . . She makes love to her husband on the dunes of that beach and then walks him to the arms of John Boyd Frazier, where he is shot once under the chin and in the head."

The prosecutor refuted the defense's claim there was no physical evidence that connected John Frazier to Brent's murder. "Circumstantial evidence is just as good as physical evidence, if it comes together properly."

Morgan Martin had stood before a jury many times to counter the claims of a prosecutor. If the jury was going to believe his viewpoint, he would have to get them to disagree with what the police and the prosecution said the facts meant. He would have to prove the evidence in this case showed the police certainly had their own agenda. They had their own set of problems. They had their own motives for pinpointing his client as the murderer.

"There's absolutely no physical evidence linking John Boyd Frazier to this crime," Martin told the jurors. "No fingerprints, no gun, no DNA tests, no hair, or fibers." In his easy conversational style and a heavy Southern drawl, which was very appealing to jurors, he assured them the police had arrested the wrong man. "There is a lot I would submit that a man would do for a woman, but there is not evidence John Frazier killed Brent Poole. John Frazier is wrongfully accused."

And second, if the jury was going to be convinced his client was innocent, Martin would have to substantiate the reasons a desperate woman had agreed to a murder plot in the first place. He would have to submit that Renee was a well-known liar and point out, one by one, the many lies she told not only to the police, but to her husband, her lovers, her friends and her family.

The jury would have to see that Frazier at the time was a twenty-eight-year-old bachelor who was only looking for a good time. He had had a brief relationship with Poole, but he certainly wasn't in the market for a wife. Especially one with a jealous husband and a two-year-old kid.

Finally Martin had to put out the brush fires of doubt that

Frazier was not home the night of the murder and out looking for an alibi. He wanted the jury to keep in mind that Frazier was at home alone on the night of the murder. Martin would argue and fight for the truth of that fact, suggesting to the jurors, "You can't prove that you were home, if you were alone."

In the first day of testimony, there were no surprises from the prosecution's witness list. The same four Myrtle Beach police officers and two residents described the crime scene along the beach and how Brent's wallet was found in a nearby neighborhood to where he was killed. But it was the seventh witness for the prosecution that brought a wave of anticipation and bewilderment in the courtroom.

As promised by the prosecution, Renee Poole was called to the hot seat. Dressed in jailhouse blues with a white T-shirt underneath and the sleeves hanging out, she had been escorted through the back of the courthouse and a rear elevator in handcuffs, shackles and belly chains. Her hair was pulled back loosely behind her head and she wore no makeup. Before she walked into the courtroom and took her place on the witness stand, her hardware was removed and she was joined by her attorney Bill Diggs.

Renee quickly glanced at Frazier before she sat down beside the judge's bench. She looked downward as Diggs explained to the judge that her case was being appealed and that her testimony might threaten the success of the appeal. "She will invoke her right not to incriminate herself," he said.

With the jury out of the room, Renee said, looking briefly again at Frazier, "I don't wish to testify." Once the jury returned, Renee invoked the Fifth Amendment. While she spoke, Frazier looked directly at her until she was dismissed and escorted away in handcuffs by two deputies. As she made her way out of the courthouse in chains again, and back to the waiting patrol car outside, her father and a family friend briefly walked alongside and talked with her.

Dee Mishler said she was disappointed that Renee had decided not to testify. "She never ceases to amaze me," she said after her sister-in-law left the courtroom. "John Frazier still comes first with her, instead of her daughter, Katie."

Having had enough excitement for one day, the jurors then listened to the testimony of Dr. Edward L. Proctor, forensic pathologist, who told them about Brent's wounds and injuries to his skull and brain. Beach patrol officer Scott Brown followed him with a replay of the night Renee flagged him down and told him her husband had been shot.

The third day of Frazier's trial, the prosecution began smoothly enough with testimony from Lieutenant Bill Frontz and a taped conversation with Frazier from June 10, 1998. Jurors would hear Frazier on the tape respond, "Oh, my God. Oh, shit!" when Frontz told him Brent Poole "was no longer with us."

The prosecution relaxed a little. They had revealed to the jury the true nature of the defendant and let them hear Frazier's own words when told he was a suspect in Brent's killing. "My heart's going now," Frazier had responded, denying that he was the killer. Sounding startled, the jurors listened to him tell Frontz, "True, there was no love lost between us by any means because of the relationship that Renee and I had. But I mean, I'm not that, I'm not that type of person."

John showed no emotion as the jurors listened to the tape and while Agnes Poole glared at him the entire time. Even if the jurors had not already made up their minds that he had murdered her son in cold blood, she had no doubts about it.

During the taped interview, Frazier said he knew that the Pooles were planning to travel to Myrtle Beach to celebrate their third wedding anniversary, but he didn't know what hotel they would be staying at. He also admitted to Frontz that he and Renee had had an affair, but he said he was at his house in Winston-Salem when Brent was shot. Renee had had affairs with several other men during her marriage, but he didn't think that any of them would be jealous enough to shoot her husband. His memory of the day of Brent's murder was that he had talked on the telephone with a friend, Thomas Pedersen.

The prosecution would go after that statement to verify that John was searching for an alibi. Hembree later elicited the testimony of Thomas Pedersen, his questions continuing, each one leading to the next until Pedersen answered that he had not talked with John that day. It was the *following* day after Brent's murder when police had called and questioned him about John's possible involvement that he had spoken with him.

John leaned slightly forward, listening to his best friend with his eyes steady and his lips slightly parted. Pedersen was not cutting him any slack.

Hembree then showed jurors copies of a daily planner taken during a February search of Frazier's home in North Myrtle Beach. He asked the jury to take notice that Frazier had recorded March 13 as his and Renee's first date. Other dates of special interest to them were March 24, their first sexual encounter, May 1, the day she moved into his Winston-Salem home, May 12, the day she moved back with her husband, and June 9, the couple's wedding anniversary and day Brent Poole was killed.

The prosecution, courtesy of the Myrtle Beach police, had once again choreographed the trial so that witness testimony was followed by an audiotape or visual display that either confirmed or refuted the defendant's claims to the police. The audiotapes played in the courtroom would prove the most damaging blow against the defense's claim their client was innocent. Even though Renee had chosen not to testify against her former lover, the jury would now hear her interview with Sergeant King. They would be able to judge for themselves and decide from the actual interview if Renee's words and opinion were true as to whether the man dressed in black, who had shot her husband, was John Frazier. The courtroom was quiet, except for the sounds of Renee testifying as to what had happened the night her husband was murdered and admitting John could have been the murderer. The words that the defense had feared lingered in the minds of jurors. As the tape played accusing John of murder, he would wipe the sweat from his forehead, then look back down at the floor.

The prosecution was brutal in that they had supposedly exposed everything that John and Renee were, everything they had thought and done to conspire and murder her husband. Minute by minute, Hembree pointed out, Renee had woven her and her lover into a trap with a web of lies and deceit. The story about a robbery she and Frazier had tried to manufacture beforehand didn't hold water with the police and their evidence proved it was a different one from what the defense was now promulgating in court.

If that weren't enough ammunition for the jury, Hembree offered more. He wanted jurors to understand further that Renee had sounded relieved after confessing to police she and Frazier had plotted to kill her husband. She seemed to believe that since she did not pull the trigger, she was in the clear and could not be implicated of any wrongdoing—that she could go home to her daughter, grieve for her dead husband and be left alone to start a new life.

In a series of questions to the ten witnesses that followed the tape, including Brent's mother, baby-sitter Carolyn Murphy and John's coworker Bruce Sovereign, the prosecution was able to link Frazier to a relationship with Renee, to the Pooles' troubled marriage and to Brent's murder. Their testimonies forced the defense to scramble and try to explain away why if Frazier and Renee had broken off their relationship, had Renee's neighbor Jim Bollow seen a black 1996 Chevrolet Blazer with the license tag NERVUS parked outside her home when Brent was at work almost until the day they left for Myrtle Beach? They would have to explain why the three days Frazier had requested off from work were, ironically, identical to the days the Pooles had scheduled for their vacation at Myrtle Beach. How could they explain Frazier having borrowed a friend's car for those same exact days? And would they be able to explain further why Frazier's own friends had sworn to police he had once owned a TZ-75 9mm pistol that would misfire and eject the unfired bullets, the very same description of the gun police contended had killed Poole? Frazier, the prosecution continued to pound, had tripped himself, time and time again, in a misguided plot to deceive the police and cast doubt in the minds of the jurors.

James Bowman, a special agent with the North Carolina SBI, testified he had interviewed Frazier and noticed him to be very nervous when he talked with him. "As the interview progressed," Bowman remembered, "he was sweating profusely. Sweat was running down his face and dripping."

Looking over at Frazier sitting uncomfortably at the defense table, dabbing himself with a large white handkerchief and living up to his personification emblazoned across his license tag, the jury may have misinterpreted that statement. His mother had stated that John had always sweat profusely, and even as a little boy, he would sweat heavily on a cool day. No one was disputing her word, but it was hard to believe one man could sweat so much without having a valid reason to do so.

The prosecution meant to turn up the heat on Frazier with their next witness.

Since Hembree had taken office in January 1999, he had had ample opportunity to have studied Martin and Brittain's style and learned their trial techniques and strategies. He had not underestimated his two worthy opponents and swore he would not make the same mistakes twice. That was one of the reasons why he called Bruce Wolford, the bartender at the Silver Fox, to the witness stand. Wolford had befriended both Renee and Frazier at one time, but he was willing to provide damaging evidence for the prosecution. The young man whom private investigators working for both defendants had implicated as Brent's killer would testify that John had tried to fight Brent on May 30, 1998, when he took a pair of Renee's panties and a videotape to the club where she had worked as a topless dancer.

"He was wiping the sweat off his face with the panties," Wolford recalled for the jurors. "He tried to get him to fight him in the parking lot and Brent wouldn't get out of his truck. John didn't like Brent. He said he hated him and that Brent had control over Renee, and he was using their daughter to control her."

Wolford did admit to having his own sexual encounter with Renee while he was married and the filming of that affair, just before Renee began a relationship with John. But the prevailing thought among the jurors was that he had convinced them thoroughly he had no desire to be with Renee after their affair, nor to see her husband dead.

The prosecution supplied fact of the matter to end all questionable doubt when they called John's coworker Bruce Sovereign to testify.

"John stormed back into the computer room one night," the jurors would hear from Sovereign. "'Somebody should kill that son of a bitch or I'm going to kill that son of a bitch.' I said simply, 'John, you can't be serious about that?' He didn't say anything; he just shook his head and walked away to the other side of the computer room." He told jurors further that John would often spend more than an hour on the telephone with Renee soon after arriving at work at the manufacturing plant and that Renee and John were lovers.

Frazier didn't show any emotion as his former coworker spoke against him. He continued wiping his forehead and speaking quietly to his attorneys while Martin protested and asked the judge to strike the statement from the record. He said Sovereign was not directly involved in the telephone conversation, and that "you have to put assumption upon assumption upon assumption" to come to that conclusion.

Under cross-examination from Martin, Sovereign said that John had threatened Brent after he hung up during a telephone call. He said John had told him he had been speaking to Renee Poole.

But once again, the most important stage of the prosecution's case was the eyewitness testimony of the couple from Virginia. Martin had succeeded in defusing the testimony of SLED firearms expert David Collins, getting him to admit he had no proof that the TZ-75 9mm pistol John had once owned was the murder weapon. But, in spite of a relentless cross-examination of Mark and Donna Hobbs, he could not get the jury to doubt what they were saying was true. The Hobbses' memory was crystalline in that Frazier was definitely the man they saw on the beach the night Brent was shot.

Martin believed he could add enough question marks on the jurors' yellow legal pads about the couple's accounts and events from nearly twenty months ago, but he never could seem to make a stand against them. This time around, Hembree had seen to it that there would be no controversy relating to a missing ponytail and the Hobbses' identification of Frazier, coupled along with Renee's implication that John was the shooter on the beach dressed in black. It was just too big an obstacle for the defense to hurdle.

Feeling very good about their presentation, the prosecution rested.

There had been a few hints of the direction Martin and Brittain would take for Frazier's defense, but having John testify was not one of them. His attorneys knew Renee was going to be subpoenaed to testify against him, but they doubted she ever would. They did not view the sexual details about her and John's affair as very important to this case, but they didn't want John to have to face cross-examination from prosecution. Like Renee, he had far too many skeletons in his closet to survive a brutal attack and be skewered by the prosecution in front of the jurors.

Martin moved the defense's case ahead in full throttle on the fourth day. Presenting their case with a total of only eight witnesses, he admonished them to keep an open mind and remember the operative words "a reasonable doubt." He insisted that John had not been at Myrtle Beach the night Brent had been murdered, and he and Brittain spent a lot of time trying to convince the jury that the Hobbses were not close enough to get a good look at the suspect.

"Special circumstances would undoubtedly bring about factors that weaken people's memory," Tommy Brittain argued, standing in front of the jury. He then presented a videotaped deposition of himself and Dr. Elizabeth Loftus, a psychologist at the University of Washington at Seattle, to repudiate further the eyewitness accounts. "Witnesses who have a brief exposure to an event often do not remember it well," Loftus added. "Lighting and distance also affect memory."

It had cost Frazier's defense team $11,600 for her testimony, but it would be considered a small price to pay if it could work the magic they needed. In a nutshell, Dr. Loftus's testimony theorized that people's memories can be skewed by suggestions given to them after the event, and their memory fades as time passes.

It sounded like a throwaway question when Hembree asked the acclaimed Dr. Loftus how many times she had testified in the past twenty-five years. But several of the jury members winced when she later admitted that of her 225 testimonies, not once had she ever testified that an eyewitness was reliable. Her words hung in the courtroom.

In an attempt to chip away further at the prosecution's eyewitness testimony, Martin had secured the expert opinion of Donald Smith, owner and operator of a local television production company known as Lucky Dog. Smith was there to testify to the difficulties of someone being identified on the beach under the same conditions the night Brent was killed. Martin moved to introduce a video of the location Smith had made and requested officially that the jury be allowed to visit the very spot on the beach where the Hobbses said they had seen John.

But Peeples would have none of it. When he denied all defense requests for admission of the tape and the jury's visit to the beach, Martin asked to approach the bench. Those who knew Martin best could see he was scathing. With both parties at the bench, he argued John was entitled to a proper defense and this was one of their efforts to get at the truth. Some of the jurors watched Martin for a reaction. Others looked away or at their notes in their laps. Only a very few looked at John, who kept his eyes fastened on his attorneys. Clearly, he had trusted them with his life.

John had come to despise this courtroom. The Pooles were always there, watching and staring, and their eyes burned into him from across the courtroom. And he had a gnawing worry that the jury might confuse their own emotions about the Pooles' grief over their son's death with the lack of evidence against him.

The defense long ago had realized the Hobbses were the only two accusing witnesses that could actually pin John to Brent Poole's murder, and the defense had planned with Smith's testimony and the video to knock the credibility out of what they thought they had seen. Martin once again asked the judge for consideration of this vital evidence, but he was flatly denied.

During a brief recess, Martin asked members of the gallery and press how they thought the case was going. Although he didn't admit it, it was obvious that he was not happy with it. His sulky expression let on that he was not pleased with Judge Peeples' courtroom decisions. He didn't need Willard Scott to tell him which way the wind was blowing. After seeing the wind knocked out of his sails, the jurors' faces told him the verdict was already a foregone conclusion in their minds. Martin would have no choice but to dismiss his witness, rest his case and hope to regain what little ground he thought he had left in closing arguments.

Tommy Brittain addressed the jurors, in hopes he would be able to pick up the broken pieces of their case. Telling the jurors he was the son of a Methodist minister, Brittain again singled out the Hobbses' "false identification" of their client as misconstrued.

"The Virginia couple made a mistake when they identified John as the man they saw near the hotel before the shooting," he said softly. "They saw the man for only a few seconds in a dimly lit area, and investigators helped the couple pick John out of a photographic lineup by putting his picture in the lineup's first position."

Both Brittain and Martin would urge the jurors to acquit John Frazier of all charges because the prosecutors did not prove their case against him. These were headline words.

"A case of circumstantial evidence has sand for a foundation," Martin turned and told the jurors, as if he expected his words to trigger some intense reaction from them. "John Frazier has been wrongly accused. He had no motive to kill Brent Poole. . . . There is no evidence that John Frazier wanted to marry Renee Poole or that Renee Poole wanted to marry John Frazier. He had a short relationship with Renee Poole."

Prosecutors asked the jury to convict Frazier. "There was no physical evidence that linked Frazier to the shooting because he was smart enough to get rid of any items that connected him to the crime," Humphries had said in his closing summation.

"John Frazier wanted Renee Poole," Hembree reminded them. "For the love of a bad woman, he was willing to commit a lot of sins." Utilizing the same speech he had used at Renee's trial, he emphasized, "John Frazier robbed Katie Poole of her daddy. Brent Poole will not be there when Katie starts her first day in kindergarten."

The second jury now had heard the story of how Renee Poole and John Frazier had plotted to kill her husband. It was easy to see what the jurors had thought about John Boyd Frazier's guilt. They found it odd that the defense had not found outside of Frazier's own family one single witness who would be willing to take the stand and extol his virtues. No Boy Scout leaders, Little League coaches, high-school teachers or former employers to speak of his goodness or praise his acts of kindness. There had been plenty of people to testify against him, but not one there to connect with the jury in a real way. The jurors didn't like him, either; they found him arrogant, transparent and void of all conscience. In spite of the fifty-eight motions made by the defense on Frazier's behalf, there was nothing his high-dollar dream team could do or say to convince them otherwise.

It took the jurors only forty-five minutes to decide the fate of John Boyd Frazier. Brent's family sat behind the prosecution's table, silently weeping and holding hands as the verdicts were read. Sitting directly behind the defense table, John's family also held hands but showed no emotion as they waited on the final outcome.

"On the count of murder," the court clerk read, "guilty. . . ."

At hearing the announcement of the jury's verdict, Fran Humphries slid back in his chair and pulled both hands to his chest in a gesture of thankfulness. Greg Hembree took a deep breath, smiled, then dropped his head. He would tell reporters after the proceedings that it had been a long wait for the Poole family, but it had been worth the wait to get justice for William Brent Poole.

Two juries now had believed that Poole and Frazier had

plotted to kill Brent Poole. In addition to the murder charge, John was also found guilty of armed robbery and conspiracy. He showed no emotion when the verdict was read, but wiped the sweat from his eyes and face with his handkerchief when the judge asked him to approach the bench for sentencing.

For those caught up in the emotions of this trial, Bill Poole would not miss the opportunity to speak before the judge this time. "Nobody should go through the evils that have been portrayed in these trials," he said after asking Peeples not to show Frazier any mercy.

It was difficult to assess Agnes Poole's emotions as she stood before the judge. She wiped the tears away from her eyes and discussed how horrible it had been on her family to lose their son and how much they missed him. "My husband and I are raising Brent's four-year-old daughter, Katie. It's going to be horrible when she learns what has happened to her father." She began to sob again.

Listening intently, Brent's brother was poised. Craig Poole said his daughter and Katie were born seventeen hours apart and it was going to be tough on his family for Katie to grow up without her father. "I've got a little girl who spent a year praying every night that no one would come and shoot her father," he growled at the judge.

Like Renee, John had refused to testify on his own behalf. But he was quick to tell the judge that he was no murderer. "I didn't do this. I had no love for Renee Poole. And I had no hatred for Brent Poole. Me and Brent had become friends, and I tried to tell him how his wife was. I have a three-year-old daughter, who will never know me."

Jane Lovett still insisted her son was not guilty and that his family still supported him. "He didn't take another person's life for a woman," she said, annoyed at even the thought of such a ludicrous idea. "And, especially not for Renee Poole."

Ed Lovett, John's stepfather, wanted the Pooles to know, in a class act, that he sincerely offered his family's deepest sympathy "for the horrific times they had had since the incident."

Judge Peeples wasn't as poetic as Cottingham had been. "Nothing I can say can bring him back or change what happened," he said to the Pooles in a quavering voice. "There is nothing more valuable than human life. But it's always darkest before the dawn—you just have to keep faith."

Peeples then sentenced the thirty-year-old Frazier to life in prison for the murder conviction, thirty years for the armed robbery and five years for the conspiracy conviction. The sentences for armed robbery and conspiracy would run concurrently with the life sentence.

John turned and hugged his mother, then not so graciously stepped toward the police officers. The officers handcuffed him and walked him out of the courtroom. He slowly stepped down the hall like he was walking onto a frozen pond.

Members of the Poole family stood together with the prosecutors and the police and talked with news reporters. Captain Sam Hendrick, Detectives Altman, King and Frontz were there to congratulate them. Their long ordeal finally over, Craig Poole said Frazier's verdict and sentence would help bring closure and healing to his family. "It feels a lot different than it did after Renee's trial."

Bill Poole credited many prayers to God for the verdicts and sentences of Frazier and his daughter-in-law. "Murder is bad," he said softly with one arm around his wife and the other around his daughter. "But this is the worst because of the circumstances."

Frazier's attorney Morgan Martin told reporters he was very disappointed with the outcome. He still maintained Frazier's innocence and promised to file an appeal.

After hearing about Frazier's intentions to appeal several weeks later, Dee Mishler penned a letter to the *Sun News:*

> No one will ever know the pain and heartache our family has had to go through because of these two evil, wicked people. A jury found them guilty, they were sentenced to life without parole. And yet John's mom is still claiming his innocence. There comes a point when even a mother's love cannot change the hideous things that her child chose to do. John and Renee are where they

*need to be and where they will stay for the rest of their
lives. The parents of these two need to accept the fact
that no appeal will get them out of prison. They made
their choice the night they shot and murdered my baby
brother.*

Attorney Bill Diggs filed Renee's request for a new trial
with the South Carolina Court of Appeals on June 6, 2000.
As previously argued before Judge Cottingham, Diggs listed
and expounded upon what he believed were errors in her
trial. But in January 2002, the court of appeals affirmed
Renee's conviction and sent notice that she would not be
getting a new trial.

It was welcome news to the prosecutor and to the Poole
family.

"She's dangerous," Hembree told the press. "She's bad. And
I don't want to give her another shot at being out among law-
abiding citizens. Renee Poole is a cold and ruthless murderer
and she is where she should be—in a cell."

The cell Hembree was referring to was Leath Correctional
Institute, in Greenwood, South Carolina. Barring a miracle,
Renee would be spending the rest of her natural life inside this
facility.

Renee's misfortune at getting a new trial didn't discourage
John's attorneys from filing an appeal with the state. Morgan
Martin and Tommy Brittain believed John had not received
a fair trial.

At the April 2003 hearing, Martin stated before the high
court, "We didn't get a fair trial from that judge. Two witnesses
identified him as the killer and he had a right to challenge that."

John hadn't done anything wrong. His family believed that.
His lawyers believed that. His mother knew it. Jane Lovett had
asked her son point-blank if he had done this, if he had killed
Brent Poole. He told her no and she believed him. It had cost
Jane all the inheritance from her father, her retirement, her
rental property and even her automobile. She spent nearly
$500,000 on her son since he was arrested, but that was noth-
ing when compared to his life. She was rewarded for her

faithfulness, for in January 2004, the state supreme court overturned John's conviction and life sentence. Citing errors by circuit judge Rodney Peeples, the high court ordered a new trial because he erred in: 1) excluding testimony from videographer Donald Smith and his videotape depicting the scene of the eyewitness identification, 2) excluding portions of the videotaped deposition of Dr. Elizabeth Loftus concerning a "Photo Lineup Study" and 3) allowing the testimony of Frazier's coworker Bruce Sovereign.

John Frazier's new trial was scheduled to begin May 16, 2005.

EPILOGUE

This case weighed heavily on my mind from the first day I read about it in the *Sun News*. I know and respect the persons who investigated, prosecuted and defended this case. Indeed, I consider many of them my friends. During the two trials, I also got to know the families and developed long, lasting relationships with some of them. And, from the very beginning, they proved themselves to be honorable, respectable and courageous folks.

Kimberly Renee Poole continues to serve her life sentence at Leath Correctional Institute. In a bizarre twist of fate, the person she was often likened to, Susan Smith, is one of her suitemates and they have developed a platonic relationship. On November 9, Renee celebrated her twenty-ninth birthday. She, Susan and several other prison inmates celebrated with an impromptu party.

"Oh, you'd be surprised how resourceful one can get in prison," Renee wrote to me.

An old college roommate of Brent's had been visiting Renee regularly. They had agreed if she were to be released from prison, the two of them would hookup and give their relationship a try. Apparently, that friendship must have run its course, for Renee recently posted her profile and advertised for pen pals on the web.

Horry County solicitor Greg Hembree was reelected during

the last election and is currently serving his second term. He and deputy solicitor Fran Humphries now argue their cases in a much improved, multimillion-dollar, state-of-the-art complex, sitting directly behind the older courthouse on Second Avenue. They are very confident John Boyd Frazier will be found guilty in his upcoming trial.

"We'll just prepare for trial a second time, get ready and do it again," Hembree said after he received the news from the supreme court. "The videotape and lighting expert are another tool Frazier's attorneys can use to attack the witnesses' testimony, but I think what they saw will hold up. The eye can pick up better than a video camera, so the testimony may not help him much. And as for allowing testimony about the photo-lineup IDs, the witnesses picked Frazier from the pictures because they saw him, not because of a description from someone else. Other evidence made the case against Frazier so strong that the new testimony should have little effect."

In August 1999, Captain Sam Hendrick resigned his post at Myrtle Beach police and accepted the job as chief of police, in Conway. Several months later, Sergeant John King gave notice he would be joining his old boss in Conway.

Detective Terry Altman is still employed in the homicide department at MBPD. Although his job requires more supervision and less hands-on investigation of crimes, he says he still gets a rush when he has the opportunity to interrogate criminals. "It's the greatest job in the world." He smiles. "I can't think of anything that excites me more than the moment when the criminal finally breaks down and admits he or she has committed the crime. And you walk away saying, 'I got 'em.'"

Bill Diggs still practices law in Myrtle Beach and Orrie West continues to represent those who can't afford to pay for an attorney. Diggs has visited Renee only twice since her conviction, yet he continues to work on her appeals. He is eminently qualified for this task, given the fact he served as the former chief attorney for the South Carolina Office of Appellate Defense for five years and has represented approximately one thousand clients at the appellate and postconviction levels.

The last time Diggs visited Renee was with Morgan Martin in 2004. He made the mistake of asking her, "How do you like my hair?" She told him she didn't give a damn about his hair—all she was interested in was getting out of prison.

The Summeys are angry with Diggs and claim he won't return their phone calls. Marie said she was going to Myrtle Beach to have a talk with him. And true to form, she swore, "Bill is going to look mighty funny in court with a foot up his ass."

Jane Lovett says that she has never had a problem with John's attorney. "It has been wonderful to know Morgan Martin and have him. God blessed us greatly with his presence in our life. He always talks with me when I call on him, and as soon as he can, he will call me back. He calls at night or weekends or anytime I need him. I have his home number, his cell number and his car number. I truly thank God for him and know God sent him to us in our desperate time of need."

The Pooles contact the MBPD homicide office just about every time they visit Myrtle Beach and have never failed to express their appreciation for bringing justice to their son's case. Each day they think about Renee, and how she not only murdered their son but inflicted a lifetime of trauma and loss on them and their family. Life will never be the same without Brent, but at least they have Katie to hold on to. They pray Renee will one day accept what she has done, and will at last acknowledge she is a murderer. But they know they're only fooling themselves. It was Renee's failure to face her sins in the first place that resulted in Brent's death. They believe she never had any guilt or remorse for what she did or said to Brent while they were married and it is that same attitude now that has cost her her own daughter.

The Pooles listened in court when Dr. Thrasher tried to explain all the terrible things had happened in Renee's childhood that made her into what she is. But they never bought into all that psychological mumbo jumbo. Dee Mishler believed Renee to be simply evil; she deliberately chose to lie, cheat and murder, and then tried to pretend she was Brent's grieving wife all the while. It was Renee's own doing, her unwillingness to accept responsibility for all the deceit in her life, that led to her downfall and caused her to give testimony to the police that would assure she and John Boyd Frazier would be caught and punished.

But the Pooles wondered, even after all this time: how could she still proclaim her innocence, knowing she had already confessed and admitted she helped plan it? In June 1998, they filed a petition with the North Carolina court stating that Renee was not a fit and proper person to exercise custody over Katie and asked that they be granted exclusive care, custody and control. For their granddaughter's sake, they have tried to fill their home with photos of happier days with her father, but that does not include her mother. In every picture where Renee had appeared with Brent, her image has been cut out.

Katie will soon be celebrating her tenth birthday. She has not spoken or written to her mother since the conviction and no longer visits the Summeys. All of Renee's letters and cards to Katie are saved and put away at her mother's house. Marie sends word to Katie they are there for her whenever she's old enough to understand and wants to see them. Katie does not return Marie's phone calls. After knowing how her mother betrayed her father with the other men she had affairs with, it is hard to believe Katie will ever be able to have enough trust in her life to enjoy any close relationship.

After corresponding with Renee for two years now, I am convinced she thinks about the people whose lives intersected and impacted with hers. As she grows old in prison, she continues to reflect as to why she chose certain paths in her life and followed that course to certain disaster. For the most part, she will admit she had always taken for granted the people who loved and believed in her the most. That was certainly the case with her parents and then Brent, who had worshiped and adored her since they were both teenagers. She sees now that many of her lovers she dragged into her spiraling marriage were already losers, people, like herself, who abused their wedding vows and had serious troubles with their own relationships. They were people like Bruce Wolford, who spent so much energy spinning his webs of deceit and constructing excuses to explain embarrassing situations to his spouse and his lover, who were both suffering with broken hearts.

Most of Renee's friends have not written or talked with her since her conviction. She's never imagined any of her lovers agonizing over her as they sat in their homes and watched as she was handcuffed and driven away by the police to face murder charges. She guessed they considered themselves fortunate to have escaped from her long enough to *not* become the desperate man John apparently was, or they, too, could have been wearing an orange prison jumpsuit.

If everything the prosecution said about Renee was true, then she killed the one man who could afford her because he wouldn't give her enough time. It was a terrible waste of a good man's life. Renee now understands she also wasted her own life, and like so many young women who get caught in the underworld of the adult entertainment business, she threw away great opportunities for happiness in exchange for a nonstop orgy of lust and an apparently overwhelming desire to validate her self-worth by entangling herself with people who used or manipulated her as easily as she behaved toward them. During all or most of her adult life, she had cashed in on her physical attractiveness to snare one man after another, and didn't hesitate to bring in a parade of women friends to satisfy her libido. She worked her love potions on the men and women she worked and slept with, and even tried them on Terry Altman, when she posed as the poor little girl whom everyone was picking on. She often interrupted his question-and-answer sessions with threats and innuendos, yet at the end of two interviews, she asked him for a hug.

She doesn't understand any of that.

One would think if Renee had truly hungered for love and affection, all she had to do was ask for it. It was certainly within her capabilities to establish and sustain warm and loving relationships. And if she no longer loved Brent, why didn't she just find someone else and settle down with that person? The prosecution's theory maintained she was too driven by greed. She wanted it all and ruthlessly squandered all opportunities for a healthy relationship, behaving like a child caught up in a candy store. She didn't have to waste her adult life cheating on the person who trusted her the most. She was an attractive, intelligent and creative woman, who had other options besides dancing seminude at the Silver Fox. It wasn't the money, for she didn't spend it on herself, but rather on Brent and other people.

A customer once told Renee he would pay her $2,000 to come dance for him outside the club and then sleep with him. She told him no and if that was what he was looking for, she could direct him to someone who would be willing to make the extra money, but she wasn't. She then walked away from him and thanked him when he later gave her a $20 tip.

Apparently, Renee preferred the challenge and pleasure of seducing men and women over any other gainful employment as a means of boosting her self-worth. After seven years of self-introspection and others poring over her life with a microscope, there is still much she will never know about her life and why she did the things she did.

If Renee and John really did plan this murder, then they weren't all that clever. They made some terrible mistakes, beginning with John's choice of clothing to the fake robbery they created and the story they stuck to throughout the investigation. Renee's performance on the beach was believable, but it seemed after that, she did almost everything wrong. It was her cold heart and the ice in her veins that first grabbed the detectives' attention. If John planned it all and gave her directions in what to do and say, he lacked real ingenuity in both shrewdness and criminal expertise.

The most dramatic moments of the trials were not in the courtroom, but in the courtyard and breezeways outside the courtroom where the families confronted and challenged each other. It would have been so easy for tempers to have flared and gotten out of hand.

Having been involved with the families of both Renee and John, it's hard to say who has suffered the most. Marie frequently calls me in tears. She is heartbroken over not seeing Katie, who looks so much like her mother. She and Jack long for a relationship with her and believe the Pooles have poisoned her against them and Renee, but have no idea how to break through that. They hold out hope that Katie will want to find out the truth for herself someday, that she will want to question her mother about all that happened. They pray their beloved and only granddaughter will one day accept the love they so desperately want to give her.

But until then, it hurts. It really hurts.

John Frazier's loyal parents have also suffered because of the predicament they have been cast into. They were not only dragged through the hurt and embarrassment of seeing their son arrested, prosecuted and convicted for murder, but Jane Lovett has spent nearly everything she has in the world to help him get straight. John was never the type of person others sought out to pattern their lives after and he always seemed to put himself right in the middle of serious trouble. His difficulties appear to come when he falls under the destructive influence of others and can't find the words to say no. But he seems to have the care of a loving mother and attentive stepfather and they're doing their best to support him.

To this day, both families strongly support their incarcerated children. They believe they have been wrongly accused and convicted, and that the real killer still runs free. Is it possible that Brent could have been murdered by some crazy psychotic roaming the beach? Were the Pooles victims of a robbery gone bad, or was it a diabolical plan that happened exactly as Renee said it had? It is odd that no cases even remotely similar to Brent's murder have occurred in the beach area since.

Despite public opinion, the American justice system does not always find the truth. Renee and John are angry that the state has held them responsible for Brent's murder and want to punish them for their actions. Even after having been judged by a jury of their peers, they still feel they have been wrongly accused. It is difficult for most persons to feel any empathy for what has happened to them. They were caught up in a love triangle, knowing all the while something, sooner or later, had to give. They desired to manipulate and have something without following the laws of society. Did their lives not follow the laws of nature in that *whatever a man soweth, he shall also reap*?

Interview with
Kimberly Renee Poole

HUDSON: I want to thank you, Renee, for your input in this book during these many months. Is there anything else you would like to add?

POOLE: First of all, I want to say I knew this would be difficult, but just how difficult I never would have guessed. There are so many aspects of my life in which I'm not proud of and am even embarrassed by now. I'd much rather forget many things in my past as I'm not the same person I once was. There's no point in me dodging your questions or being untruthful about my answers. I hope that my story *does* help someone else not fall into the same trap I found myself in. And unlike a lot of people in this world, I've realized my mistakes and I've changed things about myself. I've grown and become a better person because I *have* learned from my past. I just hope this book helps people to understand why I made the choices I did.

HUDSON: Was John Boyd Frazier your husband's killer?

POOLE: The night I told the detectives I was certain it was John is because of the pressure everyone was putting on me.

I just wanted them to all shut up and leave me alone. To this day, I don't feel it was John. And I'm sorry I put him through all of this. I felt if I told them what they wanted to hear they'd leave me alone long enough to grieve. As it was, I was still in shock. And, yes, it angered me that my attorney was asking me as many questions as the police. He was leaving the country in a few hours and just wanted to hurry up and be done. So I guess we had that in common. We just wanted to be left alone.

HUDSON: John Frazier said you told him that Brent sexually abused you during your trip to Chicago. Is that true?

POOLE: No, Brent didn't rape me in the shower while in Chicago. As a matter of fact, the sex we had there was awesome; the best we had shared in a long time. What I believe John was referring to was that there were times (though few and far between) that I simply didn't want to be touched at all. Brent would ironically choose those times to *want* to touch me. He'd continuously ask me to have sex and I'd tell him no (for whatever reason, I didn't feel like it) and he'd do it anyway. Brent never physically abused me. He *would* verbally, mentally and emotionally abuse me, though. That is why my self-esteem remained low to nonexistent.

HUDSON: Are you aware that Bruce Wolford had mailed a copy of you and him having sexual relations to the Myrtle Beach police after you were arrested?

POOLE: No, I was not. I was under the impression that the police had confiscated the tape. Why would he do something like that? I don't know. He's a coward. I don't know why he and Courtney divorced, but the rumor mill is that she found out he killed Brent and he tampered with her [car] and caused her to wreck. And that she left him when she felt he was trying to kill her, too.

I don't know if there is any truth to it—because I've been locked up for almost eight years—but Bruce is a control freak. Courtney seemed like she was a lot like me—weak, spineless, willing to do whatever it took to keep the men in our lives happy. Maybe that was just the last straw for her.

I didn't know until recently that Bruce was attempting to be the first in line to collect the reward money on Brent's murder. Figures, though. He was trying to get the heat off and away from himself obviously. Creep. I still don't know for a fact that Bruce killed Brent (I just know what I've been told), but if he did, then he won't get away with it. Not with John and I sitting in prison for so long and neither of us having anything to do with it. The truth will come out eventually and I hope they show him no mercy. He destroyed my life.

HUDSON: After you had been arrested, there was a rumor circulating that someone had posted nude pictures of you on the Internet. Did that upset you?

POOLE: Absolutely. As I have said all along, I'm not proud of the things I've done in my past and whoever would stoop so low as to do that is the scum of the earth. I'm quite sure they wouldn't want the same thing done to them. The main reason it would upset me is because I've changed and I'm no longer the same person.

HUDSON: If you could live your life over again and change anything, what would it be?

POOLE: I would have never spent the night with my friend when I was twelve. I believe it was the night that guy took advantage of me is what led to me being promiscuous. It was after he had raped me that I felt I had no self-worth and set a pattern of attempting to fill the emptiness within me through sexual behavior. I see sex now as a temporary fix, as drugs or alcohol would be to an addict. All of that negative thinking influenced me to engage in extramarital affairs, whether at Brent's request or at my own choosing. I'd seen infidelity while growing up and when you see it and don't know any different, you believe that it is okay. I'd wish I'd known long ago how it would affect your perception of self-value and self-worth.

HUDSON: You state you were raped at a young age. Did this cloud your perception of sex in any way?

POOLE: My first sexual experience ruined my perception of how lovemaking should be. I felt as if it was just the act of doing it, the motions. It had no real meaning to me. I had no meaning. So, yeah, I developed a need to be loved. I wanted more than to just be used. That's what I thought I was put on earth for. It's taken me years to realize that I loved Brent—still do— and in his own way I know he loved me, too. But by the things he made me do sexually, it only confirmed in my mind that I wasn't here for any other reason than to please people. If there is any advice I can give to young ladies who want to become sexually active, don't lower your self-worth for a few months of pleasure. In this day and age, advertising agencies use sex to sell their products as that is the greatest thing if life, but there's a lot more to life than that. Realize who you are and know that you have value. You're just not an object. I don't ever regret becoming pregnant. Katie's the best thing that's ever happened to me. But there are many young girls who aren't ready to become mothers. There's that risk and there's the risk of STDs, AIDS, et cetera. It's not worth it. No one should put themselves in that position to be used like a porcelain doll, taken down to be played with, then cast aside until the need to play hits again.

HUDSON: Danny Shrewsbury, what does the name mean to you?

POOLE: Ha, ha. There's a name for you. What a joke! That's one of the things in life where you ask yourself, "What was I thinking?" Yes, Danny proposed to me, but it wasn't the night of my graduation as the Pooles implied. It was well after that. Yes, I accepted. And why? I have no clue, because there was no way in hell I'd leave Brent for him. It may have been because I didn't want to hurt his feelings. It's got to be a blow to the ego to be shot down and I felt sorry for him in that respect.

Danny bought me two things. Actually, it was a pair of earrings he bought from some pawnshop that he had made into a ring and a necklace . . . which equaled out to be two things.

No, I wasn't an exhibitionist. I was a stripper, so naturally I had to become comfortable in my nudity. Danny took pictures of me in my dance costumes, but I don't recall ever being totally nude. He said he wanted to make a portfolio for me. At one time, I considered trying out for modeling, but couldn't afford to have a professional portfolio made. So, yes, I agreed to let Danny take those pictures of me. This occurred when Brent was neglecting me and the attention was welcome. I've never really been "body shy," because though I may be small in size, I have a decent body. No stretch marks from my pregnancy or anything like that. After seeing other women naked, I've become proud of my body. It's not perfect, but it's nothing to be ashamed of, either. Many people considered it (nudity) art and it is as long as it's respectful.

HUDSON: How about the name Robert Cummings?

POOLE: Hee, hee. Yes, Robert is the redheaded guy who's ultrafeminine. I think he may be gay, but he's not. Maybe it's just he doesn't have a lot of testosterone. Anyway, Robert was my first *real* boyfriend. I was with him the whole while I was being raped by another guy. Robert was my bad influence. I met him and my grades went downhill. I developed his "who cares" attitude. Anyway, he wasn't much in the looks department, but he sure knew how to charm someone. Eventually I learned it was all lies, though. With Robert, everything was a lie. We broke up and I'd see him around town every now and then. The last time I ran into him was when I went to get my navel pierced. He was in the tattoo parlor about to get a new tattoo. He gave me his number and told me to call him. I called him and we started hanging out. If I went shopping or whatever he'd tag along and help me. It's hard to shop with a two-year-old. Anyway, Robert was strange. He has this thing for vampires, which I happen to like vampires myself. But he thought he *was* one. With the fake teeth and the fake blood, he had tried to convince people he was one. I let him believe I was convinced, because it was funny the things he would say and do. So, that's Robert.

HUDSON: Do you ever feel guilty or responsible for what happened to Brent?

POOLE: In a way, I do. I mean, I know that I didn't have anything to do with it, but all of the "if only's" pop up and it makes me wish I'd been the one shot that night. Had I stood up to Brent and not done the things he asked of me, we would never have been in the situation we ended up in. If only I had more of a backbone. If only . . . if only . . . if only . . . there are so many things that I wish had or hadn't occurred that could have prevented what happened. We could have stayed in that room instead of going out.

HUDSON: I was told you had suicidal thoughts?

POOLE: The reasons I cut myself and have frequent suicidal thoughts is because I can't handle being away from Katie and my family—all because I am a victim of a crime. I've seen Katie once in 6½ years. I never had a chance to grieve over Brent. I miss them both terribly. The worse things I've ever done in my whole life is commit adultery and I think I've paid the price for that several times over. The two of them are my reasons for living. Brent is dead and Katie is being turned against me and my family by the Pooles' lies. So I feel I have no reason to keep living. The *only* reason I've not ended my life is because I hope that one day Katie will come to me for the truth and I have to be there to tell her or she'll never know.

There's a song that Brent and I used to listen to often, I can't remember the name of it because it's been so long since I've heard it. But it reminds me of him and I catch myself singing it often.

"Who's the one that makes you happy/Oh, baby/Who's the one always on your mind?/And who is the reason you're living for?/Who's the reason for your smile?"

When I sing that song, I think "Brent was the reason." Since he's no longer here, I keep his memory close to my heart. The song's meaning has transferred over to Katie and it reminds me that she is now the reason.

HUDSON: My assumption is you miss being a mother?

POOLE: When Katie was two months old, she was admitted to the hospital for an infection that started in her eye. She had to have her tear ducts opened surgically. I refused to leave the hospital while she was there. My mom would come and give me a break occasionally to smoke and to bring me food. I slept in a chair beside her bed until [she] was well enough to come home. The purpose of me telling you this is because Agnes used to brag to her friends about how good of a mother I was, how I was careful to read the labels on all chemicals before I used them while pregnant so I wouldn't harm Katie. Then, all of a sudden, I'm unfit to see my child or even have any times to her because of what happened to Brent. I send Katie cards, letters and other various things I've made for her. Mom keeps them in a box for her. When she's old enough to want them, she can read them and see that I love her and know she's my sole reason for living. Mom has sent copies of these to Katie, but we doubt she's ever seen them.

I know that Craig and his wife, Amy, wouldn't let Agnes keep their kids overnight for some reason. Brent told me he talked to Craig to find out why, but he never got the whole story. He was killed before he found out everything. The part he did find out was that Agnes blamed Craig for her marital problems with Bill. When he was in mechanics' school, she didn't even want him coming home on the weekends. One weekend he came home to find Agnes sitting in a chair rocking back and forth crying, with a gun in her hand. She meant to commit suicide, but apparently Craig stopped her. Now I'm thinking that's why Craig wouldn't let his kids stay overnight. She's unstable. We were always told that Bill Poole's had a brother who had committed rape and murder in Texas and was executed for rape and murder. But that's all the dirt I can dig up, as I said they never talked about their family.

HUDSON: How does one who was so sexually active for such a long time fare in prison?

POOLE: Well . . . I'm not *nearly* as interested in sex as I was at home. As I've said, I have found some self-worth. Occasionally the urge will hit and I'll masturbate. I do have a "girlfriend" that I've been with for over a year. Julie and I have been intimate a few times, but our relationship isn't based on that. She's my best friend, the one whom I can count on to help me when I feel depressed. I've told her more about myself than anyone (except for you). Our relationship is based on emotions. What Brent and I should have had and were lacking. If we had had that, then none of these things in our relationship would have happened. He wouldn't have made me do the things he did. I've grown up a lot and am developing true self-esteem. I have respect for myself that I never had at home. I've come to realize what I felt for myself at home was a false front. It was what was expected of me. Now I have my own feelings. I see women in here who still act the way they did at home— jumping from one relationship to another. I've changed in that respect. I like my solitude and have discovered that I didn't like myself the way I was at home. Though I do have a relationship with Julie, it's not at all like my relationships at home. I feel loved because she doesn't want just sex, she's interested in me as a person. It makes a difference.

HUDSON: Are you in a cell by yourself?

POOLE: Unfortunately, I don't room alone. I have two roommates.

HUDSON: I understand that Susan Smith is a suitemate of yours. What are your opinions about her crimes?

POOLE: I've never asked Susan why she did what she did. My thoughts are that she was either brainwashed into doing

it or that she had a lapse in judgment. Maybe she didn't realize the finality of death. She does feel remorse and misses
her children. In light of that, I feel she wasn't in her right mind.
But I don't judge her for her crimes, just as I don't want to
be judged for the charges against me.

HUDSON: I appreciate you being so candid with me about
your life.

POOLE: You are very welcome. Before I discovered who I truly
am, I never would have freely admitted to the mistakes I've made
in my life. But I've inventoried my life and changed things I
didn't like. It's hard now to admit to the things I've done, but
I'm no longer that person. I have learned from my mistakes. By
learning and changing myself I've become a better person and
I've grown to love myself. I wish my attorney would have
taken the time to learn my past as you have and brought all these
things up in court. Had he, maybe I wouldn't be sitting here in
prison today. I'd be home wrapping Katie's gifts instead.

HUDSON: I know you used to enjoy playing pool. Do you
still play?

POOLE: I don't have the opportunity to play pool here.
There's no pool table. I usually stay in my room and keep
myself occupied. I don't get involved in the sports they have
here due to a heart condition.

HUDSON: Do you ever hear from any of your old friends back
home or from the Silver Fox?

POOLE: No, I don't hear from anyone at the Sliver Fox. I don't
hear from anyone I knew at home except for one person. A few
people wrote me when I was in the county waiting for court,
but that was years ago and they've long stopped writing.

HUDSON: It's true that John Frazier spent most of his inheritance money from his grandfather on you?

POOLE: That's definitely a good laugh for me. John went through money like water. He never bought me anything more than a few meals, a few cards and a couple of flowers. If *that* cost him his entire inheritance, then he must not have inherited but a few hundred dollars. If we went shopping or anything, I paid for my own purchases.

You see, I've worked since I was fourteen and was never used to anyone supporting me completely. It's hard for me now to call home and ask for money because I'm used to having my own money while at home and because I am independent in that respect.

HUDSON: Tell me about Brent asking you to marry him again.

POOLE: We were at his parents' house and talking and trying to work out where our marriage failed. We both admitted that we didn't want to lose the other and that we wanted to make things work. He brought several cards in, one at a time, with roses. Finally he left and came back with Katie. He got down on one knee and asked me if I would marry him again and we'd do things right this time. Not only between ourselves, but with my job. He said we would have whatever kind of wedding I wanted. He told Katie to tell me what they had talked about. And she said she wanted to be the flower girl. Then she told me she wanted a brother or sister. It was so precious. We both decided right then that we were going to make a lot of changes in our lives and make things right with our marriage.

HUDSON: I must tell you when my editor saw your picture, he commented that you look even better now than you did before you entered prison.

POOLE: [If I look that good] then I worry about that because people will try to misconstrue things. I want it to be understood that since I was taken away from my family, I've basically had to "adopt" a family within the fences. They keep me fairly sane.

HUDSON: My greatest concern about this book is that the readers will think it is biased and that I misconstrued the truth about you.

POOLE: I don't know what to say about your concerns about the book being too biased toward me and my family. You are the only person who has ever taken the time to get to know us fully. We've all been open and honest about *everything*, and if it turns out that you're biased, it's only because you know the *real* people you're writing about. I know I have not one skeleton lingering in my closet. How many people can say that? How many people would admit to their faults and mistakes as openly and honestly as we have. I've told you all the bad stuff I've ever done, so how could this story be biased?

(Author's note: For the purpose of this book, Brent Poole's family was contacted, but they chose not to be interviewed.)

AFTERWORD

When the South Carolina Court of Appeals reversed John Boyd Frazier's conviction in 2004 and ordered a new trial, no one doubted the prosecution would have their work cut out for them. This time, Morgan Martin and Tommy Brittain would bring nothing less than perfection to the table. In Frazier's first trial, the defense team's efforts had been thwarted by the judge in not allowing them to present videographer Donald Smith and his taped reenactment of conditions and visibility comparable to the night Brent Poole had been murdered. Mark and Donna Hobbs's eyewitness testimony was the prosecution's one and only corroboration that a darkly clad Frazier had been trolling the Carolina Winds and walking the beach the night Poole was killed. The defense believed any conscientious jury would be convinced after having viewed Smith's video reenactment that it would have been totally impossible for the Hobbses to have gotten "a good-enough look" at Frazier to later identify him in a police lineup.

In addition, Judge Peeples had in Frazier's first trial allowed certain evidence and testimony that had been critically injurious to his case. Martin and Brittain still believed wholeheartedly the prosecutors had never proven their case against Frazier—that it had been merely one of circumstantial evidence against him and he had been wrongly convicted based on misleading information and fallacious accusations presented to the jurors. Their intent was that Frazier be tried on the direct evidence against him and not from what others had testified about his relationship with Renee Poole. They had painstakingly reviewed the trial transcripts and examined in great detail every bit of evidence and single word of testimony that could have affected the judgment of the jury.

For this new trial, Martin and Brittain had crafted a more aggressive defense and planned to challenge each piece of evidence and every witness the state had to offer. Frazier's family and defense team saw it as a good omen that Judge Paula Thomas would run herd over this trial. During Thomas's seven-year tenure as a circuit court judge, she had presided over many emotionally packed cases, including a couple accused in the death of their twenty-month-old girl and the murder of Horry County Police Department corporal Dennis Lyden. To those who saw the attractive Thomas with her trim figure and soft voice outside the courtroom, she could have been easily mistaken for an elementary-school teacher. But to those who saw her inside the courtroom, it was perfectly clear she was not only capable and had a solid grasp of the judicial system, but was a tough and gutsy lady. From the very beginning of the trial, Thomas demonstrated she wasn't afraid of the job, or the press, and was bound and determined to see that Frazier would receive a fair and impartial trial.

Questions related to Renee Poole had already been asked before the trial date: If John Frazier was acquitted, how would this affect her appeal? Would she get a new trial? Would she get a reduced sentence? If she was to be released, would she file for custody for her daughter, Katie? Was she planning on testifying against John in this trial?

One of the first hurdles for Judge Thomas to overcome in the trial was to find a panel of jurors that was not already familiar with Renee's or John's previous trial. Fortunately, Horry County consists of a transient population, always coming and going, and a lot of new faces had appeared on the scene since Brent's murder in 1998, Renee's trial in 2001 and John's trial in 2002; a jury was seated the first day.

Secondly, how would Thomas handle evidence and testimony

against Frazier? Even though a lot of testimony in Frazier's first trial had already been thrown out, Thomas would preview outside of the jurors' [hearing] testimony that was questionable and decide then and there if that information was admissible. Unless Renee chose to testify against her former lover, even her words could not be used against him.

Lastly, if the jury found Frazier to be guilty, would Thomas impose the same sentence of life imprisonment without the possibility of parole, or would she consider reducing it in favor of a term sentence with a parole date? The family of Brent Poole prayed his conviction would be upheld and he would return to prison for the rest of his natural life.

On the first day of trial, May 23, 2005, John Frazier walked into the courtroom with his entourage. Prison had not been nearly as kind to him as it had been to Renee Poole. Dressed in a dark suit, he was totally bald and looked significantly older and heavier than he had in his first trial. Someone in the gallery later remarked John looked like Uncle Fester from the Addams Family. Gone was the cockiness and the bantam rooster swagger he had first presented at his extradition hearing in North Carolina nearly seven years ago. John's mother, Jane Lovett, said he had done a lot of soul-searching and Bible study since his conviction and a gentle, kind and humble spirit now prevailed within him. His lawyers agreed and hoped the jurors would notice that. In fact, they were so convinced in the changes John had made in his life that there was talk of him testifying on his own behalf.

John's defense team believed there was a lot of important information the jurors needed to know about him. Particularly damaging in his first trial was that jurors had mistakenly confused "his sweating condition" as further evidence of guilt. Morgan Martin would remind these jurors that this was nothing more than a prevalent, high body temperature John had had since birth that caused him to sweat profusely. "Even on the coldest days, he still sweats," Martin assured them.

Martin also wanted jurors to know up front that in 1998 John Boyd Frazier was a single, youthful and potent male. He admitted John hadn't lived the kind of life his family was proud of, and his unbridled lust for the nightlife and exotic dancers *had* gotten him into a quandary more than a time or two. Granted, it was a lifestyle frowned upon by many persons positioned near the top of the food chain, but, nevertheless, a common and acceptable standard among other circles of society. But should John be penalized for having lived the life of a single man when he was just one of countless others—many of whom would testify in this case—that had succumbed to the calling of the night?

To help bolster their arguments in the courtroom, John's defense team relied on an advanced collection of computerized equipment. One quick click of the mouse and the miracle of technology changed the courtroom into a mini-theater. Relevant information could be booted up at command and this dazzling stage presentation was, no doubt, impressive to the jurors. They laughed along with Martin when he lightheartedly poked fun at the prosecution for hand-pasting their little "stickies" up on poster board.

On the serious side, the defense asked Judge Thomas not to allow the prosecution's poster board to be carried back to the jury room. They believed it represented a summary of the prosecution's argument. Deputy solicitor Fran Humphries countered, "It wasn't a summary, but a timeline to help jurors keep information organized."

The prosecution started out flat. This was their third time to argue the case before a jury and their scripts were beginning to lose their luster, sounding more like a high-school Saturday-matinee production of *Our Town*. Hembree and Humphries looked tired and frustrated at having to jump through all the endless legal hoops. Some of their original witnesses were not available for trial, due to sickness or unavailability, while others had rewritten their lines and/or moved over to the defense.

Morgan Martin and Tommy Brittain were flawless in the first few days of court. They were on top of their game. The momentum of the legal sport quickly shifted to their side of the courtroom. Going after every witness with a cavalry charge, they shrewdly asked questions that had never been asked before, then demanded answers.

During John's first trial, his good friend Kayle Schettler had made a strong witness for the prosecution. Early in the investigation, Myrtle Beach detectives had firmly convinced Schettler that John had murdered Brent Poole. And because John had driven his car the night of the murder, he had implicated him in the case. Rightly so, Schettler was pissed at John for involving him in his troubles and mirrored that outlook.

But after five years of reflection, Schettler's view had changed. When asked by Morgan Martin if he now thought John had driven his car to the beach, he flatly replied, "No, I don't." His answer hung in the courtroom.

Schettler added that his car had two bald tires and *he* wouldn't have risked driving it to the beach. He also said when he got his car back from John, it was clean—the front of his car lacked the normal evidence of squashed bugs, which are so prevalent to the Carolinas. No bug juice. Mosquito wings. Or beetle guts. And that seemed odd to Schettler, who had made a similar trip from Winston-Salem to Myrtle Beach shortly after John had been arrested and his front fender was covered in bug splatter.

The defense team made mincemeat out of another key prosecution witness, Bruce Wolford. In Renee's trial, her lawyers pointed at Wolford, saying he, too, had had an adulterous relationship with Renee. Couldn't he also be considered a suspect in Brent's murder? Wolford was not called to testify in Renee's trial, but provided very damaging information against John in his trial. Wearing tennis shoes, blue jeans, and a green pullover cotton shirt, falling loosely outside his jeans, he sat at the back of the courtroom looking more like Shaggy from *Scooby-Doo* than a star witness. Strutting around the courthouse with the distinctive air of a prize stud that breeds well in captivity, he would return to his seat after court recess, then immediately focus on the female reporter operating a television camera in the back corner. When he finally made it to the witness stand, he was so quiet and reserved, the attorneys had to remind him several times, for the sake of the court, to speak up. Only when Martin asked him about his affair with Renee did he then perk up, explaining in great detail how it all began and took place.

"Mr. Wolford, didn't you make some type of memoriam to remember this occasion with Mrs. Poole?" Martin asked bluntly.

Wolford smiled, then admitted he had made a tape of him and Renee having sex. His face brightened as he revealed the slippery truth about his relationship with Renee and the other women he had known in that same time period. He sat up straight and pulled in close to the microphone, acknowledging there had been other women in his life besides Renee that he had pleasured for the benefit of him and his ex-wife. He said his ex-wife had also been an exotic dancer at the Silver Fox Gentleman's Club and had been friends with Renee. The purpose for taping his and Renee's affair was because his ex had wanted to watch them have sex, but didn't want to be there. That was not out of the ordinary, for he had brought a lot of women home for that very reason.

Bruce was coming in loud and clear. Short of tongue, Martin asked Wolford, "Would it be fair to say, for lack of a better word, that you and your wife were swingers?"

"Well, we had an open relationship," Wolford said proudly. He looked around the courtroom as if he were the "American Gigolo" expecting applause from a nighttime talk-show audience, then added, "That would describe it best." He never realized he was the only one amused by his sex tales.

Martin continued to build his case that Wolford was not only unscrupulous, but wouldn't think twice about lying in court. Using Wolford's own testimony about dates, times and events, he compared those against evidence submitted in court and forced Wolford to admit he had not told the truth on more than one occasion. Wolford was caught by surprise at having been exposed in the courtroom.

It was apparent throughout the trial, John's lawyers were putting on one hell of a floor show. Ripping witnesses apart. Tearing through testimonies. Keeping damaging information away from the jurors. By midweek, they had quieted the prosecution's side and even had the detectives and other law enforcement officers who were there to testify squirming in their seats. John was feeling very good, laughing and joking with family members and friends.

Winston-Salem police officer Darrell Mills, who had first approached John's house during the early-morning hours of June 10, 1998, to see if he was home, admitted he had made a vital mistake in not checking the hood of the parked car to see if it had been driven.

"All you had to do was ask," Martin suggested, then got Mills to agree. "If you would have done that, found out whether or not the hood of the engine was hot or cold, then we might not have been here today in this courtroom."

The confidence level was high in John's family and his supporters, and at the end of the day, they walked with a lighter step. Martin and Brittain had been merciless and showed no signs of letting up. Even before Mark and Donna Hobbs took the stand, they sought to have their testimonies discarded. After John's trial, Bill and Agnes Poole had contacted the solicitor's office. They felt so moved by the Hobbses' courage and conviction to testify that they insisted on giving them each a gift of $10,000.

John's lawyers exhausted all arguments to strike the Hobbses' testimony and the photographic lineup. The Hobbses were an imminent and present threat to their client's acquittal. If they could keep their testimony out of court—the only witnesses who could put him at the crime scene—then he would stand a good chance of walking out a free man.

But after hearing the Hobbses' testimonies and lawyers' arguments outside of the jury, Judge Thomas ruled no foul had been committed. The Pooles had given the money in good faith and with no intention of malice, and long before they knew John's case would be overturned.

"I don't need the money," a red-faced Mark Hobbs told the judge. "It's still in my bank account if you want to have it back. My wife and I didn't want to take it, but it was something the Pooles insisted that we do."

As in previous trials, Mark and Donna Hobbs were unshakable in that they had seen John Frazier at the hotel and on the beach the night Brent Poole was murdered. The defense went after them, time and time again, shaking their heads and murmuring to the jury, "And how can you be so sure?"

Donna Hobbs testified that even seeing John again in the courtroom convinced her she was right. "When I first saw him, he made a certain move and I thought, 'Oh, no. He shouldn't have done that. It was the same move he made on the beach that night.'"

After the prosecution rested its case, the defense opened with the testimony of videographer Donald Smith. The long-awaited video, by Smith's video production company, Lucky Dog, produced for the first trial and two years after Poole's murder, raised a lot of concerns about whether the Hobbses could have seen John clearly enough that night to recall his face in the photographic lineup.

John's lawyers had also secured the services of university professors, Brian Cutler and Elizabeth Loftus, to explain mistaken eyewitness identification and memory selection. It all sounded plausible, but was the jury buying it? Even if they didn't, the defense maintained that the Hobbs' identification of John still didn't put him at the crime scene. If indeed they had seen him at the hotel, Martin postured, he was still some two blocks away from the crime scene.

A critical point in the trial arose when the defense called John's sister, Christine Micholatti, and his former roommate and exotic dancer, Sharon Haymaker, to testify that Renee Poole didn't mean anything to him. Both women insisted it wasn't a big deal to John for a girl to move in with him, have sex, then move out. John would always move on as if nothing had happened.

But on cross-examination of Micholatti, Hembree reminded her about John's Day-Timer, garnered in a search at his mother's beach home in February 1999. Listed among its pages were significant dates, such as the beginning of his and Renee's relationship, the first time they had sex, the day Renee moved in, and Katie's birthday. The last entry was written the day of, or the day, Renee moved out. The note read: "FUCK YOU RENEE!!"

Hembree continued to paint a clear picture of how upset John was when Renee moved back in with her husband. He wanted the jurors to see that John did care for her and believed he would have a future with her. Brent's sister, Dee Mishler, was called as a rebuttal witness and revealed a phone conversation she had with John.

"It was Mother's Day," Mishler began. "Brent called me and said Renee was moving back home. He asked me if I would help him clean the house and get everything ready for her arrival. . . . He had grilled steaks and prepared a surprise dinner, but Renee never showed. And when it got very late that night, I called her on her cell phone. In a few minutes, John called me back."

Mishler stated John was very upset and used vulgar language.

"I had never been called any of those names before. He used the 'F' word, and told me my brother and family was 'f-ing' crazy. Then it was G.D. this and G.D. that, and Renee was never coming home. . . . He was really angry."

John was collapsing under the pressure. Up until Mishler's testimony, he had done very well holding his emotions. But as she walked away from the witness stand and past him, he quipped in a voice loud enough for her to hear, "Thanks for lying." Mishler wheeled around, then leaned into Hembree and reported John's taunt. Hembree jumped up and demanded that John be reprimanded.

The jurors believed they were now seeing a side of John Frazier that had been cleverly disguised in court. In the eleventh hour, Mishler's testimony confirmed what they had suspected all along. Her words were the last words spoken from witnesses in reference to John's character and, no doubt, would carry a lot of weight in their final decision.

Still, there was hope for an acquittal.

Renee's parents, Jack and Marie Summey, had been present every day of the trial, sitting in the row behind John's family. After Martin announced, "The defense rests," Jack leaned over to Marie and whispered, "If our daughter had gotten that type of defense from her lawyers, she wouldn't be sitting in prison today."

As Fran Humphries began his closing argument, it looked as if the case could go either way. Humphries' job was to be brief and set the jury up for the final act—Hembree's closing arguments. He looked a little sheepish, but was his usual calm and methodical self.

Tommy Brittain, on the other hand, came on like a roaring lion. For forty minutes, he preached that the state's case against John Frazier was all circumstantial and that they did not have one shred of evidence to prove him guilty. "And don't you think if there had been any evidence," he boomed, "four law enforcement agencies and their forensics teams would have found something by now?"

Morgan Martin held the jury captive for seventy minutes as he went through a laundry list of the state's evidence and pointed out the discrepancies between that and the witnesses that testified. "All they did was infer that John had been at a certain place or committed a certain act," Martin emphasized. "It's all circumstantial evidence. And you can't pile inference upon inference and call it evidence to say that a man has committed murder. . . . There is nothing here that rises to the level of a motive for murder."

Martin apologized for the length of time he had taken, but wanted the jury to know a man's life was at stake here. Spectators in the courtroom squirmed and shifted from the discomfort of sitting so long in the wooden pews. One young attorney sitting behind the prosecution turned to his associate and whined, "We've been sitting so long that my ass is hurting."

Greg Hembree had been silent during most of the trial, leaving a lot of the courtroom drama to Humphries. But the time had come in Hembree's career for him to reach deep inside of himself and grab hold of the best he had. He grabbed a fistful. Walking the jury through the entire scenario from beginning to end, Hembree explained how Poole and Frazier had plotted her husband's murder: they lured him on the beach, where Renee made love to him; they executed him; then they tried to cover it up. During the one hour and twenty minutes it took Hembree to make his case, John fidgeted in his chair with his head down, mumbling underneath his breath and shaking his head in quiet protest. Morgan Martin listened carefully to every word, determined not to let his opponent get by with some inferences he considered misleading. On four separate occasions, Martin rose to his feet and objected to Hembree's discourse, prompting Judge Thomas to intervene and call for a sidebar. Without realizing it, those short interludes of discussion may have benefited the prosecution more than the defense, in that it gave the jury periodic breaks to digest and ponder Hembree's final arguments.

"John Frazier did not kill Renee Poole," Hembree pointed out in his closing remarks. "He left her alive because *he* wanted her. He wanted her, but he hated Brent Poole and wanted him dead."

But in the end, it was Hembree's reference to the movie and screenplay *Chicago* that would stand out and provide the greatest sting to Frazier's defense.

"My daughter loves theater and we recently attended the production of *Chicago*," he said. "And I remember the lines of Richard Gere's character, Billy Flynn—the town's slickest lawyer—who sang this song." (Hembree then assured the jury he was not going to sing):

> *If you put on a good enough show, it doesn't matter what the truth is. It becomes a razzle-dazzle show.*

Hembree asked them to remember all the paid experts for the defense. "One hundred five thousand in total dollars . . . *it's showbiz, razzle-dazzle showbiz.* Look at all this equipment—you've got an Alabama Theater here. You know what your eyes can see.

"John Adams once said, 'the truth is a stubborn thing.'" Hembree moved in closer to the jurors and lowered his voice. "No amount of money. No amount of experts. And no amount of *razzle-dazzle* can stop the truth. They spent all this money on all this equipment just to shake your beliefs."

It seemed to fall directly on the captive audience.

"In the words of Billy Flynn, *'Give 'em enough razzle dazzle and you'll get away with murder.'"*

Hembree was relentless.

"Yes—a man will commit a lot of sins for the love of a bad woman. John Boyd Frazier sinned. He sinned when he entered into an adulterous relationship with Renee; he sinned when he took advantage of his friends; he sinned when he lied in an effort to cover up his crimes.

"He sinned in so many ways—he sinned when he committed the robbery of taking a father from a daughter." Hembree paused to let the jury ponder that thought, then offered, "There is no father for this daughter."

Martin rose to his feet and objected that Hembree was leading the jury with such an emotional reference to Poole's daughter. Thomas overruled.

"Don't allow the old *razzle dazzle* to cloud your judgment," Hembree concluded. "Let the truth prevail."

The case was finally handed to the jurors at approximately 6:00 P.M. Spectators and the press estimated the jury would reach a verdict anywhere from two to four hours. Word came earlier than expected. At 7:30 P.M., Judge Thomas slipped back into her robe and announced a verdict had been reached.

"Guilty on the charge of murder," the foreman read. "Guilty on the charge of armed robbery. And guilty on the charge of conspiracy to commit murder." Sobs were heard on both sides of the courtroom.

Brent Poole's family asked the judge to send their son's murderer back to prison for life. "My son was just twenty-four years old," Agnes Poole cried. "He had just come back to the Lord about five weeks before this happened. . . . His daughter asks about him all the time."

John Boyd Frazier faced the judge at the front of the courtroom, still maintaining his innocence. His face was void, without emotion, as if he had expected to be found guilty. In a soft, gravelly voice, he told the judge he could never kill anybody.

"I have a daughter myself," he told Thomas. "And I beg you

for a parole date so I might have a chance to spend time with her sometime in the future."

Judge Thomas sentenced Frazier to concurrent terms of thirty, thirty, and five years. He would be required to serve 85 percent of that time before being eligible for parole. But with credit for the time he had already served, "supervised" parole could be possible in twenty years. Any way you looked at it, it was a partial victory for both sides—a reduced sentence instead of the life sentence he had received in his first trial.

After John was led out of the courtroom, his mother, Jane Lovett, stood among her supporters and said loudly, "Sorry? Sorry. . . . My son is going back to prison, and all she can say is she's sorry?" She was referring to an informal apology Renee Poole had sent through her parents.

Brent Poole's brother, Craig, expressed his disappointment with the sentence. "It's the same case, and the jury saw it the same way. It should have been the same penalty."

Greg Hembree praised the jury's verdict. "I think this says the evidence was clear, even though much of it is circumstantial."

A noticeably disappointed Morgan Martin responded, "There is no question the key to the case was the eyewitness testimony. We put that to a strong test, and you live with the result."

As expected, Renee Poole had made a brief appearance at John's trial to act on her Fifth Amendment right not to testify. Shackled at her wrist and feet, her long curly hair hung down and across the shoulders of the prison-issued orange jumpsuit. It broke her mother's heart to see her daughter in chains. On the way out of the courtroom, Renee looked toward her smiling mom and dad.

Two days after the trial, John Frazier was transferred to Perry Correctional Institute, in Pelzer, South Carolina (southwest of Greenville), some two hundred miles away from his family. He has not spoken or written to Renee since their bond hearing in 1998.

When Renee received the news of John's conviction, she was disappointed but not crushed. "I knew from past experiences not to get my hopes up too high," she wrote from prison. "So, I didn't have far to fall this go 'round."

Even if John would have been found not guilty, the status of Renee's conviction would have remained the same. Barring a miracle, she'll never get the opportunity to drive a car, sleep in her own bed or shop at the mall. Two juries were convinced that John Boyd Frazier murdered Brent Poole, but because South Carolina law deems one hand is the hand of all, Kimberly Renee Poole is considered as guilty as if *she* herself had pulled the trigger.

At this book's writing, it has been two years since Renee received a letter from her daughter. She has accepted the fact they may never be together again. Right now, she is just trying to stay one day ahead of yesterday.

GREAT BOOKS, GREAT SAVINGS!

When You Visit Our Website:
www.kensingtonbooks.com
You Can Save 30% Off The Retail Price
Of Any Book You Purchase

- All Your Favorite Kensington Authors
- New Releases & Timeless Classics
- Overnight Shipping Available
- All Major Credit Cards Accepted

Visit Us Today To Start Saving!
www.kensingtonbooks.com

All Orders Are Subject To Availability.
Shipping and Handling Charges Apply.

MORE MUST-READ TRUE CRIME
FROM

M. William Phelps

__Every Move You Make $6.50US/$8.99CAN
0-7860-1695-7

In December 1989, in upstate New York, thirty-five-year-old Gary C. Evans, a master of disguise and career criminal, began weaving a web of deadly lies to cover a string of murders. Evans first met New York State Police Senior Investigator James Horton in 1985. For more than thirteen years, Evans and Horton maintained an odd relationship—part friendship, part manipulation—with Evans serving as a snitch while the tenacious investigator searched for the answers that would put him away. After Horton used Evans as a pawn to obtain a confession from a local killer, Evans led Horton in a final game of cat and mouse: a battle of wits that would culminate in the most shocking death of all...

__Lethal Guardian $6.50US/$8.99CAN
0-7860-1587-X

Beth Carpenter, thirty-one, wanted guardianship of her two-year-old niece, Rebecca, daughter of Beth's estranged sister, Kim. On March 10, 1994, along a lonely stretch of road, Anson "Buzz" Clinton, Kim's husband, was shot five times. Behind Clinton's death lay a bizarre murder-for-hire conspiracy that found privileged professionals and local misfits joined in a cold-blooded plot against an innocent man. The paid killers were two buddies, organizer Joe Fremut and triggerman Mark Despres, who brought his fifteen-year-old son Christopher along for the hit. The aftermath of this brutal crime would set investigators and prosecutors on a long and twisted path strewn with lies, treachery, and deceit that would cross the Atlantic Ocean before finally bringing justice home.

__Perfect Poison $6.50US/$8.99CAN
0-7860-1550-0

From August 1995 through February 1996, nurse Kristen Gilbert dealt out wholesale death. Her victims were helpless patients who trusted her as a caregiver; her weapon was a drug capable of causing fatal heart attacks. But she got away with murder until three of her fellow nurses could no longer ignore the proliferation of deadly "coincidences" on Gilbert's watch. Investigators believe Kristen Gilbert may have been responsible for as many as forty deaths. As the law closed in, she struck back, faking suicide attempts, harassing witnesses, stalking her ex-boyfriend, and terrorizing the hospital with bomb threats. In March 2001, after being found guilty of four counts of murder and two counts of attempted murder, "Angel of Death" Kristen Gilbert was sentenced to life imprisonment.

Available Wherever Books Are Sold!

Visit our website at **www.kensingtonbooks.com**

HORRIFYING TRUE CRIME
FROM PINNACLE BOOKS

Body Count
by Burl Barer   0-7860-1405-9   **$6.50**US/**$8.50**CAN

The Babyface Killer
by Jon Bellini   0-7860-1202-1   **$6.50**US/**$8.50**CAN

Love Me to Death
by Steve Jackson   0-7860-1458-X   **$6.50**US/**$8.50**CAN

The Boston Stranglers
by Susan Kelly   0-7860-1466-0   **$6.50**US/**$8.50**CAN

Body Double
by Don Lasseter   0-7860-1474-1   **$6.50**US/**$8.50**CAN

The Killers Next Door
by Joel Norris   0-7860-1502-0   **$6.50**US/**$8.50**CAN

Available Wherever Books Are Sold!

Visit our website at **www.kensingtonbooks.com**.

MORE MUST-READ TRUE CRIME
FROM PINNACLE

Under the Knife   0-7860-1197-1   **$6.50**US/**$8.50**CAN
By Karen Roebuck

Lobster Boy   0-7860-1569-1   **$6.50**US/**$8.50**CAN
By Fred Rosen

Body Dump   0-7860-1133-5   **$6.50**US/**$8.50**CAN
By Fred Rosen

Savage   0-7860-1409-1   **$6.50**US/**$8.50**CAN
By Robert Scott

Innocent Victims   0-7860-1273-0   **$6.50**US/**$8.50**CAN
By Brian J. Karem

The Boy Next Door   0-7860-1459-8   **$6.50**US/**$8.50**CAN
By Gretchen Brinck

Available Wherever Books Are Sold!

Visit our website at **www.kensingtonbooks.com**.

MORE MUST-READ TRUE CRIME
FROM PINNACLE

Slow Death   0-7860-1199-8 $6.50US/$8.99CAN
By James Fielder

Fatal Journey   0-7860-1578-0 $6.50US/$8.99CAN
By Jack Gieck

Partners in Evil   0-7860-1521-7 $6.50US/$8.99CAN
By Steve Jackson

Dead and Buried   0-7860-1517-9 $6.50US/$8.99CAN
By Corey Mitchell

Perfect Poison   0-7860-1550-0 $6.50US/$8.99CAN
By M. William Phelps

Family Blood   0-7860-1551-9 $6.50US/$8.99CAN
By Lyn Riddle

Available Wherever Books Are Sold!

Visit our website at **www.kensingtonbooks.com**.